AF413222

DEFIANT GERMAN
DEFIANT JEW

A HOLOCAUST MEMOIR FROM INSIDE THE THIRD REICH

WALTER LEOPOLD

LES LEOPOLD

ISBN 9789493056565 (ebook)

ISBN 9789493056558 (paperback)

ISBN 9789493056688 (hardcover)

Publisher: Amsterdam Publishers, The Netherlands

info@amsterdampublishers.com

Holocaust Survivor Memoirs World War II, Book 10

CONTENTS

Dying earth,
No water, no forest,

Home and love so far.
The night is so dark, the furrow so cold,
How fearfully the stars do flicker!

Burning sun,
How I fear,
How I am ill, oh so tired!
I climb up the rocky slope
And find not rest not peace

Walter Leopold, September 1943

INTRODUCTION

Could German Jews have done more to rebel against the Nazis and resist their deportation to slaughter?

Dr. Walter Leopold faced this question in real time, and in his diary shares his daring version of Jewish "resistance." Willing to take his own life rather than to be captured by the Gestapo, he carried a weapon at all times.

Born in 1898 in Ottweiler, Germany, the son of a cantor, Walter grew up in small villages with very few Jews in the southern Rhineland. Sincere about his faith but not Orthodox, he fought in WWI for the German Imperial Army, along with approximately 100,000 Jews, and received an Iron Cross for bravery in the Macedonia campaigns. After the war he attended Heidelberg University, earning his doctorate with the hope of serving in the new Weimar Republic, the first democratic government in German history. His dissertation focuses on the health and welfare of Jews in Palestine, and concludes with the statement that Zionists should not determine the future of the Jews. He, like many assimilated Jews, is Jewish *and* German. Germany is his home, his passion, his calling.

Like many other young people in that era, he was drawn to radical politics and eventually aligned himself with what he called "left-wing socialism." When the Soviet Union was born in 1917, he witnessed the fracturing of the German Socialist Party (SPD). The militant socialist wing formed the German Communist Party (KPD), which failed to lead a revolution at the end of WWI. The SPD was more cautious and participated in the Weimar government. Party politics was intense and bloody throughout the 1920s, with the Socialists and the Communists battling each other. While suffering from draconian war reparations, the Weimar Republic faced extreme economic hardship, including Germany's infamous hyper-inflation. During this post-war chaos, the far right – captained by the young Adolph Hitler, groomed and supported by German business and military elites – led a failed coup d'état in 1923 (The Beer Hall Putsch). Hitler was arrested and sent to prison for a five-year term but was released after nine months.

Although closely aligned ideologically with the Left, Walter, a keen student of these events, claimed to be completely independent of all parties and political clubs, a stance he considered a badge of honor.

During the 1920s, Walter was unable to find public employment in the Weimar government commensurate to his high-status academic degree, even though that social democratic government was much friendlier to Jews than the pre-war Bismarck monarchy. Instead, he found work within the Jewish community as a director of the Reichenheim Orphanage in Berlin. There he met his future wife, Hilda Blümlein, a pediatric nurse and daughter of a prosperous factory owner in Leipzig, a city with a population of about a half million. By 1930, Walter relocated to Leipzig, married Hilda, and lived in a wing of her parents' spacious 10-room apartment.

Leipzig was home to the seventh largest Jewish population in Germany as of 1933 (approximately 12,000). Unlike most German cities it allowed this Jewish community for nearly a hundred years to run its own governing body – the Gemeinde. Since the 14th century, at least, Jews had come to Leipzig because it was home to one of the largest trade fairs in Europe. Between 1688 and 1764 municipal records show that more than 80,000 Jews had attended these fairs.[1] By 1866, Jews had been granted equal rights to live within the city and they formed a vibrant community (but not a ghetto) that ran its own affairs. The local government authorized the Gemeinde to raise taxes from Leipzig Jews and to administer its schools, places of worship, and cultural activities. Starting in 1933, the Gemeinde found itself increasingly in the grip of Nazi repression.

Walter became a public official of the Gemeinde and throughout the 1930s he directed plays and other public performances, ran its orphanage and then became an auditor in its tax department. When the roundup of German Jews began in mid-1942, part of his job was to collect the "exit" taxes from those on the next transport to Theresienstadt, a concentration camp in Czechoslovakia, which the Gestapo claimed was a Jewish "resettlement camp." As the deportations commenced he was ordered to go to the homes of soon-to-be deported Jews to assess their valuables. Walter urged these families to hide their cash and jewelry to avoid confiscation, but often he found they were too fearful to take the risk.

* * *

Given the Gestapo's ironclad control of Jewish life in Nazi Germany, was it actually possible to resist in any meaningful way?

Overt acts of sabotage led to immediate interrogation, torture and then deportation to concentration camps or even summary execution. Nevertheless, Walter believed he could be a disruptive force, a significant obstacle to the Gestapo's plans, assuming he could avoid detection and draconian punishment.

He knew the difference between collaboration and resistance, and claimed to see it clearly within the Gemeinde leadership as younger, less politically reliable, leaders rose to power there. What he sees are collaborators who do the Nazis bidding as a means to maintain power and gain favor. To Walter there is always a clear distinction between working from within to disrupt the Nazi machine, no matter how minor the acts, and helping it run more efficiently in pursuit of selfish opportunistic aims.

Through his underground political contacts Walter learned that Theresienstadt was a death camp, or at the very least, the first stop to other camps with ovens. He couldn't bear to watch as his Jewish neighbors meekly arrived at the deportation location, a former school no less, passive, defeated, forlorn. There they were pushed, robbed and beaten by guards who reveled in their brutality and absolute power. No resistance. None at all. "It's a work camp. It won't be so bad. We will endure," his Jewish neighbors claimed.

Walter had other plans. Because he was certain that eventually all the Gemeinde officials would also be deported to concentration camps, he arranged with his working-class political contacts to gain access to an empty apartment of an army engineer with anti-Nazi proclivities. Walter prepared by carefully hiding the family's valuables in safe storage, including his library of 2,500 books. Then in the fall of 1942, when the Leopolds' names appeared on the deportation lists, he made his move. Instead of turning up at the appointed time and location, he and his family vanished into the engineer's flat. And so, their odyssey began.

Walter never claims in his diary that every German Jew should or could do what he does. Nor does he offer any concrete alternatives for others who find themselves on the lists. But he is appalled by the passivity and the excuses for inaction – "If you run away, it will only make more trouble for others." He is angry at German Jews who for decades placed their hopes in establishment elites that abandoned them as soon as the Nazis arrived. Instead, he believed more Jews should have reached out to working people who also detested the Nazis, and he was furious that Jews allowed themselves to be so humiliated, without any resistance at all. The gun Walter carried always was his ultimate act of defiance.

* * *

One big question stands out: Why was Dr. Walter Leopold, PhD, still in Germany in 1942? Was he really this heroic anti-Fascist fighter who risked his life and his family's to fight against the Nazis? Or was he yet another German Jew who, for one reason or another, simply failed to emigrate in time?

The diary provides many clues, but the final judgement is left to us.

When the Nazis rose to power in 1933, we have no indication that Walter made preparations to leave, even though 37,000 of the 500,000 Jews in Germany fled. From 1934 to 1937 another 100,000 German Jews emigrated, but Walter was not among them. In 1938, when the final wave of 40,000 German Jews legally exited the country,[2] including his two younger brothers, Walter did not join them. (Germans received 19,552 American visas that year, with 139,163 on the waiting list.[3])

In October 1938, Walter was still in Leipzig when nearly the entire Polish Jewish community, accounting for a third of the Gemeinde, was forcibly deported. And he was still there during Kristallnacht, on November 9-10, 1938, when the Nazis organized a national pogrom that destroyed thousands of Jewish businesses, killing one hundred Jews and beating hundreds more at random. In Leipzig alone, "193 businesses were destroyed, along with 34 private homes, three synagogues, four smaller temples, the cemetery chapel, an old-age home (the Ariowitsch home, only open since 1931 and a showplace, with three separate kitchens for meat, dairy and Pesach), and a school."[4]

The next day, Walter along with several hundred men from Leipzig were sent to the Buchenwald concentration camp. (His notes written during his three-week ordeal there form the first chapter of his diary.) After he, along with others, were released because of their WWI medals, the Gestapo tells them to emigrate immediately. Nearly all do, but Walter, his wife and one-year-old daughter, Anneliese, stayed behind.

* * *

Did Walter remain in Germany because he believed he had protected status as a war veteran with an Iron Cross? It does appear that the Nazis, at first, looked favorably upon the 18,000 Jews with such medals. After all, his medal did get him out of Buchenwald in 1938. But most of his modern-day relatives believe that he was simply unable to obtain the visas necessary to come to America – that he was a victim of the miniscule American quotas which were totally eliminated after Hitler declared war on the U.S. in December 1941.

This explanation runs counter, however, to the fact that Walter was the oldest, most esteemed, most credentialed and most capable member of his family, and had more financial resources than his two younger brothers. If his siblings were able to secure visas, it is hard to imagine that Walter could not have done so as well, assuming that was his primary objective. Even his elderly widowed mother made it to the U.S. by 1941 after several months of confinement in Camp de Gurs, an internment facility in the French Pyrenees.

What about escape to Palestine? Unlike the Orthodox Leipzig Jews who were strong Zionists, Walter had no interest in becoming enmeshed in an area ripe with conflict with the indigenous Arab population. Remaining in Germany, for whatever reason, seemed to be Walter's preference.

If so, did his desire to stay relate somehow to his educational status? "Herr Doktor" was a prestigious title in Germany. Unlike his brothers, Walter already had a distinguished career of service within Germany. He may have sensed that at age 40 it would be very difficult to regain that status abroad. Also, despite Nazi

xii

oppression, in 1938 he still had the remnants of an elite lifestyle (including the 2,500 books in his collection), which may not have been something he wanted to leave behind. And finally, Walter loved the German language, the German culture and many of the German people. He believed that as a German Jew, he could share his passion for freedom, justice and peace. He wanted to serve Germany – the true non-Nazi Germany – so that it could become the fountain of progressive ideas and hope within the Europe he dreamed of.

Perhaps Walter's radical politics, which are far to the left of any of his kin, provide the most important reasons for why he stayed. Could his self-identification as a "left-wing socialist" and a "revolutionary Jew" be why he did not emigrate in time?

Although Walter fiercely maintained his independence from any of the communist and socialist parties in Germany, he had close ties with the working class in "Red Leipzig," as the city was called after WWI because of its very strong Communist Party, the KPD. Like other radicals, he was totally committed to fighting against fascism. In his diary Walter refers to himself again and again as a freedom fighter, an anti-fascist resister.

But, is he so committed to the cause that he would willingly risk the lives of his wife and infant daughter, born in 1937? Walter does not come across in this diary as a foolish zealot who throws caution to the wind for a cause. Rather, he seems measured, cautious, careful and extremely caring towards his family. If anything, his demeanor more than anything suggests he may have missed the emigration deadlines due to an error in timing, rather than due to a political choice.

But viewing Nazi history from our vantage point is fraught with potential distortions. That's because we already know the grotesque outcomes, which Walter does not as he makes his fateful choices. Based on his writing it seems likely that he viewed events as they unfolded as more hopeful than as we see them now. He may have believed that mass political resistance to the Nazis might succeed, or certainly was worth the risk and effort.

From 1933 to 1936, there was arguably nothing inevitable about the survival of the Nazi regime. Their claim to power was tenuous as they waged war against German communists and socialists, starting with the setting of the Reichstag fire in Berlin which they blamed on the KPD. It also was not clear then that the Nazis would be able to eliminate KPD domination of key working-class strongholds in the major German industrial cities, including Leipzig.

The Nazis also had to surmount a significant socialist problem within their own ranks. Its paramilitary formation, the SA (Sturmabteilung) vied for power by advocating for a follow-up socialist revolution to produce a more egalitarian Nazi society. It was only in mid-1934 that Hitler put an end to that upsurge by summarily executing the SA's leadership during the "Night of the Long Knives." In addition, the balance of power within the Nazi coalition that seized control in 1933 was not set in stone. Shifting alliances between the large industrialists, the military establishment and Nazi Party forces meant that Hitler was not yet an absolute dictator, so it might have seemed both sensible and patriotic to Walter to support the socialist and communist fight against the Nazi Party in "Red Leipzig."

Furthermore, the incredible successes Hitler achieved geo-politically from 1936 to 1938 were not foreseeable. Who could have predicted that the German remilitarization of the Rhineland (1936) in violation of the Treaty of Versailles would not be halted militarily by France and England? Who knew that at the infamous Munich Conference in 1938, the West would appease Hitler by allowing him to annex Sudetenland, the German-speaking area of Czechoslovakia? And who could have possibly predicted that Stalin would sign a non-aggression pact with Hitler in August 1939, thereby crippling what remained of the united anti-Fascist front against Hitler? Finally, who could forecast with any degree of certainty that the Nazis, in the middle of an extremely taxing two-front war with heavy losses mounting on the Eastern Front, would redirect badly needed resources to institute the Final Solution against the Jews? None of this was pre-ordained.

So, it is possible to imagine that a politically talented and committed activist might choose to remain in the fight at least until Kristallnacht, November 1938. Why Walter didn't flee after that is a mystery, but it could very well be because his options by then were extremely limited.

* * *

What did Walter do as a self-defined resister?

His diary is largely silent about actions that we typically imagine as resistance fighting, like actively joining with others to sabotage the Nazi regime, or providing behind-the-lines intelligence to the Allies. Of course, he may have purposely chosen not to mention names and related activities in case his diary was confiscated by the Gestapo. Nevertheless, when first reading his papers, it is hard not to yearn for some mention of clandestine cells and co-collaborators. But as modern-day readers our entire notion of resistance is shaped by our images of history – namely by the French, Norwegian and Dutch resistance movements with their many heroic acts against the occupiers.

It is prudent, however, to consider that resistance in the home country is very different from resistance in the countries occupied by the Nazis. Historian Ian Kershaw reminds us:

"What constituted 'resistance' in Germany itself during the Third Reich is indeed less easy to define than 'resistance' in those countries occupied during the war, where it was synonymous with all attempts to oppose and work for the liberation from an invader and conqueror. Resistance by the German people to their own state, and for six years while the state was at war, raises quite different problems of analysis."[5]

In his detailed review of Bavaria during the Nazi era, Kershaw provides three categories of resistance-like activities: dissent, opposition and resistance. Together these are best viewed as concentric circles.[6]

- In the center sits the smallest circle of "resistance", defined as "active participation in organized attempts to work against the regime with the conscious aim of undermining it or planning the moment of its demise." These are the French resistance type of operations like sabotage, assassination attempts, mass leafleting, retribution against informers, etc.
- The next larger circle is "opposition," which "can be seen as a wider concept comprising many forms of action with partial and limited aims, not directed against Nazism as a system and in fact sometimes stemming from individuals or groups broadly sympathetic towards the regime and its ideology." Included here are worker job actions to protest management policies, absenteeism, disobeying various Nazi rationing decrees, etc.
- And the largest circle is "dissent," "the voicing of attitudes, frequently spontaneous and often unrelated to any action, which in any way whatsoever ran counter to or were critical of Nazism." This would include not giving the Hitler salute as the "hello" and "good day" greetings, telling negative jokes about the Nazis, complaining about well-fed Nazi bureaucrats during rationing, etc.

Over the entire 12-year period of Nazi rule, Gestapo records count approximately 800,000 Germans jailed for any of the above activities, all of which were illegal acts as defined by the Nazi state.

The only specifically known Jewish resistance group in Germany was formed in 1938-39 in the Siemens factory in Berlin, led by Herbert Baum. About 30 young Jews put out anti-fascist propaganda and engaged in a dramatic action in May 1942 against the anti-Soviet propaganda exhibition produced by Joseph Goebbels:

"Eleven members of the group invaded the exhibition and set fire to it at different points. Taking advantage of the surprise, they escaped but only temporarily. A few days later arrests began and soon embraced the whole group, most of whose members, after appalling tortures, were sentenced to death and executed... Not content with the condemnation of those involved, the Nazis further arrested some 500 Jews as hostages and put them to death."[7]

Why was Jewish resistance within Germany so rare?

Because there were so few German Jews. Before Hitler took power in June of 1933, there were just 502,799 Jews, 0.35 percent of the German population. By May 1938, only 194,214 Jews remained. In Leipzig, where Walter lived, there were 4,110 Jews in 1939.

Because of explicit Nazi policies to remove German Jews from all economic and civic life, 84 percent of the Jewish population was unemployed by 1939. In the entire country there were only 1,203 Jews listed as working in "Official Bureaus". Walter was one of them.

After the Wannsee conference in January 1942, when the Nazi leadership put into motion the "Final Solution," its massive program to exterminate all the Jews in Europe, the German Jewish population that remained was systematically rounded up and sent to concentration camps. From that point on German Jews were essentially eliminated entirely from Germany. By the end of 1942 the number of Jews as defined by the Nazi Nuremberg racial laws (at least one Jewish grandparent) was down to 51,257; by the first of April, 1943, 31,807; by the first of September, 1944, this number was only 14,457.

But more astonishing still was that nearly all of these remaining Jews were not Jews at all! These were people who had never self-identified as Jews because their parents or grandparents abandoned the religion long ago. They were on the list only because of the spurious Nazi racial biological laws. In fact, the Gestapo reported in 1944 that there remained only 227 self-identified Jews – like Walter. By the end of the war the total number of Jews, including those who survived either through hiding or taking other identities, was 19,000, which included all of those who were considered Jewish under the Nuremberg laws – even if they were no longer self-identified Jews. In sum, 96.4 percent of the German Jews had either emigrated or perished.[8] This is why historian Ruby Rohrich writes that, "for Jews during the Holocaust, simply surviving can be considered a form of resistance."

But Walter did much more than just struggle to survive. He also self-consciously tried to turn "dissenters" into "opponents" of the Nazi regime, and "opponents" into "resisters." He didn't join other groups, but rather he created his own through which he carefully built up anti-Nazi sentiment by encouraging others to engage in countless small acts of defiance. And in doing so he turned them into co-conspirators in violation of a myriad of Nazi laws.

* * *

Because a portion of Walter's story takes place in Austria, some background on that country's relationship to Nazi Germany and to antisemitism is needed. Austria was formed after the break-up of the Austro-Hungarian Empire following its defeat in WWI. It had its own virulent Nazi Party and a history of episodic antisemitic fervor. On March 12, 1938, to the jubilant cheers of the onlookers, German troops marched into Austria as Hitler annexed the country, an event known as the "Anschluss." This German-speaking country – Hitler's birthplace – became a federal state within the Third Reich. A month later, a rigged plebiscite showed that more than 99 percent of the Austrians voted in favor of the Anschluss.

To what degree are these Austrians actually enthusiastic Nazis?

There is considerable evidence that many Austrians were indeed fervent Nazis. In some policy areas, including the Aryanization of the economy and the "efficient" deportation of Jews, Austria served as a model for the German Nazis. Historian Bruce F. Pauley writes:

"... just three months after Anschluss, Jews had already been more thoroughly purged from public life in Austria than in the five years following Hitler's takeover of power in Germany... None other than Hermann Goering complained in the fall of 1938, that the 'deJewification' of the economy in Germany was not progressing as rapidly as in Austria."[9]

The 1998-2003 Austrian Historical Commission, which employed over 150 researchers to explore Nazi rule in Austria, found that Austrian antisemitism was endemic and widespread. After the Anschluss, approximately 140,000 of Austria's 200,000 Jews emigrated. The remaining 60,000 were sent to concentration camps, with very few surviving within Austria. The commission's reports also show that a great many Austrian people and institutions were actively engaged in expropriating Jewish property of all kinds.

Another indicator of Nazi support is the extensive involvement by Austrians in the Waffen-SS, the most brutal of the Nazi military branches. Although Austrians comprised only eight percent of the Third Reich's population, they accounted for 13 percent of the Waffen-SS. Furthermore, 40 percent of the staff at the Nazi death camps, and 75 percent of their commanders were Austrian.[10]

How deep is Austrian antisemitism still? According to a 1986 poll, 60 percent of the Austrian respondents believed that all Jews ought to move to Israel. In Germany, only 44 percent agreed with that statement compared to 15 percent in France and 13 percent in the U.S.[11] (However, a 2019 poll found "significant decreases" in Austrian antisemitism.[12])

On a personal note, while staying in a small village near Salzburg, Austria in 2005, we came upon a memorial crypt in a small graveyard. In it were framed portraits of about a dozen young

Austrians who had died in WWII. Nearly all of them were still pictured in their Waffen-SS uniforms.

* * *

Dr. Walter Leopold was my uncle. I have no memory of him since we only met once when I was three years old. My father was the youngest of the three brothers, 14 years junior to Walter. I grew up hearing tales about how Walter and his family survived in Germany under assumed names. I never heard a word about his politics or his bravery.

Our cousin Anneliese, Walter's daughter, has understandably had no interest in revisiting the disquieting and painful memories of her life in Germany. She did not want to resurrect the diary, but my sister, Evelyn Leopold (who is fluent in German and spent part of her career with the Reuters news agency as a correspondent in Germany), supervised and arranged for its translation.

In 2018, I began to transform the sprawling diary and notes into a coherent story that Amsterdam Publishers agreed to take on in 2020.

Although Walter originally wanted to create a carefully crafted and refined memoir, he never completed the task. We have tried to shape it as we imagine he would have. To assist the reader, I've added short introductions to each chapter and a timeline of political events to provide some context for the diary entries. Footnotes are also added to explain some of the many references that might be unfamiliar.

It is impossible to read this diary and not ask what one would do if in Walter's shoes, faced with so many impossible choices, all involving life and death for himself, his wife and his young daughter. One never knows until put to the test, of course, but I'm fairly certain that I would not have survived. I know of very few people, if any, who have Walter's rare combination of insight, intelligence, compassion, caring and fortitude. Cousin Anneliese, clearly, is blessed with many of these qualities. Somehow as a young child she never faltered, never gave up their secret, never put the family at risk. She suffered through bombings, hunger, and Gestapo raids. She went to school under an assumed name, but somehow was able to keep the family's secrets away from what her parents called the "wicket people." How anyone could grow up with such enormous tension, pressure, and fear, and still become such a lovely, caring person is truly incredible.

I am very, very proud to be part of this family, and to enjoy the light of life with the Leopold cousins Anneliese and Eleanor, and my sister Evelyn.

It is an honor to share Uncle Walter's story with you.

Les Leopold, 2020

PART 1
LEIPZIG
1938-1942

IMPORTANT DATES

1933

- *January 30: German president appoints Adolf Hitler as Chancellor of Germany.*
- *March 22: Dachau concentration camp opens, mostly for political prisoners.*
- *April 1: Nazi government organizes boycott of all Jewish shops and businesses.*
- *April 7: New Civil Service laws bar all Jews from holding civil service, university, and state positions (nullifying any chance Walter has of gaining public sector employment).*
- *May 10: Public burnings of books written by Jews and political dissidents.*
- *July 14: Law stripping East European Jewish immigrants of German citizenship (which impacts large numbers of Jews in Walter's community).*

1934

- *June 30-July 2: In the "Röhm Affair" (Night of the Long Knives),*

Hitler orders the purge and execution of the top leadership of the Nazi SA (Sturmabteilungen).

- *August 2: German President Von Hindenburg dies. Hitler becomes President of Germany with the backing of the Army and the industrialists.*
- *August 19: Hitler abolishes the office of President and declares himself Führer of the German Reich and People – the absolute dictator with no constraints on his powers.*
- *November-December: SS Chief Heinrich Himmler builds the Gestapo as the state's political police force under the command of Reinhard Heydrich.*
- *December 10: The SS (Schutzstaffel – the elite para-military force) takes over the command of the concentration camps.*

1935

- *September 15: "Nuremberg Laws" enacted that take away German citizenship from Jews and prohibits Jews from marrying Aryans.*
- *November 15: Germany creates a racial definition of a Jew as anyone with three or more Jewish grandparents, even if grandparents or parents had converted to Christianity.*

1936

- *March 3: The Nazi government bars Jewish doctors from practicing medicine in "German" institutions.*
- *July: Sachsenhausen concentration camp opens.*

1937

- *July 15: Buchenwald concentration camp opens.*
- *October 14: Uprising in Sobibor death camp*
- *October-November: Rescue of the Danish Jewry*

1938

- *March 13: Austria is willingly incorporated into the German Reich (Anschluss). All German anti-Jewish laws immediately go into effect.*
- *April 26: Mandatory registration of all business and personal property held by Jews inside the Reich.*
- *August 1: Adolf Eichmann establishes the Office of Jewish Emigration in Vienna to increase the exodus of Jews from Germany.*
- *September 30: The infamous Munich Conference occurs during which Great Britain and France attempt to appease Hitler by agreeing to German occupation and annexation of western Czechoslovakia (the German-speaking portion called Sudetenland).*
- *October 5: Following request by Swiss authorities, Germans mark all Jewish passports with a large letter "J".*
- *November 9-10: Kristallnacht (Night of Broken Glass): Anti-Jewish riots take place in Germany, Austria, and Sudetenland; 200 synagogues destroyed; 7,500 Jewish shops looted; 30,000 male Jews sent to concentration camps (Dachau, Buchenwald, Sachsenhausen).*
- *November 12: Government order forcing all Jews to transfer retail businesses to Aryan hands.*
- *November 15: All Jewish pupils expelled from "German" schools.*
- *December 12: One billion mark fine levied against German Jews for the destruction of property during Kristallnacht.*

1939

- *March 15: Germans occupy Czechoslovakia.*
- *May 13: German Ocean Liner MS St. Louis set sail from Hamburg with 937 passengers, most of whom were Jews. After being denied entry into Cuba, the United States and Canada, it was forced to return to Europe where 254 Jewish passengers would die in the Holocaust.*
- *August 23: USSR and Germany sign non-aggression pact shocking pro-Russian progressive, around the world.*

- *September 1: Germany invades Poland. Honoring their treaty with Poland, Britain and France declare war on Germany. WWII commences.*
- *September 27: Warsaw, Poland, surrenders to Germany forces: Poland is partitioned between Germany and the U.S.S.R.*
- *October 16: Germany bombs military ships in England.*
- *October 28: First Jewish ghetto established in Piotrkow, Poland.*
- *November 23: Jews in German-occupied Poland forced to wear yellow star.*

1940

- *April 9: Germans occupy Denmark and southern Norway.*
- *May 7: Establishment of Lodz Ghetto in Poland.*
- *May 10: Germany invades the Netherlands, Belgium, Luxemburg, and France.*
- *May 20: Concentration camp established at Auschwitz.*
- *June 4: After the failed Dunkirk operation to retake France, the British evacuate over 338,000 soldiers.*
- *June 10: Fascist Italy joins Germany in the war.*
- *June 14: The Nazis march into Paris.*
- *August 13: Battle of Britain begins with German incessant air raids.*
- *November 16: Establishment of Warsaw Ghetto.*

1941

- *January 21-26: Riots in Romania killing hundreds of Jews.*
- *March 11: Over the objections of Congressional isolationists, Roosevelt signs the Lend-Lease Act to aid Great Britain.*
- *April 6: Germany attacks Yugoslavia and Greece.*
- *April 13: Japan and U.S.S.R. sign a neutrality pact.*
- *June 22: Germany invades the Soviet Union.*
- *July 12: Luftwaffe bombs Moscow for the first time.*
- *September 28-29: 34,000 Jews massacred by Einsatzgruppen at Babi Yar outside Kiev.*

- *October: Establishment of Auschwitz II (Birkenau).*
- *October 23: Nazis prohibit Jews to emigrate.*
- *November 16: U.S. extends Lend-Lease Act to USSR.*
- *December 7: Japan attacks Pearl Harbor.*
- *December 8: Chelmno death camp begins operations and U.S. declares war on Japan.*
- *December 11: Germany declares war on the U.S.*

1 THEY SEIZE A RABBI AND TEAR OUT HIS BEARD

On November 7, 1938, the German diplomat Ernst vom Rath stationed in Paris is assassinated by a Polish-Jewish student, Herschel Grynszpan in retaliation for the mass Nazi deportation of Polish Jews that included his parents. Hitler and his top lieutenants seize upon this event to launch a "spontaneous" pogrom, called Kristallnacht. Thousands of Jewish businesses and places of worship are destroyed and hundreds of Jews are injured and killed in Germany (which by then also encompasses modern-day Austria and Sudetenland). The police and fire departments are told by the Nazi government not to interfere as Jews are beaten on the streets and fires rage. The Jewish population of Leipzig, a city of about 500,000, is hard hit.

In the two days following the pogrom the Gestapo rounds up hundreds of German Jewish males in Leipzig and transports them to the Buchenwald concentration camp, near Weimar, Germany. One of these is the 40-year-old Herr Doktor Walter Leopold, an official of the Gemeinde – the Jewish community's administration in Leipzig. He leaves behind his wife Hilda and one-year-old daughter, Anneliese.

Walter's notes below are written covertly while incarcerated at Buchenwald, which until this time is used primarily to hold political prisoners, mostly members of the Communist Party (KPD). Buchenwald is not as yet a full-fledged death camp with Zyklon B gas chambers and blazing ovens. This is the first time that German Jews have been rounded up en masse. Who is released from the camp by when and why is left entirely to the whim of the Nazi SS commanders.

The camp itself is a sprawling detention center with dozens of buildings and barracks, parade grounds, electrified fences, search lights, dog patrols, canteens and clinics, all under the command of the SS, the Nazi's most elite para-military force. The references to medal ribbons concern those awarded during WWI to German soldiers, which included 18,000 German Jewish recipients. Walter Leopold fought in the Germany army and received the highest order of the Iron Cross for bravery in the Macedonia campaign.

Notes from inside the Buchenwald Concentration Camp

November 12, 1938

Breakfast, courtyard roll call run by a police doctor, constantly new arrivals. The supervisor collects money and distributes cuffs around the ears... Electric fences. Machine guns. Filth. Beaten people. Barrack huts. Distribution of identification numbers.

We are moved into emergency barracks, where the floor is covered in mud and water collects in puddles. The Kapo[1] is looking for money. I can hear whipping in the barracks next door as I go to the latrine. "Whoever is ill dies, whoever pretends is beaten cold." We are not allowed to smoke.

November 13, 1938

At 6.30 am we muster on the camp parade yard. I discover people from Leipzig (Grübel, Rabb, Cohn, Jaffé, etc.). My first view of the camp by day: I can make out a bear pit and an aviary. Somebody is lying motionless on a pile of rocks.

There is another roll call, and more new arrivals. Touring the camp, I see a man tied to a post. Guards gather at the bear pit. The prisoner is "liberated" from the post, tied to a stretcher and brought out to the gate. We hear shouts: "No, that can't be!" The guards load their weapons. After a while the executioners appear with the stretcher at the bear pit, around which guards have gathered. The stretcher is carried down, and is soon brought up empty. We hear a fenced gate fall. The bears go down. A scream pierces the air and the guards smirk. Then everything's quiet. I talk to my comrades about what has happened. Squad leaders appear with small jam jars, go down to the bear pit, come up, go to the aviary, take a few pieces of flesh and throw them to the birds of prey. They come back up grinning.[2]

I don't touch anything, no food, no drink. It is a beautiful day.

The flag on the administration barracks is at half-mast, since today the funeral of Vom Rath[3] will take place.

I suffer from terrible thirst, but there is no going out. We urinate where we are. New transports of old men and small boys arrive from Herne, Frankfurt, with nearly everybody beaten bloody. Names are called out by loudspeaker, echoing back from the nearby forest. Late in the evening, we march to a barrack under the searchlights.

There is confusion, and people are shouting. A Rabbi seeks shelter. I am next to Carl and Erich Freund. I rummage out a few biscuits from my suitcase. There is still no water.

We can hear shooting followed by shouts and the chatter of machine guns. Carl's foot is getting more and more painful. We pass a restless night without a proper latrine or toilet paper.

November 14, 1938

Monday morning, and we muster again. I try to relieve myself beforehand. Men have slipped and fallen, smeared all over with excrement. Further up somebody is lying in his last throes. It's the one who ran into the electric fence – nobody's going to bother about him.

The Jews are led by the Kapos onto the roll-call grounds. The SS dogs bark and fight among each other. The ground is black with people; thousands more must have arrived during the night, making a total of 10-14,000. A steam-roller levels the ground. Prisoners pass by, carrying large buckets of liquid manure in twos. If they spill any, the squad leader strikes them in the face until they lie unconscious. They keep separating people out. At midday we are served a bowl of soup, but half of the people don't get any. Our barracks are separated from the actual camp by wire netting. They are covered with tarred paper, which fixes extremely well. Behind them is the camp registry office, and opposite the "sick-bay" with its painted red cross.

Max, a fellow Jew from Leipzig, becomes our Kapo. Loudspeaker wires are laid to the barracks. We can see several aircraft. After each separating out, we change location. In the evening, some of us are driven from the roll-call grounds and we gather behind a dividing fence. We watch the camp workforce march in by searchlight. Carpenters, glassmakers and locksmiths are needed. They should report to the barrack buildings, Jews excluded. Then we too are driven away and once again seek shelter for the night. After a while we are taken from yesterday's barrack to the so-called "laundry".

We thirst. Max brings water, tirelessly, in peril for his life. Prisoner-fitters lay high-voltage cable and fastenings through the window along the ceiling, two cable ends hanging to the floor.

We are driven into nearby rooms. Then the slaughter begins. After about two hours we are driven out of the laundry. I see many corpses smeared with blood. An old Jew whose tongue has been cut out runs to and fro, howling. We are transferred to barrack 5A. The people from Leipzig gradually assemble here, and are registered. Strauss from Frankfurt appears.

We have bread. Water is sold for the first time. The "salesman" names his price.

November 15, 1938

We hear of suicides with pocket mirrors. It is raining, so we drink water from the roofs.

There are rumors going around the latrine, repeated by optimists and pessimists alike. They announce the laws of atonement. Motor vehicle owners are summoned to the big gate. What do they hope for? I do not report.

What actually happened? In the morning there was a parade in the yard, and the fitter was killed. "Who killed him?" The squad leader comes over with sniffer dogs. The word goes around that a Jew has escaped.

We have to sit down on the sharp gravel. The path to the big gate is directly in front of me. To the right sit old Jews with food tins on their heads and the Jewish star smeared on their foreheads in their own blood. Lashes rain down on people bound to trestles.

The midday meal is a bowl of milky rice. Squad leader Oberkrich is armed with a club. In addition to their pistols, all guards are now carrying clubs. Max gets too little food for his Leipzig people and swears.

The squad leader with sniffer dogs comes back. Behind him, two guards lead the escapee, a sturdy man in black overalls between them. He refuses to go on and sits down. They take him away, probably to the oven.[4]

It is the afternoon and we should get dressed. Tables have been set up. A few groups make their way over to the big barrack. It's not our turn yet and we can go behind the wire. Camp officers and squad leaders hang around and shout: "Caps off, hats off." They seize a Rabbi and tear out his beard, and mock a Leipzig acquaintance, a high school teacher, who has just been brought forward, beaten black and blue.

In the evening smoking is allowed outside the barrack, but how to obtain cigarettes? The camp workforce marches back in. Everyone grabs bread. For the first time there is a piece of sausage. Thieves roam. We chat about our neighborhoods. Lights go out.

Loudspeakers summon Jews to the big gate, and there is fresh hope and new rumors.

November 16, 1938

I hear the name of my long-sought friend and go and search for him. Then I am summoned again to the parade grounds.

During roll call the squad leader mocks the Rabbis. The camp commander, who has a Nazi decoration, goes by on a motorbike to the records office, gesticulates wildly, wants to establish whether or not a certain Jew has actually been admitted – it is difficult to be certain.

Lunch, a thick pea soup, is fetched in huge containers amid clouts from the Schupo guards.[5]

A catering van arrives and bread is unloaded. I find a corner to eat, then I am summoned again to stand in the yard. Clips around the ears. Fitting out for new clothes is aborted. Bloodstained shirts are everywhere. Tea is shared out, as are clobbers with sticks. Medication and shaving things are collected. The assembly point is beneath a tree, where a branch sways in the wind. Brooding and pensive, I am feeling sorry for myself.

Work is allotted to us prisoners: carrying stones, hauling and clearing the outhouses.

Aeroplanes, more and more aeroplanes. Mud and clothing. When it is time for supper, the usual men with lists fetch the food and distribute it. I chat with Frank. Later, my rest is punctuated by an attack of fever and much shivering. During the night, we are once again summoned to stand in the yard. I hear the sound of the guard's night-time warning signal.

November 17, 1938

Sickness in the form of itchy and scaly skin, rashes, intestinal bleeding and constipation takes me to the doctor's cubicle. I write letters and deposit them at the camp post office.

We don't go out. Blackmailers flog their wares: one bottle of watery coffee costs two Marks. Chocolate. Cigarettes. Pralines. Bread rolls. We have no admittance to the camp canteen.

I hang around the assembly point or take a walk around the barracks. The "laundry" has become the hospital. Lennhoff injures his hand. Jews are called up, leading to talk of emigration and complaints. They congregate by the big gate and stand for hours listening to the list of names. We are taken to the barber and reappear, shaved bald, late in the afternoon. We stand and freeze until nightfall. Having been constipated for a long time, I am passing blood. I sit on the latrine. Carl is off to buy pralines or chocolates. Frank has a fit. We continue talking into the night. I listen to the other men snoring.

November 18, 1938

The loudspeaker blasts early in the morning. Every inmate has to hand over three Marks for lost or damaged metal bowls or cutlery. New roll calls follow and we report in the yard for further checks and beatings. Lennhoff's hand is much worse. I meet a long-sought friend. I become weak and seek permission to rest in the barracks. No one can wash or clean their teeth. Everyone is filthy. The beatings continue as the soldiers practice their drill. I am growing a beard as my razor has disappeared. The damp has turned my mattress musty. Carl searches for his pralines and finds an empty box.

November 19, 1938

Frank and Danziger are called up for discharge. I give them a secret message.

Dr. Michael and others run around without a coat or jacket; all their possessions have been stolen. The discharged are transported down to the woods. There is bad news, we will only be discharged after a quarter of a year. Despair takes hold, but after a few hours there is a new rumor: someone has heard from the camp leader that everyone will be discharged in one week. The new toilets are to last until Christmas. More roll calls.

The barracks are flood-lit. There are new discharges in between snow flurries, alphabetically checked. Lennhoff's name is no longer called out. We are able to buy soda water, as well as extra bread and food. Lennhoff has bandaged his hand.

A further contribution of two Marks for crockery is demanded. They call out names of people who received a parcel. Parcels are unpacked in the presence of the recipients. All woolen articles, shoes, gloves, beverages and smoking materials are taken away. Money remains at the camp post office.

Two Jews are led out of the big gate, and two minutes later we hear shots. Max, speaking with tears in his eyes, says, "Too late, you will not see that friend again." We hardly ever come to the camp yard now, only to ascertain the total number of inmates. There is no sign of Lennhoff.[6]

Everyone has to buy cutlery and a bowl for three Marks. After a few days, we have to report again. A death transport comes in, while the branch of the tree continues to swing. The cutlery and bowls we have purchased are taken away. Discharges have ground to a halt; no names are called anymore.

A rumor is going around that those remaining are to be fitted out with inmate clothing. A sense of resignation spreads – in fact, despair.

I sit on the toilet next to the children's doctor, Dr. Adalbert Stein. He is owner of a certificate bearing a cross[7] confirming his participation in WWI-frontline action. There is a sudden announcement over the loudspeaker: owners of WWI frontline fighter crosses, who have their identity cards, are to come immediately to the big gate. Stein quickly pulls up his trousers and tramps through the quagmire. Hundreds follow. I don't have the identity pass on me. The registration of identity passes is not recognized without the actual card. I doubt they will acknowledge my prestigious Iron Cross. The crowd cannot be processed immediately, and the majority of the men are sent back to the barracks. Gloomy days follow while the WWI-frontline fighter cross bearers wander off.

More than three weeks have since passed. At 8 o'clock in the morning the loudspeaker blares. My name and date of birth are announced. I nearly pass out. My neighbors shed tears of joy and sorrow.

I share my few belongings in handkerchiefs with Schick, who is completely unable to shake hands. I give a handtowel and underclothes to others and pack up the rest of my things... On the way many offer me their hands and congratulate me. I stand in front of the big gate and hear Carl's name.

We stand until we are stiff, but no food or drink is brought us. At two o'clock in the afternoon we trudge to the barber and are let into lovely warm barracks. Dirty washing has to be handed in if fresh clothing is available. We go through a physical inspection. Those with injuries have to remain behind until healed. They shave our heads with electric shavers. Then we queue for money at the camp post office. Standing for over an hour in the rain by the big gate, we freeze because of our bare heads. We are checked again and some latecomers arrive. Fountain pens, pencils and woolen blankets have to be given up, but I hand over nothing. We are escorted to the big gate in front of the administrative barracks, let in 50 at a time, and given instructions.

Rules of conduct are established. Use the fast train, go to a foreign country, there will be a possibility of re-admission in the future. We are given transfer tickets to Leipzig.

We report again, only to stand outside. It continues to be draughty around the head. An SS dog with a rifle strikes and punishes everyone in turn. "Do you know who's the cop here? Lie down, get up!" The grass has been trampled flat. The squad leader arrives and chases him away. We put on hats. "Show that you are men." We march on hard concrete until we reach a guard house in the woods where we wait for cars to pick us up. Carl has no money, so we share cigarettes. The camp can be seen lit-up in the distance. A car arrives, we pay for the ticket and get in. At Weimar Station there are police.

We stand for two hours in mud. We are to register immediately on arrival with the Gestapo in Leipzig. We are to take the next fast train. We eat in the station restaurant without having to pay. The local community pays for everything, even tobacco.

On the fast train, we are given ham sandwiches and are met by the welfare service from Leipzig. They say everything is fine, including in our homes. Our women, they say, are packing and applying for emigration. I know that my wife will be at the station. Carl shivers and feels faint. We disembark. My wife Hilda is on the platform. We fling our arms twice around each other's necks. I decline the free rations. At home there is a female friend, a relative of my wife's, and Carl. Mäuslein, our dog, sniffs me but does not recognize me. Anneliese, my one-year-old daughter is asleep.

Next morning, we report to the Stapo.[8]

I am issued a new driver's license. Our names are now Israel and Sara.[9]

2 MÄUSLEIN THE MARTYR

On May 15, 1942, the Nazis require all Jewish residents and cohabitants to wear the Jewish yellow arm band on their outer clothing at all times. As part of that decree all Jews also are required to deliver their domestic animals to special collection points for euthanizing.[1]

As insane as this pet slaughter seems, the British also kill 750,000 pets at the start of WWII in 1939 to avoid food shortages.[2]

Walter mourns the fate of their Great Alsatian.

September 24, 1943

We had a beautiful home. It was not ostentatiously furnished, not tarted up like an exhibition of club furniture and highly-polished showpieces to which the housewife would be slave; it was made light through spiritual warmth. Like all Jewish dwellings, it was degraded to the area of operations of the race fanatics and decimated to the bare necessity of shelter for father, mother, child and dog. Yes, in spite of everything, our dog had equal rights to us, and after every move found his own little place and modest little pleasures, insofar as war and the Jewish laws allowed.

Especially on September 24 he had his day – for the last time two years ago in 1941. His birthday, when during the good times he could breakfast on a hard-boiled egg and receive a few sausages to go with his favorite lunch of potatoes with sauce. It was truly an exquisite meal in memory of the event which set a whole household in uproar. For what crawled out of the body of the Alsatian Nora in the sixth hour of the morning was not much bigger than a mouse and would therefore be named Mausi, also called Mäuslein or Maunz. But the little chap grew up quickly, looking half like an angora cat and half like a dancing bear. His curly dark brown coat brightened to a gleaming rust-brown, the floppy ears rose and the snout became more pointed. After just one year, Mausi had grown into a remarkably beautiful dog, who was midway between a fox and a wolf, and drew looks to himself from afar. With his silky, slim, elegant and lithe body, the reddish-brown color of which changed to a black at the snout and the tip of the tail, but to snowy white on the neck, breast and paws, it was no wonder that he attracted every friend of animals to stroke him, but also people who knew nothing of dogs were quite fascinated by the expressive eyes and the attentive ears.

Yes, Mäuslein. You were just a feast for the eyes. With your sturdy appearance and meticulous cleanliness, you were also a clever and thoroughly good animal, and even willing to learn and obey when you hovered between life and death after irresponsible handling in a training institution. Then, in the absence of the longed-for child, you remained our dog-child for years, until you became the untiring playmate and most loyal companion of our little daughter. You shared joys and sorrows with us, prosperity and deprivation, and suffered from a longing which turned into lethargy when vacations separated us. You were all the more fanatical about trips which took the three and sometimes four of us off into the mountains, where you jumped around in carefree boisterousness when the human friends of nature had already sunk worn out into the grass.

True, at times you were badly behaved. In your early years you chewed at furniture and tore down curtains, even pinched what came in reach of your licking tongue and hairy paws, whether it was goose or kippers, but your fox's nature also did not despise fruit. Apples, pears, grapes, figs, nuts and dates disappeared sometimes by the bowl-full from a table set for company, and lacking that, you pilfered a raw potato from the cellar where you accompanied your mistress. Like that you remained young, year for year the same Mäuslein with the face of a child, always curious, and played the role of a child's governess at the age of over 11 just as nonchalantly as in your youth. You were averse to every member of your species, but all the more devoted to us and our friends.

We paid you back with love from the depths of our hearts, took quite some unpleasantness and forgoing of things upon ourselves, and got through a few tussles with new janitors and fearful tenants. You understood that and afterwards let yourself be led, also to the police station, where with wobbly knees and beating heart I had to present you for inspection.

Sensing what things they had in mind for you, before we got in the door you turned yourself into a mangy cur and stood with spread legs and hair on end for the police uncle nicely talking to you, trembling with your whole body and playing the poor, sickly and heavy-legged dog, who paid no attention to even much-loved sugary things. For years we had managed to dodge the real executioners, who had such "Yid dogs" on their lists. Until the terrible people came, until the Nazi swines decided with their insatiable sadism that the animal children of the Jews should also suffer death. By May 30, 1942 all of them, dogs, cats and birds, were to be unconditionally handed over to the relevant animal protection society.

You good dog, you never knew what your foster parents suffered in the 14 days and nights until our separation, all that we tried to keep you alive, our "firstborn", how we ran after every friend of animals who we might ask to take you from the society, and implored them to take pity on you. But they were fearful and reluctant, as they could attract suspicion by taking on a "Yid dog". A brave neighboring woman, the owner of a dachshund, wrung her hands and started up a true advertising campaign for the red fox known around the town, but it was in vain. So, we counted the hours, took you into our arms and caressed the hair on your head, which smelled so nobly, and lavished on you everything that belongs to a last meal before execution.

And then came the moment when your mistress and your playmates tearfully hugged you once more, your master fetched the collar and went out with you into the alley. No, Mäuslein, you did not guess that it was your last walk, and wholeheartedly enjoyed the long-missed pleasure, while Mutti and Annekind[3] waved to you from the balcony.

I walked the long way with you to the place of execution and wept inside when you gratefully looked up at me with your faithful eyes. Then a woman stopped us to say that tomorrow the slaughter of horses would provide good bones for the dog. Tomorrow, for Mäuslein, tomorrow... Should I tell her what tomorrow would be? Thank you, dear woman.

After an hour we were there. It looked inhospitable and smelled of food going off and steamed potatoes. Mäuslein lifted his nose and sniffed, resisted and began to strain, dug his claws into the floor cracks and reared up. He buried his head in my hands and tried to force me out. Then a woman led us to the cages, dirty, horrible cages, where my dog would be locked up until execution. No, I would not allow that. What was this torture for? I wanted to have Maunz with me again. The woman called the manager. Yes, he could be killed at once.

Now the woman leads our Maus animal, our lovely animal, into the electric cage, where he stands with feet in water and she makes his neck wet and lays a thick chain around it. Mausi turns towards me with a look that cuts into my heart. I cannot help my dog. I have a wife and child who they would lay their hands on. "Will the dog really die immediately?" "Immediately. In here I have already killed the largest dogs. Your dog is a small wolf." The largest dogs killed, by a woman. How? When she turns the switch, is Mausi dead? No, he isn't! Then a click, a dull sound. Mausi collapses as if struck by lightning and hangs in the chain with his head pulled up for several seconds. Then when he lies before me again on the flagstones with broken eyes and half-open snout, I collapse over him and my tears flow onto the still warm and sweet-smelling body. Are you dead now, Mäuslein? Quite dead? Forever? No! That must not be so, cannot be so! Dead! Dead! Bring them here, the criminals, the murderers, the vampires, Mäuslein, our dog-child! Finished!

With a wounded soul I come back and drag myself up the stairs one by one. In our home there is one less. Only a dog. A "Yid dog". Now he is dead. Gone for ever.

Mäuslein the martyr.

3   HOLDING OUR BREATH

For five long years between 1938 and 1943 we have no diary entries from Dr. Leopold. We do not know if he simply stops taking notes, or whether they are lost or destroyed. It may be the case that he does not decide to write his memoirs until he is driven underground in 1943. As a result, we lack his contemporaneous insights into a time when the Nazis nearly conquered all of Europe.

We do know some of the events that shaped Walter's life in Leipzig:

- *By 1939, most of his socialist and communist allies are arrested or driven underground.*
- *For the first time in Leipzig a Jewish ghetto is created by the Gestapo as they confiscate Jewish homes and relocate families into rooms within other Jewish homes. Walter makes references later in his diary to moving to smaller and smaller living quarters, ending up in one room with his wife and daughter.*
- *Starting in 1940 all Jews are required to wear the Star of David on their outer garments.*
- *Jews lose their German citizenship and their official documents must list their names either as Sarah or Israel.*

- *The ability to participate in public life is greatly constricted. The following are prohibited for all Jews in Leipzig: Contact with and employment by Aryans; Entering hostelries, cafés and hairdressers owned by Aryans; Entering public parks, green areas and woods; Use of benches on streets and in squares and all public transport; Resorting to Aryan doctors, dentists and non-medical healers; Use of public telephones and leaving one's home between 8pm and 6am.*

We gain a sense of these horrible constraints in Chapter 6 in which Walter tells the sad tale of the "simple-minded Jew," Hans Meir.

Efforts to join his brothers, who moved to the U.S. in 1938, also come to an end in 1941 when the Nazis shut the door to all Jewish emigration. At the same time, Walter's work within the Gemeinde becomes more difficult as the Gestapo uses it as a tool to control and suppress the Jewish community. To compound these difficulties, Walter becomes increasingly suspicious that the new Gemeinde leadership is working far too closely with the Gestapo in order to consolidate its own power and privileges.

Sometime during this period Walter gains sufficient information to become convinced that Jews are being exterminated in concentration camps. He does not yet know the scale and scope of the "Final Solution" developed by the Nazis at the Wannsee Conference in January 1942. Nevertheless, he is certain that deportation to any of the camps means death.

The driving events that shape all of Germany during these years stem from the state of the Nazi war machine. From 1938 to 1942, the Nazis ride a wave of astounding victories, having conquered and/or annexed Austria, Czechoslovakia, Poland, France, Norway, Luxemburg, Belgium, and the Netherlands. England is hanging on by a thread as the German Luftwaffe pummels its cities. The Nazi Third Reich is basking in what seems like an aura of invincibility. Most Germans are enormously proud of these "successes." The idea of a "Reich that would last a thousand years" seems quite realistic as the humiliation of German's defeat in WWI is replaced by pride in the Fatherland.

At the peak of these military successes, Hitler turns on his Russian allies and launches Operation Barbarossa sending hundreds of thousands of German troops deep inside the Soviet Union reaching as far as the gates of Moscow. There, destiny takes a turn as the German war machine grinds to a halt in the long winter of 1942. Moscow does not fall and Hitler's forces lose key battles along the Volga River. From this point on, the Nazis are in retreat on the Eastern Front, suffering enormous casualties. They also lose ground to the Allies in Northern Africa and prepare for what they know will soon come – a massive Allied invasion of France and the opening of a Western front in Europe.

As we return to the diary, the German people are experiencing mounting casualties, food shortages, increasing military call-ups, and severe production pressures within war industries. Aerial bombardment of German cities begins, killing thousands of civilians, night after night, ripping up the infrastructure and destroying the housing stock. For the Jewish people, hardship is transformed into death as the Nazis institute the "Final Solution." If Walter once thought his Iron Cross would save him from the need to emigrate or from deportation to a concentration camp, he realizes now such protection is gone. As a Jew and a socialist, he's a marked man.

As we return to Walter's diary, it is the fall of 1943. His first entry reflects back on the Polish Jewish calamity that took place five years earlier. At that time the Nazi authorities in Leipzig conduct the first roundup of Polish Jews, who comprise nearly one-third of the vibrant Leipzig Jewish community of more than 12,000. It is a sad anniversary for Walter.

November 11, 1943

A day heavy with memories, its dreadful events capable of unleashing trembling and anguish after five long years, a day in October 1938 that is the epitome of horror, the incarnation of the evil deed!

Throughout the last three weeks, the deportation of Jews of Polish origin had us holding our breath. The Nazi regents, who for years had been trying to solve the problem of how to drive away ill-favored foreigners, particularly Jews, with impunity and rob them of their possessions and property in peacetime, at last found the desired opportunity in the refusal of the Polish government to prolong the passports of its Jewish citizens in Germany beyond the year 1938. This gave the Nazis an opportunity to get rid of the Polish Jews cheaply, saddling the Poles with these Jews, as long as they possessed Polish citizenship.

Hardly had day dawned when the Nazis posted policemen at the entrances to a number of houses in which Polish Jews lived, rang to get others out of their beds, ordered them to get dressed, tie up their bundles and come with them. Those concerned were so surprised by the suddenness of the intervention that they overlooked the most necessary things in their panic and pulled together trivialities. Then they tried to talk with the policemen while trotting next to them on the way to the station. When we at the Jewish Community Administrative office started work, the evacuation was already under way. The directors and Rabbis ran in consternation to the authorities in order to engineer at least a temporary postponement of the expulsions, but the officials shrugged their shoulders and took refuge behind their orders.

Our leaders called on the Polish Consulate and received assurance that refuge would be provided. Meanwhile, the news of the Jewish abductions spread like wildfire from house to house. Whoever still had time, and money, closed down their apartment and fled to acquaintances or relatives of German citizenship. Hundreds sought protection in the Polish Consulate, where they camped in the corridor, on steps and in the garden, but most were taken by surprise in spite of this, snapped up and transported to the main railway station. There they were closely guarded by soldiers with fixed bayonets and then dispatched in several trains.

The Nazis made no distinctions by age or sex. From the white-haired great-grandmother to the smallest infant, they tore people out of their homes, even taking them straight from the dining table and driving them out; however, their power faltered before those who had knowingly "lost" their passports, without which they could not be expelled.

We at the Jewish Community Administration were extremely busy. Our employees, insofar as they were not affected by expulsion themselves, were on the move day and night, in order to supply provisions and the permitted pocket money of 10 Marks to those leaving, amongst whom were often their own relatives, and not only Leipzig Jews.

Transport after transport rolled through Leipzig from south, south-western and western Germany heading eastwards. Supported by well-disposed railway officials, we could hand out warm food. But on one train coming from Munich, a hard-necked Nazi escort tried to stop any contact with the occupants with the words: "Get away with you! They are prisoners! If you talk with them, you'll be punished."

"What are you saying, prisoners, they're not that at all. It is peacetime. And anyway, we've got permission from the authorities to provide for the people, and you can't do anything about that!"

He snorted but withdrew and we could get back to work. The deportees were mostly in good cheer and took their fate more lightly than we did, thinking they would soon return, as the Polish government would show the Nazis what's what. The Polish government, however, did nothing of the sort.

What then happened was entirely worthy of the Nazis. Amongst other things, it was reported to us from sympathetic railroad workers that the deported Jews had to leave the trains shortly after dark, just before the frontier, and were then driven with their few belongings into Poland, suffering blows and machine-gun fire that left many dead and wounded. There they are said to have fared not much better, with a few exceptions. The Polish government, which had taken the first step towards the destruction of its Jews, might now enable their return to Germany for slaughter. They were the first among Hitler's victims, and their deportation became the prelude to the events of the coming November.

4   I RAN OFF LIKE A MADMAN

Walter Leopold writes about key events that occurred while serving in the Jewish governing Gemeinde administration in Leipzig. This passage refers to the first roundup of Leipzig German Jews in 1942 (as distinct from the expulsion of Polish Jews which occurred in 1938). A list of a specific number of Jews is posted by the Gestapo for deportation to concentration camps. No one is certain why these particular names are chosen and most of those on the list believe they are headed to labor camps, not gas chambers. Once the lists are compiled, escape is nearly impossible.

To achieve full compliance, the Nazis hold the Jewish community administrators liable for any Jews who do not show up for deportation at the specified date and time. In such cases, a specific Jewish administrator is ordered by the Nazis to find the missing deportee. If that administrator fails, he is deported instead of the missing deportee. Walter is ordered by the Gestapo to go on one such suicide mission.

Undated

In the last hours of their presence here, I only remember their lethargic, almost sleep-walking indifference to what was happening, and their veiled eyes already turned away from the happenings of the cruel world.

I saw them in their last hours sitting in the entrances to their houses on steps and on landings, next to their few belongings, waiting for their abductors. Officials of the thieving tax authorities, hurrying from house to house, had already sealed their rooms, after the dispossession of their property as "hostile to the state" and the withdrawal of their state citizenship had become "legally effective" through the signature of the relevant Jew.

Outside, SS guards drew up with steel helmets and guns with safety catches released, and were greeted warmly by Aryan neighbors hungry for sensation, to whom they appeared as guarantors that the damned "raggle-taggle" would finally disappear. And then the Jews disappeared. Some with their load on bowed backs in the sad trot of exiled people – among them the sick, the crippled and mothers with suckling infants in their arms, others climbing with difficulty onto wagons drawn up by one of the dirty, blood-spewing Himmler dogs.

All of them, hundreds in each transport, came into the assembly camp in the 32nd elementary school in Yorkstrasse. Here, in some classrooms and the gym hall, Jews not yet ripe for deportation had had to strew the floor with straw, so that the measure of their degradation, condemnation and proscription was full. The poorest wept silently to themselves or squabbled from time to time for a place at the wall to lean on it or hunt through their stuff, until they were snapped at again, pushed around and driven up- and downstairs to the clear amusement of the Stapo gang.

A few dozen of these Nazi swine, among them even a lady official from Berlin, had set up their Eldorado in several rooms to subject their welcome victims to a body and baggage inspection, so that they could diligently relieve them of anything desirable that they still bore with them. Briefcases and purses with their contents, pocket- and wristwatches, fountain pens, pencils, razors, knives, clippers, pocket lamps, toiletries and wedding rings, which people had been allowed to keep until now, all made their way into designated boxes and receipts were given in the form of slaps on the face and well-placed kicks. What a joy to let muscles and snouts once more get to work without restraint on outlawed creatures and to relish the facial expressions caused by threats of the worst torture!

Below in the icy schoolyard, to where these people frightened into passivity were chased with prods and shouts together with their bundles and suitcases, moving faster down the stairs through a few well-placed kicks, one had the opportunity to practice one's art of command on human toys, so that for example, after the order "Left turn, march!" the suitcases had to be left behind. In that way one brought more freedom of movement to the troop and its bundles. Their loads were to become even lighter with every mile these people were transported.

Now they stood there as some wanted to have them: the previously well-to-do Jews, no richer than the professional scroungers among them, the old even more helpless than the children, the healthy even more miserable than the ill, and the intelligent mentally even poorer than the stupid. They stood there like that, shivering, and next to them children blue with cold, cried, cut off from the world and without hope of help, just objects of fun for a band of serious criminals. The ill soon collapsed and were dragged off to the police doctor and – later they were not so "humane" – sent back to the community. There they would be freshened up for the next transport.

The resulting gaps had to be filled, so new candidates were summoned from the community, all ready to go. A healthy man, who had slit open his body with a razor blade in utter desperation, was taken into the Jewish hospital and stitched up, but already on the next day was brought to the loading station and put on the train, to the delight of the Stapo.

Nearby the enterprising Stapo policemen swarmed, picking up unsuspecting star-wearers[1] from the street and seizing the best of the people going in and out of the school with a white band on their left arm, who had been engaged by the Jewish community to provide food for the "evacuated" and to run errands. They kept them there and ordered the Jewish community to take care of declarations of property, travel food and luggage.

I was once chosen to chase up a replacement man whom the Stapo louts had not found at home, and I was made responsible for his handing over to the committee at a given time. I was already poised to flee, but the Jew reported himself at the last minute. Then I ran off like a madman.

I had been told in a telephone call that my wife had gone to the school as a helper; she had heard I was away on a dangerous task and rushed up to Grunsfeld[2] to ask where I was. She was calmed down, went back home and felt her blood curdle when suddenly two ruffians, among them an acquaintance from the house, stood at the landing door and demanded two empty suitcases – not for me, as it turned out, but for their victim, whom they had seized along with her sister. When I came storming up the staircase, my wife was leaning against the wall with deathly fear in her eyes.

For two days and nights, while the remaining Jews were locked in their houses, the Nazi brothers drove the Jewish deportees into the school, and took them off to the Engelsdorf loading station.

With more beatings and more kicks with boots, the many hundreds of people were stuffed into the carriages, unheated little coaches – it was a bitterly cold January – on which long icicles hung. Here they received thorough instruction in starving and freezing.

Here also ends my knowledge of what went on, for no "unauthorized person" could now enter the station area, let alone observe what happened to the Jews. But a railway man who accompanied the transport for part of the way gave away that shortly before departure, a troop of heavily armed SS men climbed onto the train. After a few hours these men stood on a crowded siding, in order to pull Jews out of the compartments and beat them half dead, and others, children too, were locked into the brake wagon. When the railway man left the train the following frigid morning, having done his stretch, he also saw the SS thugs pull out people from the carriages, who were frozen and beaten to death, and throw them into the bushes.

The Jewish men and women who were tasked by the community administration to clean the school found not only a mountain of seized suitcases in the rooms of the Stapo, but also the remains of emptied beer- wine- and Sekt[3] bottles, and several empty boxes of cigars and cigarettes. Thus, Commissar Ebeling[4] and comrades had worthily smoked and drank to their efforts for the Third Reich.

PART 2
UNDERGROUND

1942-1943

IMPORTANT DATES

1942

- **January-June:** 230 Allied ships sunk by the Germans in the "Battle of the Atlantic".
- **January 20:** Wannsee Conference held near Berlin that develops concrete plans for the "Final Solution" to exterminate 11 million European Jews.
- **March 17:** Gassing of Jews begins at Belzec death camp in Poland.
- **May:** Gassing of Jews begins at Sobibor death camp in Poland.
- **June 4-7:** Battle of Midway Island in the Pacific – first U.S. victory over Japanese Navy.
- **Summer:** Deportation of Jews from Belgium, Croatia, France, the Netherlands, and Poland to death camps; armed resistance by Jews in ghettos of Kletzk, Kremenets, Lachva, Mir, and Tuchin.
- **September-October:** 110,000 Japanese living on the West Coast of the United States are sent to prison camps.
- **November 8:** Allies invade North Africa.
- **November 19:** Russians launch massive counter-offensive

at Stalingrad that destroys the German 6th army, ends the German progress on the Eastern Front and sends them into a grueling three-year retreat.
- **Winter:** Deportation of Jews from Germany, Greece and Norway to death camps; Jewish partisan movement organized in forests near Lublin, Poland.

1943

- **March:** Liquidation of Jewish ghetto in Krakow, Poland.
- **April 19:** Warsaw Ghetto revolt begins.
- **May 12:** Allies re-capture North Africa.
- **July 5:** The Soviets win the Battle of Kursk crushing the German Panzer and Luftwaffe.
- **July 10:** Allies land in Sicily.
- **Summer:** Armed resistance by Jews in Bedzin, Bialystok, Czestochowa, Lvov, and Tarnow ghettos.
- **September 8:** Italian government agrees to armistice with allies. The Nazis occupy Italy to prevent surrender.
- **Fall:** Liquidation of large ghettos in Minsk, Vilna, and Riga.

5 OUR SOUL HAD LONG LEFT

Walter Leopold and his family run out of good fortune in the fall of 1942 when their names appear on a deportation list for transport to the Theresienstadt concentration camp. At the time he does not know for certain that the plan for the "Final Solution" already had been conceived by the Nazi leadership at the Wannsee Conference near Berlin in January 1942. Walter soon discovers that there will be no more exemptions for German Jewish WWI Iron Cross recipients. All 11 million Jews in Germany and its occupied territories are marked for extermination. The passage below is written about what had occurred a year earlier.

September 17, 1943

Today, together with wife and child, I mark the most memorable anniversary of my life so far: the day of our flight from the snares of the Gestapo. On September 17, 1942, after the clock had struck two in the afternoon, my wife and child took leave of our home, which had shrunk to one room, and set off with the last luggage. Meanwhile I myself crossed the limit of "the ghetto" with coat and briefcase somewhat later, for I had to take care of a rucksack and other pieces of luggage which had been left with a trusty friend. Seemingly quite calm, just having to get along this one last important stretch, I sauntered through the streets of the station and

Reudnitz quarters, keeping my coat over my arm to carefully conceal the tell-tale Jewish star from unwarranted looks. For I had to eliminate any trace of a Jew who for once was not willing to obey the order to go to slaughter.

Far to the east I caught up with my wife and five year old daughter. They were accompanied by the wife of my friend, who transported our hand luggage on her bicycle, laughing merrily, and followed us the rest of the way to our temporary lodgings – the family of a worker put us up first and showed us to a child's room, which as an isolated domicile would be hard to discover.

After days of agitation and spiritual tension, we were overcome by deep shock which exhausted us, and for hours this kept out every feeling and any kind of assessment of our new situation.

Only late in the night, which I spent awake by the side of my wife on a hard child's bed, to which our fleshless bodies were not accustomed, did I find my thoughts again. They jumped around, recapitulating the course of the agonising days which preceded our flight.

The deportation formalities had been the usual ones. First a call by the Stapo to their accomplice Grunsfeld, administrative director and unchecked ruler of the "Jewish Worship Association Leipzig", a communication that meant no less than the announcement of new deportation lists, then the feverish preparation by the surviving Jewish community personnel, and finally the task of informing the victims.

I did not have to wait for the ominous circular with the many rules of conduct and the deportation numbers. A look from my colleague betrayed everything to me. It had been determined that Jews not living in a mixed marriage, Jews over 60 years of age, all war-wounded and holders of the highest war decorations should also be transported to Theresienstadt in Bohemia.

"Resettlement action" was what it was called on the official notice for deportation to human slaughter, while the scoundrels of the security office declared with jovial gestures that care was being taken at the place of arrival that the "emigrants" would fare well. Tens of thousands of Jews from Germany – it was forbidden to speak of "German" Jews – had already been sent to Theresienstadt by the bearers of European culture, and once stuffed in the former fortress, they were cut off from the outside world and could get no news to friends or relatives. It was recounted here and there that one or the other had sent news from Theresienstadt, but those were probably a few resourceful heads from the first transport. Once taken away, all of them were struck from the book of the living and were not even recorded in a list of the dead.

This fact alone justifies the worst fears, as did other versions according to which Jews dragged off to Theresienstadt were treated as prisoners-of-war and shipped off at intervals to Poland, an assertion that did not lack logic at all in view of the endless stream going to the old Bohemian fortress. Had it not been declared to the "participants" in the First World War before the first deportation in 1942 that they could "settle" in the places where they arrived in the Baltic provinces, and make a comfortable life for themselves? At the end of the war, it would be seen what Himmler[1] and his comrades have understood by "comfortable".

As mentioned, the three of us and the 73-year-old, ailing mother of my wife were also on the list. I have the highest war decorations, my mother-in-law is over 60 years old, and the remainder of our large families are in Germany. And that despite earlier assurances by the Jew-eaters that soldiers on the front with decorations from EK I upwards and their families may stay in the German Reich. This disturbed the ambitious Grunsfeld,[2] who like many assimilated creeps regretted nothing more than that he was a child during the last war. Every decorated front soldier he measured up with a disparaging look, with the exception of his father, whose "officer's blood ran in his veins", as he liked to boast.

He is still pained by the mishap he underwent with the last transport, which he tried to bundle me on by the dirtiest of means.

Through the malevolent concealment of my war decorations he had had me classified as ready for deportation in June, 1942, as the final link in the long row of my deported friends. The cunning plan failed thanks to my title deed,[3] which even for the executioners' henchmen was an adequate piece of evidence. (Grunsfeld was not taken into custody in spite of his failure to make an official report and deliberately giving false testimony, one more reason for suspicion that he stood against his own people in alliance with Himmler's hordes.)

Time will tell what really happened, whether the constant rumors of active participation even by the "Reich Association of Jews in Germany"[4] in the extermination of its members corresponds to the facts. To an experienced person this apparent fairy-tale does not seem absolutely improbable; one had to see how many a Jewish functionary sacrificed his colleague for the sake of a temporary reprieve, and how the granting of insignificant advantages, with which the Nazi officials lured the lickspittles, created willing informers, or at least people of weak, spiritually impoverished natures, who still lived in the crazy hope that the sacrifice of their neighbor would bring their own salvation. Time strode roughly over them too, and drove them after their victims, whose fate they believed they had evaded through their services to the cause of the Nazis. Many of them may have known how to continue their misdeeds in Theresienstadt, Poland or other places. For them there will be no peace and no return. Like all criminals, they will end their unworthy existence on the scaffold, so that the Jewish community is cleansed of this stain.

The hope that I may live to the day of liberation and justice calmed me down during the first night in our sanctuary. However, the fate of my mother-in-law and many fellow-sufferers who believed our protection would bring them God knows what relief was like a throttling grip on my throat. Besides my mother-in-law, we had let only two other Jews in on our plan, people who we knew would sooner go to their deaths than betray us. Nobody had the slightest suspicion.

For we too had fulfilled all formalities, beginning with the declaration of property, through which each deportee had to cede his worldly goods to the state, up to the preparation of the prescribed "travel luggage" and tying up beds and mattresses. Nobody noticed that for months, with the exception of our furniture, we had brought to safety everything we considered useful and necessary for our future: firstly, our extensive library, bed linen, clothes, shoes, my optical instruments, jewelry, the stamp collection and much else. The smuggling continued also during the night before last, suitcase by suitcase and basket by basket; under cover of night but also in bright daylight, they were brought unobtrusively down the stairs and through the streets of the Jewish quarter to various Aryan friends, after they too had received their shares as payment for protecting us.

The rest of the clothing, bed linen and necessary travel kit we kept back in case we should be taken into custody as runaways – one had to reckon with that – in spite of all the security measures. We provided ourselves with food supplies and calmly dealt with the numerous visitors who rang the bell, partly to say good-bye and partly to receive advice as they believed us to be companions on the journey.

The last 13 days were unbearably busy and they could be, since contrary to its custom the labor office had released me from employment in view of my imminent "emigration". What I clearly had to do in front of my fellow human beings was to play the tortured and nervous man, who spends the rest of the day away and seeks relaxation for a few hours with friends. The last person with whom we spoke was a doctor friend. He kept us company for our last meal in our home, without realizing that our innocently chewing mouths took in more air than food.

Taking leave of our home was painless. Our soul had long left it. What had been dear to us for so long had turned into dead inventory. And an hour later, in the early afternoon, we had flown, unnoticed and unheeded. Next to me my wife wept silently to herself. She mourned for her dear mother, whom we had to leave to the killers, without any possibility in her state of advanced illness to drag her through misfortunes and perils into hiding, the duration of which was unforeseeable. It was already extraordinarily daring for three Jews to flee – one more and there would be even fewer people who would have the courage to extend a helping hand.

An ill person was not to be helped, even if it was one's own mother, and even if one of us three – we had to look this danger in the eye too – had to go to hospital for a long time, one would have to reckon with voluntary departure.[5] For they had dragged away my mother and 87-year-old grandmother nearly two years earlier to the Pyrenees, where the matron went mad with grief and died a lonely death.[6] They also burned down the house of the relatives of my father over their heads and drove them away or deported them, and in the end did not stop at eliminating "Jewish dogs, cats and birds."

Nothing was sacred anymore to these bandits, not the lives of humans nor animals. Nothing could sate their thirst for blood, and it almost seemed as if they would not rest until the last heart had bled out.

We three still lived. And as we listened to the peaceful breathing of our child, who slept carefree in her little bed next to us, we slumbered into the first morning of our freedom.

6 HE ONLY PRETENDS TO BE SO

Walter is extremely cautious when writing about their life underground. He never uses full names, perhaps as a precaution against his diary falling into the hands of the Gestapo. The World Holocaust Remembrance Center records the following about Georg Jünemann (whom the Leopolds call Grandpa J) who was one of those who provided shelter. The details about Walter's employment, the number of hideouts and whether Jünemann was the first to take them in may not be entirely accurate. But we get an excellent sense of Walter's political reputation – he was a known socialist.

"Georg Jünemann, b. 1876, a teacher and pious Catholic, was forced into retirement by the Nazis because he objected to their views. In 1942, he shared a home with his widowed daughter, Josephine Zauzich, also a believing Catholic and anti-Nazi, and her five-year-old son. Walter Albert Leopold, b. 1898, who was employed by Leipzig's Jewish community as a lecturer at an adult-education center, was on the list of Jews to be deported to the Theresienstadt ghetto, together with his wife, Hilda, and their five-year-old daughter, Anneliese. The transport was to leave on September 18, 1942, but the family decided to go into hiding instead. The day before the scheduled transport they went underground and adopted false identities.

Leopold was a socialist, and anti-Fascist activists in the city helped the family find refuge. They moved from one hiding place to another, with at least 12 people helping in different ways to hide them.

Their first place of hiding was in the home of Georg Jünemann and his daughter. It was then, on the eve of a transport, that the danger was greatest, as the Gestapo mounted intensive searches for Jews who had fled. The Jünemanns, however, were undeterred. On one occasion, indeed, their home was searched, but fortunately it was not a thorough search, and the fugitives were not discovered (the little girl hid under a bed).

Jünemann and his daughter could not hide the family indefinitely, as food was scarce. The Leopolds hid in their home twice, for five weeks each time. Georg Jünemann and Josephine Zauzich took a great risk by hiding Jews in their home – an offense, which could have led to their internment in a concentration camp.

They received no material compensation, and even reduced their own food intake during periods of shortage, in order to share what little they had with the persecuted Jews." [1]

Fear of the Gestapo hovers over Walter's meticulous plans as he creates false trails about where they are headed. Because he is so certain that death awaits them if they are caught, he and Hilda arm themselves and agree to commit suicide rather than face capture. He does tell us what then would happen to their young daughter.

The effort to gather sufficient food becomes more and more difficult as Allied bombs explode throughout Leipzig from late 1943 through 1944.

It is worth noting the careful planning involved in each aspect of their escape. Walter knows that their survival depends on his ability to understand and think several steps ahead of the Gestapo pursuers. It also depends on their young daughter playing her part unerringly. One revealing utterance, one telling reflexive motion that suggests they are not who they pretend to be, and they all die.

The following passages are written in September and October 1943 while still in hiding.

Fall 1943

Our escape plan, however early it had been drawn up and carefully worked out, very nearly fell through. For the friend, a young electric engineer, who had offered us a definite place of safety as well as food, and had insisted that we come when I pointed out the difficulties of accommodation for an unforeseeable period of time, suddenly moved with his military repair column to Russia one bright day in June. He said goodbye with the friendliest of assurances that everything we needed had been provided for, and that he had again reminded his wife and his parents, who lived with them, to give us a warm reception.

But once he was far away and out of sight, sound and communication, and our names appeared on the deportation list, his relatives pulled dubious faces, and pointed out in bright colors all the dangers we could plunge them into. We comforted ourselves and awaited the young man's return, which did not come, despite my long beseeching letters. The uncertainty weighed more heavily on us with every day that brought us closer to deportation. Already the name Theresienstadt hung heavily over our heads, and another friend advised us to choose the way into the concentration camp over the constant humiliation of having to beg for accommodation – advice that bordered on madness. The decision was ripening within us to escape the stranglehold of the Gestapo by committing suicide, when a worker from among the engineers without further ado offered to hide us for five weeks to begin with. After that we would have to see.

Although he lived with his wife and two children aged 12 and one in a modest little home with three small rooms, if we would make do with the smallest room, there would be nothing in the way of our coming. Forced by circumstances and after long consultation with our confidants, we accepted, and the savior appeared with his wife. We dragged a lot of cutlery, kitchen utensils and other useful things with us, partly as a gift in return for his compassionate deed, and partly to rescue them for us.

During the last night in our house I wrote two weighty letters of significance, one to the Leipzig Jewish Office, and the second to our best friend Friedel. They were intended firstly to mislead any bloodhounds tracking us down and secondly to protect our friend from the suspicion that, with her constant coming and going in our home, she knew about our flight plans.

I wrote with a stub of pencil, pretending I was writing in an emergency. In the letter to the Jewish Office I gave Bitterfeld station[2] as the place of postage, in the second, however, Dessau,[3] and arranged with the friend that she should hand over the lines written to her to the Gestapo immediately upon receiving them. The Nazi gentlemen, who I knew by experience did not have the cleverest of heads, would be deceived and release Friedel from any suspicion, and would not search for us in Leipzig but give greater consideration to the rumor that we had fled to Switzerland. By the time the rumor was circulated, no gullible person could miss the indications I repeatedly gave about Hochstein[4] being the best crossing point.

A few hours after our arrival at the first place of refuge, I pressed the letters into the working man's hands of the asylum provider, which were gloved to avoid fingerprints, and sent him on his way with ample money for travel and provisions.

In spite of all this we still did not feel entirely easy. The wife and mother of the engineer kept us company as we settled into our new accommodation, secretly glad that –now that they were at least temporarily relieved of the burden of finding us a home – they could convince themselves that we were settling into the new situation. Even though Anneliese played with the children of our hosts and was seemingly untouched by the events of the day, and although no one present betrayed any agitation, we still felt wretched. The thought of possible deportation, which could befall my mother-in-law the next morning, when the Gestapo hunters, together with their steel-helmeted seconders, failed to find us, left our faces as white as cheese and made our intestines revolt.

We left the abundant provisions and the hard sausages decidedly meant as iron rations to our hosts, and we were glad that they tasted better to them than to their exasperated charges.

Our own situation worried us not so much. For hardly any Leipzig inhabitant – never mind a Stapo man – might have a notion that we were situated only a few kilometers from the Jewish Quarter in an inconspicuous little proletariat house in the east of the city. And so the Stapo man would hold my letters from Bitterfeld and Dessau under the nose of someone who seemed cleverer than himself, and yell at him whether he thought the good Leopold was so simple-minded that he would remain in Leipzig, so that one day, as sure as two times two makes four, he would run into the grasping arms of the upholders of the war laws.

"No, you who are nine times cleverer, he is not that daft, he only pretends to be so, as if he were a tame sheep and ready, like all people of his race, to let himself be led to the butcher."

"No, and again, no. Should you, however, really want to know where he has fled to then we will tell you: to the Swiss border. Yes, he has chosen the same fate, as we explain to the Jewish community more than once through insinuations. Much as he seems cunning to himself, he goes to the same fate as all those who tried before him. Our border guards have been alerted and will welcome him and his brood. And now go to hell with your self-important pretensions. We alone know how to deal with runaway Jews!"

In the Hindenburgstrasse they would make deductions and speculate and shout, send radio messages, set up secret letter drops and boast that they knew how to handle disobedient Jews. Therefore, we need hardly expect any unpleasant surprises from this quarter. We also had at our disposal a modest sum of money, which we had extracted from the snooping Nazi thieves little by little over the years, and this together with our pieces of jewelry, which friends had taken into safekeeping, would suffice for our immediate needs.

One big worry remained though: whether our six-year-old child could behave quietly enough for months on end so that the other occupants of the house would not become suspicious, and whether she could remain discreet in front of the acquaintances of our hosts and other nosey people, who might show interest in the child and her origin, and not to be misled to express her Leopold name rather than our pseudonym: "Freiherr" from Mannheim.

We taught her this easily memorable name on the day before we left, with the explanation that we were not allowed to call ourselves Leopold anymore, as long as "the wicked people" were pursuing us. In addition, "Freiherr" (free man) was a nice name and everyone would like it. The dear little soul did not disappoint us, adhered to our admonitions through all temptations and house searches until today, and hopefully it will remain so.

The first days of our taking refuge brought neither novelties nor surprises. Conversation with our hostess, her children and her husband when he returned from work brought us some diversion, and their old-fashioned radio, which as genuine proletarians they had not declared, kept us more or less informed of happenings in the Nazi camp, the position of the British, and the progress of the war in general.

Somewhat awkward and not without danger was the way to the toilet – a small hut in the yard, which was used by every member of the house and therefore not protected from curious looks. But even these excursions passed without incident, moreover my razor allowed the beginning of a beard, a change which in a short time made me old and ugly. This change affected me less than the people with me, who got worked up thinking that a stubbly beard would damned well make me look like a Jew and arouse suspicion. With the objection that then I too would be arrested and deported, I withdrew for the time being from the disapproving looks to our lonely little room.

I buried myself in setting up a coding system that would enable me to keep in contact and exchange thoughts with a few friends, especially with Friedel, while I did not dare to leave the house. Hardly waiting for the hour of our getting together again, she appeared ten days after our departure, deliriously happy to see us unharmed, and brought us bread and a pot of jam. Then she told us in great detail about the excitement and consternation that our escape had triggered in the Stapo and the Jewish community office. She told us how Grunsfeld went pale on hearing the news that of all people, the main objector to Stapo orders, Leopold and his family had slipped away contrary to all calculations, and how swearing he crashed from office to office, telephoned the Gestapo, questioned the staff and was finally given a formal ultimatum from Ebeling of the Gestapo that his head would roll if the Leopold family was not captured within 24 hours.[5]

And then she told us about her official visit to those awaiting deportation, who, like everyone before them, were lying on straw in the sports hall of the 32nd Elementary School, and on hearing that "Leopold has left!" lamented the loss of their friend, and the danger to which he had "wilfully" exposed himself and his loved ones by his impossible attempt to escape.

But when I began to speak about my mother-in-law, she hesitated. Only so much was forthcoming, namely that the sick, old woman appeared to mourn the puzzling disappearance of her children, but otherwise lay still and submissive among her fellow sufferers. To our question about whether they had done harm to this suffering person as revenge for our flight, Friedel lowered her head and remained silent. In the afternoon, she continued, shots were fired in the school playground, but she had not been able to find out anything more.

Then the conversation took an unusual turn and her eyes began to sparkle again when she told us how the Jews who had lost the capability of logical thinking in their Stapo psychosis and submission to Hitler's bloodhounds, and could not distinguish between the force of the state and domination by terror, quite openly disapproved of my obstruction against deportation and slaughter, while the majority broke out in shouts of enthusiasm when it became known that we had escaped the executioner.

With these words Friedel laughed out aloud, but became thoughtful again when she asked who would continue to provide food for us if something was to happen to her. Indeed, that was the cardinal question upon which the success of our plan depended. I thought that we could gradually search out several sources and then the edibles would flow in greater quantities. Feeling calmer, Friedel said goodbye with the firm promise that we would see each other again soon and of the continued transmission of coded letters with which she would keep us informed about everything worth knowing in-between her visits. I could send answers via her sister, who lived in the Bayrischestrasse and was married to a non-Jew, and would hardly be suspected of being our *postillion d'amour*.

After only a few days our core rations of butter, cheese, sausage and other provisions, which we had stored with our hosts, were eaten up. The first worries about our existence crept in and rubbed off on our hosts, whose facial expressions darkened, and who became taciturn and sometimes even cold. Finally, they let all their good intentions and encouragement be forgotten, as the first flames of enthusiasm and willingness to take us in died down.

What helped us most then was when Friedel managed to get hold of a weekly loaf of bread, and another friend and her mother, who had the bulk of our precious belongings in her care, surprised us with a sausage or a little bacon, or an acquaintance from work, disguised as an old man, brought a head of cabbage or a few beetroots and potatoes. The worries which our friend on the Eastern Front had shrugged off with the words that he had provided for our safekeeping for at least a year, came back to me and took on enormous proportions as I realized we were only at the beginning of a long journey. And when the engineer returned on leave, unexpectedly and coughing, he had forgotten about all those dreams of the future on which he had raised our hopes, but he at least kept his promise to take us in at the end of the four weeks on the condition I get rid of my beard.

We breathed again on hearing these words, which removed the worst of our worries, took new courage, wanted to do everything we could and go without much, if only our child, for whom we were taking these risks, could get enough to eat. For the time being we were satisfied with this not exactly wholesome emergency accommodation and to have headed off any searches by the Gestapo, who could have targeted the house of the engineer, who was known to be friendly to Jews.

On one of the following evenings I dared to take the first step into the outside world in the company of my landlord, camouflaged with glasses and cap, tottering, unused to walking, thoughtful. I was glad when we had climbed the two staircases to our engineer friend's apartment. We met him surrounded by his family and one or two friends, who had come to visit him once more before his return to the front. After a few moments he put on his rucksack, declared that he had agreed to our coming, and said goodbye with a warning to be very careful, as well as other bits of advice which were in no way marred by any familiarity with the nuances of the Nazi hounds. All the same, I was at last certain that I could protect my wife and child from going under, that I could keep them from sinking, so with this not inconsiderable piece of change in my pocket, I discussed the details about our move in with the engineer's family. I had to accept the condition of a completely separated kitchen, a new, unexpected obstacle which we would have great trouble making our way around.

7 YOU SIMPLE-MINDED JEW

In the passage below Walter describes Hans Meier, a Jewish man who gets crushed by the ever-tightening noose of Nazi oppression in Leipzig. But who is Meier? On the surface it seems that he is a friend who tells Walter of his horrific fate. But the dialogue below also includes behind-the-scene Nazi discussions when Meier obviously is not present, nor is Walter.

In Germany at that time, the name Meier signifies a Jewish person. It is possible then that the tale of Meier is more like an allegorical play, a composite of true stories about passive Jews who allow themselves to be led to slaughter. It is the polar opposite of how Walter sees his own defiance of the Nazis.

At first glance, the Meiers and the Leopolds share a common plight. Like Meier, Walter and his family are forced from their large apartment into smaller and smaller quarters, losing their decidedly bourgeois standard of living.

Like Meier, Walter's WWI medals no longer protect him. Like Meier, he must wear the Jewish star after September 1, 1941, and adhere to an ever-growing list of prohibitions against Jewish participation in public life.

But Walter, of course, wants to highlight the obvious differences. Meier's fate and demeanor is what Walter desperately struggles to avoid. Unlike Meier, Walter defies the Nazi commands, even if his actions do little or no harm to the Nazi machine. Most importantly, he rejects the passive Jewish mind-set that acquiesces to unjust power. Walter is reminding himself and the rest of us why he chooses the deprivations of underground life for his family – why he chooses dignity and even death over abject humiliation.

September, 27, 1943

The rumor goes around that the Jew-basher and general spy Gebhard has lost his post, and sought refuge with the fire protection police. For a long time, he was the feared executor of the notorious triumvirate Freyberg-Furch-Voigt, whose main occupation was making the Reich trade fair city cleansed of Jews.[1] A trade fair without Jews seemed to them an ideal no less worth striving for than a Gewandhaus concert hall[2] without Mendelssohn,[3] whose statue a deputy mayor described as an "arse with ears" and had pulled down from its plinth – contrary to the order of the artistically inclined mayor Dr. Goerdeler,[4] one of the few men in his position who dared to defy Hitler and was dismissed for his pains. The destruction of the monument lent a new, long-awaited impetus to the Jew-bashers. Underhanded elements, who had been waging a feud against intelligence, hard work and peace, and lived as perpetual loafers, threw themselves vehemently on the Jewish representatives of arts, science and capital, whom they hated.

"Office for Promotion of Home Construction" is how they harmlessly and inconspicuously named a city office of the Gestapo, in which the men plotted action against the seven thousand remaining Leipzig Jews. Expropriation laws for Jewish property eased their handiwork, which offered public office candidates in all departments enticing premiums and rapid promotion.

Nothing more was demanded of them than a good portion of unscrupulousness, an appearance as terrifying as possible, and the ability to drum orders in a concentration camp tone into the heads of dangerous Jews, while a gift for snooping and a certain bearing, like that of a policeman, could only enhance the aptitude of the zealous official.

Gebhard counted among these types, who were so admired by the Hitler Youth. Before his cupola-shaped head surrounded by red stubble and his effusions stinking of head rot, fussing like a true Saxon with words learned from the Stapo canon, victims trembled like mice in front of a swaying snake's head. Woe betide the Jews whose knowledge of human beings and presence of mind were not enough to parry the hook to the jaw by the reputed master boxer who had run away from the S.P.D.[5]

In complete contrast to his intellectual potency, Gebhard's activities were manifold and indeed all-encompassing. They were by no means limited to carrying out the plans hatched by the triumvirate for "Promotion of Home Construction," which were: expulsion of Jewish home-owners from their own property, the creation of a ghetto and restrictions on purchases to three shops and specific goods for a few hours a day. Finally, with the help of his ears and Argus eyes,[6] he spied also on the most sacred moments of Jewish families. The methods he used were like those of the rest of the Hitler clique: first the stealthy casting of the noose, then its tightening until the victim is driven out.

What happens when Jews are driven from one home to another? Little or nothing. One has the new home redecorated, moves and goes on living.

We are told: You Jews are arrogant, impudent and on top of that demanding. You live *eo ipso*[7] in houses which have to be Aryanized, because as goods stolen by Jews they are part of the wealth of the German people. So, get out of the stolen property! And Gebhard carried out his task in masterly fashion; he first snooped around the properties, and then made a report to those higher up and called in the owner. The latter knocks shyly and is let in.

Jew: Morning, Herr Gebhard. Hans Meier is my name. You asked me to come.

Gebhard: Wait until you are spoken to... You were supposed to come at seven! Now we are at half past seven.

J: Sorry, Herr Gebhard, I am a sick man.

G: You Jews have all sorts of excuses. I'm ill too, we're all ill, and our soldiers have their mouths shot to pieces. And why don't you immediately show your identity card when you come to see the authorities, huh? And I suppose you have forgotten that you are called Israel?

J: You told me to come, Herr Gebhard.

G: Just a moment! (he touches his forehead with an outstretched index finger, sticks the same finger into the air towards the visitor, pulls a dossier out from under the papers). Yes, we've got it here. So you are the Jew with the property in Ehrensteinstrasse? What date is it today?

J: The 18th, Herr Gebhard.

G: The 18th... You've to leave your house by the thirtieth and look for another home, understood? ... Did you understand me?

J: Herr Gebhard, I am a very sick man...

G: You shouldn't keep trumpeting on about the same thing. You could long be dead, and then we'd have less bother.

J: But the property belongs to me, Herr Gebhard.

G: Belongs to you! Did you say belongs to you? Stolen it, that's what you've done, you rascal, stolen it from our own people!

J: But I fought on the front and took to the field for Germany...

G: Well, you were lucky that you got out of it. And what you did out there, I don't care a damn about. If the Jews had not been there, we'd not have lost the war.

J: I am not aware of being guilty of anything!

G: I believe that of you, you hypocritical criminal. So, get a move on. I've no time! By the thirtieth, do you understand?

J: Yes, where then should I get a home so quickly, Herr Gebhard?

G: Where you get it, I don't give a shit about. How many people are you?

J: Three. My wife, my daughter and me.

G: How old is your daughter?

J: Fourteen, Herr Gebhard.

G: And how many rooms do you have at present?

J: Two, Herr Gebhard. A living room, a bedroom and the room of my daughter.

G: Three people... three people... Hmm. One room is enough for that.

J: For goodness' sake, Herr Gebhard, with our daughter we can't really...

G: Course you can! You just put in a room divider curtain, then it's all OK. Go to the Jewish Community, Riess should give you a room. Off with you! And if you are cheeky again, you'll get it! Off with you!

J: (Goes away).

G: (Takes the receiver from the telephone and calls the Jewish Community). Gebhard here! Get me Riess! Goddammit, where's he got to! Have I got to run after you? Gebhard! Riess, I just had Meier from the... the.... yes, the Ehrenstrasse. He's moving out on the last day. He gets a room.... Don't grumble, if I said a room, then that's it. Stick a room divider curtain in, then he can go on with his copulating. Done, finished.

(Calls the Labor Office). Gebhard here! Herr Inspector Mühlich, please. Yes, Gebhard, Heil Hitler, Herr Mühlich, there's another of those Yiddish pig litters in Ehrensteinstrasse 17, a man and a woman and a daughter.

All absolutely healthy pickpockets. Shut them up properly so they can't stand it. How? Yes! Push them really hard! And if they don't do what they're told, you just need to tell me. Yes. Let's do it. Heil Hitler.

In response to this, Herr Meier, his wife and his daughter the following day fell into the hands of this notorious Mühlich, Senior Inspector of the City Labor Office Leipzig, once a tobacco trading company in miniature, today the "Deutschen Rauchwaren GmbH"[8], a type of fat-bellied Nazi boss in fashionable dress.

Herr Meier, kept alive by insulin injections, chopped wood from early morning to late evening, day after day, until the skin of his hands broke open. And then he sank half-unconscious to the ground and awaited the lashes from Herr Mühlich, which were soon forthcoming. Meanwhile, his wife and daughter had to muck out pig sties with their bare hands. The faces, hands and clothing of these poorest of people showed that at times they were forced to work through cold showers and blows of a stick.

And to such mortals were the Leipzig Jews totally crushed; no, not only the Leipzig Jews, but all Jews in the whole of Germany and until today all European countries. For it's a matter of bringing their movable goods and then themselves under the hammer as quickly as possible.

That was not difficult to achieve after the "taming of the shrews." You simple-minded Jew, believing that you could pacify Hitler's hyenas through conscientious fulfilment of eight thousand orders! You have lost the roof over your head and had to sell off your much-loved pieces of furniture at bargain prices to squeeze your wife, child and modest belongings into a single room.

Like all your suffering companions in straitened circumstances, you have used part of your money to turn this corner allotted to you into a snug home, in spite of the beds, cupboards and table, and look, you have proved yourself a master of making the most of space and to be of good taste. You don't want to let things get you down and want to make visits for guests pleasant and stimulating. The two sofas harmoniously pushed together are your beds, and beneath your magnificent lamps you and your family can be seen smiling contentedly over a homely meal. It is tasty despite the lack of the right ingredients, which you have been deprived of for a long time, not because of wartime rationing but because you are a Jew!

And woe betide you if some Gebhard blundering in discovers fruit, compote, fish, sweets or any other food or drink products which the Consumer Association Authority for Jews does not make available or sells to Germans with lucrative connections. And woe betide you if his baleful glare successfully censures the bread bin for moldy bread. And woe betide you if you should dare to use ice to keep perishable foods fresh. The brown-shirted manager of the food business, Jung, a concentration camp torturer, would have you arrested directly at the ice-cart! Yes, he can do that. But if anything spoils, you or your wife have to pay for it.

And one more piece of advice I would like to give you: eat up what you have bought on the same day. Keep only as much money at home as is granted to you monthly by the Finance President. If for example it is altogether 200 Marks per month, then on the 15th only 100 Marks may still be found in your purse. What is left over you have to deposit in your savings account. Constantly think that not only Gebhard but also the Gestapo are on your heels, day and night. Unexpected, they stand on your doorstep, these dogs, they chase you, your wife and your children out of your beds, throw the contents of your cupboards on the floor, kick around for anything suspicious, and pinch what is desirable, e.g. razor blades, skin cream, hair oil. They burrow around for genuine jewelry, diamonds, gold watches, chains and rings, silver light stands and fine cutlery, all things which you as a Jew are not allowed to possess and should have handed over long ago.

You bring them to the Gestapo the next morning and have to stay there. Your family will only find out days later that you have wandered into a police prison and from there to Herr Mühlich, where you wait with your skin beaten black and blue for your dispatch to Buchenwald, Sachsenhausen or Dachau, without the slightest prospect of ever seeing your family again.

Yes, my dear patient, war-decorated front soldier Meier, a thousand-fold are the tortures which they have thought up to improve your spiritual, bodily and mental wellbeing. Don't make any objections, a whole book would not suffice to record them, and your memory would be too weak to recapitulate them daily and hourly. You were disturbed in 1938 when you were forbidden to go to any public places, including theatres, cinemas, concert halls, baths, swimming pools, fairs and museums. You grieved when you had to bring the radio sets to the handing-in place.

Did you thereby believe you had banished the tormenting spirits? Not at all. Week after week, announcements, decrees, and prohibitions for the protection of the Aryan community hailed down. Specifically:

<u>Prohibited</u>
Contact with Aryans
Employment by Aryans
Entering hostelries, cafés and hairdressers
Entering public parks, green areas and woods
Use of benches on streets and in squares
and all public transport
Resorting to Aryan doctors,
dentists and non-medical healers
Use of public telephones
Going out between 8pm and 6am

You gasp for air, my dear Meier, you fear you are going to choke. Calm down! No "Jewish haste!" It is the task of a higher authority to have you kick the bucket only very gradually. It does so according to a daily, monthly and annual plan, so that you snuff it in such and such a year, in such and such a month, and exactly on such and such a day, and endeavors to lend a hand if there should be any hiccups.

For this purpose, you were branded in the first place, i.e. you were obliged to brand yourself. At the Jewish community office, you received wonderful yellow Jewish stars similar to those stuck on Jewish shops a few years ago, so that the "seething soul of the people" did not first have to seek out the sales outlets of the haters of Germans. Sew (clipping or sticking forbidden) the state persecution pieces onto your dress, blouse, or coat, on the left side of the breast, but in a way so that a raised arm could not conceal it. If this happens but once, voluntarily or involuntarily, you must be prepared for something to happen. For spies are all around, Aryan and Jewish, and not only Gebhard and the Stapo men. Don't let yourself be seen in front of Grunsfeld or Steinert[9] anymore without a star. They are greedy for credit in Aryanizing Germany.

And now do take off your WWI ribbons, also your decoration for being wounded, for you should know that no German wants to hear or see anything about a Jewish front soldier ever again. (Which is not difficult to attain due to the memory deficiency of the Germans.)

What do you say, that your seriously wounded and half-crippled friend, almost without the top of his skull, is not allowed to wear his EK I medal[10] and his golden decoration received for being wounded and is sworn at? Why are you surprised at this? Don't you know that this war cripple is not even allowed to use the tram to carry out his official errands? Yes, he has even been forbidden to rest on a park bench if he loses his breath on the way! Now he leans against a wall because he cannot go further, to the scorn of passers-by and his own torment. Yes, my friend, that is National Socialism!

Be careful that when you are out you are not thrown to the ground by a stroke, as happened last week to an old Jew on his way to the Police Presidium. He lay in the middle of the pavement for three or four hours in agony, laughed at by the crowd of people "disinfected of the Jewish spirit," until a Jew came along by chance and saw his plight. What to do? Call the Jewish Community Office. Impossible, because Jews are forbidden to telephone. He was not allowed to ask an Aryan. So, he ran to the Police Presidium and asked them to notify the Jewish Community Administration, which happened after a long delay. When the Jewish doctor finally appeared at one o'clock with two other star-wearers, the man was dead. So that you recognize, my dear Meier, what a proud Aryan heart is, that is why I am telling you this. Now wait for the next blows, then we will talk again.

* * *

My thoughts wander back to you, my dear fellow sufferer, Meier. Yes, one can see that your diabetes has got worse and that your war wounds are painful and discharge pus. How so, the labor office has ordered you to the garbage heap, the stinking rubbish pile of Leipzig, where you have to collect cans and other old materials from the putrid pile of stinking refuse? And the two other orders, over there on the table, what do they read? Your wife and your daughter are to report to the rag sorting facility? Well, one really cannot say that Gebhard runs a bad office. It will be useless, my dear fellow, to ask the Jewish doctor for a certificate in which it is plain to read that you cannot carry out this hard work due to your illness. He has been threatened with arrest were he to encourage Jewish shirking. You can register with the municipal medical officer. If you are lucky, you will be allowed in, and if you are very, very lucky, you will be examined. But whether the city doctor will dare to plead for a sick Jew is highly uncertain.

The Jew Meier, like so many before him, had no success with his complaint. Therefore, he procured for himself, his wife and his child – it was considered a perk – permission from the Jewish community through Gebhard's middle man to travel to work on the front platform of the trailer, designated for the purchase of food and a few other supplies for old neighbors, who were hardly able to crawl, and were without work.

The three reported at the appointed time to their workplaces, were first yelled at according to the rules, and were then saddled with very dirty handiwork, as ordered by the labor office for Jews. The father collapsed after only a few hours. He was taken to the Jewish hospital, that porter's building in Dösen magnanimously left to the Jewish community by the Lord Mayor of Leipzig as a replacement for the large institute stolen from them. Mother and child came home from work every evening dirty and tired, and then had to think about a warm meal which was refused them in the work canteen.

Winter was coming, the best time to devise new villainies against the Jews. So, let's go. Hand over all fur items to the Jewish community! You are not entitled to payment or any kind of compensation. Also, remove fur collars and trimmings from coats and jackets. It was useless, my dear Meier, that in good times you had to pay two thousand, and the tears which fall on your magnificent fur jacket, cap and muff, which sit on the table ready for delivery, will not help you, Frau Meier nor your daughter. You may stroke them once more and press your face into the sweet-smelling fur.

Say farewell to your beautiful things, off they go to the community where, with many hundreds of similar luxury items, they will be sorted and registered and then shipped off to the Gestapo, and from there into the hands of the Nazi bigwigs, their wives and their daughters, who hoard countless diamonds, gold, and silver jewelry in the vaults of Hitler's "connoisseurs and patrons of art".

So, are you ready? Now deliver also your woolens. All of them! Also, your woolen socks and stockings, your underclothes and scarves, your gloves and wrist warmers and wool muffs. And no dallying! Do you Jews perhaps think that it was for nothing that you got no clothing coupons? Also, your still smart and clean clothes, dear Meier, even those socks that are not yet darned and those shoes that are still not worn out by your wife and daughter have long become thorns in the side of the outraged Gebhard and his companions. And always remember that everything that you own is not yours at all. How often must you be told until you get it?

Meier is discharged from the hospital but he can no longer walk. Gebhard's threats no longer help, nor do any new orders from the labor office. The man is a ruin. Even so, his wife and daughter are not allowed to care or cook for him. They must continue to sort rags and have to entrust the patient to the care of ancient Jewish neighbors.

À propos, dear Meier! Haven't you got a valuable stamp collection? Ten thousand Marks, you say? Declared years ago, at the currency exchange? A pity. You must have it assessed by an official within a week and deliver it with a valuation certificate to the currency exchange.

Go on, your typewriter is also due next week. You cannot manage without it? There's no such thing! Only the municipality and the Jewish lawyers, now called counsellors, are permitted to continue using machines. So, don't forget it either. The Stapo does not understand jokes.

What can you do? Nothing, my friend. A year ago, you dismissed my well-intentioned advice to put whatever valuables you still had into a secure place, with the reproach that it was against the law. Now you must follow the Nazi regulations. I'm sorry, but there is nothing you can do.

But Meier would like to hear from another acquaintance about this matter and reaches in the old way for the telephone on the bedside table. He reaches into space, then to his forehead, as the memory dawns on him of the two postal officials who dismantled his telephone the previous week, as they did for all Jewish subscribers.

Then he asked to see the official announcements in the newspaper. I'm sorry, poor Meier, surely you know that newspapers have not been sold to Jews for some time now. One can see that you are ill, very ill. I must leave you now. I will come and see you again, get well soon. And give my regards to your wife and daughter. Goodbye.

PART 3
AYRANIZATION

IMPORTANT DATES

1944

- **March 19:** Germany occupies Hungary.
- **May 15:** Nazis begin deporting Hungarian Jews.
- **June 6:** D-Day – Allies send 5,300 ships with 176,000 men to land on the Normandy beaches.
- **July 20:** German officers fail to assassinate Hitler: 7,000 arrested, 4,980 executed.
- **July 24:** Russians liberate Majdanek concentration camp in Poland.
- **August 15:** American and Free French forces land in southern France. Hitler orders retreat of the German 7th army from Normandy.
- **August 1:** Russians arrive at the gates of Warsaw. Polish resistance movement starts uprising against the Germans that lasts 63 days before being crushed by the Germans. The Soviets refuse to aid the uprising. The Germans destroy much of the city and kill tens of thousands of resisters and civilians.
- **August 25:** Paris is liberated.
- **September 11:** First allied troops enter Germany.

- **October 7:** Revolt by inmates at Auschwitz; one crematorium blown up. The revolt is crushed with more than 450 Jewish inmates killed.
- **November:** Last Jews deported from the Theresienstadt "labor camp" in Czechoslovakia to Auschwitz in Poland.
- **December 16:** Battle of the Bulge – massive German counter offensive that nearly cuts the Allied forces in half in the Ardennes forest in Belgium.
- **December 25:** The Americans stop the German advance at the Battle of the Bulge.

8   THE CHILD CRIED AND SHIVERED

While underground, Walter's contacts provide him with a blank military pass (pilfered from the Leipzig Fair office) which he uses to forge a new identity for himself. Working with a loupe and a fine pen he recreates the proper German stamp so that the card looks as if he has a military exemption for illness. And most importantly it gives him a new name: Kurt Freiherr. He hopes the pass will help protect him and his family if their hideout is raided, or if he is discovered while walking around the city searching for food.

Walter realizes that he is running out of places to hide. His old contacts are starting to worry about detection, and new contacts are difficult to find. Emotionally, he is cut off from the society he valued. He is alone. To add to his worries, in the fall of 1943 Allied bombing of Leipzig begins in earnest with a massive raid on December 4, 1943 during which 1,815 residents die, 4,000 are wounded and 20 percent of all the apartments in the city are destroyed. Walter becomes a chronicler of destruction and fears even more for their survival.

From these ashes, he seeks new opportunities to avoid detection. Can they change their names and claim to be dispossessed German refugees from a different city?

Even if that becomes possible, entering Aryan Nazi Germany involves many entanglements with the official Nazi bureaucracies controlling all social and economic life. Passes and papers are needed not only to verify his military exemption, but also for employment, housing, transportation, food, clothing, post office use, travel, and residency. Also, to move from Mannheim to Leipzig, as Walter/Kurt would claim to have done, requires deregistration from the former city and re-registration in the new. To have any chance of success he must play a deadly form of bureaucratic chess with these all these Nazi officials... and win.

Undated

It may sound like a paradox to maintain that detention in a concentration camp could also bring good to the person whom fate selected to survive. Well, this apparent contradiction was my savior and my way out of the claws of the Stapo executioners. In the notorious concentration camp Buchenwald, in the year 1938, they performed all their terrible deeds of cruelty, beginning with the test of strength of their victims tied to the "vaulting horse"[1] and finishing with the quite unimaginable crowding of the living quarters with arrested detainees. From then on, I knew what awaited me and my family if we would ever be delivered up to the bloodthirsty bandits, and would have to set out with the many thousands of fellow sufferers on the march of death to the slaughterhouses of the East. Our intention to emigrate to my brother in America had become unattainable through Hitler's declaration of war on the United States.[2] So, being chased from one home to another, and subjected to the endless harassment and humiliating laws and measures of dispossession, with the help of my non-Jewish friends I drafted a plan, which was to come into effect at the moment of our deportation.

On September 17, 1942, it had come to that. The sister of my wife and her husband had already fallen prey to the slaughterers and most of our friends and acquaintances had been turned to ashes in the furnaces of the sadists, when I together with wife, child and mother-in-law appeared on the death list. We signed the declarations about property and the withdrawal of state citizenship, including giving up the most necessary objects for our daily needs together with our valuables and fur coats.

After a heart-rending goodbye to the ill mother-in-law, who was no longer capable of such a difficult undertaking, we "vanished" in the bright light of day through the ranks of Nazi spies and landed under the pseudonym "Freiherr" in hiding at our friends'.

To cover our tracks, I had our first asylum-giver post two fictitious letters to the Leipzig Jewish Office and to a third person in the stations of Bitterfeld and Dessau, and spread the rumor through our Jewish friends still living in Leipzig that we had fled to Switzerland. This maneuver meant all investigations by the police hit dead ends.

Only a few trusted people knew where we were staying, visited us regularly, kept us informed about all happenings in the community, and provided us with food which they saved in spite of all cutbacks, until they too were sent to their deaths by the vampires. Now deprivation and want entered our lives and, together with the sharp-eared Stapo spies, threatened to cause our efforts to fail. We slipped from hiding place to hiding place, often begging a piece of bread for our careworn child, and at times our situation seemed so hopeless that, rather than run into the arms of the thugs, we saw suicide as a last resort.

But like a miracle, new saviors, sometimes completely unknown to us, came forward at the last minute, and they gave us further courage. We gladly bore hunger and danger and the humiliation which is natural in any asylum, if we could only succeed in keeping our child alive.

To reach this goal, we had to above all sail around one cliff: I possessed no kind of personal identity document in my new name of Kurt Freiherr. And after darkness fell, when I walked through the streets like a cripple, in order to receive bread, a few kohlrabi and potatoes from charitable people, it was all too easy for my return to my family to be cut off by the Kapo[3] police and their agents. After long, fruitless efforts to get an identity document, I used blank forms which some of my friends obtained at the Leipzig Fair office to prepare a Military Pass according to original samples. It gave the place as Leipzig, the papers named me as a freelance auditor, and they indicated I was not suitable for military service. These documents brought me greater freedom of movement, but I had to remember the serious limitation that no Leipzig person to whom our existence had to remain secret must recognize me, a condition I fulfilled with only a few exceptions. I dared to go out in public during the day, visited friends and sympathizers and could more than once delight wife and child on my return with a rucksack full of food. I also went shopping, so far as our nest egg allowed it.

In the middle of these happy moments, we suddenly had to pack our belongings when the son of our host, who was in St. Blasien[4] as a soldier afflicted in the lungs, was arrested by the Gestapo and thrown into prison for supporting the enemy and undermining military morale, an event which entailed the danger of a house search and our discovery. Our situation appeared hopeless in view of the fact that we had used up all feasible hiding places and that comrades[5] had become fearful of me. Finally, a young married couple with a little daughter, who were complete strangers to us, saved us and took us without conditions or time limit into their comfortable home under our legal [Jewish] name. They let us take part in their meals and treated us all in all like family members, always telling us that they had to make good to us for what the dear people's comrades had done against the Jews.

These people were so ready to make sacrifices and brave death that they took us to the cinema with loaded pistols, presented us to their acquaintances and relatives, and fought steadfastly with the father and brother, the main tenants, so that we could remain.

The evenings we spent in pleasant hospitality around a glass of wine and cakes, told jokes, listened to forbidden radio stations or practiced pistol shooting in the corridor, which enabled me to note that after all these years and spiritual shocks I had lost none of my accuracy.

On the day of the dethroning of Mussolini, July 25, 1943, we all got on a bus together and drove out to one of the large, splendid open-air swimming pools, jumped around in the sun, air and water. On every summery day we repeated this pleasure, acting like children. We then temporarily went to stay with a previous asylum provider, so that our young friends could catch up on their repeatedly postponed trip to Garmisch[6] before the cool of the autumn made the leaves wither.

October 1, 1943

Whoever flits with wife and child from one hiding place to another for a whole year to save his life becomes hypersensitive. Sensitive not only to the dangers constantly lurking around him, but also to the remarks of those around him, confidently trusting in the nature of his asylum-givers and grateful for the self-sacrificing courage of his friends. He flutters like a feather in a gentle breath of air, registers high and low pressure like a barometer, and the warmth of his providers like a thermometer. Experiencing surprises and disappointments, he looks eagerly for every ray of hope, like a prisoner grasping with trembling fingers for a sunbeam which may stray into his cell, as if it were a lifeline. The darkness lasts for far too long and repeatedly I babble my fearful words: watchman, what time of night is it? It is dark still. Only the encouraging words of friends flicker like stars in the distance, far from this world. But their help and courageous sacrifice are like rays of sunlight on which the hope of freedom and human dignity rises upwards.

They come from many different camps, our friends. Their attitude to the events of our time is as manifold as their concept of life, but they all agree on one point: the unbridled hatred of Hitler and Hitler's comrades. They all loathe his war, his lies, his slaughter of foreigners and Jews. They are all weighed down by vegetating under the heel of the barbarian; their words speak of restrained anger against this worst scourge of mankind. Some among them have advocated for him and welcomed him as the saviour of the Fatherland. Others, on the other hand, are out of principle the sworn enemies of Hitler, independent freedom fighters, or unflinching Communists.

They all see the Jews as the main victims and afford them all possible support. Only one among them was driven to offer assistance through greed. He was generously rewarded and sank back into the mass of weak characters who fear the blows of the swastika perpetrators more than the painful screams of their massacred objects. But let the praises be sung of all the others, starting with the daring electrician who already in 1938 acted quickly to extricate Jewish men from the Nazi hunters and, some time before the fate of deportation befell us, slipped me the key to his apartment so that our escape route would be accessible every day and night.

He and his parents, called Grandpa and Grandma B. for short, resolutely took us into their community, despite all the dangers that beleaguer a rented apartment in the Third Reich, after a "quarantine" stay of four weeks in that workman's dwelling, which we willingly underwent so as to cover our traces. They also hid a great part of the belongings we could save.

As they trembled about our lives no less than about their own, the clouds of disaster gathered over the rebellious boy (the apartment key-giver) who was discharged from his duty on the Western Front. A charge of "high treason, aiding the enemy and undermining military morale" followed him to the hospital, where they cured his tuberculosis only to hand him right over to the judge. That he brought the process on himself, regardless of his earlier skirmishes with the Stapo, in naive high spirits and unforgivable light-heartedness, is one of the inexplicable acts of carelessness and provocation that the "average German" is always capable of in both great and small matters, and which has brought upon him hard wars and the loss of generations.

Now they fear the verdict of the Reich court martial, they, the young man who is ill again and practically an invalid, and the parents with their faces furrowed by worry and eyes swollen with tears. They had hoped for acquittal, until I brought their fragmented thoughts to the conclusion that their existence would suddenly turn to disappointment and pain, if they could not see sense. A Reich judiciary, taking into account how he neglected his personal safety on the front, might be ready to consider a prison sentence unless new testimony emerges that completely discharges their son. That a prison sentence, no matter its length, would be ended by Hitler's fall, while the carrying out of a death sentence can never be undone, was simple logic no one in the family could come to terms with for a long time. In this way, good and helpful people suddenly became companions in suffering and had to take care to save their own lives.

The most urgent concern for us was to change our dwelling again, at night. Experience had shown that the Stapo dogs could turn up to conduct a search in any apartment where they smelled a rat, and that would have cost us our heads – not only ours but also our hosts'. But where does one find a courageous, unselfish soul who can hold us back from the final exit, the flight to Hades? Twice one stepped forward after a long and desperate search. First it was an old acquaintance who, when the air raid wardens threatened to capture us, took us in answer to Grandpa B's persistent pleas, housed us for several weeks in his roomy apartment. Although we feared that both would refuse to step forward again, a happier outcome for all could emerge if only another place to stay miraculously appeared.

One clings to a straw.

October 16, 1943

I was overcome by the urge to loosen the bonds of my voluntary imprisonment and take my body, which was hungry for light, for a late summer afternoon walk in the sun. With my pistol ready to fire and a homemade military pass in my pocket, I sauntered along the railway line which led to Leutzsch, and much further on to our friends in Garmisch. I went past allotments in which shirt-sleeved gardeners pinched and checked thick-skinned pears on trellises, as if they had been charged with delivering an earthshattering judgment. Only when one of the few trains with electric or steam locomotives thundered past did they look up, stroked their moustaches, shaded their screwed-up eyes and looked up into the sky, then again for a second to me, only to resume caressing their pears.

Behind a bridge which crossed one of the dirty Leipzig rivers rose a mountain of rubbish, the martyrs' mound of our cultural friends. A few French prisoners stirred things around in the stinking pile before scattering the rubbish high into the air. More city rubbish heaps appeared and spewed out new dirt. In a few generations, Leipzig wants to erect a tower on the summit of the rubbish heap, from which the descendants should enjoy a great view from a platform. I'm of the opinion that the people of Leipzig do indeed need a good view, albeit from this rubbish heap, since the sight of once-Red Saxony[7] has been blocked since Hitler mounted the throne. And like everywhere, in Leipzig too they move around the rubbish or destroy a square in order to make the existence of citizens living like moles pleasant and attractive. The mounds of earth typical of fields and meadows now decorate all intersections and parks in gigantic dimensions, and indeed you do not need enemy intervention to enhance a big city such as Leipzig. Somebody like Hitler does achieve that with his "Strength through Joy"[8] organization, and indeed this "patron of work" seems to still impress the people.

Only where my walk led me through an undisturbed world did my disgust for the Nazi filth recede. What remained was a feeling of traumatic isolation. It increased from hour to hour and became a nightmare at the sight of the largest and most beautiful Leipzig entertainment park on Lake Auen, which was derelict and overgrown with grass, bearing a large banner: "Resettlement Wolynien, Camp Leipzig".

Where years ago, dance tunes sounded among joyful people, everything is horrible. Anglers sit motionless staring doggedly at the place in the water where a fish should snatch the bait. And behind them, their wives crouch, knitting next to open baskets ready to take the catch. They will go on sitting, the anglers and their wives, even when nothing but rubble remains of the former magnificence.

I have become a stranger among these people, who cherish martyrs' mounds where death holds a dialogue with their works. I have become a stranger, not only because they have extinguished me from their lists, and not only because I secretly walk their hallowed paths, but because I am horrified at their master and their views about race.

* * *

Five weeks have since passed and already autumn with its debilitating melancholy is scattering the faded leaves over the grave of nature, and the smell and coolness of the season fills the air again. I took my little daughter, now six years old, by the hand, scurried out of the house and led her along remote streets into the open air, for which she has been longing for weeks like a trapped animal seeking a way out. She wants to walk again, further than from wall to wall and from room to room, and she wants to see what is new and wonderful. Railways are a representation of freedom for her, the big farm the playground of her fantasy, and a fresh bread roll her tonic on the way. And my child had much to ask. She looked at the locomotives which have no other tasks than to pull, but she rejoices at the express train racing by, from which she promises herself the greatest delights, once the "wicked people" have gone away.

The aircraft hulls looking like Zeppelins caught her curiosity no less than the huge statues in the park. Why wonder why she also celebrated seeing the Monument to the Battle of Nations[9] again, that square stone colossus for the dead, the material of which would have sufficed for the construction of hundreds of sanatoriums and schools for the living?

We go to the pool in which one can see one's own reflection as always, and in it wild ducks cavort and the dirt of the Nazi regime is piled knee-high, in the high-tide bed of magpies. I explained to my child about everything that fed her thirst for knowledge, but to two of her questions I had to reply an untruth: the question about the destination of a freight train with cattle for the slaughterhouse and the one about the purpose of the big anti-aircraft guns by the main market hall. Should I tell her that cattle transports and guns are symbols of the suffering of beast and human?

October 26, 1943

A busy week lies behind us. Leipzig had its first air raid. On the twentieth, shortly after eight o'clock in the evening the sirens wailed, and after a few minutes one could hear anti-aircraft flak. For our friends, this was a signal to hide three floors deeper down, hoping Leipzig would only be a marker for more distant targets. But it was otherwise. Heavy guns near the main market hall drummed out concentrated salvoes, and from afar vibrations rolled through the houses, which creaked in their joints. For the former front-line slave,[10] this was an unmistakable sign of the dropping of bombs and a signal that the lights of people's lives were in danger of being blown out.

With a prying look under the blackout blind, I caught sight of searchlights casting around restlessly in the sky, which was already red. I perceived the short flashes of exploding flak, which rained down splinters on roofs and courtyards, while a drumroll of artillery filled the air. Suddenly a bird spitting fire crashed down with a terrible din, and I just had time to disappear from the window before the house began to dance, rattling the doors, and to echo with crashing, breaking and crunching. No doubt the impact had been near us. I felt a bit apprehensive. Wife and child had crouched down in the bathroom, the most protected corner of the flat; they clung to each other tightly at every impact and were startled at the roar of the bombers thundering over the roofs.

In a pause in the noise, our dear hostess came out of the cellar and fell around our necks, her face white as wax, trembling and half weeping. Her husband, the air raid warden, was not yet back from an evening visit and we were all worried. The witches' Sabbath lasted almost two hours. Then everything was quiet again, as if nothing had happened. Leipzig fire engines, screams, fleeing people, the smell of fire and clouds of smoke became the epilogue.

A tour the following morning led past heaps of shards of glass shovelled together through streets completely without window panes, past houses in which doors hung out of windows instead of curtains, courtesy of the numerous explosive and incendiary bombs. Here a few buildings had collapsed into ruins, over there a block of rented dwellings still burned brightly. Household belongings stood gaily in the open air, and birdcages, night pots and clothes horses stretched far into one of the main shopping streets, which had spat thousands of display windows with their contents onto the street.

In a suburb a bomb had struck on open ground, taking the roofs off all buildings in a large radius. It had made such a mess of the small church that, with its naked roof timbers, its bent tower, from which the dial and hands had fallen down, and its empty window and door frames, its pews and organ parts thrown all around, it looked like a plucked cockerel among its hens.

In the course of the next few days news came of destruction and human casualties not only in the Leipzig city area. Whole villages were said to have burned down. All the same, this attack seems to have been only a foretaste of things to come, and not a heavy one as the British maintain.

October 27, 1943

When clear sunlight pushes through the soft mists of autumn and their sparkling breath clouds the window panes, I caught myself sometimes in a sullen mood and, despite all good intentions, oppressive memories flutter into my martyred brain.

During the warm days of the past summer I had found peace even though we were still in hiding. There were indescribably lovely weeks in June, when we romped with our friends in one of Leipzig's open-air swimming pools, so untroubled, even childishly boisterous, as if all danger was banished, and all need and deprivation forgotten. The first visit I made in the company of our loyal, self-sacrificing friend. After limited nourishment, I was just skin and bones, and at first somewhat helpless in the pool surrounded by the many splashing, happy swimmers. But I got over my inhibitions and after a little while I was again master of the wet element, and beat my well trained and powerful companion by more than a body length. On the horizontal bar I managed to do belly-swings, the big wave and about 20 pull-ups.

We lounged in the sweet-smelling grass, bodily refreshed and spiritually relieved. Following this successful reconnaissance, we went out into the summery freedom for the next six mornings. My heart skipped with joy while I swam backstroke through the wavy wetness, accompanied by shrieks of joy from mother and child, who as non-swimmers were amusing themselves in the shallow pool and on the slide. We were roused from this delightful and idyllic interlude by air raid sirens – first just a few but then they kept us far from tranquil for hours. When our friends hastened off to Garmisch, our week of freedom came to an end.

Now my friend is back working his profession, and his wife busy with her housework and all the odds and ends of Hitler's everyday privations, and Tillchen[11] has to go to school. While Mutti shares in the household duties of her companion, and drives away her grave thoughts at the stove, I again have only too much time, not only to brood over our lot, but those of our Jewish friends and relatives, those unlucky creatures, whose ashes might already be fertilizing the local fields. I think about my mother, of whom we know nothing, and wonder whether she can still think about us, as we do of her.

Then I get fidgety and rummage in all pockets and containers for a cigarette or a pinch of tobacco, and as I am everything except a magician, I take refuge in our child, get her ready to go out and sneak away with her. The tram, its tracks, carry us to the south of the city, where we get off, and Anneliese notices wonderfully tempting things in a shop window, a brooch of a white stately bird with spread wings, colored pencils and a whisk for a doll's house kitchen. I do not begrudge her this modest pleasure and allow her to buy one of each plaything. Proud and happy she wears the bird on the collar of her coat and will not let go of the colored pencils and the whisk, which she confidently carries in her bag like a carpenter carries his ruler.

Two blocks further on her interest is momentarily diverted by the menu in a restaurant. She knows her talent, and suddenly she remembers the holiday in Augustusburg, where we "like the posh people" were served all sorts of tasty dishes at a table with a white tablecloth, silverware and flowers. She wants to do the same again and forgets that we no longer live in the year 1938, when a certain amount of money sufficed to please both palate and stomach.

Still she will not give up, and I finally notice dishes exempt from ration vouchers – soup, mussel meat with potatoes. Anneliese sits opposite me with beaming eyes. Tables no longer have tablecloths, the cutlery is no longer silver, and soup is served on a bare wooden table and tastes as if it has gone bad. The mussels have a flavour that is a conglomeration of herring stock, muddy water, and frozen soil, supplemented with crunchy grains of sand. But the potatoes really tasted like potatoes.

For her sake I fight to swallow the stuff, and even Anneliese accepts her fate with visible fortitude, though giving me pleading looks while eating the last three mussels. I understand and pay the bill. Anneliese has had her "fun" and is satisfied. Then she trips "home" with me for her proper midday meal, nourishing swedes which I got hold of in yesterday's raid.

Towards evening I become restless again. Our friend gives me a cigarette, a second one she pinches from her husband, who is a non-smoker, and a third one he himself brings from the shop. But when the ciggies are used up, I continue to rummage in every pocket and container without success, which does not surprise me at all.

October 29, 1943

I once stood before the counters of the Leipzig Finance Office in order to renew my motorbike tax card. Before me, next to me and behind me were petitioners on a similar errand. On the other side of the fence were four officials, who were giving religious attention to the deed of breakfasting. The public for their part waited with amazing patience, but dared to audibly breathe a sigh of relief when one of the privileged ones at last conscientiously folded his bread paper, wiped his mouth, stretched, groaned and rubbed his hands together, only to take another pack of bread and butter from the drawer.

This was too hard a test for the patience of the spectators and led a burly leather worker to request that he should finally be served, since he had been standing around for an hour. This insubordinate opinion resulted in a hook nose armed with a pince-nez rushing up, striking a pose and releasing an unambiguous warning from contemptuously curled lips: "Watch it, you – you –! Don't molest the officials!" Whereupon the work of chewing resumed according to regulation.

That's how it should be. Who dares to grumble?

Even the people who have been bombed out do not dare to complain when they go to the damage office, the opening of which has raised so many Nazi Party comrades to the rank of civil servant. They have more important things to do than concern themselves with houses with roofs blown off, ceilings broken through or flooded cellars. But they thaw in front of Party comrades who have overcome their inhibitions and prove thorough training and exercise of lungs and biceps. A brusque, snappy tone of giving orders darkens the halo even of a well-endowed Nazi official, since nothing in the Greater German Reich is more productive than to humiliate and cheat a partner by shouting.

This method has been tried and tested countless times, but was most blatantly demonstrated to me on a train on the Höllental railway, which brought me home from military service in February 1919. A private who had also just been demobilised turned it into his hunting reserve, and appeared during the journey at the door of our carriage, where he put his arms on his hips and thundered to the passengers:

"All of you, listen to this. I am a defender of the fatherland and have rendered services for your sake for years. Now I have no money when I come home, and I demand each of you do his bit so that you don't get to know my other side. Open your purses and give voluntarily, otherwise I will make a report!"

The word "report" was enough to set the hands of all listeners moving towards their trouser pockets or handbags, as if hypnotised. The word "report" turns off all independent thinking, even the notion that the worthy soldier had cashed in his demobilisation money like everyone else, and was probably better off than most of the passengers.

When he came up to me, I delivered this explanation, also in a barking tone, and unleashed a general blank thoughtlessness and weakening of the will tirade, whereupon the stunned man quickly cleared off. From this it can be concluded that the Hitler pomp comes to an end as soon as a courageous opponent appears on the scene. One still waits for him, almost desperately, like that helpful woman in the tram who smilingly pressed the fare into the hand of another woman who had forgotten her purse, and remarked that she can spare two Groschen, that in any case they are not worth any more than a scrap of a ticket, whereupon a passenger got up, arrested her and led her off at the next stop, without showing any identification or meeting any resistance.

Resistance against the Himmler dogs, and those who still want to become one, one dares to show in Germany only in secret, passive resistance – and in the best case through sabotage.

One person tried this in his own way by emptying the heavy contents of his guts at night at a place with busy traffic and crowning it with a swastika pin. Under the current circumstances there is no more open way of documenting one's disgust for the excrement of authority.

However, whoever wants to put an end to National Socialism must master three things in order to catch the attention of the people and be popular: barking, arresting and beating. That impresses. The old ones no less than the young ones, who each day train noisily in the alleyways.

November 20, 1944

This time it is practically only explosive bombs, and fewer incendiary bombs. There are dreadful explosions, but not many large fires. Our block is spared. In our area a phosphorous and an incendiary bomb fall, both duds. An old lady found one in her room and wandered around with it unknowingly. All day long people are moving around the streets again. Around midday I go for a walk. There is a further air raid warning, and I seek shelter in the Connewitzer Holz.

There are sudden detonations. Old women in fur coats come running, shaking with fear. We take shelter under the boat houses amid ear-splitting explosions.

American planes fly in ordered formations above us. I worry about my wife and child. The singing of grenade splinters is in my ears as I arrive home and am served potato dumplings.

Thousands are dead, mainly foreigners. There are new trenches, and parts of corpses can be seen in meadows and on trees.

December 2, 1943

Since Whitsun,[12] which is celebrated on the seventh Sunday after Easter, we have been guests of our young friends. It is a long time, measured by their courage and the selflessness with which they have concealed us in their home, and from time to time let us share their meals when my foraging has had meagre success. For on that depends our energy to get through, whether our bodily strength rises or sinks, whether our courage grows or dwindles in the face of our child, whose eyes already shine at the sight of a piece of dry bread.

It is bitter and painful and of little use against feelings of despair, which were alien to us also in the days of the hardest struggles, even when faced with death. More powerful is the creeping decimation when time, hunger and faltering support by political comrades come together. The times when I could surprise my loved ones once a week with a full rucksack are long past, and three pounds of bread, a few spoonfuls of jam or a meat coupon for 50 grams for seven days today mean something extraordinary for us, and it is true luck that our young friends can still bring enough potatoes to the table.

The old adage that a friendship demanding sacrifices eventually goes flat like beer has come true among a number of political comrades, including from the Communist camp. One of them once filled my rucksack together with his wife with visible satisfaction every Friday and valued an hour of chatting and exchange of political thoughts almost as highly as I did. I looked forward to these meetings in my voluntarily involuntary mental exile, but he has allowed the curve of his affection to plummet noticeably since those two nights when he reluctantly granted us asylum. He fussed around trembling, and with a face red with fear cast doubts on my promise to leave his house punctually, withdrew his offer to help me as an expert in making military identity cards, and invented all sorts of excuses to keep me away from his home and business.

The neighbors, who were already muttering about the man with the ominous rucksack, or the Gestapo, who were once again on the heels of him and other comrades, watching him and reading his letters, they were the men in black who should scare me off and make me disappear from his field of vision. Another one became incensed about a comrade who once advised me to let myself be deported with my wife and child, since he could do more for us in the place of banishment, but on the other hand warned him against meeting with me. Another constantly insisted that none of his friends were in a position to let us have any of their food, but then had to witness how several of them after a brief, anonymous greeting slipped me bread and other food, even whole loaves and meat coupons.

Then there was the one who, to put it briefly, fancied that further contact with me would put Jews roaming illegally into danger, and did not trust my discretion, and furthermore did not consider my Communist education and convictions equal to his. Others in turn have remained constant until today, giving either money or food, some of them both. For me and my wife, who all our lives have given and rarely taken, this scrounging pushes us into depression, disrobing us of human dignity and autonomous action.

I do not want to be unjust. Everyone who has contributed to the salvation of unfortunate victims of the Nazis has earned distinction in the struggle against the Fascist henchmen: everyone who without reservation and afterthought has given and sacrificed something, even just a little, will count among the chosen ones of humanity to come. But whoever gives in feigned love and takes it back again in his thoughts, whoever believes he can draw a bill of debt for the future with his contribution, or who even enriches himself by taking in helpless people, cheats them of their few belongings, and then rushes out on the street in a rage because the business has not been worthwhile, that person will be no more named in the book of true fighters than those who see themselves disturbed in their well-earned rest by the distress calls of the persecuted.

However, time is pressing. The sincerest friendship must crumble too, if it is strained for too long. I admire our asylum-givers, who bear this burden in the struggle against the dangers inherent in our game of hide-and-seek, and in opposition to their relatives, with their endless reproaches, and paint the end of the undertaking in as bloody terms as possible. There will certainly be consequences. Already the joyful mood which helped us overcome difficulties begins at times to give way to an oppressive silence, and the facial expressions of our friends already betray impatience and often even feelings of vexation.

We are certain that this asylum will be the last, and that no door will open to let us in elsewhere. The way out of the house of our friends will inevitably lead to a bitter end, and they know that as well as we do. And therefore, they grit their teeth and make honest efforts to banish the threatening shadows and lighten up the approaching darkness. That is difficult, that demands self-control on both sides, and here only strength of character can triumph.

December 4, 1943

3.30 am sirens, in contrast to the relatively few air raid warnings which always came between 7.30 and 8pm in Berlin, followed shortly after four o'clock by the first detonations. I was in the bathroom. During the first wave of the air raid windows were shattered, the house shook, and plaster fell from the ceiling and the walls. We heard the noise of approaching Stukas.[13] During the second wave, doors were ripped from their hinges, and the house shook alarmingly. We hugged each other. The child cried and shivered. I took her in my arms.

I took my wife and child and air raid baggage into the cellar. On the way down, I noticed the flicker of flames in the house. I alert the other inhabitants. Fire extinguishers and rescue equipment are brought out. (I forgot my typewriter.) Washing, clothing and household goods are piled up in the cellar. We must interrupt extinguishing, because the third wave is coming. After that, the third floor is already in flames. Household goods were even more quickly saved. The Lausches family had only taken essentials into the cellar. The Richter family provisions through the dividing wall into the neighboring house.

Once more we had escaped death. We also aroused no suspicion of any kind with the assertion, which was credible enough, that we had been surprised by the attack the previous evening as the bombed-out Mannheim friends of our hosts, and from the district air protection leader, who lorded over the whole company, we earned applause for our "selfless" effort. Our child was taken care of by the neighboring wife of the head of the Leipzig Butchers' Guild, gradually calmed down while with her children and was fed with bread and sausage until she was full. When there was nothing more to talk about we joined our daughter and remained as the neighboring wife's guests with our friends, who had also become homeless, and about 20 other bombed-out people.

They collect the dead. The drunk. After daybreak I go out onto the street. Our house is ablaze. The burning dog. Smoke and dust black out everything. All around there is rubble and fire.

The wall of a house collapses into the street. There is no fire engine, they are only allowed to extinguish public buildings.

Later we go to the reception center. On the way we get our first impression of the devastation caused by the air raid attack. In the square in front of the Carola High School aerial mines came down. The institution is bombed out, a wing completely demolished, and other damaged buildings spill out into the street. The Elisenberg Hotel is almost totally burned to the ground. Adolf-Hitler-Strasse is not quite in such a mess. The tower of the Andreas Church has collapsed onto the steps leading up to it. The air is full of smoke, soot and dust. The reception center (a school) is burned out.

We go back home. Later I go for a stroll through the town with Erich L. to his shop. The northern end of Adolf-Hitler Strasse is more damaged. Houses are still on fire. A huge crater has opened in the road. Many houses are demolished. A firestorm whirls soot and dirt through the air. The blood-red sun shines dimly through the smoke.

The nearer we come to Königsplatz, the more unbearable it all becomes. Königsplatz is unrecognisable. The Ury, a department store, is burned to the ground. Textile Exhibition Center 1 (Grassimuseum) is also burned to the ground. All the other houses around the square are razed to the ground. The District Court is undamaged, Police Headquarters only slightly damaged. The tower of the Market Hall stands deserted, the Hall almost completely destroyed. The Tower clock shows 4.05 pm. The Windmühlenstrasse is engulfed in flames. Flames as high as houses leap out of the windows of the right wing of City Hall.

We have trouble walking and are already as black as chimneysweeps. A dozen automatic hoses are pumping water out of the pool in the Schillerhain onto the New City Hall. We have a panoramic view – all other houses have been destroyed. The Kurprinzstrasse is in a sea of flames. The district governance building is totally destroyed and the Sternwartenstrasse partly so.

The shop, owned by Erich, is still there. The door handle has been ripped off, and the door frame is shattered. Behind it Breitkopf & Hartel is in flames. Water is running, the lights are on. We take cigarettes, guns and ammunition. Erich is drunk. With a great deal of trouble and effort he drags himself back home.

The Bayrischestrasse is still impassable, so we take the same way back home.

Müller's house is besieged by all the people from neighboring houses. Children are crying. Grandpa L eats incessantly. Ilse is "down" with a nervous disorder. There is talk of the heightened risk of air raids... I take a nap on a chair and read a book on Furtwängler[14] who distracts me. The rooms are all packed with saved possessions and the corridor is stuffed full. We look like swine.

However, a new danger emerged after we were thrown back against our will into public view after the air raids. On the one hand I could not exclude myself from going as a victim, together with other sections of the population thrown together, to the newly-set up care services without arousing suspicion, and on the other hand I was afraid of the moment when my homemade Military Pass would undergo its baptism of fire.

Next morning, we go to the reception center. It's the school in Herderstrasse. After the crossroad there is practically no damage, but the reception center is overcrowded. Officials talk into the crowd. No benefit or travel tokens are issued. People are told to come back in a few days, but they won't be put off. The mood is very irritable – everybody swears and curses. After two hours' queuing it's our turn. I gathered courage and took the best precautions I could against being recognized and held the Military Pass under the nose of a gold-encumbered Nazi functionary. He checked through it, made a somewhat commiserating gesture towards me as a poor fake cripple and had a food card reading "total aerial bomb damaged" made out for me. My last asylum provider and companion in destiny, with one hand constantly on the firearm in his pocket, did not turn his gaze from me and the identity card during the procedure and prodded me in the side with a mischievous look for good measure. Afterwards he took my arm and thus we brought the documents to our loved ones, who breathed out with relief.

For the first time since the day of our flight I received food and smoking cards with all the supplements for people hurt by bombing. We have food for the first time in a year and a quarter and don't need to beg any more. It was the only way after the catastrophe. The hunger was at an end; we ate a fabulous amount of the butcher's sausages, with bread rolls or the long-missed butter rolls and felt no weariness after the experiences of the past few nights. Only Anneliese grew pale and trembled, clung to us and cried at the dull thunder of the exploding of dud bombs. It soon became apparent that she had suffered shell shock, which would cause her and us considerable worry for a long time to come. In addition, there were other tasks, such as registering with the economy and residency offices, which I could not omit doing without exposing ourselves to undesired inquiries.

The fires continue to rage, thousands lie under the rubble, and survivors have marked their houses with chalk to show where they can be found. Singed cats and dogs roam abandoned and whimpering through the streets. Our friends have taken themselves off to their relatives. The brother is on leave from Warsaw. The library has burned down.

I am obliged to walk further on the way to my legalisation. I report to the solvency office and withdraw 200 Marks as a part payment. I then obtain coupons for groceries, cigarettes and other purchases after an hour of queuing – but constantly shake with fear lest the whole thing come to light. All it would take is for a record to be kept of the relative ration coupons and vouchers on my legal family document, which is not available at all since I have not reported to the police.

I am aware that my wife, my child and I are either on the way to freedom or to certain death, and I think through every step I have to take very precisely, suffering horrible, endless mental and spiritual martyrdom, without reaching a satisfactory outcome. I find peace neither in our shelter among the self-sacrificing people, nor on my wanderings through the burned-down city, which is most horribly destroyed in the area around the Bayerischer Station. Our hosts take care of us, we, the Freiherrs, with exceptional love.

They have handed over their two daughters to an old friend who is to take them into the country. Everyone is rushing to the Konnewitz and Wahren stations in order to get away quickly, and there are endless caravans of fleeing refugees with suitcases, bundles tied up in bedsheets and hand trolleys moving through the still smouldering streets. I visit Grandma B. She is seriously ill with phlebitis, Grandpa B is still on convalescent leave, and the daughter-in-law has left to visit her husband in Berlin.

The window in our room is broken, bombed-out refugees are sleeping in my bed. On the way home I saw the burned-down university in Augustusplatz, the ruined opera house, the completely destroyed square building of the Main Post Office, the disfigured New Museum, etc.

I walk on the Georgi Ring, where no building remains intact, past the damaged Main Station, through the Wintergartenstrasse.

There I discover that along with the house of our acquaintance, most of our belongings which we thought we had brought into safety have also been burned – together with my library of two and a half thousand volumes, bed linen, clothes, crockery, suits, dresses, etc. (Everything else is at B's holiday house in the Rhineland.) Some of the windows are shattered, including the one in our little room.

I take my coat and also my wife's, together with a suitcase, and wander through the ruined quarter of the printers and bookstores, finally crossing the unrecognisable Johannisplatz, where the church is destroyed, and the upper crossing street flattened.

The next morning, I report to the police station and say that the deregistration form from Mannheim has been burned. Fortunately, the B-Card suffices as identity card, and thus obviates presentation of my Military Pass.

Days of uncertainty, helplessness and frightening fancies follow. I suffer terrible internal turmoil. The thought that a police check back in Mannheim might uncover the fiction and get the police and Stapo going spins around in my head. The three of us would then be taken away to the great surprise of our hosts and new acquaintances, first to be interrogated under the most severe torture, and then taken to a place from which no one has ever returned. This causes sweat to run from every pore and I can hardly conceal my anxiety.

The offer by that watchmaker's wife from our burned-out sanctuary, who had conjured up an apartment for us just next to the first home we had before the start of the many evictions, I had to decline under the pretext that living near the only slightly-damaged Main Station would be very risky. Instead I followed the advice of her husband to go to a place about 30 kilometers away, a whole day's journey through snow-covered fields, where he had pleaded with the district governor on our behalf.

I find only a woman in a beautiful country house, but when I explain my situation, I discover that her only son was killed as a member of the SS a year ago and receive the promise that she will speak with her husband. I do not attach much hope to this pledge; behind my doubt lies the worry that zealous civil service officials in a small place into which a stranger might wander only every ten years or so might have enough time and enthusiasm to find out about our background, to check my military and other credentials.

My Military Pass is stamped Leipzig and bears the recruiting information "a-v" (incapable of work), which did not protect me from the imperative of notifying my change of address to our relevant military service registration office, and it was never once ascertained whether the police headquarters in Leipzig made any report to the military service registration office of the labor office. I registered. Should I not be successful in discovering a new and practicable way of settling the question of a pass, we would not be spared rapidly floating from place to place, having to leave behind almost all of our possessions. The very last solution, should everything fail, would be to grasp for the big revolver.

My agitation mounted each passing hour and increased on my way to the economy office and cost centers. It subsided occasionally during stimulating conversations with our hosts and their acquaintances, only to return for the night with renewed vehemence.

Our hosts greeted our plan for a speedy departure with dismay and asked whether we were no longer happy staying with them. They said, our intended plan to go to the countryside was foolish for they were doing a lot of good for us. Their political and humanitarian leanings, that I sensed were reliable, permitted the thought to come into my mind to reveal my true identity, and so on a following evening, when I was alone with her, I confessed our origin. She showed no surprise of any sort, and instead expressed pleasure and increased concern for our welfare. She promised to keep our secret, including from her husband, and tried to lessen our fear and worry and agreed to make inquiries in Mannheim.

It is Christmas time and Anneliese is ill. Our host wants the rooms empty. I must go to the Housing Welfare Association. I live in fear of a police search. As we inhabit our new lodgings, we receive news of the total destruction of Mannheim. All the same one could not know whether individual registration offices did not possess double lists, through which it could be immediately ascertained that a family Freiherr was unknown in Mannheim. Much less dangerous was our registration with the economy office which, because of the total destruction of the south branch, had to newly register all those entitled to handouts. Many bombed out people, and others who designated themselves as such, made really good use of this and received twice-over the special food and smoking material handouts.

Meanwhile, I prepare to obtain a Post Office card, a clothing coupon, then made friends with Untergruppenführer Reimer. Police investigations fail to materialize. The fear subsides gradually. I went with Reimer to office manager Bauer regarding resettlement of bombed out victims, and our reception was friendly. Fourteen days later I repeat the errand. He had marked us down for collective transport[15] with the central National Socialist People's Welfare.[16] He recommends I go there and curses the Jews. I clear up the misunderstanding and discover that we are on the list for the next collective transport to an unknown destination. My request to negotiate private accommodation is refused. I report again the next day, this time I succeed in getting myself crossed off the list, and receive a blank permit to visit relatives.

With my new departure permit I also get free travel tickets. I search for fictitious relatives in vain. Grandpa J. delivers a sermon about fasting and we drink wine punch.

There is still no police investigation, nor any word from the economic authorities. There are continuing good relations with the Müllers and new acquaintances: Frau Kaufmann, Frau Lehmann and Frau Reichenbach. The Pastor visits with his inexhaustible supply of smoking materials. I continue to collect and buy stamps. I visit Eric's wife for cigarette rolling papers.

I continue visiting Grandpa J and think about money. My wife and daughter's birthdays pass us by. Mine is brought forward with my new identity. Friendships are diminishing. We are ready for more raids, carrying around our luggage. My heart disease is on my mind. Our belongings are now in the cold storage depot. We remain on our guard, sleep on the sofa and chairs, but in our clothes.

Where we could turn to in an emergency is a mystery. The searches for courageous friends in the countryside fail because of the over-crowding of villages and small towns with bombed-out refugees, and are succeeded by all sorts of brooding over the possibility or impossibility of our getting to Switzerland. In our naiveté we overlook not only the strict body searches and frontier controls, but also the jumpiness of our child.

9   I TOSS AND TURN AND RACK MY BRAIN

As Walter/Kurt Freiherr enters into German society as an Aryan, for the first time in years, he is free to move above ground. He also is free to form new friendships based on his new identity.

At the same time the possibility of discovery looms large. He is still in his home town and well known in certain areas. He needs to be wary of any slips, especially from his six-year-old daughter, that could alert the Gestapo and its many neighborhood informers. Also, he fears for the survival of his family as the Allied bombings continue. The time and space allow him to some room to also reflect on Nazi Germany from this most unusual vantage point.

His primary goal at this point is getting his family out of Leipzig, away from the bombing and away from his former identity. His location of choice is the alpine areas of Austria and Southern Germany where he and Hilda vacationed shortly after marrying. The verdant valleys and majestic mountains of the Alps, he hopes, will provide refuge from the Allied bombardment as well as the Gestapo.

The problem, however, is finding employment. In tightly regulated Germany one could not simply move and hope to find a job. The job must already be secured and a place to live established before a move is authorized. That proves exceedingly difficult for a Jewish man with forged papers, one among thousands of bombed-out Gentile refugees struggling to find shelter and employment.

Furthermore, Walter wants a job in public administration more suited to his skills and which provides a higher perch for keeping an eye on his pursuers. The quest for this type of job would likely require that his employers check his background information. Employers might even demand that he take an oath to the Nazi Party and to Hitler. Navigating these existential demands without losing his soul proves exceedingly challenging for Walter's health and well-being.

His first venture takes place in the Garmisch area of the Bavarian Alps. His notes reveal the day to day chaos of travel and job hunting at a time when the Allied bombing and Nazi defeats in the East against the Soviet Red Army are taking their toll on German society.

Spring, 1944

Emil L. goes to Garmisch at the beginning of April. He writes that there are jobs available but no rooms. Then he writes that I could be taken on immediately. I would first have to be allotted work by the Garmisch Labor Office in order to obtain a room through the local council.

The new departure permit arrives, along with summons to the "Office for Family Support." I see a well-wishing secretary and the department head. I need to be released by the Labor Office in Leipzig as an "independent auditor". The secretary pleads in vain on behalf of the sick man who is to be sent away by the Nazi People's Welfare Organization with his family. My permit remains unsigned.

I apply to the Labor Office. It is a labyrinth. I present my Military Pass and make a young man proud. I experience temporary dysfunction of the muscle controlling the rectum. I receive a certificate that I give no cause for concern and return to the Labor

Office court. The secretary is absent, but the department head is absolutely friendly. The departure permit is extended, signed and stamped, followed by a cordial farewell.

Erich's news from Garmisch is problematic, and I decide to go there at the end of April. I don't feel good about this. I buy tickets. I dress myself smartly in a clean suit and good shoes for the first time in ages. I bring an umbrella and a winter coat.

I observe the filth on the way to the railway station. It is muggy and thundery. I secure a standing place. On my first journey since 1938 I converse with private soldiers while the rain falls.

In Regensburg there is an announcement through the loudspeaker that the train will travel only as far as Landstuhl because of bombing in Munich. At Landstuhl everybody has to get off. There is crowding and questions are asked on the platforms, and later in the waiting room. I am thirsty and gulp down a half a liter of beer and eat the first sandwich made by Hilda. I begin to write postcards in the ticket hall. At the sound of an alarm we take cover in an air raid shelter. Rain, rain, rain. It is ten o'clock in the morning and I should already have left Munich for Garmisch.

There are no Allied aircraft, only a German one, turning around in the air. A connecting train to Morach is pushed in. I tell the people waiting about it, and they storm the carriages. I arrive in Morach dirty as a pig. The train travels in stages to Pasing, passing overcrowded platforms. I see swallows and rain showers through the window as rail traffic slowly resumes. Mainly these are suburban trains.

At a quarter to four the Garmisch-Innsbruck train is announced, and there is cheering. As I get in, somebody treads on me with rough-nailed shoes that go through to the bone. I cannot stand anymore, so a woman gives up her place for me. Starnberg passes by. Then we are back in sight of the mountains, and arrive in Garmisch, which is cold. I send greetings home. My phone call to

Frau Keil about lodgings is fruitless. Erich is said to be with acquaintances, but when I call him there, there is no answer.

My chats with passers-by about lodgings are just as fruitless. I put through another phone call to Frau Keil. She says she may possibly have lodging for emergencies in the neighborhood. I should come there. It is a long way to walk to 114 Zugspitzstrasse through the pouring rain, and water is flowing out of my shoes. I get to know Frau Keil, who shows me the lodging in the house in which I would meet Erich. I briefly clean it and smoke, then have supper. I go to find Erich at the place of his girlfriend Irma, and get a friendly reception. I put the wet shoes to dry.

A long and animated conversation about Erich's successes and mishaps in Garmisch and Kohlgrub follow. I sleep badly and freeze in the cold room. Next morning it is still raining.

After coffee, I go into Garmisch with Erich. My application for accommodation at the NSV is hopeless, and I am told to apply at the regional council. The regional council in Munich has been bombed out. After lunch I go to write in a nice café.

Garmisch makes no impression on me: neither the locals, the displaced persons, the "chums" nor the bombed-out people. I spend the afternoon and evening with Erich at Irma's place. She generously cooks for me. Irma's cousin is coming. The place to sleep is disgusting. Early in the morning I observe the Alfspitze Mountain against the rising sun, a marvelous sight. There is new snow down in the valley. I drink coffee in the kitchen and think about the bombed-out people (Rhinelanders).

The fat mama constantly wails because the landlord's wife shouts so much. The son is on leave and has to return to Russia the next day. I tell the landlord's wife that she should try shouting at me, and I would soon sort her out. She laughs. The old man with the pipe curses at the Nazi dogs. He says there are no native Garmischers among the authorities, they're all rogues who've turned up from somewhere, "such ones" (he makes the Hitler salute). I spend a short time with Erich in Garmisch. I'm to report at the regional council building at two o'clock in the afternoon.

We agree to meet at this time. I eat in the "Kaiser Franz", as all other restaurants are closed. It is wretched as hell, but I converse with the ladies there. One is the daughter of the owner of a Leipzig printer. The business is bombed out and she is here with her daughter. The behavior of the Garmisch people to the bombed-out ones give me pause. (It is forbidden to cook, no using the lavatory after nine o'clock in the evening, and electric sockets and lamp fittings are covered with sticky tape.)

At two o'clock I am again at the regional council office with two underlings. My torrent of words elicits their sympathy, and I receive a recommendation for Erich and me to the mayor of Oberau. Oberau urgently requires a replacement for the only men's hairdresser, who has been called up to serve in the military. Maybe the mayor can also provide me with a place to stay. There should be rooms available.

I travel to Oberau and have a conversation with the mayor, who shows enthusiasm over the arrival of the hairdresser who is said to be coming to take over the business. For me he unfortunately has nothing free. The job of Chief Inspector of the local council he has recently had to fill with an old bone of a man, since the Labor Office in Garmisch didn't send him anybody else. He had to put a woman from Leipzig in the Economic Office. He recommends me to the Chief Inspector of the Labor Office in Garmisch, since there are certainly possibilities of employment in Oberammergau and other places around Oberau. Then I could well live in Oberau. I go with Erich to the house of the wife of the hairdresser. She swears like a sailor and sends him away. He thinks I may have more luck.

At Oberau station I send a somewhat more confident postcard home and look around a bit, taking in the town. I return and spend the evening at Irma's. Next morning, Friday, I go with Erich to the Labor Office. After the fiasco of Oberau Erich wants to ask for a labor card for Kohlgrub. I hesitate, and suspect nothing good.

I talk to the Chief Inspector, who finds fault with my departure permit. He says a public service post would be out of the question for me. He decides on Oberammergau and indicates I should have a medical examination. I should walk up to Oberau in the afternoon and report there (without further details). With Erich, who has received his labor card for Kohlgrub, I leave the Labor Office downcast. Under no circumstances do I want to go to the armament dump at Oberammergau.

I tell the landlord's wife I am leaving tomorrow, then talk with Erich at Irma's place. Further talks at the Labor Office in Garmisch prove pointless, since it is under the Chief Inspector's control. The Chief Inspector wouldn't depart from his directive to go to Oberammergau. We decide to go home, and during the stopover in Munich Erich wants to finalise the matter in Kohlgrub.

During the night I toss and turn and rack my brain about how I can come home having made some progress. I consider putting off my departure and making a detour to Mittenwald. I sleep for a short time and wake up bathed in sweat.

At four o'clock in the morning the landlord's family leave in traditional costume for their relatives nearby. It is raining again, and cold. There is no chance of undertaking anything else in this weather with my clothes and shoes. I take leave of (Oberbraunsberg) Garmisch. There is a control on the train. The rain clears up only in Munich.

I have a slow and boring return journey through a shabby region. Voigtland is more interesting. There is a noticeable difference in temperature between South Bavaria and the mid-German plain. Arriving in Leipzig I take leave of Erich on the Augustusplatz and we agree to meet on Easter Monday at our home.

I arrive home and creep unnoticed into the room, where the child is already sleeping. I lie down, put house shoes on and hear my wife speak in the kitchen. She is talking with the daughter of the house, who has just arrived from Berlin, about the bombing of her train, and is very afraid for me. Suddenly I stand before her.

My new plan: Application letters to the Reich and Railway Head Office in Munich and the mayors of over a dozen communities in South Bavaria, Tyrol and Vorarlberg.

PART 4
ESCAPE

1943-1944

Walter gets a positive response from the government office in Bludenz, in the Voralberg area of western Austria, (now merged with Germany and therefore governed by German Nazi administrators). This is precisely where he has vacationed with Hilda many years before. But securing the job is fraught with danger and Walter must carefully size up each Nazi official he encounters.

May 25, 1944

A great surprise penetrates through the hopelessness: Bludenz, the invitation letter.

My journey begins on 25.5.44, at 20.10 hours, via Weissenfels, Nuremberg, Augsburg, Buchloe, Lindau and Bregenz. Until Weissenfels I have a conversation with a woman friend from the high mountains. We look at photos and she wishes me good luck. Fear and doubt, coupled with self-reproach, encroach. I send my first greetings home from Weissenfels station, then the journey continues. A young man gives up his seat for me, and I converse with my fellow travelers. There is an odd similarity with old, long-forgotten friends in Habitus, with their expressions, tone of voice and way of thinking. One traveler recounts how he took the Berlin

Damage Center for a ride: "You've got to earn a few pence and a bit of old clothing from the shitty war. So, what do you do otherwise? You can't chat openly about it anymore. There's only one really effective means, you've got to moan about what's to moan about. So, aren't I right, or what? Well, they caught one of them. On the very same day they cut off his head, so they could give his things to other people. So, the scoundrels once again spared themselves a dowry."

One of the railway policemen pushes through the corridor. The story-teller jumps up, seizes him by the jacket and shouts in his face: "Come over here, you old twerp, you can listen in to what we have to say about you people. You're also from that association, the so and so, aren't you?"

Whereupon he made a gesture of stealing. The person he is addressing panics, looks around fearfully, smiles with embarrassment and vanishes. Laughter and jeers follow him. "We hit the fool right on the head, didn't we, ha, ha, ha."

In Nuremberg, lots of people rush into the train. We move slowly between Donauwörth and Augsburg due to restoration of the railway bank, which was hit by bombs a few days earlier. We pass Augsburg and Buchloe.

The Munich express to Lindau is overcrowded on my first journey through the Allgäu. The mountains around Immenstadt (Grüntem) appear, behind them those not yet covered with snow around Oberstdorf. Then we have a beautiful journey with tight curves and steep climbs past the Alpsee Lake to Lindau. I see Lake Constance again when crossing the linking causeway.

The wait before continuing the journey to Bludenz is used for a short stroll along the harbor. On the left is Bregenz Bay with Pfünder, to the right of that is the Hochälple and Three Sisters. Straight ahead in the distance I can see the Swiss shore, behind that the Säntis Mountain. To the right is an endless, shimmering, fragrant stretch of water, sparkling in the light. The old seems new-born.

I arrive in Bludenz and go to Tourist bureau – my search for a room, even in a hotel, is unsuccessful. I telegram home and encounter a saucy woman official. At three o'clock I telephone to the Regional Council Office. There is distrust and annoyance that I'm without lodgings, because I'm dirty, unshaven and sweaty. There is a weak prospect in the Arlberger Hof. I walk around and sit down in the grounds. Agitated I then go into the Regional Council Office. I read the name Dr. Czinglar on a sign. In the reception I am told I should come back at five o'clock. I sit down in the grounds again and wonder if I should travel back home. It's muggy and a few raindrops fall. I watch the fountain and listen to the traffic: cars, motorcyclists.

There are many people on the street (bombed-out people). A guard notices me. I walk morosely back and forth. At five o'clock I enter the Regional Council Office again with the intention to swallow my annoyance and be friendly. I am received nicely and admitted immediately to the Chief Inspector. I apologize for the way I look. He introduces himself. I take my coat off. He maintains he never received my written appointment request and apologizes for asking me to come on Whit Saturday. He has in the meantime freed up a room in the "Hohen Frassen" hotel through the police, but the people don't believe I am coming. He calls there at my request and confirms I'm coming.

The first interview begins immediately: "What do you say to our invitation?" I have to tell him about my activities. He asks me about documents, references, etc. Since I have it with me by chance, I show the testimonial of B., which he reads with a steadfast gaze, then my Military Pass, which he leafs through curiously. I am a teacher of commerce with teaching qualifications. I rigorously observe his expression for any doubt about the authenticity of the Pass, but nothing stirs, and he gives it back to me smiling contentedly. In his manner and appearance, he bears a great resemblance to Dr. Rudolf Neumann,[1] from which I conclude that he is similar to him also in restless mind and finicky attitude to official matters. However, his appearance is more sedate, mature and balanced, he shows he masters the situation, speaks with carefully considered fluency and puts all his official colleagues I have seen so far completely in the shade.

Then he asks me why I want to give up the lucrative profession of auditor, to which I explain the enormous difficulties caused by the continual bombing, making dedication to my tasks impossible, then the necessity to do something for my health, my heart troubles and finally my duty to save my wife and child.

He understands this, but draws my attention to the fact that the salary which he can give me would not be remotely equal to my pay hitherto, to which I ask a counter-question. Would he be ready to exchange his fixed employment with an official salary for that of an auditor with a large salary?

He categorically rejects this idea, and with that I have convinced him that I am serious with my application. He gets his secretary to give him the salary table in order, he asserts, to calculate the highest possible salary for me. He comes to a net salary of about 310 Marks, which I consider appropriate.

Meanwhile I look around his room. It is light, airy and spacious, as indeed are all rooms in this modern building. At the back of the room looms large the Holiest of Holies, the picture of the great prophet and favorite of the Gods. Next to it hangs a beautiful relief map of the Vorarlberg and a large bookcase recalls a lost fortune – the destruction of my 2,500 books.

But in the midst of my observations I get a question from the Chief Inspector: "You are of course a Party comrade, Herr Freiherr?"

"No, Chief Inspector!"

To this he made a concerned face, wrinkled his forehead, looked at me through his glasses and said: "That would of course be a precondition for your appointment."

"I would very much regret that. I have never belonged to a party organization and will in future continue to keep to my basic principle of absolute freedom from political ties!"

"But Herr Freiherr, it is for you personally so inconsequential if you become a Party member. You have no sort of unpleasantness or even guilty conscience to fear!"

"Do you think so? That would look hypocritical and exactly that I consider as the greatest evil of cultured humanity."

"Well, I want to bring your matter to the attention of the Regional Councilor. It is quite possible that he insists on your belonging to the Party."

"Then regrettably I would have to withdraw my application!"

"Well, you may rest assured in leaving it to me. The Regional Councilor gives much value to my opinion, and in the way, I will present it I believe I may take it that your employment is secured."

"I thank you kindly, Chief Inspector."

Now, as the service is closing at six o'clock, he asks me to accompany him, so that he can show me to my lodging. The way leads back through the little town, then in bright May sunshine through the gardens and meadows which I knew from earlier in Oberdorf, where numerous new buildings were put up in the 18th century.

I talk about my earlier stay in Bludenz, where we almost melted from heat; he says the pension "Hohe Fraßen" is excellent and recommends me to spend the Whitsun days there eating well, which I intend to do if things go to plan. He shows me in the direction of my accommodation and asks me to come to the office again tomorrow morning at ten o'clock, so that he can introduce me to the Regional Councilor. He takes leave of me with best wishes.

I set off alone, wearing my winter clothing in the heat, gradually climbing the steep track which leads up to my accommodation. It is the last house and lies at the foot of the Mutterberg Mountain, with a magical panoramic view over Bludenz, the valley and the mountains.

I am allocated a room. It is small, with only a bed, wardrobe, table and chair, but with running water, which allows me first of all to enjoy a good wash and to clear my throat. I have a good stretch and change my clothes. Then I light a cigarette and go on to the small wooden balcony. I stand spellbound and utterly transfixed by the splendor of the view. Bludenz snuggles in the valley below so peacefully, as if it did not yet know that war had broken out. Above it, to the northeast, one can see the foothills of the jagged Rutlikamm, while to the left the valley splits into the Montafon and the Kloster valleys on the way to the Silvretta and the Arlberg. It is similar to the Tschaggenau and the Landschau, and to Laugar, Stute and the Flexenpass.

There is no proper evening meal served in the guesthouse, because it is Friday, a meatless day. Instead I eat soup and bread and butter with cheese. I go to bed after sunset but excitement keeps me from sleeping. Serious problems ferret around in my brain, especially the matter of my tax card, which I will have to present on an eventual return to work, and my child's schooling, for which, especially here in Bludenz, a certificate of racial descent will certainly be demanded. I harbor the fondest wish that the job will not happen and that the Regional Councilor will refuse me because I do not belong to the Nazi Party.

Full of impatience and torment I await the break of day, and when it is light, I step onto the balcony and am overwhelmed by the fairy tale magic of the awakening mountain. The peaks of the Rhätikamm are bathed in the early sunlight, birds twitter and warble, meadows and woodlands smell of fresh dew, and from the Montafon a smoke trail along the entire valley enhances the immensity and majesty of the mountains in contrast to the sleeping town of Bludenz carefully embedded with its houses and gardens. It is the most bewitching sight I have ever seen. It surpasses even Garmisch.

I truly believed I was dreaming, held my forehead and called myself a fool who dared to believe in a stroke of good luck, which I was denied even in the best years of democracy.[2] And while Garmisch left me fairly indifferent, this place seized me with heavy yearning and the burning desire to bring my wife and child this joy, to carry them off to freedom, and accompany them through the meadows and up the mountains, which my child does not yet know, her hard young life having been spent only in the lowlands.

This desire and the sense of impending danger struggled within me as I walked down to Oberdorf at the appointed hour through the gardens, the villas and the cottages to the important interview with the Regional Councilor. I breathed in the fragrant air like a creature from whom one has withheld the elixir of life for years.

Chief Inspector Kühnl introduced me to the Regional Councilor. He had an imposing appearance with his powerful figure, wide, smooth and cheerful face and his snow-white hair. Here "Heil Hitler" was naturally the non-committal greeting. He bade me take a seat and offered me a cigarette.

"Chief Inspector Kühnl has already told me everything worth knowing about your person and your career, and your political leanings and non-membership of the Party are irrelevant in judging you. I, on my part, put no emphasis on whether you become a Party comrade or not, since I am mainly interested in a competent employee."

I then had to briefly re-state and explain all the information I had given Kühnl the previous day. The question of accommodation was discussed and the Regional Councilor thought accommodation in the Tyrol settlement was a possibility, which was a new housing estate for evacuees from the South Tyrol. I told him that as "total air raid victims" we no longer possessed any furniture and therefore were obliged to take furnished accommodation.

"I would not like to recommend that you make do with wartime furniture. Such trash will give you little joy, Herr Freiherr. Wait a minute, I will call the mayor."

This he did forthwith and announced, "Freiherr from Leipzig is here with me", and asked him if there was any possibility of furniture being made available from the community store on the basis of the Reich service law, to which the person being questioned appeared to reply in the positive.

The Regional Councilor wondered if I could not for the time being move without my family to Bludenz. In view of the permanent danger of bomb attacks on cities like Leipzig, I had to reject this idea.

"Yes, but for a few weeks you will have to live in a hotel anyway until we get your accommodation sorted out."

An informal conversation followed about the danger involved in traveling from Leipzig to Bludenz, my previous sojourns in this town, its splendid surroundings, and "Red Leipzig", as the Regional Councilor called it, and its dreadful current condition.

Then he sent me back to Kühnl, who had one or two more things to settle, and who bade me call again around midday in order to hear his decision about my accommodation, for which he requested the certificate of bomb damage from me.

Again, I sat in front of Kühnl.

"Now everything is arranged to the best, Herr Freiherr."

"Yes, Herr Chief Inspector. And as I assume that the success of my application is largely due to your recommendation, I cordially thank you."

The Chief Inspector gave me a satisfied smile.

"So, now we have a few more formalities to deal with. I have to ask some questions about your personal details."

Personal details? Why? Oh my God!

"You must understand, the Regional Councilor could give permission without the approval of the Reich Governor in Innsbruck. However, as you are not a member of the Party, he wishes to be sure of the facts. I am sure you understand that?"

I felt a slight apprehension.

"Please, Herr Chief Inspector, ask your questions!"

"So, let's begin!"

"Surname?"

"Freiherr"

"Christian name?"

"Kurt."

"Date of birth?"

"February 23, 1898."

"Where?"

"In Mannheim."

"Occupation?"

"Auditor."

"Sworn auditor?"

"Yes."

I could feel myself sweating.

"Are you of Aryan descent?"

Kühnl gave me a penetrating gaze and I could feel the sweat slowly pushing through my pores.

"Are you of Aryan descent?"

Kühnl gave me another piercing look. A tingling feeling crept up from the soles of my feet to my knees.

"Yes, Aryan descent."

"Have you got an Aryan identity card?"

Again, he looked me up and down.

"Not anymore. It was burned along with all my other personal papers."

"No longer available," he says as he writes. "But you certainly possessed one?"

"Yes."

My knees become soft.

"Where was it issued?"

"In Mannheim."

Again, there is a sharp look.

"I can be sure that you are telling me the truth, can't I?"

"Certainly, Herr Chief Inspector."

"Mannheim," he repeats slowly and writes down.

"Member of the NSDAP?"

"No."

"Do you belong to any of the associations of the Party?"

"No."

"Not even one?"

"None, apart from the fiduciary association."

"Hmm, that is very little. But you could still become a member of the NSV, Herr Freiherr. I would highly recommend it."

I too thought I would like to recommend it. It is too late. The trap snaps shut. My heart races. Still I control myself and using my last strength, I attempt to hide my agitation.

"Were you prior to 1933 a member of a political association, party or lodge?"

"No."

"Any other association?"

"No."

"How long have you lived in Leipzig?"

I hesitated and he looked at me again.

"Since October 1943."

"And before that?"

"In Mannheim."

"Street and house number."

"M 3 Nr. 5."

"Have you ever lived anywhere else?"

"No."

"So, this seems to be going reasonably quickly. Now it will depend on the enquiry at the Mannheim Party offices. The people in Leipzig hardly know you."

Party headquarters in Mannheim? Good heavens! That will not do, that will be the end! I pull myself together with a great effort. "I don't think you will quickly get a reply. Mannheim is almost entirely in ruins, and the authorities there have not been functioning properly for a long time."

"It doesn't matter, in 10 to 14 days the staff at the District Administrative Office in Innsbruck will be able to process the matter, and I think your employment will be confirmed, assuming that no objections exist against you."

"So," – he pulls his watch out – "now everything is completed, Herr Freiherr."

He looks at me and smiles contentedly. I force myself to reply, taking the greatest pain to make sure that my agitation is not noticeable.

"Didn't Herr Regional Councilor want to speak to you again?"

"Certainly, about the question of my accommodation. And now many thanks, Herr Chief Inspector, you have indeed made a big effort on my behalf. I will come to see you again after talking again with Herr Regional Councilor. In the meantime, goodbye!"

"Heil Hitler, Herr Freiherr!"

The Regional Councilor seems to be in a great hurry, for as he hands me his card, he tells me abruptly that he has not yet spoken to the mayor about my accommodation. That, he says, I must settle with the Herr Chief Inspector. He shakes my hand and says, "And now, Heil Hitler and goodbye!"

Thereupon I left, somewhat disappointed at the abrupt parting, and went across again to Kühnl and reported the failure to him. He excused himself, saying he had a mountain of work waiting for him.

"If you do not need me anymore, Herr Chief Inspector, perhaps I can go home?"

"Yes, indeed, Herr Freiherr. For the time being there is nothing more and nothing has been found against you. And that will certainly be the case!"

Nothing found against you? No, nothing. If this man, to whom I have lied for a whole hour, in a way which no Jew ever conned a

Party man before, had been tickled by one molecule of suspicion, there would be no seeing my wife and child again and for my wife and child not one more week alive. My brain is doing roundabouts, my vision is blurred and my hands are sweating.

"So, Herr Freiherr, with that these formalities too are complete. And if all signs don't mislead, you will soon be able to move to your beloved Bludenz."

"Hopefully, Herr Chief Inspector."

"I can hardly see any obstacle."

He sees hardly any obstacle. Not yet, good Heavens!

"Will you report again to Herr Regional Councilor?"

"Yes, at 12 o'clock, about the accommodation."

11 TO COME CLEAN IS NOT POSSIBLE

Walter faces a potentially lethal problem. Securing the job in Bludenz requires a much bigger background check than he anticipated. The local authorities will not hire him until the higher-up Nazis in Innsbruck verify his story. This raises the possibility that they will reach the Mannheim officials who will tell them that there is no Kurt Freiherr from Mannheim. If that occurs not only would he fail to get the job but, in all likelihood, would be sent to a death camp with his family. Walter must escape from a trap of his own making.

May 27, 1944

I smoke one pipe and cigarette after another, repeatedly looking at my watch to see whether it is time to go to the station. At last, I say goodbye, throw my coat over my arm, take my briefcase and the unavoidable umbrella and tiptoe off, feeling like throwing up. If only I were already at home with my wife and child. But how could I reverse all that has happened and how could I rescue them? This fear would not go away as I stood on the platform waiting for the fast train to Lindau, and then in the overcrowded corridor of the train, taking in once more the glorious countryside. When a compartment became vacant, I saw Czechs or other foreigners eating.

Once more I see the sparkling Lake Constance, Lindau. There is a special train to Augsburg. Travel companions from Leipzig, childminders of the NSV in Dornbirn, keep me company. Conversation drags as my mind dwells on the imminent danger. Once more I have a heavenly journey through the Allgäu, zigzagging upwards to Konstanz, then through the middle of Immenstadt, Kempten, Kaufbeuren, Buchloe, and then – in twilight – Augsburg. I have to stand for hours on the platform with those accompanying me for the train to Halle to arrive.

Under normal circumstances, I would have given God knows what for such a journey. As it was, I cursed it with all its probable and possible consequences. After Augsburg I again stood in the overcrowded corridor with my companions, smoked my pipe and racked my brain about how I might find a way out of my hellish predicament.

The thought that the whole escape plan, which I had set up for the three of us, might collapse like a house of cards made me feverish, so that I started to speak aloud to myself. "Out!" I shouted, losing my self-control. My companion hesitated and asked astonished: "What is out?" "My pipe has gone out, the weedy tobacco is worth nothing, like everything at this shitty time." She pulled the corner of her mouth into a bittersweet, disbelieving smile.

I sat on the railing and tried to calm my brain through a nap while she leaned against the wall opposite. A couple of SS bigwigs, who had chatted her up between Feldkirch and Lindau, were sprawling on the floor of the corridor, snoring like bears. Then I hit on a solution. Immediately upon my arrival in Leipzig, I would telegraph the Regional Councilor and ask him to hold back my approval application until he receives my written explanation. Then, as long as the application had not yet been sent to Innsbruck, I would find enough time to construct excuses in such a way that the gentlemen in Bludenz would willingly withdraw my contract of employment.

Yes, that is good and quite safe. I will therefore have to cheat these gentlemen once more. From then my spirits began to rise a little, but I was so tired I could have fallen over. Such marathon tours without sleep and yet again without a seat get to my bones like hell, and as the misty morning dawns, we go through Probstzella.

Everything is suddenly quite silent, and the only discussion is whether we should change in Weissenfels or go straight through to Halle. In Halle we can get the connecting train to Leipzig and be there an hour earlier. My companion beams from ear to ear at the thought of surprising her parents for Whitsun in Borsdorf, and hopes to get an immediate connection in Leipzig. But between Weissenfels and the Leuna works the train stood still for over half an hour. We hear that bombs fell during the night and that the track is largely destroyed. Then we continue slowly on our way and reach Halle more than an hour late.

Naturally the connecting train has long departed, and a second train from Magdeburg is not expected for the time being as there were air raids there too. We get on the local train which is just coming in, and trundle off after 15 minutes at snail's pace, stopping at every little station, and when we come into the main station in Leipzig, my companion has only one minute to run to her train to Borsdorf. She takes my leave with her best wishes and is gone.

I stand for a long time on platform 8, in brilliant Whitsun sunshine, sweating in my winter coat, looking anxiously around, before finally leaving for the Bayrischestrasse. I reunite with my wife and child. She is more in control of herself than I am and listens to my adventures and does not see any difficulties – I however feel dreadful after all the strain and excitement, but I manage to draft a job withdrawal telegram to the Regional Councilor.

I send my wife to the post office. She calls on Grete in order to send her up to me, and when she comes, I lie exhausted on my bed and make my report to her. The story is getting to her nerves, she is afraid of being caught as an accessory, but comforts me and assures me of a favorable outcome, a point of view which she stubbornly defends.

After more than an hour – it has become very warm – my wife returns hot and bothered. She had to go to the post office in the main station because at Whitsun all other post offices are closed. She was spotted by an old friend on the way but ran on and managed to deliver the telegram to the man despite initial difficulties. Scarcely is she back than air-raid warnings sound.

All afternoon I worry about the draft of the letter to the Regional Councilor and come to the conclusion that I should express myself in such a way that the danger of making him and the Chief Inspector nervous is minimal. To come clean is not possible, otherwise they would be duty-bound as officials to report me, and the grounds for my negative reply must ring imprecise and non-binding, and be expressed in the most charming way possible, so as to give the impression that I took the step of withdrawing in a completely relaxed way, but with the greatest sorrow about the loss of the pearl of Bludenz. In the following days I write a second letter to the Chief Inspector.

12   I AM NOT ABLE TO FIGHT OPENLY

The Bludenz officials do not accept Walter's withdrawal letters. They want him to start the job as soon as his background inspection is completed. He should not worry, they say. At this point it's just a formality. But Walter knows the inspection will fail to find any information at all on Freiherr from Mannheim, so it is far from a formality. Nevertheless, Walter decides to wait a few more weeks to see if he will be fortunate enough to receive a formal letter of acceptance. Meanwhile, he adds to his patriotic credentials by supervising a prisoner work detail in Leipzig. Here, Walter, a socialist who sympathizes with the Soviet Union, must guard Russian prisoners while wearing a Nazi armband – an irony not lost on him.

July 2, 1944

Just at this moment Sergeant R came to see me and asked me for a "labor of love". I am to supervise prisoners-of-war on Saturday morning as they perform tidying-up duties. Subject to other duties, I said I would.

Things are getting madder. But what was I to do? Carrying out this request could give me a chance in case the people in Bludenz ask the people in Leipzig for information about me. Naturally I made it a precondition that I do not have to carry a weapon. Then no one would expect me unarmed to chase after a runaway.

This is a timely bit of fun from the treasure chest of the goddess of my destiny, in regard to my fate! If Bludenz was not on my mind, I would laugh hysterically like a tortured man whose soles a goat is licking for salt.

Freiherr, guarding of prisoners-of-war. It is truly mad.

July 7, 1944

I have just received official confirmation that on the coming Saturday morning, I have to do prisoner-of-war guard duty. The group leader says that, in the order he gives in the name of the NSDAP[1] of the district of Leipzig, he has to employ me as "an honorary official" to guard six or seven prisoners and also emphasizes that I must be recognizable at least by means of an armband.

Now, should the people in Bludenz want to check on my legitimacy, this remarkable document would be very useful. "Honorary official" – that is indeed an important title quite designed to lighten the worry and bother of the Regional Councilor in Bludenz with regard to my employment. Were I not so edgy, because he has not yet given the postman any comforting news to bring me, I would do a somersault and submit a prize question to the experts in racial discourse.

The Allies, without knowing or wanting it, have rendered an inestimable service to me and my wife and child. Their bombs not only bury people, they even spread a shroud over the past of the one who understands how to use their thunderous fire-spitting. May their burning sign also inspire my friends in Bludenz, and illuminate the Gauleiter[2] in Innsbruck who is authorized to grant concessions, so that the last syllable of the fateful crossword puzzle may be completed.

Time is pressing. Already the Russians are attacking in East Prussia, while the Nazi cohorts according to the latest army report "fight back westwards", these gifts to humanity, who now pant back down the hill they so craftily scrambled up. By the time they get down again, I want to have found a firm footing. My nerves are torn to shreds. Let's go, people of Bludenz! I am waiting.

July 9, 1944

I have fulfilled my obligations as a guard. It was both interesting and amusing to observe my "comrades", also wearing official Nazi armbands, and to see their breasts swell on the way to the mission. And what worthy plans they had hatched! They wanted to show the scoundrels from Russia what work means and how one gets down to it without wasting time, and if they don't obey, a punch on the ear will help them achieve their goal.

The way of dealing with them, which was read out to us, seemed designed to achieve a maximum effect through "strict treatment", "sharp supervision", "the most stringent measures, in case one of them decided to disappear underground amongst the rubble of the flattened houses or even be caught nicking" and "prosecution or alternatively reprimand of national comrades who intended to slip provisions or tobacco to the enemy, as the Bolshevists are well supplied." One of our watchdogs had the necessary knowledge of the language, and could himself bend obtuse elements to his will.

All the same I softened the Teuton hearts of the guard column within an hour by diplomatic means. I first carefully tested the waters and then proceeded to speak more openly, and with all the more success since the others felt offended by the bosses who arrived in official cars, wearing safety pins,[3] and waited in vain for at least one of these self-important guards to offer a sip of beer or a few cigarettes.

And then, as the sun rose to its highest point and burned down not only on the heads of the unhappy prisoners-of-war but also caused sweat to pour out of the pores of their guards, I got the company as far as to curse the whole "Nazi shit racket" in chorus. They looked on happily as I put my cigarettes into the Russian faces beaming with gratitude, and quite willingly followed my example. Inflammatory and insulting words were no longer heard, not even when the prisoners lay down for a nap after their work. "We can't do otherwise, let them be." And when one man, who was snapped at when he flung himself to the ground early in the morning, told us that he had malaria, they even sympathized with him and let him lie down as long as he wanted.

Yes, they even dared to use really crude words about the meagre provisions which the German military authority condescended to call prisoners' food, and even got the troop commander to extend the midday rest period from a quarter of an hour to one and a quarter hour. Then we were relieved by six other chosen ones, who took over our Russian column with the same good intentions "of showing them what work really means".

Naturally my collaborators could not refrain from thoroughly celebrating the success of their mission with the old Germanic tradition of drinking beer, which the Germans are accustomed to do on every happy and unhappy occasion, even when they have borne their nearest and dearest to the grave. However, I greatly prefer that as opposed to when they bump off friend and foe with a shot to the neck in cold blood during the night.

What may the Russians have thought of me? I am ashamed to appear in their eyes as one of those who consider themselves upholders and custodians of European culture, and yet not once did I dare let my mask fall in front of them. Even with them, like with everyone, there are treacherous elements. It is well known that they too have in many cases denounced trusting and helpful people in the camp of their enemies for the sake of an advantage, causing their downfall.

As in my present state I am not able to fight openly and do the good that is in tune with my inner feelings, I will try to prevent being entrusted with such a task for a second time. Hopefully the time will come when I can undertake it with stronger fervor! Only the objects need to change!

13 NOW WE ARE IN A REAL MESS!

Because Walter's work permit in Leipzig expires on July 15, 1944, he desperately wants his new job in Bludenz finalized by then. If not, he will have to get an extension which means more dangerous visits to the various offices in Leipzig, increasing the risk that either someone will recognize him as Walter Leopold, the Jew, or that someone will sense that his Freiherr papers and explanations are suspect. He also must depend on now seven-year-old Anneliese not to reveal their secrets as she attends school as an Aryan.

July 11, 1944

Our golden child brought home her first school report today. Leadership and attitude: very good. Performance: satisfactory. The teacher told me that no child in the first class had received a better mark, since a thorough assessment of her abilities was possible only towards the end of the full school year. Furthermore, Annekind gave him great pleasure to teach, once she got over her initial shyness, behaved beautifully and always gave precise and well-thought-out answers. Although she had only been at school for four weeks, she had caught up with all her classmates, which for this whipper-snapper was a respectable achievement.

The holidays start on Friday, which for me is cause to ask the school for a letter of referral in case of a move to Bludenz. I also had to shake up my protectors over there yesterday with a telegram, in which I let them know that my exemption notification expires on July 15 in case they have not reached a decision.

The real motivating force was naturally the gnawing uncertainty about the things that could come out about me in Bludenz and elsewhere, which could pose a real danger to me, my family and my friends, a nightmare that can only be forgotten through knowledge of what was actually going on. That is why I telegraphed and now have at hand the cabled personal reply from the Regional Councilor that he is approaching the employment exchange in Leipzig by telephone and by letter and has asked for an extension of my residence papers, as my employment is expected to receive official approval. I should call at the labor office, he instructs me.

Now we are in a real mess. Just what I wanted to avoid the most, namely to make the Leipzig Labor Office aware of me, has now happened, despite the fact that I had asked the Regional Councilor in the telegram to let me know the news personally. Now any old official, who because of the lack of a declaration of my unobjectionable status, cannot explain to himself its origin, can make a fuss and decide that I have not observed the deadline for filling in the employment documents. He can demand a health certificate and may not, like his predecessor, push the certificate discreetly towards the authorized person to be signed, but see some merit in declaring me indispensable for employment in Leipzig.

True, I could self-importantly lay out on the table the telegram from the Regional Councilor, and claim that the contractual agreement was in fact dated May 27, and that as a public employee, I am no longer obliged to fill out labor cards, and whatever other convincing arguments there might be. Hopefully, the Regional Councilor was clever enough to follow the hint I gave him 14 days ago and explain in his letter that I am de facto already an employee and that this will be confirmed by the Gauleiter. Hopefully!

Should putting my head in the lion's mouth for a second time be successful, my legalization will doubtlessly make a big jump forwards through a back-dated entry into the labor card and the eventual completion of a labor book. Much more important for me is the knowledge that for the time being the Nazi administration has not dug me a grave. And if it should go to the opposite extreme and my "installation" be confirmed – all under the condition that the labor office does not obstruct it – then even the most resourceful criminal could not have even the slightest suspicion that I am not Freiherr. After the day of the hanged Nazi hangman I could find it difficult to present this proof myself.[1]

In the end I fear, old pessimistic realist that I am, a dreadful outcome of my strange adventure, because I cannot imagine that the Bludenz officials will say yes and amen to a false report from Mannheim. If they do, I know of no explanation anymore and would have to fall into humble silence before the mysterious workings of the heavenly power.

July 12, 1944

I once more have the way to the Labor Office behind me. For a long time, I was tormented by doubt, whether I should go immediately or put it off and await the arrival of the Regional Councilor's letter. It seemed important to me to be put in the special position of my intentions. On the other hand, I am no friend of waiting. Storming off afresh to the goal brought me the best result so far...

I got going, constantly on the lookout for known faces, and stumbled through luck on the young man who a quarter of a year earlier had helped me with the blessed testimonial document.

Understandably he pulled a surprised face on seeing me, because he imagined I had long disappeared over the hills, and to start with, listened to my explanation with a somewhat morose look.

This young altruist is called Würker. I have promised him a greetings card from Bludenz.

July 13, 1944

I wrote to the Regional Councilor to say that the matter, despite the confusion in the twice destroyed Labor Office, had been solved. Because of the death of the former referee and the shortcomings of the filed documents and of an official who had not been informed, and wishing to avoid any further complications, I request a weekly progress report.

And I much regretted that I did not follow his well-meant and far-sighted advice to ignore all doubt and move to Bludenz and wait there for further developments, with the result that I and my family are exposed to further bomb raids. I add that I recognize that I am partly guilty for the additional troubles which I have occasioned to him.

I wonder whether my fatherly friend, who is unaware of the true reasons behind why I want to be informed by him weekly, understands this hint? Will he invite me to follow his earlier advice without delay? Be as it may – this fear stabs me incessantly in my spinal cord like a bundle of needles – that waiting for the wretched, disappointing news that the Mannheim inquiries will reveal there is something wrong with me.

So, what then?

Is it not pitiful that one has to so profoundly trick two people[2] who one admires, as one loves one's dearest friends, only so as to wrest oneself, wife and child finally from the clutches of the Gestapo?

And is it not even more dreadful to imagine how, if they suddenly crashed from the height of their boundless trust, they would inwardly bleed and turn into people-haters?

I curse the day I made their acquaintance and long for the hour when I can face them with an open visor in front of the gallows where my enemies may hang. There is no one who can advise me, no one is strong enough to help me. Only the Almighty, who guides our destiny, is able to save us.

May he have mercy on a man who shrinks from no sacrifice or risk to save his loved ones from evil.

14   THE WORST OF ALL TORMENTS

Walter often chronicles the news of the war as gleaned from forbidden shortwave Allied radio broadcasts. Due to space considerations most of these geopolitical editorials are not included in this volume. However, we share his original insights concerning the relationships between German culture, Jewish resistance (or the lack thereof) and the mass killings.

His generalizations about the German character are tempered by knowing that not only did he and his family secure underground refuge with Germans gentiles, but also that the two Nazi officials in Bludenz are truly trying to help him get a job and move his family out of harm's way. Under better circumstances, he believes they could become true friends. Now they are his potential executioners.

July 14, 1944

It appears the Nazi power is coming to an end. Vilnius has already fallen and the Russians are driving three wedges into their Polish and Baltic spheres of interest, scattering the cohorts, grabbing one of Hitler's generals every day and with them thousands upon thousands of mercenaries, the infected and the immune. What does it matter against this that the bloodsucker makes propaganda with flying bombs,[1] like the Rex Imperator[2] in 1918 with his miraculous long-distance heavy artillery, which was supposed to force the French to their knees?

Germany's artistic capital, Munich, the city over which once hovered a glorious translucence of the noblest tradition, lies in ruins or is engulfed in flames, where exploding bombs have left work over for their incendiary brothers. The residents, displaced and fleeing, call for help but the fire departments of all Bavaria are quite powerless against the violence of the avenging might of Hitler's enemies. He sees his luster fade, the scoundrel, and his numerous helpers, already fearful of death, tremble and grasp their necks to feel them one more time before they are caught in the noose. And to crown their doings, the beloved national comrades hurtle in multitudes to their deaths, some into the turmoil of battle, others to concentration camps, and the last into a hailstorm of bombs.

They haul hundreds of thousands of Jews from Hungary into poison gas chambers at Auschwitz, where they murder up to 8,000 each day, until not one is left alive.[3]

And the German people continue lethargically to tolerate these shameful atrocities and acts of horror, with which the bloodhounds burden them; their sons, fathers and grandsons continue to fight like berserks on the fronts for the physical and mental well-being of their bloodsuckers, and still fervently cultivate the godly hygiene of their human race, and hide behind propaganda against the dark figure of Bolshevism.

The enemies of Hitler, and soon of the entire German people, have given openly to understand that they will raze Germany to the ground unless her inhabitants turn away from Hitler and his gang quickly and wholeheartedly. Whoever tolerates is also to blame, they say, and whoever fights for the common good is equal with his creator.

They are right in this. They judge, and claim that the majority of Germans are only too well informed and are to blame for the nastiness and irredeemable guilt of their seducers, that they on the day of reckoning would be branded like receivers of stolen goods and punished.

Cowardice is no excuse, however little I can certify that the Jews, at first submissive, then in their fear willing, and finally depressed and murdered, did the slightest for their own salvation. Their guilt is suicide by negligence, but the guilt also belongs to their brothers, friends, yes, and relatives, who have been saved in America, England and Australia; they shut themselves away to the cries for help of the tortured in criminal self-satisfaction and self-sufficiency, and will be sentenced on the day of judgement.

However, the origin of the devilish plans for the destruction of the world is and remains Germany, Adolf Hitler's Germany. If he wants, it can die with him. If not, it must fight for its life against him. There is no third way, except possibly in the insane minds of those who madly turn with the wind.

July 16, 1944

Again, the postman went past our home without knocking and delivering the final acceptance letter from Bludenz. Anyone who needs something, or wants to order something or bring something, has to knock on the door of the landing, as the bell has not worked since December 4. The postman passed by with his bent posture and old, tired tread. And again hope, doubt, fear and sorrow are one day older, and tomorrow becomes the day after tomorrow and the day after tomorrow becomes a week, and new British and American squadrons continue to roar overhead in a dreadful sing-song, lay their eggs and tear up more railway lines, destroy locomotives and cut off the last road to freedom.

More than five weeks ago, the first encouraging letters arriving from Bludenz and the two telegrams offered a small glimmer of hope. But since then, I have had to endure enforced silence and uncertainty. On them grew the dream of travel I was hoping to be able to undertake with my child and her careworn Mutti, far away to the south in jam-packed compartments, but still onwards to freedom in the mountains, fresh air and sunshine. Our child, who inhaled the ozone of the Alps in her mother's womb, and took her first steps in the forests of the Erzgebirge mountains, but then had six long, tantalizing summers, one after the other as a Jewish kid on urban streets, and had to remain locked up for a year and a half like a song-bird in a cage, in order to protect her from the gaze of curious people; we wanted to make our first big trip with this child, to show her a corner of our beautiful world, the mountains of the Allgäu, Lake Constance, to be in the southern sunshine and under linen-white clouds that playfully hug the peaks and pinnacles of the Vorarlberg region.

In my mind's eye, trembling slightly, I saw her wide-open eyes full of wonder and amazement, and her questioning cherry-red mouth and her little hands dirty from the journey. Yes, we dreamed of all this and still dream of it day and night, so long as the minuscule glimmer of hope from Bludenz continues to smolder. Its will-o'-the-wisp temptation still outshines the Leipzig sun and to a large extent it is like lightning through our spacious apartment let to Freiherr, the gentile, with its lovely balcony, where I am just planting some flowers, a gift from a friend. Our home remarkably and challengingly creates copies of the objects in our Humboldtstrasse apartment, from which we fled as people condemned to death on September 17, 1942.

Superstitious fantasists would say this is an unmistakable sign that we have turned the corner away from danger, and started going up towards better days, while those who want to be considered prophetic aim at the downfall of our enemies.

Dreams, dreams about the knot which the goddess of fate has tied and which I, a weak human being, am supposed to unravel, without there being anybody in this world in a position to lessen the tantalizing torture. And those in Bludenz will languish in vain for the redeeming word from Innsbruck, disappointed and finally perhaps repulsed by the unheard-of breakdown of trust. They have fallen into a meaningful and – who knows! – dangerous silence. Two men, who I know could become my friends, steadfast and forgiving, even after I have degraded myself so deeply in their eyes... I am still enslaved to them and can still fall to my death with my wife and child, if the uppermost rung of the stepladder of this affection, so rare in Hitler's period, collapses.

And no one can hold us. May God protect us!

July 19, 1944

No news from Bludenz. Our old postman said that mail from Tyrol is arriving regularly again, so that cannot be the reason for the silence. How could the post deliver the requested weekly report if the Gauleitung does not release it? It must sit on the application until Mannheim confirms our existence. And the people in Mannheim are at a loss of what to do, as no records exist. "Never registered in Mannheim" the ominous dispatch will say.

The officials in Innsbruck will send it on to Bludenz shaking their heads and shrugging their shoulders, and my good comrades will turn pale, stare at each other and slowly trot home with their faces down to sleep on what they have heard. And what will they do the following day? Nothing? Nothing at all? Oh yes, they will do something! And that scares me terribly. But when, when?

The burden of not knowing is the worst of all torments...

July 21, 1944

I receive summons from the Labor Office regarding a "telegram from Bludenz", but as feared, there is again no word from the Regional Councilor. Then there was an air raid alarm. Annekind, once bitten, twice shy, with her ashen face and fear of death since the December 4 bombing, could be dressed in her basement clothes only with great trouble by her poor mother, who could hardly get herself ready, and carry our heavy luggage down two flights of stairs.

While I stared at the sky from the back door in anticipation of danger with the other habitually nosey people, a harmless creature fell on the asphalt and lay there wriggling with spread wings. It was one of the large native swallows, a swift. I picked it up. It panted for air with its wide-open, split beak, its heart beating loud and fast in my hand. The abandoned creature's round black eyes looked around listlessly, then clung tightly with its sharp talons to my fingers and allowed me to stroke it. For Anneliese, who had yearned for a long time for an opportunity to hold a swallow next to her cheek, despite all her fears of aircraft, chuckled with delight over the happy encounter with a bird she had previously only admired as it flitted past. What had brought it down so unexpectedly, whether a bomb or only some other bird, was not possible to ascertain from the unscathed bird. And before the large steel birds came roaring along, the swallow was up and away, stretching and spreading its wings, and sailing high into the sky. I wished it well on its way south and saw it fly off across the rooftops.

Shortly afterwards they droned over Leipzig with music typical of enormous bumblebees. Hundreds came with a dangerous load, for which they sought victims. I hear muffled blasts somewhere in Leipzig or its suburbs...

Again, I had to break off. The alarm went for over an hour. Today it must have been the turn of either Chemitz or Zwickau... Now, let's carry on. There was no smoke to be seen. It must have been mostly exploding bombs falling. Otherwise one would still hear them. Word of whatever has happened will spread throughout the entire city in no time.

Until then, as a "liquidating auditor" (unemployed), I will have some free time and can enjoy my usual afternoon nap, so as to supplement my meagre night's sleep of only a few hours. But I actually only close my eyes for a little while, I do not sleep. The summons to the Labor Office buzzed in my head and set it new tasks. Was it still the old telegram from the Regional Councilor, which only now had been registered, or already another version?

And what do those up there want from me now? They have everything in black and white! I will give myself time.

Then an official from the housing department wearing a safety pin came to ask about the whereabouts of the arriving inhabitants. I had to drag some information out of him, but he was reluctant to come inside as he had more calls to make. Nevertheless, he gave in, came inside, made himself comfortable and assured me that as we were bombed-out we would under no circumstance be evicted.

This news led comfortably into political questions, and I quickly noticed that our unexpected guest was in his element, for he was no longer in a hurry to carry out his other official duties. After initial reluctance to have a cup of coffee, he gave free flow to his thoughts locked in the Nazi cage and bellowed and wished everyone a quick and proper salvation from the wretched plague.

I considered this still young-looking man to be about 50, an old private with a "sewn-on cap". He, however, said he was about to reach his seventies, and when I accompanied him to the door after two hours of heartfelt conversation, he beamed like a forty-year-old, thanked me and promised to return. He was hardly out when I heard the sound of the all clear. We had again missed the warning sirens, as so often – also at night – the threatening wail of the distant sirens barely penetrated into our bedroom in spite of the open balcony door.

Downstairs at the house warden's I rang Granddad J. His voice was usually vigorous, but now, still trembling, he told me about the terrible attack they had endured that morning. In Gohlis, the houses collapsed row upon row, the street where they lived was in ruins, and the Landberger Platz was like a ploughed field. There was nothing left undamaged in his flat, yet they were all well, even if shaken through and through with fear.

Then the house warden, who returned just then from his trip to the city center, confirmed the extent of the damage. He had also seen many dead zoo animals, which had fallen victim to bomb fragments. Suddenly Sergeant R., in his beloved air-raid shelter uniform, shouted in a highly excited, menacing voice: "Assassination attempt on Hitler! He is only slightly injured. Could nevertheless welcome Mussolini. Radio announcement!" Then he ran on dripping with sweat, bearing this news so terrible to the hearts of the Germans.

What was it? A real assassination attempt? How? The propaganda men would surely not make this known! No, that could be a second burning of the Reichstag – a poor imitation of the 1939 edition[4] – an attempt to wrest itself out of the present awkward dilemma by reminding the people again of the divine powers that be. The intention is to get rid of annoying dissidents and to bring about a new bloodbath among the people who dare to doubt.

And then I heard the radio announcement myself:

"Assassination attempt on Hitler. Hitler is not injured. An attempt on Hitler's life was committed today. People around him were severely injured: Lieutenant General Schmidt, Colonel Brandt. Light injuries were sustained by Senior General Jodl, the Generals Koster, Buhle, Bodenschatz, Heusinger and Scherf and Admirals Voss, Puttkammer, Captain Assmann and Lieutenant Colonel Pugmann. Hitler has only suffered slight burns and bruises. He has immediately resumed his work, and as mentioned before, received Mussolini and had a long discussion with him. Shortly after the assassination attempt the Reichsmarschall[5] came to see Hitler."

The radio commentator continued:

"This assassination attempt on the life of our Führer is in the interest of our enemies, who in Adolf Hitler want to strike at the soul of German resistance. Just as during the assassination attempt in Munich on the November 8, 1939, so also this time providence has shielded the Führer. The German people are happy with the turn of events through which an appalling disaster has been prevented.

Whoever the criminals might be, their deed, had it been successful, would have delivered Germany to the enemy, and it would have meant the extermination of the German people. This aim was voiced so often and so clearly in London, Washington and Moscow, that there could be no German left who did not know the fate that awaited him and us if such a thing had happened: the deportation of men to foreign lands as slave workers, and for the remaining people liquidation in the bloody manner of the Bolsheviks or according to the cruel English-American practice of starvation and misery."

We recognize anew from this incident, that providence lies with our Führer. The love of the people is directed towards the Führer at this time in silent response and is stronger than ever, and our plea to destiny is that it may preserve the man in all battles, and sanctify his work, the liberation of Europe from the influence of hostile powers. However, we will help the Führer, everyone in their own way by tireless work for the war effort to the victorious conclusion of the struggle for life and death, to which we will make our way successfully through our labor. That shall at the same time be our response to the assassination attempt."

There we have it. Their deviousness is obvious:

Question: What do the enemy powers intend with this war?

Answer: The eradication of the German people.

Question: Who can prevent it?

Answer: Only the Führer.

Question: Why the Führer?

Answer: Because providence has determined it.

Question: How can this be proved?

Answer: By its hand, which has already saved him twice.

Question: Why is providence with the Führer?

Answer: So that his divine mission, the liberation of the peoples, can be realized.

Question: And why do you tell us this?

Answer: So that you can help the Führer to end the war victoriously.

Question: And why should we win?

Answer: Because otherwise you must die. And that is why the German people are "happy about this turn of events, because this terrible disaster has been prevented." And "that is our answer to the assassination attempt." Amen. Amen.

15 THE BRAVE WERE SILENT

This next passage is worthy of special attention because it is one of the most savage Walter writes about the Germans, especially former radicals and members of the elite who have failed to stand up to Hitler. In it he also makes reference to the hostages that may have been killed when he and his family went underground. It stands in sharp contrast to other passages in which he shows sympathy with those who saved his family and those who are bombed by the Allies.

July 23, 1944

We have just had an unexpected visit, an old friend from my bachelor days. I was his mother's tenant. He saw me on the balcony while cycling past. We considered it right to lay our cards on the table so that our presence would not be made public. The tall chap had aged considerably during the time we had not seen each other; his hair is grey and his face lined. Grey and furrowed is also his attitude.

His former Communist tendencies and willingness to make sacrifices have given way to the typical laissez-faire attitude of the masses, frightened of any criticism, and today he refers exclusively to the handbook of the Nazi canon for his knowledge of Germany and the world. He would have been deeply upset had anything happened to Hitler in the attack. The inevitable consequence would have been a terrible confusion resulting in Germany's surrender to the enemy and collapse.

His only concern is that the people's sacrifices of life and property at home are grossly exaggerated. The number of prisoners and dead is so insignificant that it is not even debatable. They, the fighters on the front, have no time for the moaners, and justly so...

He sought to prove the advantages of Hitler's dictatorship through what had happened to him. Before Hitler's time, he was constantly out of work. Since Hitler, who tore up all agreements through which Germany was being squeezed like a lemon, there are no more unemployed, and for that reason things are better for him.

I put a few counter questions to him, such as:

1. Who were the saboteurs who until the year 1933 continually brought the labor laws of the black-red-gold[1] government down, and artificially exaggerated unemployment by means of all sorts of Machiavellian tactics?
2. Why did the enemies of Germany postpone their attack to such a time when Hitler had armed his men to the teeth, despite the fact that the best opportunity had presented itself earlier?
3. Were the French, the Americans, the English, the Russians and the Jews so poor and needy that they had to steal Germany's wealth?
4. Why did the Nazis stick to this assertion, while at the same time screaming in everyone's ear that the Jews and their vassals had usurped all the world's goods?
5. Why did Hitler nevertheless proclaim self-sufficiency?
6. Why could not or would not Hitler find any other means of remedying unemployment apart from strengthening the military? Etc., etc.

To these and many other questions my one-time friend knew no answers. He could not find them, despite having gained an insight into the pre-history of Nazi domination through days and nights of discussions and lectures during the years 1928-1933. He could no longer listen to them, for his capacity for Hitler's propaganda was filled to overflowing. His mind is like a cornfield full of weeds, because like all average Germans, he was too comfortable to bother to weed, and rather liked to leave this work to others who pretended to weed. Instead they planted new and ever more weeds, until everything had grown to such an extent that people consider thistles, vetch and bright poppies as cultivated plants and pull up and throw away vegetables and cereals.

The mass of Germans are heartless too. I heard from the lips of my friend that the Jewish wife of his best acquaintance, the daughter of a former Rabbi in America, was arrested a year ago, and taken to a concentration camp and bumped off. Why? Because like many Jewish women who lived in "privileged marriages,"[2] she did not have an identity card. It seemed to him to be a sufficient reason to be killed.

Max G. quickly consoled himself and married again. That too was supposed to be understandable. (As for me, I know that Max was weary of his wife, who was registered as a Jew, which, as is known, does an aspiring Nazi little credit. She was very foolish to return from a trip to America which she undertook shortly before the war into the arms of her husband. The good man may have himself denounced her to the authorities snooping for hidden Jews. Now he is a well-to-do policeman, and no longer an arm-raising functionary).

We spoke about our escape and the hostages, who were said to have been arrested, kidnapped and killed because of us. I asked him whether the thousands of other Jews who were not captured on our account were still alive. Yes, he said, in Theresienstadt, where they are well looked after. In Theresienstadt, from where in the previous month the bloodhounds had transported the rest of the Jews from Germany to the gas chambers in Poland. He shrugged his shoulders, showing no emotion.

Germans are able to sink to such depths! Do not come to me with the hackneyed argument that not all Germans think like this man. Not all, which testifies to the emotional and spiritual decadence of the majority, from workers to university professors. How many representatives of the intellectual elite addressed the issue and raised voices or a pen when Hitler initiated his widespread murder of people with the slaughter of the Jews? How many?

The brave were silent, and the able and the thinkers too cowardly or just yes-men. They sacrificed the Jews so they themselves would remain unsullied. And the generals and the soldiers, to whom the massacre of the Jews appeared as a necessary evil, now see Himmler's knife at their own throat and attempt to rebel. Still there are too many traitors among them, like that major who betrayed the *coup de main*[3] on Berlin to little Joseph and thus brought the putsch into a dead end.[4]

Should someone have the courage to claim that every country has the Jews it deserves, I venture to add when looking at this lot: also, the leader it deserves. And I believe that these 80 million people have the riffraff they truly deserve.

May that now be the end of them.

16   ENLIGHTEN THE FOOLS

As the wait for the final employment acceptance from Bludenz drags on, Walter's own commitment to rational thought teeters on the edge. Though thoroughly steeped in enlightenment philosophy and science, Walter is so distraught that he is willing to listen to the advice of an astrologer friend, who among other things, encourages Walter to pen a scathing anti-Nazi leaflet that could be reproduced and widely circulated.

If caught, this activity is a certain death sentence as in the case of Elise and Otto Hampel, a Berlin gentile working class couple, who went on a three-year anti-Nazi card writing spree after a loss of a loved one on the Eastern Front. Like Walter, the couple hopes these messages will stir up resistance. However nearly all are turned into the Gestapo before they are opened and read. The couple is captured, sentenced to death, and executed by beheading in 1943. (Their story is the basis of Hans Fallada's best-selling novel, Every Man Dies Alone, *and the film, "Alone in Berlin.")*

July 26, 1944

In this way one day follows the other, and one summer gives way to the next, and still I am waiting with my wife and child for the hour of our return to a life of truth. Bludenz would at least have been able to give us greater freedom of movement and financial independence. To be recognized as free people again, without fear and able to breathe fresh air under the open sky, that was our wish, our modest hope. From time to time rage grips me. I have become estranged from my dear friends, I want to look them in the eye and open their mouths, so that they relieve us of this severe pressure. But I cannot do that. I don't want to do it because I fear the tough, naked 'no', the suppressed accusation which would be more dreadful than the silent uncertainty in which we have been languishing for the past two months.

My wife is right when she thinks there is still hope for us as long as the reply has not been decided and the contract has not been cancelled. And as long as the contract has not been cancelled, the employment exchange is powerless. Should the letters from Bludenz to the employment exchange really have been burned, they would prepare new ones, and give the liberating signal. Far better they remain silent regarding whatever they could accuse me of. And a thousand times better still the unsatisfied hope of freedom than the stranglehold of the Gestapo! Thus, we remain modest. And so long as we are alive we remain hopeful. We hope for the day of freedom, truth and peace.

July 27, 1944

No, my Bludenz hopes are not yet buried. The Regional Councilor has said it to me today. Yes indeed, said it! And it happened thus:

Yesterday evening I again complained about my misfortune to my friend the astrologer. Like before he had no understanding for feelings of pessimism, but insisted with annoyance on his precise calculations. They left no other conclusion than a happy outcome, at least a harmless one. He tried too to refute the fact that because of the unfortunate times, letters from the Regional Councilor addressed to the Labor Office or to me could have simply been burned, that even telegrams to Bavaria with a reply-paid service cannot be trusted. Only a call to Bludenz could bring me certain knowledge and confirm his reasons for optimism.

Much as this explanation enlightened me, for a long time it did not overcome my fear that I could be told all sorts of offensive stories, be given the hard 'no'. My wife only smiled at my fears, which spring not from outer circumstances and situations, but rather from my own disposition; she spoke vehemently to me and gradually convinced me to make the call.

I had already tried it weeks before without success, because the person at whose place I had booked the call had no registered number, which is a requirement for a long-distance call. Old neighbors, with whom we are well acquainted, are fortunate owners of military industry telephone. They immediately declared themselves ready, and as the astrologer recommended, I called the Bludenz number between 9.50 and 10 o'clock.

I waited nervously until shortly before twelve, complained and emphasized that it concerned an important long-distance call which had to be put through before 12 o'clock, and heard the longed-for ring tone. At the other end of the phone was the secretary I remembered well, and she connected me with the Regional Councilor.

I had to make an effort to construct into a whole what I at first heard only in snatches. His words came through thinly, so very thinly and from so very far did his words come over the wire already torn and mended a hundred times far away somewhere in Bavaria. What he said soothed my excruciating wound like morphine. No, the matter has not yet been decided. He has complained frequently in Innsbruck and is awaiting information.

Whether my matter is promising? His recollection, yes – he has received information about the success at the Labor Office. He asked whether he should write the letter and send it once more. No, I said, my statements were sufficient. He thought I should not be so impatient. These things need time and he would send me word as soon as he had it. Please kindly greet the Chief Inspector. Yes, indeed, and a warm goodbye. I replaced the receiver with a sigh of relief.

The astrologer has indeed calculated well! Who would have thought that! Is there really still hope of going to Bludenz, to journey with my wife and child into the mountains, into freedom, real legalization? Yes, it seems so. I should not be so impatient. The Regional Councilor can talk persuasively. What does he know of my anxieties though? His charming Tyrolean voice sounded somewhat depressed and muted. Why? He will have thought, what does the impatient Freiherr know about my troubles? He only thinks about his position. I am still concerned with totally different things. Yes, who knows, wholly different things.

How much longer will I have to wait again until I have certainty? Will the solution to my equation be correct? Perhaps. Hopefully! And then up into the mountains! A long, tormenting period would end so beautifully.

July 31, 1944

The astrologer has begged me to draft an appeal to be distributed among the people to get them on their feet, now that a constellation promises the final overthrow of the Nazi regime.[1] Good, here it is:

Friends in the battle for Freedom!

You have been suffering for 12 years under the yoke of the world's greatest butcher, Hitler, 12 expensive and precious years. Caught up, they now dread the day when they must surrender and account for their shameful conduct to the people and all mankind.

So that it continues to remain secret and unatoned, they stifle every uprising by means of bloody terror and beg us for "more fire, sulphur and grenades" so that we all go to hell if the "God-sent Hitler" and his henchmen are allowed to remain in charge, instated over the mass grave of the German people.

As they fear being exposed, they create new concentration camps and daily send thousands of innocent men, women and children to their deaths, making use of their well-paid spies, organized criminals and favorites in secure positions, the so-called "indispensable officials", but also the perpetually simple-minded, who still believe in a miracle at the hand of those bandits and sons of Satan:

- <u>Adolf the Holy</u>, a sexually and spiritually abnormal individual, utterly devoid of any sense of family or responsibility in regard to neighbors, a spiritual confidence trickster and morally bankrupt man, a seller of souls of the first order, a high priest and butcher dripping with human blood.
- <u>Himmler</u>, together with the hundred thousand working Himmler dogs, who have only learned one trade: murder. A hobbling lecher, diabolical impresario and tout.
- <u>Joseph Goebbels</u>, who in atrocious imitation of his predecessors in Hamelin, with soothing incantations and long-debunked conspiracy theories, lures into the abyss not only the rats of our life, but the very best of our people, and other people's wives into his bed, the wandering priest and dubious bearer of academic degrees.
- <u>Dr. Robert Ley</u>, head of the Nazi labor union, whose trembling dirty snout always calls upon providence with mockery and foul language, when as usual he stinks of alcohol and in his drinker's madness knows no better than to address old and perspicacious generals as "blue-blooded pigs", the fatso Falstaff, master of the Reichstag fire and Adolf's Great Mogul.
- <u>Hermann Goering</u>, a tremendously zealous registered morphine addict, who at the first evidence of enemy aircraft wanted to be called Meier, but in the meantime had to search through the entire list of names, because the enemy bombers increased like fleas and bugs behind his dreams of retribution. With hordes of cronies and drinking pals, he is always feuding against intelligence and honesty, and even in good times idly loafed on the fringes. Even

today he has nothing better to do than to erect a Valhalla of the swastika on the blood-soaked soil of Germany.

They, who are branded as criminals on their foreheads, recognized by all who are not blind, want to crown their work of destruction by extinguishing Germany completely and smoking out the people with poison gas before the avengers capture them.

Against them and only them is our battle for freedom and the deliverance of our suffering and bleeding people! You too must bring your powerful longing for freedom, your will for goodness and all your strength!

If you tarry, it will be too late.

Enlighten the fools, the unknowing and everyone who might still be prepared to spill blood and sweat and slave away for rascals!

Copy this appeal five times, 10 times, 20 times, but with a duplicating machine so that you remain immune to Hitler's thugs, and send it out to friends and acquaintances, to the military and soldiers, to workers and farmers, to town-dwellers and country-dwellers, especially to the lazy thinkers. Furiously growing enemy armies await them, if they continue to identify with the monstrosities of the Fascists. For there will be harsh judgment not only of the murderers and seducers, but also of all who silently noted their crimes or even approved of them.

Act in such a way that you help to demolish what Hitler and his executioners still plan to do before the end. Act for our poor people, for you and your children. They will all thank you. We and they have confidence in you and place our hopes on you.

The fighters for truth, justice and freedom!

17 CURING THE LITTLE HITLERS

It is clear that the Nazi Party officials in Innsbruck will be unable to discover any information about Walter in Mannheim, since, he (Kurt Freiherr), never lived there and, in fact, doesn't exist. Walter also knows that the Bludenz officials need him because it is extremely difficult to find skilled employees who also have disabilities that exempt them from military service, especially as the war increasingly turns against the Nazis.

However, the longer Walter waits for the acceptance letter, the greater the risk that his colossal fraud will be revealed. With his nerves in tatters, Walter finally decides to send a telegram to the Bludenz officials withdrawing his name from consideration. But, as luck would have it – bad luck that is – a day later a Nazi investigator visits Walter to check out his bona fides in Leipzig which signals that the Innsbruck Nazis have curtailed their search for information in Mannheim. Walter now realizes the Bludenz job is his, were it not for the god-awful fact that he already has sent his withdrawal telegram to Bludenz!

August 12, 1944

Naturally I am perfectly clear in my mind that we would be spared some wretchedness if we could move to Bludenz now. That I, driven by unspeakable fear in the merry month of May, threw a spanner in my own works, as it later surprisingly turned out, was good in itself. If after the brilliant success of my presentation, we had pushed off to Bludenz without considering the consequences which the application approval from the Gauleitung[1] could have led to, I would have had to take up my position without my tax form and without my legal status from the labor office in Leipzig. My child would not have been able to attend school without a certificate of origin, a knot I would not have been able to unravel in Bludenz.

The local school inspector would have made trouble when registering my child, and not let the certificate of origin nicely fall under the table, as the generous people in Leipzig did. In the numerous follow-ups which my boss would have had to report me for, I am dead certain, yes, dead certain in the truest sense of the word, that I would have been found out and be already rotting in Dachau or somewhere like it among the corpses created by the Hitler men.

All these stealthy traps gave me a fear of people seeking information. Now they must follow the scent from Leipzig to Bludenz. A "new person" can surely, as all are dispensable, and many even "permanent", move into the Regional Council office, and only appear then, when despite all follow-ups in Leipzig, he remains unfit for military duty and therefore becomes a welcome filler-in of the gaps left by the departed droves of ghost officials. And this one man from Leipzig is quite indispensable to them, even when he no longer possesses the red discharge papers. This will be evident even to the chairman of the draft board in Bludenz, for a Regional Councilor's word must count for something. Certainly, my wife might be forced to work there. But that is something quite different to employment in a constantly exposed armament factory in Leipzig, as well as being hellishly anxious about our child left alone at home. Actually, it is not that bad yet, but it could happen any day.

Now there is nothing we can do with, just "if" and "should" and "had we". The people in Bludenz were not, as it turned out, courageous enough to take responsibility for my employment, but hoped, happy and cheerful, that a satisfactory "report" might still turn up from Innsbruck.

Stop thinking, hold my breath – whoops – what's this? An official from the Party. Oh dear, I sensed trouble – do the Nazis want to take us off to do forced labor on the Eastern Front? We sat down opposite each other, this corpulent inquisitor with an indolent questioning expression and I with heart palpitations, yet ready with counter blows. He placed a questionnaire in front of himself, which looked damned like the terrible Bludenz report/statement, took a pencil from his pocket, pulled its top off its point, plugged it onto the other end and then he began to squeeze out of me the familiar details of my smoldering hell.

When born, where born, creed, married, how many children, occupation, how long resident here and moved when, where living earlier, whether bombed out and where, whether a member of the Party or an associated organization, whether a front fighter and when, whether a member of earlier political parties, and in particular of a lodge, why not liable for military service, am I currently "working"?

"I am waiting for my appointment to the district authority in Bludenz."

"That is what we are concerned with here. I tell you this with discretion. Please do not talk about it."

"Thank you. I will keep it quiet."

"Are you living in ordered circumstances?"

"Certainly, even if modestly after my great impoverishment following the bombing raids and illness."

"Hmm, you must have arrived here on December 2, 1943 only after being bombed out in Mannheim."

"Yes."

"Hm, can you name some Party members who can give information about you?"

"That too. Chief Air Raid Warden, here on the ground floor, and Mrs. K. at number 57."

"So, you know Mrs. K.?"

"Yes."

"Good, thank you."

And he placed the top back over the pencil, stowed the questionnaire in his briefcase, stood up and disappeared with a "Heil Hitler".

Oh, bloody hell, so what now?

My wife came out of the kitchen looking pale, eyes dilated and lips trembling.

"A trap from Bludenz."

"Bludenz?"

"Yes, Bludenz. The questionnaire from the Gauleitung."

"And it is still in progress?"

"It appears so."

"Was he nice?"

"He could not be otherwise."

"And what now?"

"Now he is off to H. and to Frau K. for information."

"If they don't babble..."

"Hopefully not."

"Should I snoop?"

"Try."

My wife searched for a pretext. She rummaged around for a meat voucher and went shopping, although she had taken care of that an hour ago. Soon she returned and told me that Otto could not keep the secret and affirmed he had given a very good report regarding us. And what about K? She is fearful, but I do not have any worries about her. What could she say? We are not in the Party and indeed not even in the Kapo.[2] There is nothing new there, it's of little importance. And what else? I am not a staunch supporter of the regime. She knows that too. What else? I don't know. Let's wait and see.

The people in power in Innsbruck seem to need so many weeks to make the square stone roll. And the poor Regional Councilor cannot help it that I constantly declare my loyalty. He has certainly moaned to the ruffians at the Gauleitung that they are entirely responsible were I to become impatient with him, be snatched away by the labor office and slip through his fingers. And he needed me so urgently and could not get hold of a cripple like me again. But what has become of the questionnaire from Mannheim? Nothing, absolutely nothing. Freiherr left Mannheim over three quarters of a year ago. Much has happened since then. However, the people in Leipzig should know the fellow if he hangs about legitimately. Let's ask them. And so, they have indeed asked.

I served a formal ultimatum to the Regional Councilor one day too early. When he receives it, he can take it up and the whole thing will finally fail, just as things were beginning to go right. What to do? The letter can arrive at the earliest in Bludenz on Sunday morning. My wife has a splendid idea. Could one not have the letter taken into custody telegraphically and have it returned to Leipzig? I ought to try it. I went to the post office and at the door added a few bread coupons for Mrs. K. And I was successful. Of course, there was much scribbling with double addresses, power of attorney and authenticated certificates – identity cards, showing that I am the person I profess to be. It took 30 minutes and three

German paper Marks, for which the official in a peaked cap promised the most accurate processing. I trotted home, sweating a lot under my unseasonable mock disguise and stopped by once more at Mrs. K's and gave her the bread vouchers.

Mrs. K.: "But only if you can spare the vouchers."

Walter: "Even if we needed them, we would give them to you... One good turn deserves another."

Mrs. K.: "You flatterer!"

W: "Goodbye."

Mrs. K.: "Heil Hitler!"

W: "Heil... Hitler..."

Mrs. K.: "Please, with conviction. That's better!"

W: "Bread vouchers are also good!"

Mrs. K.: "Your eyes twinkle too little. Bread vouchers? What has that got to do with it?"

W: "Oh, a great deal."

Mrs. K.: "Don't understand."

W: "In that we are indebted to the Führer for our daily bread, don't you understand?"

Mrs. K.: "You cunning one! Now you must be quiet!"

W: "No, I can amuse you most with a present from Hitler. And I will continue to do it when you are so obliging."

Mrs. K: "Today too I have done you a great favor," she says blinking meaningfully.

W: "You, to me?"

Mrs. K.: "Yes, yes, I must keep quiet, I'm a member of the Party."

W: "I must ask my wife about that, perhaps she knows."

Mrs. K.: "Yes, indeed, a very big favor."

W: "Thank you."

Mrs. K.: "My pleasure."

W: "Good bye."

Mrs. K.: "Heil Hitler. In the future, please, with conviction, my friend!"

In the future? In Bludenz? I would cure her and all the little Hitlers if I were there already, so cunningly and effectively that they would return to their senses. The Nazi who is so infatuated with my child has vouched for me. A Hitler youth and a Hitler girl are persuasive witnesses to my blameless political change in Leipzig – that ought to be sufficient even if the people in Mannheim are still unsuccessfully poring over their singed files.

The more I think about it, the more amusing the whole business appears. The people in Bludenz inspected me to the bone marrow with their ominous questionnaire, so that an infallible Nazi administration could establish by dubious means whether I am politically blameless. And because it cannot be what must not be, the Gauleitung had no better idea than to submit by means of the Leipzig district branch exactly the same questionnaire and skipped the most important thing – my Aryan descent.

August 17, 1944

The late summer again awakens an insatiable Wanderlust. It seizes me so powerfully when in the early morning and in the evening twilight the autumn air penetrates right into our room and the slanting sunbeams show their real power. This suppressed urge threatens the body to bursting point. They are tormenting me these gigantic mountains, the gurgling and frothing white water, the murmuring woods and waving cornfields. Yes, even the smoke from a railway engine going through our neighborhood transports me to the softly rocking motion of a fast train wagon, so that we finally go to freedom.

Soon it will be the second anniversary of the first leap from the Gestapo net and our venture into a new phase of life, since that late summer afternoon when I, my wife and my child left for the asylum, followed the tracks which led to the Upper Bavarian holiday home to which our friends had flown; this leap has turned into a miracle akin to resurrection. We have a home again, we have something to eat again, and we can go out again without having to avoid questioning looks. We can be happy with our little daughter, who does not have to be enclosed between four walls, and can freely frolic with her borrowed doll's pram and other toys or can amuse herself for half a day with her playmates over at the overgrown Schmuck place when she has done her homework with Mutti. Who would have dared to hope for such a change of things a year ago! She does it well, the little darling. In only a few weeks she has caught up with what her school comrades needed a whole year to learn. She reads, writes quickly and does arithmetic and is already in the second class.

Yet they live in constant fear that bombs might fall during their lessons, and lie in wait like foxes in a clearing, so as to be ready to jump when the alarm rings, pale with fear, and to run. This constant, unspeakable danger has become our companion on the way to freedom, and remains also the other, to be seen and recognized before we reach our destination.

How frequently acquaintances have crossed our path, how frequently we have suddenly stepped into a trap and only reached solid ground thanks to a determined leap. For that reason, my wife goes only on short shopping trips, while I always wear glasses, a peaked cap and a summer coat. Since a few days ago I go armed with crutches, which my wife provided, so that my inability to enroll in military service or work is recognized and appears credible when I make my usual excursions to friends or necessary errands to various offices, constantly looking around me like a hunted animal – especially on the tram, where fellow travelers have enough time and opportunity to spy an old, well-known face, despite the glasses and hat.

It's no wonder that we cannot risk offering our child what she would be entitled to demand, that is a daily outing to a green space or a ride into a neighborhood which is safer from air raids – light, air and sunshine. Even the slightest attempt causes me fright and to turn pale, and there remains unease, exhaustion and consolation at the move to the remote location which will give us back our freedom of movement.

The matter in Bludenz is still not dealt with, yet we hope in not too many days to pack our junk, spread our wings and escape to the sunny south. All this costs stamina and brain power, peace and sleep. But would we not sacrifice everything, if we could only bless our child with this very, very great pleasure? Everything!

The past year protected us. May the next free us and everyone who is under the whip of these man hunters.

18 GERMAN JEW ALONE

As Walter lives with his new Christian identity, he clings to the old by reflecting on what it means to be Jewish. He also ponders the slights he suffered even during the heyday of the tolerant Weimar Republic and thinks about his Communist comrades who display their own brand of antisemitism.

August 19, 1944

Germany has become an enormous concentration camp. I watch a group of eight men from my balcony, well dressed and guarded, chained two by two with handcuffs to each other, being led by one of the bastards, slowly and with bowed heads to the military prison. Why were they were arrested? According to allegedly well-informed sources it was because they have held political talks in their lodgings. Others think they did not report for military duty, while a third group asserts it knows these men had obtained smoking materials with smoking vouchers due only from August 21 and had thereby damaged the state.

Could it really be because of voucher violations? The sad Nazi state has made known today that men are henceforth entitled to only two, and women to 0.933 cigarettes, instead of three and one point four, which is why consumers, when they manage to obtain the earlier quantities on their new cards by surreptitious means "have sinned against the said legal state" and are to be punished, amongst other things, by death. Why not? The government surely has the right to do with its little sheep what it likes, after the people have so clearly expressed the will to commit or accelerate suicide.

Nazi propagandists dare to mock the German people, saying that 12 years ago there was radical change, which tasted, with the help of artificial trimmings and use of some force, of chocolate, almonds and of fruit juice, creating submissiveness and even denying the right to object when they are gradually killed off by their confectioners.

In effect, the propagandists ask: "Did Hitler promise you that he would spare you the war, you stupid sheep? If your sympathy for the Nazi regime came from this hope, then you deserve nothing better than to snuff it."

After the downfall of a people, who are totally derailed when they believe themselves to be politically at full speed (and have to derail because they lack tact and true culture), they go down in noisy heroics, in cowardice of soul and spirit, in lack of criticism and insubordination. Those people then cry out, give orders or attack as the signs of all disintegration all around them show. They have for generations counted themselves as the nation of poets and thinkers and this has turned out to be unjustified.

The Jews too once had to watch their downfall powerlessly as their cathedral, their temple in Jerusalem, undoubtedly the most beautiful and largest structure in antiquity, was razed to the ground by the conquering Roman legions. However, to this day they learn from this event. They confess complicity in the loss of their land, in that they say it is the punishment for their rebellion against the divine laws that Moses, their teacher, handed down. These laws were the condition of their national existence and laid down to guide their actions. That is self-criticism in the highest sense, not belief, not superstition. It is made sacred through reflection, changing one's ways and making good deeds.

This ethnic purposefulness based on knowledge and self-criticism has remained the common property of the Jewish community. This onus, this honorable onus, the rest of humanity has not seen, let alone recognized, and where it was seen, accusations of business machinations and attempts to spread fear did their hateful work. May they remain so, my Jews. May they remain afraid of the ruffians. May they remain enemies of the war and friends of business. Sadly, in our time, in their hundreds of thousands they have failed to convert their fear and capacity for action into timely flight from the brutes. They had scarcely any understanding of the non-Jewish environment.

Even the so-called liberal and helpful Americans were too narrow-minded to respond to the Jewish cries for help, which were stifled in a lot of money, affidavits and medical examinations, ridiculously small entry quotas and never-ending queues. The self-important people with their friendly relations with the SS bigwigs and the American Jewish community inconspicuously got their protégées across the big water. Even the Americans could not refrain from denominating the Jews expressly as of the "Hebrew Race" on their immigration papers.

The other "Christian" peoples stood even further aside and were even more aloof and reserved after the ruinous conference in Evian, France,[1] which, not unjustifiably, read in reverse, was called "naïve" and in the book of human liberators does not make for a glorious page.

In spite of this, the representatives of Christianity cannot refrain from approaching unswerving Jews who have a firm faith – my person not exempted – with the purpose of making their Christian faith attractive. They rely – how clumsily! – on the values of the New Brother, according to which the Jews remain disreputable, as long as they do not believe in Christ. They studiously overlook their own shame, in that they as brothers, happy in pious belief in

Christ for the last two thousand years, choose bishops, preach, proselytize and cut each other's throats in all the more Christian manner, which even well-known people among their representatives try to gloss over through Christ's words – saying that he did not come to bring peace, but the sword.

They claim there must be wars in spite of faith, love and hope, and only when humanity has run through all the bloody deserts will their remnants be partakers in the resurrection. In such a way they engage in the most absurd contradictions concerning their savior, who came among the people 1944 years ago to redeem them. And on top of everything else, they play the offended one and act superior to the little Semite outcast if he should dare express his own opinion. That is true even if that Jew does so in a respectful way.

But it is not only Christians who indulge in absurd discourse about Judaism and the Jews. Indeed, one comes across those who despise us even among Communists. Not only so-called Communists, fellow travelers and amateur Communists, but among thorough-bred, convinced Communists with a dialectic at their disposal that amazes not only the layman.

Judaism, that's old hat for them, reactionary superstition, a humanity-destroying amulet that is worthy of being finally wiped out with all its far-reaching roots. The Jew is for them a fellow who ekes out his eccentric existence, is not concerned with universal problems, cannot be a significant socialist because he was molded in a five-thousand-year-old tradition, and represents by his person the biggest obstacle to world enlightenment and the revival of mankind.

"The Nazis have spared us a great job when they smashed Jewish shops and burned down Jewish schools and synagogues. Had they not done that, this task would be ours, the Communists. Certainly, there were some poor wretches among the Jews. They have not deserved their lot. But with most Jews, who were rich, reactionary and anti-people elements, regret is hardly in place. In this respect the Nazis did the preparatory work. I am still looking for the first intelligent Jew who has the courage not only to finally break with his Jewishness, but also to preach energetically and unwaveringly in his circle against Judaism. We thought we had learned something. Everything went well until one day he surprised us by saying that he wanted to emigrate to Palestine, and threw all our objections and advice about his basic Communist convictions to the wind; the Jews are a special kind of community and as such will always be scorned whether they are capitalists or Communists, conservative or liberal, militarist or pacifist, Orthodox or Reformed or religious disciples. So, they are right, the Nazis."

I dared to ask the Communist friend whether he ever made any effort to think about the arguments of his Jewish comrades, and received the answer: "Does not interest me at all."

It does not interest him. It interests him just as little as the army of German thinkers and intellectual workers, who master the teachings of the Germans, the history of peoples from antiquity to the present time, and are fully acquainted with the philosophical system, but know nothing, absolutely nothing about Judaism, its ideology, its teaching, its unique social creation, its struggle against idolaters, against superstition and the incantation of spirits. And as long as they do not want to know anything about them, any attempt at discussion, at tackling the difficult problem of grasping the Jewish soul, is nipped in the bud.

I am talking here particularly about the German people's attitude towards the Jews, which is different from the English and from that of the Americans, because both those ethnic communities, it must be repeated, are dealing with the problem of Judaism more than all others. The German, however, sees the highest of all missionary achievements as converting individuals. Even in the learned circles of the black-red-gold republic,[2] people turned up their noses at Jews, which is why I, even in that "pro-Jewish" era, was completely excluded from being a consultant in public service.

Hatred of the Jews is endemic in Germany whether it sails under a black-white-red,[3] black-red-gold, white-yellow or red flag.[4] The German, when the Jew is the talking point, will always mention the word Jew as a marker of someone foreign, inferior and excluded, even if this Jew is highly educated, capable, honorable and helpful. This is an eloquent testimony to the arrogance and lack of critical thinking from the German. Hence his hopeless, contemptuous attitude towards these foreigners, and in general towards all non-Germans, his absurd, blustering patriotism in hundreds of shades, extending far into Communist circles, and a disregard for contracts and obligations, even in the face of the "much praised German loyalty". All races know how to sing a song about this, but with another ending than that of Hoffmann von Fallersleben:[5] "Not to acknowledge and feel this, as happens to many people, proves a spiritual dullness which makes one despair of the German soul."[6]

19 THAT IS SWASTIKA LOGIC!

Walter's story continues on two levels. First, he sees the war turning rapidly against the Germans as two fronts emerge – the Russians capture more and more of the East, and the Allies liberate Paris on the Western Front. There is little question that the Nazis will eventually lose the war. The big question is whether Walter can live that long.

August 24, 1944

Paris re-conquered by the French insurgents!

Hitler's stewards have taken to their heels together with their like-minded comrades – Pétain, Lare and the entire Vichy pack. The *Tricolore* flutters once more from the Eiffel Tower, cheering and shouting crowds pushing through the boulevards of the metropolis, hugging and congratulating each other, and the old *Marseillaise* rings out from thousands of throats. The old *Marseillaise*, spurred on by its sound, the children of France have often broken out of their shackles and put an end to tyranny. Their revolutionary spirit has proved itself this time too. They have torn up the streets and erected barricades and have driven out the Nazi vermin from their own ancient property, from the city of cities, from their beloved home which carries the proudest of names that history has given birth to: Paris.

Anglo-American tanks roll onwards through France, assisted everywhere by the brave Maquis,[1] who rose to a man at the given hour to flay the German tormentors. And how they are flaying them! Hours, even days before the Allied troops drew near, they occupied traffic centers, bridges and major cities, and today they have already cleared Hitler's soldiers from most of the territory south of the Seine down to the Pyrenees, including the cities of Bordeaux and Toulouse. Meanwhile those English, American and French troops who landed on the Riviera have pushed northwards with unimaginable speed and liberated Toulon, Marseille and Grenoble. They have already reached the Swiss border, and have thus cut off every point of contact with the remaining occupying national Fascists in the south of France. All the French are rising up and are cleaning their land of the Nazi excrement with iron brooms.

Allez, enfants de la Patrie!

It was extremely hot again today in Leipzig and marching music roared from loudspeakers. When the Titanic sank, the captain issued an order to the orchestra to play marching music so as to keep down the panic among the passengers. And the Titanic sank. Today another captain allows marching music to bellow out so that his protégés do not notice that the ship is slowly sinking into the waves.

It was a very hot day today, even for cool heads. And for hotheads? Oh my goodness! *Allons enfants de la Patrie.*

August 25, 1944

The Bludenz story can neither live nor die. It cannot live because, as the Regional Councilor wrote yesterday, the information from Innsbruck just doesn't want to arrive, and it cannot die because the Regional Councilor will not let it die. Rather, as he wrote just now, he expected the information "the very next day" as he had asked for a return telephone call from the district personnel department. However, the Party members in Leipzig have not yet reported back. And those in Mannheim? Not them either, despite the fact that they have nothing to report about me.

The personnel department in Mannheim is working despite incessant air attacks, as one of my friends found out through an inquiry about a fictitious acquaintance formerly living there. "Not entered in the register of residents. Not known here." That is sufficient for Innsbruck and Bludenz to disqualify me. But this conclusion has still to be drawn. Why has it not been made public? And if it has, what are the people in Innsbruck still waiting for? Does the report from Leipzig make a difference? It's laughable to assume that. Perhaps behind my back at the Regional Councilor's, they're telling fibs with the SD[2] in Berlin about further searches for deserters, a woman and a child?

Freiherr and his family were not registered in Mannheim, he gave false information, then he must have lived somewhere else, for secret reasons. Assuming that he did something wrong in his actual home, why did he try to provide himself with an alibi? Let us continue to give him a feeling of security and see what happens.

But even this is improbable. At the slightest suspicion both the Gestapo and criminal detectives would immediately call up the Leipzig end, the labor office as well as the military recruitment office, etc., which in my case, as in the case of a Party notification, would not remain hidden from me.

Since the Regional Councilor's telegram, the Labor Office has not been in touch, and the departure permit issued in April has not been revoked. But even more astonishing, they have not once reminded me of the final submission of my labor book documents, the deadline of which, July 31, has long passed. I do not want to nurture any false hope. The nature of a bomb is that it explodes in a split second. I am in constant fear of such an explosion. I have been afraid since the May 27, day and night.

Incidentally, it strikes me that the last sign of life or official activity from Regional Councilor Czinglar dates from June 28, namely the telegram in which he let me know that my employment was in "process." Since then a telegram and two letters have been issued and signed by the Regional Councilor. What has happened to the Chief Inspector? Is he no longer in Bludenz? His departure would not be good for my situation. He was, after all, a reasonable man without bureaucratic pretentions and he became my friendly protector after only a short conversation.

If only I could somehow bury or forget the Bludenz matter which is consuming all my nervous energy. I wanted to, but the Regional Councilor does not think of throwing in the towel, simply because he cannot guess the game being played. His patience and insistence are truly admirable, and if I were as sure of my situation as he is, I would be able to sleep in peace despite Goebbels' latest decree of total war and the news, "that the Gestapo proceeds with all ruthlessness against elements which because of indifference, convenience, neglect of responsibility or even firstly with intent to sabotage the measures for the totalizing of the war. In particularly serious cases prison or the death penalty is imposed."

Now my wife and I are two of these typical war criminals.

Nevertheless, the war "of the Teutons" continues. The bosses now sacrifice all the cultural development which they have preserved. The Nazis in the name of the war effort are shutting down all orchestras, music schools and conservatories, their "exhibitions", competitions, auctions, crafts, anything aesthetic, entertainment, literature, the daily press apart from a few print and two illustrated magazines, their "strength through joy" entertaining of the troops carried out by the National Socialist community with about 200 guest performance organizations, concert agencies and theatres, all artists' homes and gymnastic clubs, household management and commercial schools and even the universities to a certain extent, so that the freed-up resources can be steered towards combat troops, armaments and other production related to the war effort.

On top of that a young pilot from Leipzig, holder of the German Gold Cross, formulated his demands clearly, spelling out "that all theatres and concert halls should be closed in order to be able to give the German soldiers arms which these soldiers will use to protect the everlasting values of German culture and the German soul from the barbaric hordes of our enemies." That is swastika logic: closing and disbanding all cultural facilities so as to protect them from the hostile barbarians. In the name of the German people against the Jews? No, against the people!

20 IGNORANT BELIEFS

As Walter follows the WWII retreat of the German forces from Macedonia, he recalls his own WWI escape that earned him an Iron Cross. He worries that the Germans never seem to learn from their mistakes. And he struggles to understand how the German people could lose all touch with truth and instead swallow the alternative facts of their demagogic leaders.

August 28, 1944

Back then, yes back then, 27 years ago this month, I found myself an Imperial German soldier decorated with the cross on a ribbon, the prize for youthful courage. With me were thousands of dejected, yes, despairing, privates, deserted by all their staff, without ammunition and food, and any hope of escaping the cauldron that was Macedonia, on an adventurous flight from the pressing French, Serbs and Italians – the whole lot of us were to be delivered up to them in accordance with their agreement with the Bulgarians.

We fought our way through the canyons of southern Serbia, climbed the mountains of Albania, waded and swam in the raging torrents and swollen mountain streams, camped demoralized by continuous rainfall and the bullets of the enemy in the impenetrable forests, flogged off the last of the horses and mules to the original inhabitants who knew the swamps and easily lured us into ambushes, shuddered at the thought of the death of the entire column in bottomless pits and followed in the end only the bloody footprints of those who had preceded us shoeless and had perished of hunger and fatigue somewhere.

We had no time to rescue them, let alone drag along all those suffering from malaria, typhus or dysentery huddled in holes among the rocks or crawling on all fours through the dangerous rocky desert of Montenegro. When the desert ended, we suddenly saw the blue Adriatic far below. In one day, we staggered down a hundred zig-zag bends and were happy to reach the harbor that would save us.

What we few succeeded in doing bordered on the miraculous, and we could be happy that the Bulgarians did not intervene early enough and that the Allies with their provision trains could not follow us over the high mountain trails. The enemy had not recovered, the Hungarians mostly fought against us in the west, the Romanians and Russians had long ceased to be war combatants, and the Balkan Peninsula south of Macedonia was not touched by German troops, on the special command of William II. As a result, his armies were not as exposed as Hitler's, and so the chaos they got themselves into through the blockade of the Yugoslavian territory is unimaginable. Even if smaller units succeed in breaking through to the north, Hitler will have to write off the greater part of his southern storm-troopers.

The most amazing fact is that the Germans not only politically but also strategically continue making the same mistakes. They base their calculations, regardless of all historical experience, on the one hand on past speculation that an opponent taken by surprise "can never rise again" and secondly, no less dangerously, on disagreements among the opponents and the imminent boiling over in their heartlands.

This attitude reminds me of an amusing habit that we observed in the mother of our sheepdog Mausi, murdered by the Nazis. She liked to do her business on a piece of turf at the side of our house but could only accomplish it when she had skipped over a 50-centimeter high timber fence. One day we got rid of this obstruction, after it had been flattened by a supplier, which made the dear dog's excursions easier. Far from taking advantage of this convenience, she paused for a while, took a jump and indulged herself in her grass, happy that she had triumphed over this hurdle. For weeks the silly fence continued to exist in her imagination. She had believed she saw something even when she had long convinced herself of its non-existence with her own eyes.

They see many imaginary things, these worthy Germans. For example, the invincibility of the German armies. Defeat of the German soldiers is virtually an inconceivable concept. When they recognize the trouble, they are in and have to surrender, there will be something not right about it. Then some secret, devious powers will have had a hand in the game and made all German strategy and bravery powerless. In the last war it was the stab in the back from the Jews and the Social Democrats in Germany. Now there is a stab in the back and the front from dishonorable generals who have broken their oaths, a criminal rabble of corrupt comrades, and the Jewry outside Europe. And in the next world war, from which may heaven protect us and our children, we have the good Lord himself, who, in the pay of the Jews, brings down the poor Germans from behind.

In Germany everything is possible. Germany is the land of unlimited political impossibilities. It takes only a dozen scoundrels who have the ability to switch off the memory of the masses and divert their attention to appealing slogans. Then this people sees only the thoughts and ideas imposed upon them and jumps through the hoops, seeing Christian blood-drinking Jews – Russians slaughtering their children, and Americans raping their noble German maidens, despite knowing all too well that Jews never consume blood, let alone human blood, and that the

Russians see their future strength in the European camp, that and noble German maidens are not exactly commonplace – although they should be.

Their faith is diametrically opposed to their knowledge. And because belief means more to them than knowledge, they are able to swallow the most extreme stuff and to commit the greatest stupidities and – unfortunately, yes, unfortunately! – the most scandalous deeds, crimes which they nevertheless hesitate to profess. And when they have to, they lay the blame on someone else.

This people needs to be re-educated from scratch, if its name is to regain its reputation. It is to be hoped that future educators will bring with them the divine gift to accomplish this indispensable work. May they agree that decency, tact and political education will be of more interest than the highest contribution of money and material goods. May they also remain aware that false compassion with criminal elements leads only to new, even bloodier excesses, and that they must eradicate what is no longer capable of moral renewal. May they also remember what camp they come from, so that humanity does not degenerate into absolute meaninglessness.

21 THEY FEAR HITLER MORE THAN THE ENEMY

As the Allies drive the German army back in the East and West, the basic infrastructure in Germany begins to collapse. This makes it very difficult for Walter's would-be employers in Bludenz to communicate with their higher-ups in Innsbruck and to get any answers about Kurt Freiherr from Mannheim. The Allied bombing of the railway tracks may also make it impossible for Walter and his family to reach Austria. Again, Walter ponders the withdrawal of his application. Meanwhile, he assesses his recent efforts at anti-Nazi propaganda and finds them wanting. Walter also watches how the Germans respond to the realities of imminent defeat.

September 4, 1944

They, who have not yet fully digested their mothers' milk, are to replace in their thousands the infantry in France, Belgium and Holland, devoid of modern weapons and especially tanks.

The Allies will make short work of them, and furthermore need to seize the actors of the "people's war", if they do not want to find a completely ravaged, burned down and blood-soaked Germany after the collapse of Hitler's defense.

That the collapse is imminent is evident above all in the increasing disorganization of German rail and postal traffic. Letter boxes are only emptied once a day,[1] if at all, parcels only accepted to a limited extent, telegrams delivered only if the postman happens to be in the relevant district, and the express train service has already nearly halted. Since one nevertheless still hopes, dear Regional Councilor, for an employment position, you no doubt are writing undelivered letters to the Innsbruck Nazi officials until your fingers are sore.

You believe one can either wait calmly for the assessment of me, the aspirant, or let the letters intentionally burn to death so that the Regional Councilor will give his problem child the departure ticket. Then again, the sleepy, disrupted railway transport may, of its own accord, make the beautiful Tyrol unattainable for the Freiherr invaders from Leipzig.

It is difficult for an old Jew to understand this, because such malice lies beyond his soul's capacity to comprehend. Therefore, I simply could not avoid indicating to the Regional Councilor, that vehicles, like old Jews in hiding, can run out of juice, and it is therefore not kind to keep me on tenterhooks waiting uselessly.

I wrote this to him the day before yesterday. By the time he moves himself to act on this together with Innsbruck, the scrambled tracks of the Arlberg railway will convince him that no way remains open to Bludenz. We would then have to wait for the end of the war in Leipzig and search for means of survival, which will not be so easy, and finally I must prevent myself being recruited into the people's armed forces.

Limping through the streets with my weighty crutch, I act the bogus model invalid, send my wife for two hours a week to the Red Cross to keep up appearances and hope thereby that the Nazis come to terms with our shirking, and that the labor office will not get in touch soon. Moreover, I am busy writing my memoirs, and no suddenly appearing Nazi rascal would know that it is not some report on an audit or suchlike.

September 7, 1944

The appeal for mass anti-Nazi resistance that I drew up for my friend M., the astrologer, has fallen flat. Not one of the recipients summoned the truly small amount of courage needed to copy the sheet and hand it on anonymously. Another, to whom I sent the specimen, and whose political confidant I was, even shied away from making the smallest mention that something was stirring among the people, while others began to tremble even when reading the appeal, and feared an agent provocateur had set a trap.

One suspects that the recipients count themselves amongst the intelligent Germans, and in conversations give full vent to their feelings of displeasure and depression with the disgusting Nazi mess without inhibition. Only one addressee referred to it in one of his frequent letters, and this lover of justice seems today to have composed a catchy jingle with which to do his bit, using a children's stamp box to print on sticky address labels. It reads:

"Don't wait till Hitler falls by means of foreign weapons. Stand up and show the world you can do it yourself!"

Tonight, I am going to stick the label onto one of the much-frequented letterboxes, so that those usually using it, when looking for collection times, will get the hoped-for or irritating information.

The others are waiting for – yes, for what are they actually waiting? They are waiting for someone else to do something so that they too may be set free, but these others are relying on the Allies, who are still marching through the rubble-strewn German cities and saving her inhabitants. And these "others" are finally cringing at the thought of the Gestapo, and put out feelers like snails, imagining themselves invisible in their fragile, threadbare houses. They prattle on telling fairy-tales of black men, of the murdered and deported Russians and the impoverished Anglo-Americans.

In the meantime, their eyes nearly popping out of their heads, they whisper meaningfully about the German secret weapon, the V2-VX rocket bombs, admitting, gulping for air, "please, only among ourselves" as enemies of Hitler, and in the next moment do a turn-around so as to persuade others that Germany can still win and must win, because, yes, otherwise "everything is over". Their common sense is not sufficient to recognize that the civic submissiveness will not prevent the almighty authorities from finishing the cruel murder of its citizens.

They fear Hitler more than the enemy, and they shudder, true to Nazi propaganda, and are more frightened of the defeat of Germany than of their own tyrants. Thus they tumble, helpless and wretched, from one mawkish emotion to another, alter their viewpoints as often as Goering changes his dress uniform, live on the memories of Germany's high culture, cling to the threadbare icon of an undefeatable German army, and bewail the damage to the cathedral in Strasbourg more than the deaths of millions of people. At the same time, they have a ready excuse for Hitler's failure on the tip of their tongue or make a coincidence or a spiteful fate responsible for the defeat of the German army.

22   WILL LIFE AWAKEN AGAIN?

As summer fades, Walter knows that much is completely out of his control. Death could come from one errant word from his daughter to a neighbor. Or from just one person in Leipzig who recognizes him as a Jew. Or from an Allied bomb.

He does not pray. He does not ask the fates to spare him. Rather he uses all of his acumen, his learning and his cunning to make precise plans, to slither through each and every bureaucratic crack, and to charm everyone into believing that his fraudulent front is real. Then maybe, just maybe, he can find a semblance of a normal life for his family in the deep shadows of the Holocaust. Yet, he knows that is much too much to ask and it is a constant struggle to avoid self-pity.

September 8, 1944

Autumn is in the air. The wind again brings the scent of ripe fruits, of faded foliage and of late flowers. The diversity intoxicates like old bubbling champagne, a mixture imitating the last breath of a dying nature. We enjoyed it once on our rambles in the north, it washed over our bodies and tousled our hair when we drove the horses along the streets, happy and unrestrained, so as to dream away the summertime somewhere on a hillside or in a faraway lane. It accompanied us on our return from the hills in Bavaria and the Tyrol and even managed now and then to make us anxious when it pulled, like a naughty spirit, at our heartstrings, in poor, empty realms... That was once upon a time.

When, when will life wake like that again?

When can we leave the stone and rubble paradise, and great meadows, fields and woodlands again? When will the people stop damaging peaceful nature with evil and snatching her soul away bit by bit?

Her body is being cut open with graves and stretched with bunkers, her forests fragmented by bombs and grenades and she is sated with the blood of thousands. When will the people stop ruining creation so horribly?

When will life once more wake life? The crown of creation, you pitiful conceited fop, you see the goal of your mission in fireworks. The more it sparkles and the louder it bangs, the greater is your delight.

But I would like to follow the autumn scent into a world where there is peace and truth. Winter is approaching, homesickness threatens, I ache for a home on distant shores.

September 9, 1944

It is early morning, a quarter to seven. There is violent knocking on our hall door. My wife jumps out of bed and returns white as a sheet with a telegram... from Bludenz.

"Employment approved as from now. Furnished room with cooking facilities shortly available. Regional Councilor Dr. Czinglar"

We stare at each other, at a loss. Annekind jumps with joy and hugs us around the neck. Bludenz. How come? How come? True, indeed, Bludenz. We are speechless. Oh, away to the mountains, into light and freedom!

We remain speechless. It's all too much. Autumn has returned. Bludenz.

PART 5
AGENT PROVOCATEUR

1944-1945

IMPORTANT DATES

1945

- **January 17:** Nazi evacuation of Auschwitz; beginning of death marches.
- **January 27:** Beginning of death march for inmates of Stutthof.
- **January 30:** Battle of Bulge ends with a loss of 100,000 German soldiers and nearly all their tanks and aircraft.
- **February 13-14:** Allies firebomb Dresden killing more than 35,000 civilians.
- **March 19:** Americans fire major Japanese cities; more than a million civilians became homeless and more than 5,000 killed.
- **April 6-10:** Death march of inmates of Buchenwald.
- **April 15:** Liberation of Bergen-Belsen concentration camp in northern Germany by British Army.
- **April 26:** Soviets enter Berlin.
- **April 30:** Hitler commits suicide.
- **May 9:** Allied victory in Europe is declared.
- **August 6:** Americans drop atomic bomb on Hiroshima, 100,000 die within five days.

- **August 9:** Americans drop atomic bomb on Nagasaki, 40,000 die instantly.
- **August 14:** Japan accepts unconditional surrender.

23 NO LONGER THE DANGEROUS ADVENTURER

September 15, 1944

Bludenz is ours. We arrived this morning after ten o'clock, following a journey of 37 hours. Sixteen were planned and should have been carried out according to my rehearsal in May. However, the trip took a long time and much sweat and worry.

Since last week Allied airmen have subjected our escape routes to a thorough change, torn up most of the tracks, driven us several times a day from our packing in Leipzig and chased us tired at night from our beds.

After working hard for three days it took two loads and much effort from friends to get it all to the Leipzig Bayerischer station. To complete the formalities, which, as is known, is the sole justification for the existence of the inhabitants of Germany, we only had Wednesday. We made a last visit to the cellar in Leipzig and to meet our many acquaintances and friends, but even that kept us at a gallop as we had to push the last visitors out to finally be able to shut the door behind us.

Then at last came the journey accompanied by friends to the rubble heap, formerly Leipzig's main station. There was indescribable chaos and destruction. The colossal diagonal entrance hall has collapsed. Its concrete structure, scaffolding and supports are piled high as if shredded by a gigantic fist, dismembered and mixed and shaken into sky-high piles, or have plunged into the lower spaces, burying those seeking shelter below. Above the 29 platforms a star-studded sky formed a dome and Anneliese cried and shivered and asked ten times every minute when the train was coming that would take us from this frightening place. To distract and calm her down we walked her around.

Loudspeaker announcement: Express train to Weissenfels expected to be delayed by half an hour. It arrives earlier and we squeeze into the corridor with our luggage, and wait and wait and shake hands with the farewell entourage, so that they can find their way home before the new alarm that is expected.

The train stands still for half an hour, a whole hour. Then it crawls away at a snail's pace out of Leipzig, only to stop suddenly in Grosszschocher. Why Grosszschocher? That is the route to Zeitz! So, a diversion. If we are not in Weissenfels at 11 o'clock, we will miss the train to Munich. The train stops everywhere. At around one o'clock we reach Weissenfels, where the connection is long gone. We get out onto the platform and run through the subway. The child cries and cannot follow. The station staff has no information and suggests returning to Zeitz at four o'clock, where the next scheduled morning train to Bavaria passes through. We decide on continuing onwards to Naumburg, and just manage to get the train with which we came. In Naumburg we hear of a train at 16.48 to Saalfeld, where the express train Leipzig-Munich arrives after ten o'clock. If only we did not have to limp out of Leipzig 12 hours earlier! Now, the poor child doesn't complain despite heavy eyelids. She is content with everything her parents plan and only wants one thing: to go.

The waiting room is crammed full of foreigners and Eastern workers. A stench denies entry, so we set up camp in the booking hall. The child dozes off on our hand luggage, then jumps up again and using my walking stick takes a round trip through the waiting rooms.

We nibble, I smoke my nightly travel supply. If only there is no air raid warning. This journey by day through the danger zone has already cost the lives of some run-aways. We fear for our child. Still, the hours pass. We stand in the early morning cold on the platform and wait. We continue to freeze in the train to Saalfeld. Dawn is breaking, and it becomes light. The mist floats over meadows and creeps out of the forests. Annekind is happy. There are new impressions and the view changes continually. Her little face shines at the first sight of the Thüringer mountains, more than 200 kilometers southwest of Leipzig. That is what a mountain looks like. Very high, nearly a thousand meters, and with many flowers. It is wonderful. Can one go for a walk there with Mommy and Daddy without any wicked people coming? Yes, my child, we can do that. But where our journey ends the mountains are far bigger and much more beautiful. As high as the clouds? Yes, that big. Poor, happy child!

The armament factories are at the foot of the hills to be protected from enemy bombs. The war is more important than mountains, forests and people. In Saalfeld we have three more hours of waiting. We refresh ourselves with coffee and our picnic provisions, wash away the dirt clinging to our hands and faces after the short stretch of travel and send greeting cards to friends in Leipzig, who will think we are already traveling through the Allgäu in the Alps. It is a little cloudy, smoke rises straight up. If only rain fell instead of bombs!

On the express train to Munich we have wonderful window seats, and the journey is quick and smooth. Fellow travelers grumble about Hitler and his damned economy. We see the Probstzella,[1] the house of the people, now renamed, brings back memories of the stay on our motor car trip eight years ago. The great watershed. Schloss Bay. Dreizehnheiligen. Bamberg. Nuremberg. A light rain begins to fall, thank heavens. Annelie is happy. We are too.

In Treuchtlingen there is an announcement: the train will not go to Neuenwirth-Augsburg, it has been diverted via Ingolstadt due to a collision on the scheduled route. People are talking about the express train we will miss and the 180 dead. There is speculation about a fast train between Munich and Lindau and the choice of staying overnight in Bavaria and traveling through to Lake Constance. Around seven o'clock we arrive in Munich. It is pouring on the platform as all cover has disappeared here too. The express train is already well filled but we get good seats. Mutti got fresh rolls and sliced cold meats, for we can always eat. The change of air is demanding. It is a pity that darkness covers the splendor of the Allgäu Alps. Those under my protection do not know them.

After midnight we get to Lindau, just across the lake from Switzerland. The restaurant in the waiting area is closed. We crawl into a waiting room for ship passengers where many train dawdlers are snoring. The child is put to bed on a ship's bench. I try to sleep against Mutti's shoulder, dozing for two hours. At dawn I look out into space, where the contours of the Swiss mountains rise over Lake Constance.

The drizzle eases off. My wife remained awake and as the child wakes I take her out to the quay and past sleepy steamships towards the Bavarian lion, that grand monument at the harbor entrance at whose feet the waves break. Annelie can hardly speak for astonishment, and when she does, she asks for an explanation of these wonderful things. It is warm here, swallows soar towards the light filtering in, the mild south wind chases away sleep and the hotels on the shore are still there, white and tempting as during times of freedom – they did not foresee the worry and the need in which we would see them again.

The police still have enough fuel to search the lake for deserters. The boats have been removed, an old seadog tells me in dry Alemannic dialect of this region, after a vessel exploded. At seven o'clock the hospitable waiting rooms open their doors and we breakfast until full and happy. And when we left Lindau on an express train, the green lake smiled in the blazing sunshine, allowing a view over the Swiss mountains. Near Bregenz they were quite close, bathed in snow-white fluffy cotton-wool clouds; on the Austrian side the Three Sisters soared out of the mist.

Sixteen weeks ago I travelled this way alone and returned feverishly, awaiting a pronouncement, full of fear and with a heavy heart, ensnared by tormenting images and unable to appreciate the splendor of the Vorarlberg landscape, this wondrous area in the Austrian Alps that engulfs destination Bludenz. How my soul cried out then for the rescue of my wife and child from the deadly danger into which I had brought them through my hazardous business! Today, however, I breathed in the fresh wind drifting along the train and feasted on my wife's delight in celebrating a reunion with the mountains, forests and walking paths of our first holiday. Our child's eyes gazed on all that was new, and sparkled brightly as they took in the slopes and fixed on the cloud-covered summits. Today I was no longer the dangerous adventurer for them, today I became their guide to freedom, life and joy.

September 16, 1944

Feldkirch. A shrieking young woman, apparently recruited for labor service, yells through the compartment window at her mother standing on the platform. We enter the valley of the River Ill through a tunnel and the mountains of Bludenz appear. The mountains surround us. To the left is Hohen Tauern, to the right Mondspitze, Schottenkopf, etc. In Bludenz there is bright sunshine. We hand in part of our hand luggage and go to the post office. We post the first greetings to friends and I phone the office of the Regional Councilor. Kühnl answers. We have been allocated to the Arlberger Hof Hotel and are well received and given a comfortable room. After a general clean-up we fetch the hand luggage at the station. After lunch at the Arlberger Hof I take my first afternoon nap in Bludenz. We take a short walk to a viewing point and Annelie cries. After supper I fall into a deep sleep.

I meet Kühnl again and tell him about the journey. I, in turn, hear about information from Mannheim and Leipzig which corroborates the statements made by me about my political indifference, and which in no way justify a challenge. I get cigarettes for Kühnl and the Regional Councilor to share. The Regional Councilor then appears and declines the cigarettes with thanks. Kühnl telephones a colleague who arranges for a porter to take our luggage and accompany us to take a look at the rooms which have been commandeered for us.

24 MY GOD, ISN'T THAT A GREAT STORY!

At last, Walter Leopold and his family can breathe freely in the high mountain air of the Austrian Alps and enjoy a modest, almost normal, bourgeois lifestyle. For the first time in years, he experiences a modicum of happiness. Although their fake identities could still be uncovered, the risk is considerably lower than in Leipzig.

Much hinges on the ability of their remarkable seven-year-old daughter to play her role, and play it perfectly. As always, Walter must wade through the ever-intrusive Nazi bureaucracy.

Ironically, for the first time in his life, Walter gains a high-status position in public administration beyond the Jewish community, something he had trained and longed for, but had been denied because of his religion. Of course, he only gets this opportunity by serving as a faux Aryan. This irony is not lost on him.

Because of his job and fake identity, Walter experiences the Third Reich in a completely unique way. Even though he is relatively safe, keeping up the deception is draining his energy. He is driven to initiate more anti-Nazi resistance when the much-anticipated Allied surge into Germany and Austria slows considerably as the Germans counter-attack in the Battle of the Bulge.

Walter also senses a new empowerment. If he lives to see the Allied liberation, he will be a most unusual witness to the behavior of Nazis in Bludenz. He is a now a spy within their ranks who may help decide who shall live and who shall die. That's quite a shift from scurrying about in Leipzig scrounging for food.

September 20, 1944

The municipality inspector, in whose office I wander around like a ghost, returned today feeling upset. His resemblance to a well-known person in Leipzig is striking, yes, even the sound of his voice is so alike that even a different dialect cannot hide the similarity. The employees call him the most experienced auditor and most competent reorganizer of municipalities. I can see him from the seat I have taken, engrossed in his examination reports. While I too take great pains to penetrate the secrets of governmental accounting theoretically and pursue the practical implementation, I keep company for a while with the young man at the huge, complicated book-keeping machine. It seems as if I have suddenly become unbelievably perplexed, so difficult do I find the first steps on the way to my future field of activity.

True, it is not yet even a beginning, but I am used to climbing up the scaffolding of a business and jump straight to the top. Depressed by this realization, I discovered from the Chief Inspector that in a short time I am to accompany the local administration auditor on his official trips so that he can carry out the work more smoothly. Now, as they say, bite the bullet, and grasp what still appears incomprehensible, if I am not to be punished for my false statements about my occupation as an auditor. I have to succeed, otherwise...

My wife obtains all the essentials at the household supplies authority. The applications for coal and a child's bed have also been made. But we have still not handed in the questionnaire to the labor office, because I am still sniffing around the problem of how I can free my wife from working. It is raining, but warm and hazy, and Bludenz knows how to protect her beauty spots in a foggy mist.

This fog appeals to me. The journey was almost too much and the soul must meander through much refinement. These mountains, encircled by a belt of clouds, capture one's attention and entice the spirit towards them, where it struggles to fulfil its mission. Jagged rocks, green hilltops, fresh young woods, Alpine huts and enticing slopes seduce one into contempt of official doings and ensure that the four letters, N A Z I, never remain in their appointed place. It is raining. But this view! Wonderful.

A stray suitcase has arrived, as acquaintances kindly telephoned to inform us. It came from Innsbruck and had lost its address label. They ascertained the recipient from the dispatch number. It contained of all things our linen. Again, a marvelous coincidence!

I have missed my usual radio newscast this past week. I will probably not be able to listen for some time. Thus, I am politically isolated, and the only information that I can summon is from the Bludenz regional newspaper with its Nazi ox-tongue salad.

The Regional Councilor and his Chief Inspector – he actually holds the title of Regional Chief Inspector – are harboring some fears, which they confidentially confessed to me. The two good chaps actually believe that they will be devoured if there is an Allied victory. If they give me time, I will pour a tonic down their throats. They will recover if they do not feel too guilty.

The advance of the liberators appears, if I am not deceived, to have temporarily come to a halt. And they were almost at the finish line and the liberation of their fellow sufferers.

Tomorrow we want to move into our new place. In Bludenz.

September 21, 1944

Our home in Bludenz is now occupied. Our extremely comfortable hotel quarters have been superseded by a bedroom with two beds, which my wife supplemented with a child's bed from the N.S.V.,[1] and a light spacious kitchen with a storeroom. From the kitchen one can see the mountains which flank the Montafon valley, while the view to the south is blocked by huge treetops, one of which bears green walnuts. The landlord and landlady, after their initial fuss, received us in a friendly manner, brightened our move with flowers and happily offer every possible assistance. As is our practice, we speedily made friends, piled the contents of the suitcases, baskets, and boxes into cupboards and drawers, and put the rest, which is not needed often, into the storeroom next to the kitchen.

Soon there was a comfortable ambiance in our new dwelling. The child sleeps calmly in her bed, and we sit in the kitchen in the light of our good desk lamp, which my wife once gave me for Chanukah. It required a technical adjustment to get it to work, as the people of Bludenz have kept the old power supply system, with 120 volts for light and 220 volts for power. The former works in normal power points as is usual in the Reich, but the latter requires wide plugs and because of its low electricity price of nine pence cannot be used for lighting purposes, not even with the solid plug with which our cooker and lights are provided.

Without further ado, we acquired electric power plugs, and with the help of my acquaintances converted them. The landlord welcomed this solution, for in this way we saved him three quarters of our electricity costs.

Indeed, life in the Tyrol is amusing. The hotelier family were unhappy with our departure because of the friendship formed between their daughter and Anneliese and our bill was not issued in a hurry. "Do call again," the wife said and asked us to make regular visits. While north Germans often find people of Bludenz to be reserved or even encounter rejection, we were quickly trusted and can certainly not complain of isolation. Maybe my fluent Alemannic dialect has already brought understanding smiles among the people of the Vorarlberg, but my familial protégées, who mostly do not understand a word of it, also enjoy the affection of all those with whom they come into contact.

I had permission from the Chief Inspector to stay away from work today because of the move. Tomorrow morning, I will definitely get started, so that my star does not fade. I must learn and pay attention if I am to know financial administration like the back of my hand. It seems that this is definitely expected, after a slight hint made in passing by the men in charge. Instead of the initially intended employment as tax auditor they have decided to give me the difficult Party position of second municipality auditor. If I disappoint them, everything will be over, Bludenz, the job... So, let's dig in!

September 22, 1944

I thanked the Chief Inspector for the successful housing placement, in spite of my earlier futile attempt to be received by him. Only when he entered the cashier's office as if by chance could I shake his hand. However, I requested something else. I asked him for information about his move to involve me immediately in the local audit checks and the business of finance and accounting, a position which demands a 100 per cent experienced official, and advised him against treating my abilities as those of a sorcerer. He tapped me soothingly on the shoulder, smilingly showed his gold teeth and said I had completely misunderstood him.

With the taking up of duties he had just meant my giving a small helping hand, like filling in columns, etc., dealing with details that may hold up efficient completion of a task.

My fear of expectations of training at lightning speed in all areas of cash and accountancy was completely unfounded; on the contrary, he, as an old government administration official, would be satisfied if in about three months I could declare that I had a good insight into the state of affairs.

However, it would also be quite reasonable to consider a six-month preparation period, during which he could confidently assure me that, as far as official affairs were concerned, I would still be awkward – like an infant attempting to walk who still requires the support and guiding hand of his mother. Were my life to hang on these first steps, I would not be able to save it.

"In these circumstances you have saved the life of three people!" I said.

His whole face beamed with satisfaction and he swelled out his tummy, pressed my hand in a friendly way and said goodbye.

In the afternoon the door to the cashier's office opened and the Regional Councilor appeared, leading Annekind. "Your Daddy is over there. The child needs more color in her cheeks, take her out into the fresh air."

Annelie, eyes shining bright, brought me a big thermos flask of coffee, and rummaging around in her Mutti's handbag, brought out a plate with a large slice of fresh apple cake.

Then, to the amusement of my co-workers, she told of her meeting with uncle Regional Councilor. He had asked about her wishes in the entrance hall whereupon she had answered she wanted to see her Daddy. Who is her Daddy? Herr Freiherr. Then she had searched for her Daddy with him and discovered his hiding place from the secretary. Annelie caused quite a to-do as she fluently and grippingly described the meeting. Then she was off again, wavey-wavey, back to her Mommy. She was hardly outside when the Chief Inspector came in and asked whether the Frei Miss had been there. A sweet lass, he thought, and chatted for a long time with me. He also ordered the long overdue costs of my interview journey to be reimbursed.

I remain in a good mood and of good cheer. Mutti too, as I told her about the conversation and the events of the day, whereupon we intended to have a blueberry feast, but we found this delicacy crossed out on the menu as usual. Instead we had a wonderful evening excursion through the meadows around Bludenz and concluded with a happy meal in our own home.

If only everything promised to remain as good as this day has been! If. Perhaps we can hope.

September 23, 1944

Satisfied and confident, I was working on my sketch of the system of accounting and cash reckoning, so as to understand how it all joined together, when the secretary came in and with an arrogant gesture gave me a handful of forms. She commented that I was to deal with them and return the contract with my signature affixed. The contract? Oh yes, I had not thought about that.

"Herr Kurt Freiherr will be employed from September 15, 1944 as a temporary war employee..."

Temporary war employee? A formality, the Chief Inspector had informed me in May.

"...allocated to salary band VII..."

Salary band VII? Why VII? We agreed on band VI. Why is it suddenly one band lower? What does this mean? Up to one hundred Marks less. Well, well, is that how the people in Bludenz roll?

And what about the other pieces of paper?

The first is a "leaflet" with ten requirements. Well, I never.

1) Photographs from the front and in profile.

Why photos? What do they want with my face?

2) A hand-written curriculum vitae.

Curriculum vitae? I thought I was a public employee since September 15. Or am I not?

3) A certificate giving proof of origin (proof of ancestry).

Good heavens! That can't be true.

"Immediate employment approved." And "the inquiries about you have not produced anything unfavorable."

So read the cable they sent, and that is what they said. Why then this proof of ancestry? Are these blokes completely out of it?

4) Leaver's certificate from elementary or secondary schools (Maturity Certificate) in a certified copy.

Well, well, they don't trust my level of education? They are quite right. I don't trust it either. For two years I have been called Freiherr and must not show either my matriculation or my doctor's diploma. Because I am called Freiherr I am no longer Doctor Leopold. Indeed, that's how it is. You are right. You want to see my certificates. The fact that my Military Pass refers to me as a teacher of commerce and auditor is no longer sufficient for you. You are right there too. I am neither a teacher nor an auditor. I am only Doctor L. Oh, Regional Councilor and Chief inspector, you twerps! But please carry on!

5) Certified copies of utilization certificates.

Utilization certificates? What sort of balderdash is that? Oh, I see, they want to know for what they can employ me. They still don't recognize "Immediate employment approved"? They are allowing the film to run backwards. The egg is crawling back into the backside of the hen. That is a method and a half.

What else, please?

6) Questionnaire about Party membership.

That's enough now, gentlemen. I have already flatly declared, more than three months ago, that I am not a Nazi, never mind a Party member and am not of a mind to join your precious ranks. "The strict rules of a year ago are no longer imposed." That's what they told me, agreed? That's what you told me, Herr Chief Inspector? Besides, the local group in Leipzig confirmed my position to your boss. So, you don't believe that anymore either? It is enough to make my hair stand on end and stir me up inside. They are nuts.

Totally nuts. Everything has already been sorted? No, Rabbi Akiba,[2] Adolf's scion does not know him.

7) Declaration of legal and Party court penalties.

I explain to you that in fact I am not a party man. God knows!

8) Lodge declaration.

You should have that too. Or perhaps not. I will think about whether I will take part in your madness.

9) Declaration that your economic affairs are well-ordered.

They are in order. Ask my friends. They lent me the money so I could come to Bludenz. What have you done? Carry on.

10) Declaration concerning high treason regulations.

High treason? Yes, indeed, a traitor, I'm one, I am one like in a fairy-tale. If I survive, it will be demonstrated to you.

Questions follow about the origin of yours truly, my parents and grandparents, the Aryan purity of my parents back to their great grandparents, about my activity in the N.S.D.A.P.[3], etc., then my life in the Weimar Republic, and my belonging to a lodge, an organization resembling a lodge or a substitute organization or such like. It finishes with a declaration that I have been thoroughly instructed in the conditions of employment and the law journal for Austria (1938) relevant to the regulations governing treason and high treason.

All this fuss to take me on, yet you have had no time for it between May 27 and September 15, have you? Even if you do not guess which paths our Aryanizing has taken, you know all too well that someone in your clique would find it difficult to procure new documents clobbered together as substitutes for the old ones, whose destruction I have described x number of times. However, what do you intend by re-opening the miserable matter after successfully employing me? Is this meant to facilitate contractual agreements?

"Employment immediately approved."

On what grounds? Because of doubt about our Aryan origin? Or my education? Or my criminal integrity? Or my aversion to lodges and similar dubious associations? Or my devotion to Hitler? Why did you bother for three long months to obtain information about me and my wife through the Nazi administration in Innsbruck? Why, for what? So as to let the whole stinking twaddle roll into the station once more?

"Employment immediately approved."

You are giving yourselves away, you most lovable rascals. And I, silly donkey, was prepared to vouch for you when your enemies stand at the gates of Bludenz. Yes, I would have done it. But you are such blockheads that you bite yourselves in the backside.

"Employment immediately approved."

You have done that well. Oh, you stupid oxen whom I took for good people and enemies of Hitler!

I congratulate you.

September 24, 1944

We led our little Mockel on her first proper outing today, up to the Tschengla. Our initial intention was to make this trip, which is recommended to every Bludenz visitor, in the morning and stay up there for lunch, but we changed our minds because of the unsettled weather. We took in our old specialty, the Briser ravine, from which we have in the past been able to make an easy trip to Briserburg, to the Tschengla. Between the massive and often overhanging rock walls it leads into the Klauen, then past Tobeln, a narrow climb up and over swaying bridges to small rock tunnels which one could only scramble through bent double, then far on down to the countless gurgling and spurting cataracts. From there one turns unexpectedly onto a forest path, is intoxicated by the glittering trees, fills one's lungs with strong ozone. One's nose is tickled by an orgy of scents: woods, mushrooms, water and other fantastic combinations. Then the path climbs steeply up again, leaving the roaring water far below, winds along a rock wall, turns to the right and leads the visitor to the overwhelming drama of a waterfall cascading from the heights of the mountain.

The sun's rays play in the spray. The iridescent sparkling creates a symphony of sound which echoes far away to the distant rocks. It is indescribably beautiful and at the same time powerful. We keep looking back at the unreal whiteness, whose shining light follows us, and suddenly stand in a gaping crevice which was some time ago spanned, but today commands everyone who wants to go further to stop.

We briefly consider what to do and then scramble up the steep slope, pushing the child when she can't go on, pulling her higher and further up the wet, muddy ground on which our boots lacking hob nails slide about like toboggans in the snow. We are wet through and search impatiently for a clearing which promises a crossing to a new climb; still it seems as if this dangerous section has no end. Nevertheless, all at once the sky does lure us through the trees onto a sloping meadow on which my wife skates backwards, while I, with a final effort, hold Annelie upright and bring her forward.

This outing was in no way refreshing and for our child's first expedition, it was indeed too much. That is why she constantly asks when the trip will end, drinks fresh Burserberg mountain spring water with her Mutti, and complains about the long, though comfortable, zigzag way down. Views change at every bend, showing the Ritikon with its limestone peaks and cavities, fading away in the encircling fog, barriers and ridges, then the lovely lower mountains and hills dreamy in lush green, on which cowbells can be heard. Once again, we can see Bludenz far below, protected by the massive High Frassen, the horns of the Elsespitze, and the great lump of the Stierkopf, and finally one spots the magnificent Alfang valley.

Yes, all is indeed beautiful, and we look forward to a cup of coffee, which we will drink on the Trachengl to the health of the people of Bludenz. However, when we finally reach the top, the disappointment is huge. All the cafes are closed, their owners have had to give them up for children sent to the country. The only one still intact is reserved for the highly honorable RAD[4] and is not allowed to serve anything to those not in uniform, even if their throats are parched with thirst.

The caretaker, or whatever the nurse of the hut liked to call herself, graciously let herself be persuaded to give us a jug of water, which we were by way of exception allowed to enjoy in front of the house on the highest RAD bench. Suddenly we understood why we had not met a single soul on our way through the Druse gorge and why the descent was also deserted.

Practically all able-bodied people have to work for Hitler, even on Sunday. For individual walkers, the local publicans have blocked up all the huts, places of refreshments and viewing points and know all too well that everyone prefers to stay at home rather than exasperate themselves in the mountains.

An hour later the rain clouds drove us over the heights down to Bürserberg, about four kilometers from Blundez, which is teeming with women in black. Hitler has taken their husbands and sons and sacrificed them to his folly and fear of his own self. But I have no sympathy for these people, who have patiently accepted every nastiness and this wicked mass murder, as if it is something unalterable, when they wish us good day or ask us to greet the good Lord with "grüss Gott."[5] A few steps further on we see the highly polished boots of the local spokesman of the Nazi Party, a man in a very expensive, gala uniform, who has assembled the people of Burserberg this afternoon to tell them to conquer or die. But the people of Burserberg will not be victorious, they will all die for their beloved Leader, for the villain general of all villains.

Somewhat tired out after our yearlong break from walking, we go home. Bludenz is fabulous with its many hills, hilltops, summits, rock faces, gorges, forests, valleys! Uniquely beautiful. It is much too beautiful for an administrator or Chief Inspector, who know of nothing better to do in all this splendor than insist on race purity, to sniff out three immigrants fighting for their lives.

Vae victis![6] Burserberg

September 25, 1944

The clouds that drove us from the Tschengla emptied their deluge of water on to storm-engulfed Bludenz during the night. It became cloudy and frosty, and everyone in the office tried to get warm by chattering. It was claimed that the Regional Councilor behind his affability sought to conceal his worry and a certain lack of courage, which made things ridiculous, as he is a confirmed Nazi.

Now, I know too little of his character, for all in all I have only spoken with him for less than an hour. I don't take his Nazi-ness seriously after his open declaration of sympathy for an applicant who not only refused to join the Party but also let it be known he is no supporter of Hitler. Perhaps he already regrets his tolerance and is trying to neutralize it by continual demands for documents.

At least he behaves as if he already considers me an unimportant quantity, for whom a lower-paying than promised apprentice contract is a reasonable recompense, while his political inquisition would make it seem as if a ministerial post was in the offing. Birdie, eat or die! The birdie will neither eat, nor does he hope to die, but rather he will let the foragers fidget until their gall bladders bursts.

The Chief Inspector for his part has preferred not to show himself to me anymore, but when I met him this evening in the entrance hall, he behaved as if nothing had happened, greeting me with friendly smiles, and I countered in the same coin.

I still know what I owe to myself and the enemies of Hitler, but also to his friends and devoted civil servants. They too know that I do not belong with them, and should they forget it, I will remind them in time.

September 26, 1944

It bucketed down rain all night long and when I looked towards the mountains this morning on my way to the administration office, the first snow greeted me. They looked majestic with their icing sugar coating, the three-thousanders,[7] but I prefer them in their summer nakedness. For I love the summer in the mountains with its refreshing wind and want to sniff the scent of the dewy meadows and the Alpine flowers a little longer before they lie down beneath the cold cover for their long rest.

Arriving in the office, I pull myself together, take the papers and stumble in to the Chief Inspector. What does this paper inquisition mean? After the Regional Councilor's inquiry about my personal and political trustworthiness required a quarter of a year for a response? Did he want to wait until I have been able to have my burned personal papers renewed? What is the purpose of making these demands <u>after</u> the commencement of my work?

"Now, let's have a look. It is not so bad after all. Firstly, two photos are already too much. One is sufficient. Let's see, you can surely write your curriculum vitae and can fill in the questionnaire about descent afterwards."

"Yes, I can supply the curriculum vitae, but not the details requested about our mutual grandparents in four variants. All that is in the ancestry certificate, but I have not learned that off by heart. Therefore, I cannot fill in the questionnaire."

"Do you know what? Fill it out as far as it is possible and against the other questions you put: due to lack of documentation cannot be answered."

"Good, I will."

"And then the school reports."

"I don't have those anymore either. School attendance is recorded in the Military Service record."

"Simply enclose the Military Service record for information."

"Utilization certificates."

"I will enclose them too."

"So only the questionnaire remains about membership of the Party, Party and police penalties, lodges and declarations of treason, and you can take care of that at your convenience. We need these things for our personnel files."

"And the contract, Chief Inspector. You gave it to me taken as read although it would have been better before fixing it to have spoken to me. For the content does not concur with our arrangement. You had promised me band VI plus approximately 300 Marks for days of service outside Bludenz to be calculated by Frl. M. In band VII, however, I get up to 100 Marks less, a sum which does not support minimum existence. I agreed to your proposal earlier in the year, and I beg you to honor it."

Initially he did not want to remember this part of our conversation on May 26 and 27, but when I repeated it word for word to him and I referred to Miss M. as a witness, he pulled a sour face and took back the contract to discuss it once more with the Regional Councilor. I asked for patience with the filling in of the questionnaire, etc., etc., asking to be allowed to wait until my head was clearer.

"Certainly, naturally. But you will still have to swear an oath to Hitler before the Regional Councilor, you know that, don't you?"

"Oh, yes, I know that!"

Whether I know it! That is a haunting idea! I will swear loyalty to the butcher of the Jews! If there is a person anywhere on earth who is sick because he has forgotten how to laugh, bring him to my swearing-in. I guarantee his recovery, even before my hand lies in the hand of the Regional Councilor.

Freiherr, Freiherr, you are making the servants of their master into true buffoons. Pull down their jester caps so that their drunken sayings are properly hallowed. Hitler, look at these poor sheep!

September 27, 1944

Our friends from Leipzig have written, a lot and with much melancholy. Indeed, it was a painful parting, even for some who only knew a family called Freiherr. They would like to follow us, but they are bound and sold to the rubble that is Leipzig. There was a photo of Uncle B for Annelie. The two are joined like a couple of polished chain links and earlier Mockel cried again over her good friend, and wants to write to him that he must come immediately with his parents to Bludenz. If only things were that simple, they would not need to yearn for each other any longer. Further rotten eggs fell on Leipzig, with mines very close to our home. That's how our friends live.

The snow has gone from the heights, but it's raining hard. And it is cold. One freezes in the office and one cannot see the mountains anymore. Never mind, we have no visitor's tax to pay like on our earlier visit, and don't throw our money out of the window. For we live here, and after winter another spring will come. If we live to see it! We, the residents of Bludenz. My god, isn't that a great story.

September 29, 1944

For days Bludenz was buried under a thick blanket of clouds and received the incessant rain that is usual for mountain regions. It was accompanied by a perceptible decrease in temperature which made my knees creak along with everyone else's in the office and at times even stopped the brain from working. The barometer is climbing now and the clouds are gradually lifting, from time to time proudly revealing the silhouetted peaks in their autumnal winter clothing. They stand out as colossal, the massive spine of the Hohe Frassen, as well as the many-pronged Wandau rock face, towering up out of the bottom of the valley from only 540 meter above sea level, like the Karwendel above Mittenwald, which they resemble so much that they could be confused.

No wonder that we often turn towards the view, to stamp the panorama of Bludenz in its peculiar formation on our minds. However, while the swallows still soar like minute black dots in the grey-violet mist, which has replaced the clouds, we freeze as if on the North Pole and we look forward to the celebrated October days.

The secretary delivered the new contract with its equally new compensation band 6b, which she indicates is for a novice in an inspection career path. The remaining formalities are not so pressing, she said. I can take my time. Candidate inspector Freiherr! Wow, don't laugh, you still have to be sworn in.

To Adolf, your friend. Oh, Adolf, if you could see what happens under your patronage, you would no longer need rebellious generals[8] to get really annoyed. If you survive. The Heavens still protect us from your clairvoyance.

Candidate inspector. Why, that could be right. I have found out from a third party that the office of the district municipality examiner is reserved for me, currently held by an external highly-respected expert, but in a very short time to be vacant again. With this current predecessor I have made contact, and he has given my boss a not altogether detrimental opinion of me as a hopeful aspirant.

Our friends from Leipzig and Kohlgrub continue to write. Both confessed they had wept, some due to missing us, and others in happiness at our good fortune, which no one had expected. They magnified their emotions with much desired presents of cigarettes and tobacco, which I smoke to their good health until new ones arrive. All would like to follow us, and we would be the last to scorn a reunion.

In the meantime, we are happy in our nest and only harbor one wish: that an early end to the war would permit us to fight openly. We no longer know when it might come, and how things stand on both sides. For in Bludenz there is alternating current which my little radio set does not digest. That is lamentable but permanent unless I can get hold of a rectifier. All the same, I assume the Allies will succeed without my supervision.

We, however, are in Bludenz and I call myself an inspection candidate of the Regional Councilor. Happy are those who suffer persecution.

October 1, 1944

It was glorious on the Mutterberg. This morning at ten o'clock we set off, uncertain whether Annelie as a beginner would manage the steep climb, and whether the beautiful weather would last until our return, with the barometer falling. But all went better than expected. Annelie skipped cheerfully along holding her Mutti's hand, more energetically than her parents. We old mountain goats find climbing difficult now. The years of misfortune and deprivation have demanded too much of us and have ruined our bodily vigor, so that even at a modest gradient we lose our breath and sweat from our brows drenches us like a hydrant. Seventeen years ago, on the way to the High Frassen, we climbed up the Mutterberg in roughly one and a half hours. Today we need two and a half, even without our child skipping along.

Despite everything it was glorious up there in Schwalbennest on the Hohe Frassen, 1325 meters above sea level and a little over 750 meters above Bludenz, indescribably wonderful despite light pressure and a very dazzling sun. This mountain panorama begins on the left with the Silvretta, with Piz Buin like the cut-off head of a two-branched centaur, which seems through a pair of field glasses to be the bushy-eared head of a lynx. A third formation looks like a pencil with an all too long point. Then followed the cumbersome snowmen of the Montafon, from which the black Mittagsspitze points its admonishing finger.

From the Silvretta up to here, it seems that winter has already asserted its power. It tries to be loyal to the sun with both permissible and forbidden means. We witnessed the drama, unusual for the beginning of October, of a deeply snow-covered Bludenz mountain world.

Amid this feast for the eyes the two charming daughters of the landlord served us a thoroughly respectable meal. We ate with pleasure and gave the chefs are compliments. They could still cook, one had to say that.

After the meal followed a much-desired siesta in the high-altitude sunshine in which one can soak up the sun and get a tan without the nuisance of depressingly high temperatures. It is turning noticeably cooler, even when some object such as a coffee pot throws a shadow. An iron bar became quite hot to handle in the sunshine but got frosty just a centimeter away.

While we slurped our coffee and ate the sandwiches we had brought, suspicious-looking tufts of mist appeared over the slopes, and the Hohe Frassen put on a woolen cap. This bad habit spread and at the start of the afternoon a bank of clouds covered the sun, and at the same time an icy wind brought us to our feet.

I felt lousy after this miniature hike. My wife felt the same and only for Mockel, who had used her legs to climb for the first time here in Bludenz, and romped happily about during the entire stay on the Mutterberg, did it seem that the hard walk refreshed her legs.

We still lack a radio. We are as good as cut off from the world. We know neither what happens outside nor can we counter the nonsense propaganda. I will try to get hold of a rectifier in exchange for my electric razor. If not, I must succeed in finding a completely like-minded person. Even if I have succeeded in deciphering protected secrets, with news welcome to them and to me, they need to sense that their words are safe with us. Nevertheless, I lack a radio.

25 REVOLUTIONARY JEW

It is one thing to have a false identity and live in the shadow of the Holocaust. It is quite another for Walter to display that Aryan identity in a day-to-day job while also expanding his self-appointed role as political agitator. As time goes by, he cannot help but wonder whether he is doing permanent damage to Herr Doktor Walter Leopold, the German Jew.

Such thoughts, however, fade into the background against the desperate Nazi troop call-ups. As the war continues to degenerate for the Germans, the very young and old are sent into battle. What if Freiherr must fight for the Nazis to save his wife and child from discovery?

October 4, 1944

I stayed at home today, for one can catch one's death in the office. Half the department is already laid up because until November 1 no heating is permitted. It has poured for the last 48 hours, and when the clouds cleared away yesterday, snow had fallen down to 900 meters with temperatures hardly above freezing. All the mountains, the low ones as well as the giants, compete in the race towards winter, and were one not to know that October has only just begun, and one finds meadows and trees still green, or at the most lightly autumnally colored, and the sun still high over the mountains, one would bet a hundred to one that it was December. This is too much even for the swallows. The last flew southwest and southeast over our roofs yesterday.

As that heating is not permitted in the office, I escaped several times to Mutti, so as to thaw my stiff hands and my painful back at the cooker, drink hot coffee or meat broth to bring me back to life – in other words I tried to pump myself full of warmth.

I was frightfully run down: that is why I stayed at home today and have inaugurated the sofa which the landlord has put at our disposal to complete our kitchen-living room. What will happen if the cold continues until November? Then my 104-pound skin and bone frame will fall apart, as surely as the Regional Councilor avoids chattering teeth with his opposite build.

I have told the Chief Inspector about it. The heating ban is irrevocable even if the entire department has to be closed down. Fine, just fine. Hopefully they will soon have to shut down the Hitler groups. It is really time. In fact, high time.

October 6, 1944

Curriculum vitae of Kurt Freiherr

Son of the painter Heinrich Freiherr and his wife Frieda, born on February 23, 1898 in Mannheim. This great international trade and transport center of southern Germany, with the largest inland port and trans-shipment station in Europe until 1914, and the distant white waters of the Rhine, excited carefree childish fantasies no less than my father's stories of the high seas. Seafarers seemed to me not only the bravest, but also the most industrious of all working people. To emulate them I joined the high school in Mannheim after four years in elementary school. I was there without interruption until the World War ended my schooling. I was called up for military service in 1915 after gaining my high school diploma for those going to war.

My military training in the infantry (I.R. III) and mountain artillery (Geba5) followed an uninterrupted and injury-free deployment on the front line of the Macedonian theatre of war, documented by several bravery awards. I survived the collapse in August 1918 with not too many comrades through an adventurous retreat and retired from the army in February 1919 as a deputy officer.

The political and economic conditions which now developed made the resumption of my seafarer plans appear no longer appropriate; they were completely replaced by new considerations, and thoughts of being an administrative official or a teacher. Matriculating at the Mannheim School of Economics I made my choice and entered on the then all too popular path to becoming a teacher of economics. I spent the eight study terms (six regulars, two intermediary terms) in my father's hometown of Frankfurt am Main, passed the examinations with a "good" result and after one year of practical study acquired my qualification as a candidate teacher in 1923. My hope of employment dwindled – many others were in the same position. Access to higher teaching posts, including those in public commerce schools, was blocked for years, even when the candidate teachers offered to go without payment or work as primary school teachers.

Feeling unable to financially burden my mother any longer (she has since died), I looked for a purpose in life. I decided on becoming an auditor and started building up my practice in 1925. I worked in Mannheim, traveling frequently to other cities (relieved of all military duties due to my heart condition) until the end of 1943, when I moved to friends in Leipzig because of the air raids in Mannheim, but there too my family and I were totally bombed out.

I continued working despite the many day and night air raid alarms. Further raids followed, and if I could carry on at all, it was only with the greatest of difficulties. Moving with my family to a region that was less dangerous and more conducive to my health consequently became absolutely necessary and this revived my former plan to dedicate my career to public service. I was able to realize this intention, nourished by my affection for the Vorarlberg region, when the Regional Councilor of Bludenz consented to accept me in his district administration. I entered his service on the September 15, 1944. I have been married to Henny, born Franz, from Ludwigshafen am Rhein, since 1930 and have one daughter aged seven.

Politically, I have never belonged to either a Party, a lodge or any other kind of association, also not of a military nature. My aspirations rather were and are professional and academic and should cover the tasks intended for me in the Regional Councilor's office.

Bludenz, October 1944

Kurt Freiherr

October 10, 1944

I still cannot listen to the radio. I am therefore cut off from the world and have to decide what the Nazi reports reveal between the lines. That is indeed bloody little concerning the progress of the Allies. Anyhow, there is no hope of an early end to the war – breaching German border fortifications has given way to a static war of position. In the east the Polish uprising has finally been defeated and it is, however worthy the motives may have been, a shameful spectacle which the Allies[1] have performed in view of Hitler's scandals. Even if there is no hope of strengthening German resilience in view of the heavy losses of territory with its associated immense loss of food, factory production, it is enough to overhaul a propaganda machine which astonishingly has not yet run out of steam. That is all that I can say for now, and say anymore until I can get the necessary rectifier for the radio. Nowadays that counts as a miracle for an established inhabitant, and would be pure magic if achieved by a newcomer after only three weeks.

In the meantime, my big boss, the Regional Councilor, busily preaches about National Socialism, mainly within his circle, and against Bolshevism, plutocracy and Judaism, exactly as I am used to hearing from Hitler's narrow-minded crawlers. And I have become one of his employees!

I could sabotage his business! And agitate among the staff of the district authorities against the state and the movement! I, the man with the new curriculum vitae, the supposedly full-blooded Aryan candidate inspector! The Chief Inspector has to go to south Tyrol on a four-week long accounting course on Saturday, but not by military order, no, rather by order of the Party. Three other office slaves will waltz in attendance so there should be no obstacles on the way for my office sabotage.

I have to thoroughly revise my earlier opinion of a sheep in wolf's clothing as I have discovered further troubling signs of the Regional Councilor's friendship with Hitler. The devil only knows why he thought of getting me for his office, even though I made known my views against the Party, and would give my notice if he expected me to retrospectively join his club. Forced entry into the D.A.F.[2] would be moral torment, but I would try to keep out of the N.S.V. in the face of any wishes from the high and mighty gentlemen.

Otherwise, in the end, nothing will remain of my real existence other than my shaky body with its posh sounding name. Only the papers locked in my briefcase will show my true origin. For it can very well happen, as one of my friends from Leipzig mentioned when we left, that reinstatement in the original Jewish community will become impossible. That is a danger not to be underestimated should the war go on for too long.

While our old friends, both the Leopold and Freiherr ones, write nostalgic letters bemoaning our separation, Alemannic Bludenz appears particularly reserved. It is hard to know whether it can be put down to the well-founded and traditional distrust of all Germans or is due to a fear under the prevailing circumstances of having to give something that one wants to eat oneself to friendly people. Maybe they know that much good will has been "burned up" since 1938.

Still, one cannot deny a striking egotism in the people of Bludenz and a certain arrogance, which even occasionally goes out over the requisite tact. The Saxon dialect of Leipzig is in many ways hard to digest – still it is more accessible than the local Alemannic, which is why I foresee I cannot establish lasting relationships in this part of the country. Some speak of the difficulties of integration while others, like the well-bred Regional Councilor and his Chief Inspector, refuse to make a courtesy visit.

I keep my hands free, also when facing high and mighty officials. They only have my curriculum vitae together with our valuable new genealogical tree and can make play with this balderdash if they want. And if they don't want to and push me off Mount Olympus again, well, then I have not lost much.

October II, 1944

If a Jew, together with his wife and child, slips through the Stapo clutches and instead of entering the executioners' gas chambers in Poland or Theresienstadt lands the post of candidate inspector in Group VI of the district administration of his holiness Adolf the Almighty, what is he? A rebel? A renegade? A deserter?

I can pride myself on the fact that I am not labelled with any of these three commendable titles. My friends, who have known me for years, will testify that I have never stopped being the revolutionary Jew, and my old calling as agitator against everything that calls itself Fascism still makes for the highest honor.

And those who know nothing about me other than that I am Kurt Freiherr know therefore all the better that precisely this Freiherr, whose true identity would mean danger for him and his family, is in a situation where he could rally like-minded people around him, even create them. This is true even for the Regional Councilor's office, where the walls have ears. I proceed in the hope, that unconquerable hope, that the day of our return to being ourselves and to our community is not far off.

If, however, this Jew were one day to be told to present himself, on such and such a day and at such and such a time, with the necessary personal and military papers, with deregistration from the residence and economic offices, together with his belongings, according to the Tyrol and Vorarlberg National Defense Emergency Act; and if this Jew examines his suitability for service, despite the fake Military Pass, and considers this desirable, so as not to make his wife and child suspicious to the henchmen, and allows himself to be sent to fight against the Allies, what would he be? A coward, a traitor? Oh, no, an unfortunate who, so as not to lose sight of his beloved, could not even take the path of the deserter.

Indeed, this danger threatens. The first 80 men from Bludenz, among them officials from the district administration, were called up to emergency service last Saturday by the noble Regional Councilor. They had to pack their bags and report at a given time and at a certain place, from where they were transported first to Gassenasse, including my dear Chief Inspector Kühnl, and a decent sub-manager from the district cash office. The former thinks the three week "course" is truly important but does not realize that no leader would consider such a short exercise. He takes luggage in which civilian clothing can be sent home. It seems to me there will be no return from Gassenasse, not even for one discharged as unsuitable for military service. Everyone will be called up, I too, Kühnl notified me. So, I too. With the false Military Pass. I will have to march in Hitler's columns. Well, well, the Aryan Freiherr, acting his most sacred convictions.

So that is our route to freedom. Thank you.

October 13, 1944

I have handed over all the material evidence the Regional Councilor demanded of me, faithfully and fairly, such as the freshly baked curriculum vitae, the descriptive enumeration of our parents and grandparents, together with all the paraphernalia that fully legalize employees in Hitler's administration. School reports, a commercial teacher diploma and a certificate of formal qualifications, I have declared to have been burned in the bombings, and have presented, as proof of my truthful information, the forged, life-saving Military Pass, as I had done once before on May 27, when the Chief Government Inspector showed a lively interest in me.

And look, this time too, he has not cottoned on to the forgery of this vital document, but has rather made short notes on its contents, including my being unfit for military service, and passed on my scribblings to the secretary for inclusion in the personnel files. For the Regional Councilor to research the accuracy of my information is pretty unlikely, but if he does, it is potentially dangerous. Should that happen, I have cleverly filled out the family tree so that its branches touch places that are either occupied by the Allies or in danger zones which have been evacuated. Yes, even the religious beliefs of our ancestors refer to a Catholic area. These calculations were a headache for me, but I believe that they have a hint of authenticity, especially with a few questions left unanswerable by the lack of the necessary documents.

O quae mutatio rerum![3] What has become of you, dear Walter Leopold? Yes, that is what I ask myself, and on many an evening, my wife and I look at each other for several minutes and find it difficult to grasp what fate has handed us.

Only two years ago as darkness fell we were creeping with our bits and pieces from the first sanctuary to the next, lying low and waiting for the Gestapo, or equally significant, fearing running into the arms of Aryan and Jewish acquaintances. We relied on the little food that sympathetic people might let us have, and a shelter in which every sound or loud word might betray us. We remember how our flight from the Gestapo deportation nets began, glancing around, always holding our child by the hand, making it through many difficult moments nursing suicidal intentions, until our latest friends made their home available to us, not suspecting that our departure would also be theirs.

The night between December 3 and 4 with a burned roof over our heads, we were plunged cruelly into the open under a new name, and thereby towards secret ways to freedom. The Military Pass which I had made opened the arms of the Nazi hordes for us.

Accommodation with complete strangers

Hospitable people

Registration at reception centers

References for food ration cards

Money from the government for small articles of clothing

Enrolment at the police registration center without certificate of previous place of residence

A move into a furnished room

"Personal registration" through the Party

A letter of recommendation of the N.S.V.

Registration at the employment exchange

Freedom to move through a departure certificate

A trip to Garmisch

A letter of application for a public administration department in Bregenz/Vorarlberg

An introduction to Bludenz

The purchase of an identity card

Schooling for our child

Further successful negotiations with the labor office

A move into a lovely Leipzig apartment

Consent of the Regional Councilor for Bludenz position after a hopeless and fearful wait

A move to our hometown of choice

Full legalization as an official employee

Danger of conscription among Hitler's men...

That in shorthand is the mysterious way fate has led us over the last two years.

That is why we constantly have to look at each other and ask whether this is reality or an illusion. Three more Jews were able to escape Hitler's representatives and they saved themselves. How is a poor tormented brain supposed to grasp and digest all that?

Nevertheless, what have you become, Walter Leopold? You escaped the danger of slaughter in a miraculous way, but also escaped your community, for who knows how long, and are stuck among servile Hitler cronies! You have lost your old, honest name and changed. You walk on forbidden paths as a man known to be unknown and yet an officially confirmed Aryan – a pure Jew and at the same time a full-blooded race comrade of the Jew bashers!

Over in America your brothers may be mourning you, imagining you lost with the masses of Jews transported to Poland and assassinated there, your mother mourning her eldest, without my being able to lighten her heart and by saying: "He lives, your son and brother, they live, his wife and his child, but they no longer bear our name. They pine for the members of their community with whom they remain connected to their very last breath. They yearn for a single Jew, in whose eyes their soul might be reflected, and whose voice speaks their language and through whose old heart their blood pulsates. An eternal Jew, only with his eyes, his soul and his bon esprit. We have remained loyal to you through all our madness and journeying."

The heavens have watched over us and guided us as protected Jews. We know that and want to live to see our rebirth. For we hate the renegade who welcomes his rebirth in apostasy. And yearn for our community.

26 WE HAVE BECOME LONELY AGAIN

As Walter tries to understand the culture and politics of the Vorarlberg region in the Austrian Alps, he travels as if a tourist behind enemy lines. He cherishes two fundamental purposes: the survival of his family and agitation against Hitler. More than ever, he wishes to be the revolutionary helping to undermine Hitler and lead these people to freedom. With his German Jewish eyes he sizes up the local residents and manages to turn a few people against Hitler through subversive gastronomy – reminding them in great detail of how well they once ate and lived.

But the most outstanding feature of his existence comes from breaking free from all racial discrimination. No longer perceived as a Jew, he gains access to the life denied to him since the Nazis took power, and before. Even without his title of Herr Doktor, he gains the respect of his co-workers, something he always believed is his due.

October 16, 1944

Yesterday we made our first excursion by train. The barometer was low as is usual here in Bludenz, but the clouds dissolved, soon clearing from the Rätikon and a warm summer sun threw light into the valley. Mockel greeted it with jubilation because it helped fulfil her wish to go on a train ride once again. In that, she is like her father, who was mad about train journeys like a hunting dog for stalking, and becomes excited even today when he sees the smoke of a locomotive. Not even the strain of our long journey, which is now a month back, could spoil this taste she has inherited, and already on the way to the station she showed her exuberance, wriggled with delight in her window seat as the electric locomotive started with its buzzing sound, and waved to everyone, even dogs and cows.

The mountain wall of the lower valley of the Ill River passed by, first the Hohe Frassen, then the Walser mountains. The view into the Walser valley opened up and the scenery changed in quick succession like a revolving stage, in which the Frassen stood a bit crooked and showed their narrow, north-facing, steeply falling center. They dominate the lower Ill Valley far into the distance, trembling next to the Arlberg snow in the reflection of the river, which thunders on, only to channel its way a little further on to Feldkirch through an arch in the rock, whereas the train runs into the station below the castle.

The drop of 100 meters brings a considerable rise in temperature, and a gentle breeze streams towards us from the Rhine valley. We hardly dared believe our eyes when we saw swallows swooping joyfully around, and we draped our coats over our arms.

Feldkirch is a charming little town, much more delightful than we remembered it from our last holiday 17 years ago. Modern, wide, villa-lined avenues alternate with alleys with half-timbered buildings; steep cliffs and charming hillocks look down on the old squares whose traditional atmosphere one can easily smell but describe only with difficulty. They put the searcher for words in front of the same insoluble task as an ancient staircase, a passageway through a house or a medieval shop corner, where an onion aroma on the way to the wine cellar, herbs and old wood all of a sudden produce, as if by magic, a certain atmosphere that leaves a shaky recollection of earlier centuries. It happened to me again as we strolled under the oriel windows, the colored-glass panes and the pergolas, where old fountains stood, the tower clock chimed, the pigeons cooed. Hearing the bells, we walked up to the inn, The Lion, of which we had happy memories for its good food.

This time too everything he put before us was superb, despite rationing and slightly smaller portions, and the sun in Feldkirch played on the most delightful consoles with which this house was decorated, perhaps since the time of its first owners, the great-grandparents. Anneliese too is singularly enthusiastic. She pushes through the narrowest passages, flits through the pergolas, and creeps into every church which she sees is open, becomes quiet as a mouse, questions us with a look and wants to return when we have only just gone outside.

Catholic churches have an effect on me like irresistible magnets, as I grew up in a Catholic neighborhood. That they should affect our child too, for whom they are a novelty – that is a truly astonishing development, and points to a mystical disposition. It has bestowed on me many an uplifting moment, but also times of depression.

This is how we experienced our reunion with Feldkirch, almost dreamily wonderful, disconnected from the turmoil of this world and exempted from all the sorrow that we have endured since our last journey. As we mounted the many steps up to the Antenzberger Inn, which like most guesthouses now accommodates Hitler's wounded, and looked down on the charming little town, our eyes met more than once, questioning the reality of our survival. Then we looked down to the Ill which here makes its way, straight as an arrow, towards the Rhine.

It is a crossing, but also the strongly guarded frontier with Switzerland, the land that knows nothing of tyranny, war or persecution of Jews. Freedom beckons on the other side of the Ill, over the guarded hills, where the dazzling trees of the High Canton, bathed in sunlight, send greetings. That is exactly why it is totally unattainable. If, at night and in fog we – no, that would be too daring with the child. The guards shoot immediately in the direction of the faintest noise, we were told, and to take this risk would be irresponsible after the unheard-of gift which the heavens have sent us by directing us to Bludenz. Thankful for our fate, we sit down in a clearing where the panorama of the Appenzell mountains is visible, between Meister Sinchs, as if he did not want to be seen, yet recognizable by his pointed hat.

The way back showed Feldkirch from the other side; the asphalted mountain road lies opposite sheltered, crooked little houses, against whose rocky foundations the milky-blue waters of the Ill surge, after it has split the colorful little town into two.

We have a coffee without milk but with a bitter sweetener in one of the comfortable bars and stroll once more through the alleys and squares to the station so that our home in Bludenz is reached before nightfall, though in an overcrowded train. There is a frightening crush between the platforms which are besieged on fine Sundays, in the morning from Feldkirch to Bludenz and in the evening by people from Bludenz who like us want to go back to Bludenz. For we too are at home in Bludenz and can undertake a long journey every week.

This time it was Feldkirch. Dreams become reality.

October 24, 1944

The *Vorarlberger Tagblatt,* the official Nazi journal of the districts Bregenz, Domlin and Bludenz, and at this time the only reading matter for the not exactly knowledge-hungry Vorarlbergers, is overflowing with extraordinary jokes. "Do you want that again?" is the latest from the text signed by Hans Anderle and begins as follows:

"You wake up tomorrow and over the loudspeaker comes the slimy voice of a Jew, provided that you have a loudspeaker."

"On your breakfast table lies the daily paper produced by the Jews, provided you can afford the pennies for the newspaper."

"On the bread you are eating, the coffee, the butter, the marmalade... provided that you are in the situation of being able to breakfast so opulently..."

Hans Anderle continues:

"You need a doctor – your medical insurance doctor is a Jew. You need a lawyer – he is a Jew. Your children have Jews for teachers. The book you are reading comes from a Jew. There are Jews in the theatre, the cinema, nothing but Jews. Every advertisement, which screams at you in the street, is evidence of Jewish interest. In the cars which pass you by, obese Jews with their tarted-up women. You, however, go on foot to the dole..."

Hans Anderle resumes:

"Is that exaggerated? On the contrary. We older people have all experienced it, how awful the picture is. Do you want that again? No! Wherever you seize, seize the Jews..."

"Therefore fight, fight, fight and work, work, work, with everything that hand and brain can give. For it would be far, far worse if we do not hold out. That must not happen and will not happen. It cannot happen if we do not want it to happen!"

Anderle concludes shrewdly:

"It cannot be because it is not permitted to be."

Now, dear *Vorarlberger Tagblatt*, I want to help you with the necessary correction, should you have sufficient courage to publish it with small amendments in exactly the same place where Anderle spun his tale:

You need a doctor? How come you need a doctor? A German does not need a doctor for he knows the cure, and that is steely toughness. Should you, however, conduct yourself in such an un-German manner as to become ill, then your doctor will also become like steel. His Sieg Heil attitude contains the same deterrent as the healing uniform of the Führer.

You need a lawyer? My, you must be nuts. Power comes before right. Therefore, take Brown Shirt power. Your children no longer have teachers, for the schools have long been bombed out, and the teachers have fallen into either dishonor or out of favor.

Books are only known by name, and if you take up some reading matter, it stinks of a Brown Shirt mass. The theatres are burned down or closed, and only in the cinemas do the permanently victorious newsreels make a noise. There is no advertising, firstly because there is no paper, secondly because the printers can no longer go to press because they themselves are being pressed, and thirdly because advertising is reserved for Goebbels' agency.

Was that exaggerated? On the contrary. These are sober sketches, as inspired by the Nazi tyranny and Nazi wasteland. We older people, who have known better times, have experienced how appalling the picture presented of Hitler is:

"Wherever you seize, you are to seize the Jews..." And they seized the Jews and carried them off and slaughtered them.

Do you want that again?

No.

Therefore fight, fight, fight against Hitler and his executioners, with everything that hand and brain can give. For things will get much, much worse if we follow his call and command and hold out.

But that must not happen. It must not happen that a whole generation goes to ruin because of Hitler. And it will not happen if we do not want it to happen.

Instead, one day there lies, on your sumptuous breakfast table, a daily paper edited by many minds, and with reading matter you once more enjoy your coffee and roll in perfect peace.

Your medical insurance doctor or doctor for the poor is once more the much sought-after Jewish medic. You can again search for a

Jewish lawyer, send the children to the school of your choice, to competent teachers.

November 4, 1944

Yes, even the people of Bludenz have become cheerful. Despite the friendliness they show even to the unwelcome intruder from the old Reich, they are cool, reserved and suspicious, and they keep their hands closed also where they could offer help without any personal sacrifice or hardship. These are no longer the earlier merry and hospitable people of Bludenz, they are the assimilated Eastern brand of Hitler's era. National Socialism has taken the warmth from their hearts and pumped in soul-changing politics and debased them into ambivalent natures. Ambivalent, in that they despise the Prussians, the Russians and the "loudmouthed" strangers and worship Hitler.

They want to remain genuine Austrians, despite still being proud to be allowed to die as members of the German Territorial Army and the Nazi pigs. They mistrust the Germans of the old Reich and have joined them under the banner of the swastika. They defiantly shout a good day or evening to each other, but they ooze with enthusiasm as soon as the marches and songs of the soldiers of the motherland in chopping-block rhythm stamp through the streets. That is the conflict which is eating away their native roughness, the drag of universal Germans, the mentally lazy, arse-kissing, who hang a picture of Hitler in their windows and dig tunnels into the mountains so that townsfolk can find safe shelter.

To be sure they are sweet and friendly to us, the people of Bludenz, and do not let us feel that we are immigrants. Still we feel lonely, alone with our voluntary, unalterable mission to tear the fabric of Hitler's lies and to make his despicable deeds apparent wherever misplaced hopes of a reversal may awaken. We have become lonely again. We have recognized that there are a few willing to have insight or the few malcontents who, seeing their own downfall with their muddled ideology and therefore are willing to scold Hitler. However, we also see a few of the people who have shaken off the

Nazi yoke, who curse his private war, but also curse the Jews who they say would have impoverished the German people, and yet at the same time preach holding out to the end.

Hardly are they one step along the way to enlightenment than they fall back two steps, throw up their hands and run away. They run because they are scared, or the Nazi cult is already too firmly imprinted. Many of them at least attempt a platonic opposition, and want to demonstrate that they do not want to be counted among the usurping Nazi vermin. So, when officials greet them with "Heil Hitler", they respond in defiance with the usual civic greeting, even if they frequently, either willingly or by force, wear Hitler's symbol.

Others who dare not summon this modest civil courage raise a hand and say "good morning" or whisper the Hitler greeting accompanied by a bow. The first signs of a breaking away are there, and if well nourished, will one day grow into a revolt. But for now, they are just beginnings, and as such not yet capable of bearing fruit.

For the time being, I am therefore the prominent revolutionary, still alone in a large space, seconded by a few like-minded people in the Regional Council Office, officials and employees of the School of Administration with poor or misguided political ideas. To broaden their outlook and to turn their thoughts in the direction where things can take hold – that is my job and my aim.

My innate ability to adapt and willingness to help, and my spontaneous ability to adopt the Alemannic idiom, combined with a sense of humor which did not run aground during years of suffering, of fear and of poverty, these are the tools I use to climb up again. This is not only an abstract exercise, for I honestly practice every weekend with my wife and child climbing into the mountains around Bludenz so that our diminished strength may grow again, and both our bodily and mental well-being may improve.

Oxygen brings renewal to the blood, and the pallor from nights in bunkers in big cities has given way to a healthy complexion and light tan. Hollow cheeks are a memory, one's step is winged and one's head is light. Thus, works the magical elixir of the mountains and the high-altitude sun, and it is indeed wonderful to be at home there. Whether we use the free Saturday afternoon for a short trip to the Muntiker, at the feet of which the little peaceful town dreams, or go to the fairy-like "Schass", or scamper like boisterous children up the steep slopes of the Rhatikon with its alpine meadows and springs, or on rain-free Sundays climb higher to the Tschengla, to the Mutterberg, or like today, a slow ride on the Montafon railway to the Sand and then on to the Jagerberg: every walk, even the shortest, becomes an experience and a source of strength. The Queen Zuntz greets us on the opposite side, sparkling in majestic white, the grandee of the highest point, with a sugar coating. Down to the Schum and Tschaggenau a refreshing fragrant wind blows on the high-altitude path, here and there shaking the trees a little, trees that are clothed in a hundred autumn colors.

We sprawl in the November sun and see that the thermometer registers 36 degrees while all around us snow covers the paths and mountain huts. The Drei Türme rise to dizzying heights out of fields of ice and... the valley sends the sound of rushing water, which rises up to us like seductive, ethereal music. There was a disappointment today as the reservoir being guarded by police and gendarmes denies us the choicest view of the huts, however, this is somewhat made up for by an exquisite meal given us by the works kitchen. This was altogether sufficient for climbing a few steps higher up, where despite a strict ban announced on posters everywhere, we photograph to our heart's content and scan the surroundings with binoculars.

The Vandauer Steinwand rises up jaggedly, dominated by the Jubla, from the distance the Frassen, Muttersberg, Valerberge, and Elsespitze greet us, and opposite the top of the Arlberg range looms out behind the Idenkopf, and in the south the Mittagspitze rises high towards the sun. A fairytale world in the Vorarlberg!

A year ago, as refugees, frightened beggars hiding in secrecy, we were dependent on donations of enemies of Hitler willing to make sacrifices – today we are happy wanderers in a paradise of snow-covered mountains, and tomorrow a new week begins in the Regional Council Office. A mysterious story! I think of it, though still not quite without fear.

November 15, 1944

November 9 and 11, the day I entered Buchenwald and the day we went underground, have passed again, those days whose horrors are preserved in our memories. We nourish hope of liberation and salvation among rebellious and frightened contemporaries. But still living among the oppressors and blood suckers, fear of punishment sends shivers shooting sky high.

Now the yearning of the poor remains unheard, and has given way ever more to silent resignation. The war has turned into a chemical disease of the final spirit, and the bestiality and Hitler's malice result in political dysentery and advances in the entrails of ailing Europe, which the Allies made bold to predict will finally be liberated this year. Although they have raised their heads over Germany's border walls and have bored their strong fingers into her rump in various places, although the Russians are at the gates of Germany and are triggering the impotent rage of the Nazis in East Prussia, nevertheless Central Europe remains a human prison for hundreds of millions, who according to Hitler's will and command should die if the Bastille is stormed.

He wants to offer them all up in his bloodlust and his fear of being hanged. With the help of his mumbo-jumbo propaganda man, transforming this fear into the love of the motherland of his "sworn community, family of peoples", he calls upon them to trumpet up the "home guard" and even if his announcements after the last rites might not safeguard his salvation, he calls on the women and children to throw themselves against the enemy. In this way, cleverly and by force, he tries to fool the downtrodden, the most gullible and stupid masses with the thought of freedom, and offers them the Japanese *hara-kiri* as a good option. He uncovers ever new "Allied horrors", drains the countries, lets cities collapse, gradually depopulates the "dear, holy Fatherland", announces that old fogies and the sick have willingly volunteered for the state protection battalions, and attempts now, as I have always feared, with Nazi thoroughness, to make sure that none of his chums or their families should survive the shame.

Five years of war and still no end to this scourge of mankind! How much longer? Yes, indeed, how much longer, one must ask? Unfortunately, I dare say few in Germany and the looted countries will live to experience the answer to this question.

For me and my wife and child, November 9 and 11 have not changed. The difficult path on which I marched, or was actually chased, into the concentration camp on November 11, 1938 led after years of confusion and searching to Bludenz. Here I have applied myself with much pleasure to my dangerous agitation against Hitler and Hitler's comrades, but not with the clumsiness which has already brought thousands of like-minded to their downfall and the gallows. Rather I disguise the agitation with my own personal humor, with ambiguous jokes, each immediately understandable, yet not sufficiently obvious, so that I can dodge the pressure.

Where this method does not work, there remains the last and most powerful technique, appropriate even for hardboiled heroes who kowtow to the cult, namely the enumeration of all epicurean delights, ranging from non-rationed butter rolls to fat-dripping roast chicken, with wine and a fat cigar on the way to a carefree afternoon nap. Saliva collects visibly in the mouths of the brothers when I escort them in their thoughts through well-lit streets to the patisseries, and have them served with chocolate and whipped cream and real coffee, buy fresh and fragrant nougat slices, pralines and Cohen chocolate, and then seduce them with long missed Luther rolls.

Until now no one in the office has been strong enough to resist my temptations and give precedence to "the love of the Führer" over their bodily longing. Yes, I could very well coax each of the many assiduous Party comrades with stronger capabilities to throw his safety pin in the toilet for a hundred cigarettes, and I hope, if once again one of the much-praised comrade-in-arms evening gatherings takes place, to reinforce my area of operations until it can no longer be tolerated.

I am still a long way from this goal. My call-up to the "riflemen of the Tyrol District", the private company of the well-fed Nazi Gauleiter Hofer,[1] looms. The people from the first military training course have returned, and tell of the hardships which the old warriors, sick men, yes, even invalids, were exposed to without undergoing a doctor's examination. They have had to make camp in damp barracks, in which the light constantly goes out. There are poor washing opportunities, pig food out of dirty cooking utensils, Nazi instruction, courses, exercises, field training in rain and snow and marches through ankle deep mud or over snow-covered mountains until the "volunteers" have water running out of their masks and shoes. Wear and tear of one's clothes and shoes and a written declaration of voluntary entry into the Home Guard with the subsequent swearing of an oath to the beloved Führer, those are the joys which at this point await you, exempted Freiherr.

Sabotage or reporting to be ill is futile and could lead the all too curious to investigate our past and extinguish the lives of the three of us, without my being able to give lasting service to tormented mankind.

One can say: Await a favorable opportunity to take the bull by the horns and throw it to the ground. For all this I must not miss the most opportune moment, so that call-up helps me avoid the feared danger of being militarily drafted, being found not suffering from heart troubles and finally being checked for my service availability, whereby a resourceful military doctor could possibly make me undergo a closer inspection of my penis. I have figured out the excuse that I was operated on as a boy for paraphimosis,[2] and am still taking the necessary drug for the stimulation of my heart activity.

My anti-Nazi work may be like the bearded and kaftan-robed Polish Jew who had to listen to fierce attacks from Jew-bashers in a train and to his friend's question answered, "I did not give any hint that I understood." Open resistance would be one-armed and complete nonsense, so I must use the method of the kaftan-robed. I will go to the training if called upon, as long as our guardian angel continues to look after us despite a totally inconceivable separation from my wife, child and bed for three weeks. Between all these considerations, fears and prospects, a feeling of happiness comes over me now and then sparked by what I have been through up to now – our good fortune quite unimaginable to the uninitiated.

We are not only, at least outwardly, enjoying total freedom of movement again, but also after being chased and ostracized for more than a decade, we have been recognized as respectable "national comrades". Since moving to Bludenz we have peace from bombs, fire and hunger, and can make whatever use we want of our odds and ends, as far as we were able to save them. My precious library, for which I am much starved, is unfortunately irreplaceable and is gone forever, but my optical devices, microscope, telescope and cameras can once more be used for their purpose. Only the radio must unfortunately remain silent.

We and our golden child resemble our old selves again. We focus on hiking as far as the weather conditions permit, and feel really good in our humble home. But we would like to see other Jews again. Jews in flesh and blood. Jews with whom we can think, feel and speak. Jews who have heart, soul and spirit. For Jews are irreplaceable and it is a comfort to us that at least we are Jews. We are – who knows for how long – the only Jews with whom we live. But we miss others even more. More than ever the Jewish prayers echo. It is good that this consciousness is newly awakened and strengthened, but it is difficult, as a conscious and not submissive Jew, to take the way of our enemies. That they do not see us, and even more importantly do not discover us, but still remain watchful. Thanks be to God!

Yet the longing for Jews and the people's freedom remains.

27 AGITATE, UNTIL THE PIPS SQUEAK

Walter weaves together his multiples roles – father, husband, Jew, Aryan, auditor, anti-Nazi agitator – into a decent life, one that he cherishes with some pride. But with his growing self-confidence comes danger as he uses his skills to turn his co-workers against Hitler. He believes he is smarter and more politically aware than all those around him. Usually, he thinks about every word he utters and to whom he utters it. Now he may be slipping into reckless cockiness and closer to the arms of the Gestapo.

At the same time, Walter assumes yet another role – that of a witness to war crimes. He is sizing up the Nazi officials he intends to help prosecute after the war ends, should he live that long.

November 19, 1944

The sun battles with winter. The latter has sent its heralds for a whole week now, shrouded the not yet leafless trees in thick cotton wool and laid a tall snow cover over the countryside around Bludenz. But the sun finally won and turned the shroud into slush, which squelched over shoes and dirtied clothes. The icing sugar covering only remains on the mountains and when the sun licks it away, and sets with flaming red colors, it is an astonishing experience. From the Silvretta to the Santis, there's an array of snowy peaks, an invigorating fresh wind blows in the valley, and a few hundred meters higher the snow crunches underfoot.

We have had ourselves sturdy shoes prescribed by the Economy Department, as one has to have everything prescribed in the blessed German Reich – not only medicines, which in any case have not been obtainable for years. I landed a good pair of Italian shoes and had them fixed with nails for mountains, while my wife had to walk her feet sore. She and Annelie could only get fitted out by means of a trip to Feldkirch. The child now clatters on thick hobnailed boots too and is proud to be allowed to do the same as her comrades. The officials in charge needed to be pressed for a long time to gratify our wishes and made the identity card from Leipzig the premise for our acquisition, as our card did not offer sufficient points. When the waiting became too boring for me and I turned to the head of the Economy Department, who works a floor above me, he immediately gave me a hearing on display of a motorcycle license as a supporting reference for issuing additional articles.

Saucepans, crockery, frying pans and many other things which we could once call our own in abundance, but now urgently needed, were purchased. Even a second alarm clock found its way into our dwelling, as one such example "under the prevailing circumstances" must remain the dream of all without alarm clocks! As an added bonus the watchmaker repaired – yes, that never happened in Leipzig! – two of my pocket watches which for a year and a day had lived in retirement with a broken spring, and asked no more than three paper marks and 50 Nazi-German metal Reich pennies for each, while he chased to the devil other petitioners who undoubtedly needed their one and only watch more urgently.

Whether my position in the district office fostered a greater readiness to comply or there was something heart-warming in my eyes, I cannot tell. In any case pretty much everything I undertook worked, even the seemingly impossible. My experience therefore moved me to pester my Economy Department colleague for underwear, shirts, stockings, a petticoat for my wife and a coat for Annelie. Now, however, he pulls a sour face and becomes abrupt. Wait, he will come back to it, because I have based the requests for my own person on my forthcoming conscription to the home guard, and for my wife and child with the explanation that their clothing were satisfactory for a lowland climate but did not correspond to the climate of a mountain region.

Not everything can go smoothly. Somewhere in a corner of my soul a goblin has rumbled on for a long time about possible danger. It suddenly jumped into my face yesterday when my wife brought a love letter from the State Tax Office in Leipzig into my office, in which I was requested to hand over various tax declarations, in particular with regard to my income of the last years. There remains no other option for me than to do a new thing and let Leipzig know that since 1939 I suffer from heart and intestinal illnesses and consequently have been unable to work and that my wife has also been without any income. I will add that I met our meagre living costs since the spring of this year through drawing on our small savings, but these ran out in the New Year and therefore, encouraged by a distinct improvement in my health, I accepted the request of the Regional Councilor in Bludenz to enter into his service. I will corroborate these statements by referring to records of the Authority for Front Maintenance and the Labor Office in Leipzig. Whether it will work remains an open question. If the slaves don't allow themselves to be led down the garden path, I will have to expect all sorts of trouble.

The appointment which the SS gynecologist, flag-bearer Prugel – nomen est omen[1] – given to my wife after the expiry of her four-week dispensation, set me thinking about my forthcoming conscription into the trigger-happy Tyrol Home Guard, and it weighs heavily on my mind. Truthfully, after my 46 years on this blessed Mother Earth I still wait for the sun of one year in which I could justifiably claim: the agony has passed from me and my beloved ones. Clever people will sum up that in time one becomes accustomed even to chemical evil. Today, that is the only possibility to grow old. Maybe, but I would like to grow older than the evil.

Should the Nazi dogs one day cause my downfall, then I will hold my head high and think that during the time I was in the service of the District Office, I not only worked with my utmost strength but also to my heart's content. Yesterday the local head of police was the desired victim. In answer to his discreet question when peace might come, I gave the answer: "When Hitler and his faithful followers are tied to a V2 and shot out into the universe, from where they could not possibly return."

He stormed off, covering his ears. I do not think I need to fear him anymore, as he is friendly with my female colleague, who not only sympathizes with me, but also enthuses a lot about me to him. I have given free rein to the admonition of the Chief Inspector to speak out frankly under any circumstances, and I let fly so that the blessed timbers of the district administration tremble.

Tomorrow I am to take myself off to the DAF[2] and put my name on the list of members, as is demanded from all employees in official capacities. If I refuse, then I'm in trouble. As soon as the district leadership gets wind of my resistance, my where-from and my where-to will be examined according to swastika regulations, and the lives of my wife and child will be endangered. As corpses we can no longer be of service to justice, decency or freedom.

Therefore, I will go to the DAF. I will also do the Home Guard service but not with the words the foundlings have to repeat in chorus. It will be the third oath of my life. The first I swore in 1916, when I was forced into the blue dress of William by the Grace of God.[3] His majesty relieved me of that oath in time. The second one I swore at my matriculation at Heidelberg University, an oath which declared allegiance to that statues of the state which I kept faithfully except for several lapses during demonstrations. The third I will swear with real fervor, an inner fervor that I did not manage with the others, and if it is to be fulfilled, I will bring my reminiscences to a close.

Hail to you, Adolf Hitler!

December 3, 1944

I cannot end the present day without thinking of that night that became our ordeal by fire. On this evening a year ago, we were sitting with our friends in Leipzig who provided us with the last shelter, chatting happily and not suspecting what the coming night would bring us. We did not foresee or fear any disaster, indeed we strongly warded off the thought because its realization would be the end of our days. For were our friend's house to turn to rubble and ashes, to whom could we turn, where could we disappear once more without falling into the hands of the Gestapo executioners? Who would feed us, who would have the courage after the sad escapades and experiences during our voluntary exile, or be willing to make the sacrifice and give shelter and support to three imploring creatures? Nobody!

We knew all along that a void would open up after this shelter, and we trembled at the thought of such a possibility. Especially since the food donors gradually pulled away; our child, our oh so unassuming Anneliesel, did not complain when next to her dry piece of bread she saw a thickly buttered slice but was not allowed to reach for it. To see one's child go hungry yet not complain, that is the worst that fate can burden one with. This was our hardest test. Everything else was not so difficult, even if not without danger. It was risky when I strolled carefully along the streets to search for new possibilities for the support of my loved ones, to get hold of money or bread, to look for old friends or make necessary calls in telephone booths banned to Jews. I was always watching out for sudden encounters with familiar faces, as indeed happened a few times, fortunately without apparent result. Often, I brought home what I had scratched together over a few days; often, however I came back with an empty bag and saw the sad look on my wife's face and the pale cheeks of our child. Yes, it was a severe test.

And then came that night, that night of terror, fear of death, water and fire. That night, which robbed us of our last place of shelter and so many essentials of life but presented us with the gift of freedom and bread. That night both incomprehensible and miraculous, that night which struck even our enemies blind and turned many of them into friends. We did not know it, we did not dare to know, to hope, while we escaped from the flames, wandering through the cellars, bombed out, until the butcher's wife offered us shelter. In that way we were once more reluctantly pushed back among people, ate, drank and slept again but trembled with every bite and sip, and in our shallow sleep groaned at the terrible thought of being unmasked.

That took six hours. And today? Today we eat, drink and sleep in our own home again, even if not in our own way and in our own beds. But it is our modest and beloved home in Bludenz. And we have no need to beg, either for food or money. For I sit in the Administrative District Municipal Examination Office in Bludenz and earn enough to keep material worries at bay. I would be ungrateful if I were to forget the benevolence of fate, and complacently stroke of the bountiful Nazi hands.

No, we remain as we were, the enemy of the butchers of the peoples, yes, even the child keeps alive the memory of our origin as something holy and therefore completely fragile. Even if she is fond of someone, she keeps the secret without our reminding or warning her, and only when we three are alone does she say: "Do you remember, Mutti, in Humboldtstrasse 31" or "I still remember what our proper name is". Yesterday, as she chirped a Christmas carol she had learned in school, she suddenly stopped and said: "I can also sing the 'Ma'oz Tzur song."[4]

Wounds in parents' hearts, yet at the same time melancholy joy. Annelie knows that we are not what we appear to be, and more than once she has come home from school and said with a roguish look in her eye: "Today I had to say Heil Hitler again." She does not ask about our attitude, she feels it within herself, and only once did she rebel because we refused to let her take part in Catholic religious instruction.

Annelie is deeply religious and runs into every church, although no one – certainly not us – has explained to her their purpose. Even so her spirit is deeply distressed. Not one-night passes without her crying many tears, shaking and calling out loudly. She does not sleep deeply like other children of her age, yet she still wakes up cheerfully before dawn, peeps at the mountains through a slit in the blackout curtains and reaches for her picture books and dolls which Mutti lays out ready on the table next to her NSV bed every evening so that she can converse with them as she is accustomed. She has rosy, full cheeks again, eats so that even the biggest eater has to yield to her and often romps around like a let-out puppy. She speaks often of Mäuslein and her earlier Jewish friends and has an outstanding memory. That is our child today. Our Anneliesel.

And Mutti? Well, Mutti is no less content, sees to her shopping, cooks like every good housewife, cleans, mends and washes all day long and supervises Annelie's homework. She dresses our child so that no one can get the idea she is a Jewish persona non grata, who has escaped the Stapo henchmen and has been rescued from the flames. On my free Saturday afternoons and Sundays, she comes out walking with us, dear Mutti, and then the three of us stand for several minutes always on the same spot on a path or on the country road, and silently view the mountains, our refuge. After supper, when the child is in bed, we sit together, each at our own job. We tell jokes or write letters. As midnight approaches we usually pull astonished faces. The evening was too short again, there was so much more to discuss and write. While others complain of being bored, we moan about lack of time. Tomorrow I have to go to work again, to check accounts, to prepare accounts or to create new ones and to... agitate!

Agitate, until the pips squeak, agitate so that no one in the department knows where he came from and where he belongs any longer; to make fun of the Nazis, until they bring themselves to put down their safety pins for a while; gather friends around and explain to them their stupid laws and their idiotic behavior; to imitate the "heroes" and set off a volley of laughter. Wonderful, but dangerous as in an operetta. What do I care that the Regional Councilor has microphones fitted in every telephone for the surveillance of his staff? It will no longer be any use to him. My following has become too big for him to soften me up. And it will continue to increase, that I guarantee my Regional Councilor, who is sufficiently naïve not to get wind of what I could one day protect him from.

Others are shrewder. They sniff what's cooking and have invited me to a birthday party. There was enough to drink and to eat and some in the department who conducted themselves as faithful Nazis in their duties soon lost all inhibitions, and with them the fear of listening to enemy radio stations, as if it were an old habit. They count me as one of the few chosen ones, and after they have unmasked themselves, they can no longer rise up against me.

I cannot make use of these involuntary secrets. Cursed and damned are those who feel drawn to such villainy. I want to be their friend and adviser, to lead them and, should they deserve it, to save them. I am no German hero, even less a Nazi, and for that I am all the more an aware Jew. And I act as a Jew, even in the Regional Council office. I will do the same as a "protector of the Tyrol", if it comes to that. In February I am told it will come to that. In February. But perhaps the Allies will rattle around our area in February. One can already hear the thunder of cannons on the Western front in the lowlands. The Home Guard will have to help. Me too.

One year after our liberation.

One year after the night of bombs on Leipzig.

December 6, 1944

The work which the municipal examiner and I perform proceeds without any friction. He, the routine financier, who is well versed in the double-entry technique which was established in all departments, stealing from Austria, enthusiastically explains to me the relationships among the practices, as well as unfamiliar accounting methods, and gives me practical work which I joyfully carry out. At the moment I am transferring the accounting mess of a county municipality sheet to sheet, and have real trouble in deciphering the scrawl of the municipality clerk. These are the torments of an accountant. And he is justly infuriated, for the nonsense the gentlemen in the municipality office get up to is beyond description. They record payments entering the municipal account in the outgoing column, and services provided by the municipality, substantial amounts in the business sector are not mentioned at all, while elsewhere records are entered based on fiction or fabrication.

Earlier, before Austria returned "home into the Reich," the municipal auditor acknowledged that the work was dealt with by trained officials. Since the majority of these worthies were not Nazis, let alone Party members, they were sent packing and replaced by individuals who cannot call anything their own except for their trust in Hitler based on spiritual impotence. Shepherds, cobblers and army cooks took over the offices and began to muddle through with German-Austrian heroism, yes, one of them even drew up on the order of his tanned flag-waving mayor a salary payment list with x signatures whose authenticity a superficial review showed to be unconvincing. Some of those in receipt were already off to kingdom come at the time of their signing.

Some purportedly paid salaries which the municipality princes and their supporters had to confess they used to purchase uniforms for office holders and other Hitler louts. The wish of the municipal accountant to have the Nazi rogues locked up so that they had an opportunity to get their books in order in a safe place understandably got no reply from the superior authority. From little scandals of this nature they had to expect negative publicity, and something like that is not tolerated by Hitler's chosen vassals.

My colleague and Chief Secretary, who in his distinguished position shows everything but enthusiasm for the thousand-year Reich, spits poison and bile on the Nazi scribblers. He would be ready to put a small businessman under lock and key because of meagre account-keeping, and cannot forget that the Nazi trash once drove him from his post as the administrator of a large hospital because he did not wish to sympathize with them. For a year now he has performed the Augean task of looking after the Regional Administration of Bludenz, a Sisyphean task when one considers that he has had to reconstruct all the accounting several years back and redo it. His predecessor entrusted with the revision discharged the responsibility in the most comfortable way, certifying them to the management as "exemplary" and submitted them to many other Vorarlberg beauty examinations with visible success. To wipe away these black spots in the district administration is the unpleasant and difficult task of the present municipal accountant, and I support him in this to my newly brushed up ability.

In the middle of this activity a bomb exploded this morning. I was summoned to my manager and patron as I was still not "sworn in". After all, this dreaded oath of allegiance to the master butcher of the 20th century, this official Nazi ceremony I had long believed had moldered away in the mind of the Regional Councilor. I stepped into his study, had to raise my right hand and "swear to the Führer, that, etc., etc." It turned my stomach inside out. The Regional Councilor too seemed to carry out this duty more out of obligation than of his own accord, and he followed the handshake with a long conversation, warmed by the much-desired consumption of cigarettes in which he generously let me participate.

In an odd way he was even more open and friendly today, and more interested in how I was personally than at our first meeting, after which he totally ignored me, whether on purpose or not is difficult to say. All the more so since the way he talked of my official duties suggests that he feels happy having selected me. He has not realized that, to put it mildly, he has put a political louse in his fur.

As for me, I still do not understand how an educated man with fabulous manners, with his appealing appearance and melodious voice, could dedicate himself to Hitler's rabble. Sometimes it troubles me, for I am afraid there is nothing more that can be done; I think he is still a convinced champion of Hitler's bloodhound ideology – he likes to act as Hitler's itinerant preacher.

His Chief Inspector, my patron number 2, no less reasonable than the Lord himself, has long smelled a rat, and the only thing that seems to me to be truly real about his National Socialism is his Party badge. Recently my child found such a thing in the snow. I offered the pin to my audit colleague. He politely declined and remarked that one was already one too many for him. He is right and undoubtedly to be rescued should I survive the misery. Like me he will hurry to the shameful Home Guard only in the weeks ahead, and Papa Regional Councilor has confirmed that he will assign me to the course with the reputation of the best treatment and the least effort.

While I make myself at home in my office and – apart from the misery of war – get back to a more or less normal lifestyle, while Mutti and my child enjoy their days of regained freedom in total calm, ominous news comes from our friends in Leipzig. After the series of heavy bombardments on November 30 in the inner and eastern parts of the city, the "air pirates" also reduced Leuna and Bohlen to ashes, and seriously damaged Gera, Zeitz, Jena, Merseburg and Halle. They have trembled for many hours in cellars, the poor dears, and they try to calm themselves by sending greetings to us. One of them even wants to visit us over Christmas. He was bombed out with us, got to know us and now hangs on to us with touching loyalty.

We look forward to seeing you again.

December 12, 1944

Fate has arrayed me among the bullnecked, and graced me, the full-blooded Jew, my wife and my child, and my soul, with the Hitler oath and service under the Nazis. It has placed me against my will in a position which has never been occupied by a Jew who has escaped the Gestapo and has made me play the actor until the downfall of the butcher of the peoples.

A tough test this is indeed, and a denial of self, in particular for people for whom the Jewish heritage was guide, educator, and knowledge. Instead of the Chanukah lights which once were reflected in the eyes of our child, an Advent wreath hangs from the ceiling, for the production of which we brought fir branches from our walk today. Instead of *Ma'oz Tzur*, Annelie sings the evergreen Christmas carol.

This is the second time in my life that I join in singing this Christian melody. Over more than two and a half decades ago comrades opened their mouths as we huddled in our unprotected hole in the ground around a tiny candle-lit Christmas tree under which a Jew had deposited a modest gift. Tears ran down all our cheeks, theirs because they had to celebrate their truly important family celebration far from their loved ones, and mine because I could see in my mind's eye my father and brother and the Menorah alight. Still Annelie is happy that we permit her at least this surrogate, even when we know, and the child dares occasionally to bashfully mention, that she yearns for the old traditions: "I can still sing the *Ma'oz Tzur*". Poor Annelie child!

But we don't want to complain about our fate. It has saved us from the hands of our enemies, as once the Jews before the executioners of Antiochus,[5] and through all our trials has preserved the Jewish soul and the Jewish heart. Pure and unsullied, as they were during our free confessions of our faith.

Six years ago, they discharged me from the concentration camp. Weak in body and soul, but not broken, I returned to my loved ones. But our synagogues were reduced to ashes and customs desecrated. The Sabbath was deconsecrated and thenceforth candlesticks no longer burned on our table. Since then the customs of the sacrificed human beings have gone into an unbroken decline, and further thousands upon thousands of victims will cry to the heavens until a new Juda Maccabee will come among the people.

Then the blessed Menorah will also shine in our home again to the sound of the hymn of liberation, *Ma'oz Tzur Yeshu'at*.

We have brought the fir branches with us from a walk, a walk which was so fantastically beautiful and happy that our hearts are still full of the splendor that the mountains bestow on us. We walked further along the beautiful road that leads to the Arlberg and turned right to Loruns, where rocks come out over the path and Ratikon and Drummen soar up to dizzying heights. The air was dry and fresh and smelled of snow which now glows on the mountains, and as we turned back they shone in the golden glow of the setting sun, the Vogelkopf and the little Matterhorn, open frontiers, the Elsespitze.

What a gift he made us! To three little people, alone in the wide world, he showed his sublime creation and refreshed them so that their hearts could almost burst with joy. And in this magnificent and beautiful world the bloodhounds commit murder! They defile this world and its generous creator with every means of fiendish folly!

Tomorrow I will be among them again. Work among them as their equal and agitate among them as myself. And they have confidence in me because they see that I have the strength and ability to lead them back to the right path, to make them able to see, think and feel again. And not only has the Regional Councilor crawled out of his "reserve" following my "swearing in", but even the Chief Inspector has long chats with me and has pleaded for me to give extra tutoring in Latin to his 12-year-old daughter, who attends the local high school.

He has allowed the child to come to the office with her books because I wanted to meet her before my decision. She is a lovely girl with a look that speaks of everything but Aryan descent. She could be the child of a Jewish mother and when I asked her whether we want to work together on Latin, she burst out such a jubilant yes that I could not resist saying yes either. I said yes, despite my weak Latin, despite the loss of all teaching materials, the classics and dictionaries. We will start after Christmas.

On this occasion I stayed longer than an hour. Our conversation centered almost exclusively on music, where he betrayed extensive expertise, but also told of his long-standing practical knowledge. We found ourselves with Beethoven's Fifth.

I felt he both rejoices and suffers at the sound of it. But he listens to Brahms, who is too baroque for me, and is even drawn to Bach whose work with few exceptions leaves me unmoved, because I lack the understanding of his mathematical music. Beethoven's creation, however, is an interesting undertaking, testifying to the inspiration of a fertile mind without the long stretches, fixed bars and fixed forms, with which even some outstanding composers startle and confuse. He shares this view and for that reason I can still not believe that he is a convinced supporter of Hitler – may I remain right about this!

December 23, 1944

We went to the station twice today to meet the express train from Leipzig and our friend who has promised he will visit us for Christmas. The train did not arrive, the arrivals board declaring: "Does not run until further notice". Our visitor did not arrive either. He also did not get off the passenger train from Lindau which meandered in nearly two hours later. Hilda was distressed, Annelie close to tears. I regretted the cancelation of this holiday pleasure no less, but also the absence of any news from Leipzig, and the cancellation of nearly all Christmas travel – there is no service at all on short routes, let alone the long-distance routes. Even the telegram we sent the day before yesterday to elicit a reply from our guests was, according to official Nazi information, sent as an ordinary letter and might reach the addressee for the New Year, if at all. So now it's come to that. After the disappearance of cars from public transport, the railway is falling apart too, and with it the last possibility of communication, an occurrence which has not been recorded since the beginning of postal and rail services in Germany.

Not even in 1919 did Germany sink so low, apart from the intermezzo of the General Strike.[6] Whoever has had the opportunity to queue in the Bludenz shops juggling with sales of substitutes for the past weeks could perceive that the "last reserves" were set aside for country people bringing profit, while so-called authorized beneficiaries only get to see empty shelves or at best worthless, kitschy cardboard things, wood-like woolen socks, scratchy brushes and other useless items. Those people will not have to be embarrassed by overburdening Father Christmas.

The Christmas market announced in the *Vorarlberg Daily* for today simply did not happen, but in the town masses of pilgrims from the Montafon monastery and the Walser valley huddled together, seeking their business friends, and afterwards took turns standing around the tents freezing and guzzling new wine. I could not spot a Santa Claus among them, either because he had been taken off to frighten the colleagues on the enemy side with his stick, or because he could not get any cotton wool for his traditional beard. This beard is worn with certain justification in Nazi propaganda, in which cheerless articles, lies and tidings of deliverance are supposed to scare awake the herds of people they have successfully lulled into sleep. The herald of the swastika has dug out his much-worn combat beard and as the Santa Claus of the swastika pronounces the imminent downfall of all English, Americans and Russians and the success of the new counter-attack in the West. [7]

They are supposed to have taken the enemy by surprise, to have beaten him into flight by threatening his most important positions in the area west of the Rhine. The hearts of the Nazi clowns are reveling in supreme happiness, their gobs driveling about new secret weapons which will finish off every enemy plane. Unnamed German reserves will recapture all the areas lost during the last few years; the unnamed reserves of women and girls, who have been dug out and bundled off for active military service, together with the lame and crooked. Far superior to the cursed Bolshevik gunwomen, they will roar over all the enemies of the German people.

"Isn't it so, my dear Freiherr, that this new brilliant strategy is but the clearest evidence that the Führer lives despite all the rumors, and directs our fate with his proven, masterly hand," declares the bloodstained District Inspector Briebkau, suspected of being an agent provocateur.

"That the Führer lives is no evidence against the strategic talent of the German generals, Herr Briebkau."

"May I ask what you mean by that?"

"Well, I mean it would completely belittle the German people, were one to see the sole capable head in Hitler. That's what I mean."

I had forgotten myself, and so the successful Herr District Inspector, declaring I had gone too far, rushed off to his office, where he wrote down my statement for the Gestapo using the appropriate form, to be passed on as corpus delicti[8] from the Regional Councilor to the district authorities.

A fellow worker who witnessed this exchange despaired at the danger this presented and a female colleague urged the overbearing Hitler side-kick not to take the step. She then advised me to go to him, ask for forgiveness and withdraw my statement. They thought that even his knowledge of my doubts about the capabilities of Hitler and his hangers-on and my keen liking for Allied radio announcements, which I had demonstrated pointedly, would mean nothing if it was a matter of the so-called honor of a well-known comrade.

Now it was no longer a matter of whether I was right, but the lives of my family. Thus, I went to this poser recruited from the criminal police and was made aware that I had offended his honor. I had to see "that this was an accursed mess and should not be left unpunished, when on the front hundreds of thousands were being killed – that somebody at home should discourage the people." There was only one possibility of saving my head, namely through expressing my deepest regret and withdrawing my statement.

And so, I did the disgraceful deed, for the sake of my wife and child and all those whom he would have doomed with me and sent to hell. He could not have imagined that at this very hour he not only played with my head, but also his own. For I was in a position to see to it that this rogue would not live to see our fall after his previous victims had not been able to rouse themselves to this deed.

He seems to have calmed down now, this District Inspector Briebkau. I, however, will have to be on my guard again, especially when the big boss has had microphones installed.

But what about the Allies? What happened to Churchill's and Roosevelt's announcements that they would certainly force Hitler to his knees this year? Hitler's state and Party buildings have already come crashing down, he has had to suspend proven generals so that the rebellion does not spread further, German cities lie in rubble and ashes, raw materials and fuel are running out, yet this mortally wounded colossus rises to land a new, powerful blow against the over-confident Anglo-Americans. He chases them into Belgium and Luxemburg[9] and sends missile after missile into England. A new blow. His last blow? Who dares to make predictions?

That the Allies will emerge victorious from this war is certain; equally certain is that they will only be victorious when the whole of Germany is devastated and the German people have been killed. Hitler and his disciples will make sure that no German will survive to hold them to account.

So, what do you intend to do, friends in Britain and America, if even Russian help is not enough? What? I don't know, I am not a general. That is your field. And you should know that setbacks of this kind have buried the hopes of all those who have hungered for peace and freedom for a very long time! Happy Christmas!

28 HOW MUCH LONGER?

Walter's buoyant enthusiasm for the mountains, the weather, the location, and his freedom are tempered by a sense that his body and mind are slipping. He is not as sharp as he would like to be although his Nazi bosses continually praise his work. At the same time, he is troubled by what seems like a stalemate in the war. He fully expected to be liberated by the end of 1944 as the Allies had promised and is not fully aware that the Allied offense was nearly reversed in the Battle of the Bulge at the end of 1944. But he sees that the slaughter continues. He cannot help but wonder how the fates saved their family of three while hundreds of thousands perish elsewhere.

These pressures lead him again and again to reflect on their escape, their survival and the horrendous nature of war.

January 14, 1945

Christmas is long over, a Christmas with the decent tree surrounded by gifts which a resourceful and caring Mutti had conjured up despite the poverty caused by Hitler and the stripped bare, looted shops. This was a Christmas of concealment and loneliness. Taking refuge at the Catholic Mass with its solemn pomp at least transported the child into glowing amazement, but increased our longing for the tradition of our fathers. Thus, in the evenings the Ma'oz Tzur was heard on the gramophone and other oh so yearned for Jewish airs.

And then came snow, lots of snow, and after it the cold of the mountains, and with the cold of the mountains, the New Year. It was introduced by sermons by the holy Adolf, the hero Joseph and other God-sent double-dealers, who ordered the devastated people not only to believe in victory in the year of the Lord 1945, but also in Providence to hand over the government of the world to their Führer. Still Providence can be mean, so mean that she withholds from her chosen people uniforms and underwear, both of which are actually indispensable for the continuation of the war.

I for one am dubious that dear Providence will make it believable to Hitler's followers that all that stuff that they relieved the Jews of years ago to prepare them for the mass slaughter was dispensable. The Nazis hush this up, and instead arrange a "people's sacrifice", a huge collection of textiles of all kinds starting with threadbare rags right up to the gala uniforms of retired, that is, dismissed generals, under the motto that national comrades who withhold even one dispensable, no indispensable, piece, share the blame for – it is too horrible to say! I will let the *Vorarlberger Tageblatt* of January 10 speak: "Without this communal act – why should we keep it secret? – the supply of sufficient clothing for our armed forces, and thus our war effort, would be endangered, and there should therefore be no doubt that the "people's sacrifice" we demand for the winter of 1944 has a much more decisive meaning, and therefore must be taken more seriously, than the albeit astonishingly abundant collection of textiles of earlier war years."

Well, well, you see! From that one can easily deduce that anyone who does not empty cupboards and chests and gropes around in the snow half naked would have to be hanged as a traitor to the people. Not impossible, definitely not. Let's wait and see through which decrees and ordinances the "people's sacrifice" will be hallowed.

Already a secret instruction has been issued to the leaders of the armed forces saying that all soldiers should hand over their civilian clothing, as after the war it will be either too large or too small anyway. Herr Hitler amplified the message with the most sacred order that "anybody who holds back from competent authorities possessions intended for victims will be punished with death".

Therefore beware, you women, mothers and daughters, of defying the collector when, with the justification that your soldiers at the front have agreed to it, he tears open the cupboards and hauls away all the clothing! Be on your guard, it concerns your own heads and no longer the Jews! Yours! So, give, give so that the helper and his team can accept your "contributions", so that you will not be suspected one day by Hitler and his Apostles of stabbing him in the back just at the height of his struggle. Because of that you are not worth his shedding a tear over your downfall. What need is there for any campaign name for your voluntary contribution and sacrifice? It's not like a year and a half ago when they took away your cattle from their stables under the slogan "clearing out cattle".

The people of Bludenz appear to receive the Führer's proclamations with ever dwindling enthusiasm. They followed the call to "appear en masse at a people's demonstration in the 'German house" with such eagerness that after about a hundred delegated soldiers and office workers had been subtracted, hardly a few dozen participants could be counted.

I was there too in accordance with the circular from my boss in which he asked the members of the workforce to appear in the fullest possible numbers. Besides my curious presence, it was observed by only one employee, and we froze in the unheated room with an outside temperature of 20 degrees F, as did the musicians in the gallery. The conductor of the band had turned up the collar of his coat and tried to protect himself from freezing by conducting in a naturalistic style, and as 25 minutes after the appointed time the speaker from the district authorities and dignitaries were still nowhere to be seen, I left the "popular assembly of Bludenz" under the pretense of sensitivity to cold because of my heart condition. I ran straight to our warm little home, meeting on the way processions of people who were hurrying not to the popular assembly but to the evening performance at the cinema. That is what the political enthusiasm of the people of Bludenz looks like, and I am no longer surprised that they are capable of laying hands on wine after five and a half years of war, although it is no longer allowed to be sold, as it is known that it harbors the truth.

At least I have to give the people of Bludenz credit for something. They are not that stupid, they only pretend to be. It is not wrongly stated that Jewish businessmen could not last here, not because of discrimination, but because the people of Bludenz are far more diligent and refined when it comes to business. There are not only industrious businesspeople in these parts, but completely driven businessmen, and sad-looking, quiet swindlers who play tricks. Yes, even the venerable Party members risk everything by pulling wool over the eyes of the Nazi state, not excluding the well-decorated mayors, together with their veteran comrades, when they present fictitious lists of wages, with falsified signatures to pay for Party uniforms, or when they allocate thousands from the Reich for the acquisition of goods which in fact do not exist.

In this way the Nazi State is the cheater cheated, even when it tries with every kind of falsehood and infamy to declare its cause as the only respectable one in the world. Its methods are instant classics, especially this one:

The National Socialist Party customarily labels as assassins or bandits all those in conquered lands who defend their plundered and looted countries. Elements of this sort, including all those who are not ready to take action on behalf of the Nazis, were and will be "butchered on the spot" by Nazi bands of soldiers, and whole areas have been turned to ashes as "atonement" with their inhabitants wiped out in the most atrocious way. Those willing to collaborate, especially informers and traitors to their own people, were taken into the ranks of the "German conquerors" and given the highest praise. From the point of view of the German Nazis, it was thoroughly honorable to make a pact with the enemy conqueror, as long as he appeared as a German. Opposition means death.

American, English and French soldiers have not only got back practically all of France, Belgium, Luxemburg and part of the Netherlands, but even occupy a few sectors of German territory and bombard cities on the east bank of the Rhine. The Nazis, before withdrawing from German villages, are burning everything flammable, blowing up everything that can be blown up and dragging off the inhabitants, who are their own people. Only the National Socialist kangaroo courts remain, "an honorable service in the sacred German cause." According to public proclamations, they have "carried out a just sentence" on a large number of people who have offered to allow the approaching Allies to take over public offices. It is obvious that the Allied conquerors make short work of such "executioners", and other raging Nazi scum whom they capture. Whereupon bearers of Hitler howl and write the following:

Berlin, January 12

For reasons of natural moral law every person is obliged in peace and in time of war to stand by his family, his clan, his lineage, his people and his nation, to defend justice and even to fight for his life so as to fulfil his duty. Therefore, demands by enemy powers that compel a German to perform duties which could harm his own Fatherland are grave offences against natural moral law.

Coercion to carry out hostile services is not least a serious offence against the most elementary principles of international law, as Hugo Grotius, the father of this international law, determined. We know full well that this international law was violated in the First World War by British and American misdeeds and that now in the Second, because of the united effort of the Anglo-Americans and the Soviets, it was given a knock-out blow. As American General Eisenhower came closer to the German frontier, he announced to us Germans that the Americans came as conquerors, not as "liberators," as in Belgium and France.

If the American generals and military courts of justice wish to make us aware of their conquering qualities through such criminal judgements, then, as in the Punzeler case[1] they will soon experience what seeds of discord they are sowing. Predatory instincts and a craving for revenge are well known from the history of the U.S.A. – wherever these gangsters are, they naturally trample human justice underfoot. They torment and torture, plunder and steal, bully and violate and lay waste and kill, exactly as they did in their own land against the natives. The seeds of their discord and hatred will bear fruit, you can depend on it, a hundred and a hundred thousand times over. (Vorarlberger Tageblatt, January 12, 1945)

They're going to let you have it. Yes, they're going to let you have it, the Americans, and hopefully in our time will deal with the National Socialist judges of public morals in exactly the same way as the latter dealt with the occupied inhabitants of Europe. They have already started. When will they continue? When will the final strike begin? When? When?

The "Allied March on Berlin" has come to a halt for the past four weeks in the Netherlands. It also makes no significant difference to the "great German offensive" so it is not yet possible to see when the Nazi combat strength will be thwarted. And the people of Bludenz do not seem to take much notice of rumors, and not one among them ever knows what is written in the newspapers – so the majority still humbly submit to the Nazi dictums.

It is now the middle of January '45. And before the end of the year 1944 the Allies wanted to shake hands in Berlin. Did you not say that this summer? What has happened in the meantime?

Since September 15, when we folded our tents in Leipzig, I have hardly heard anything more, and if I had, you did not have anything else to report except the reality, namely stalemate. Stalemate means retreat. And that is worrying. Because you too are neither willing nor capable of waging war forever. Because not only Europe, but much more will be destroyed, and because this war will do most harm not only to the Nazis and their accomplices, but to innocent people and the cultural values of the European people, which once meant something to humanity.

So, what has happened? Something like in the last World War? That would be water on Hitler's human mill. And Hitler's mill continues to grind, grinds on dreadfully, until there is nothing. Until we are nothing.

January 16, 1945

In the middle of all this misery which Hitler and his hellhounds have brought into the world, our rescue, our way to Bludenz, remains the inexplicable miracle. Even if 20 degrees of cold freezes sticks and stones, and even if the people of Bludenz are so unsociable, and even if physical isolation has given way to spiritual and moral isolation, we are not so ungrateful as to forget how the divine hand of God has brought us here. No day passes in which we do not remember the hour of our arrival, and hardly a week passes without looking back at the steep path which led us here, carefully avoiding all ambushes and abysses which could have killed us.

And when I talk of the unsociable people of Bludenz, I have to admit that during our entire stay no one let slip a bitter word against us, with the exception of the insults that Annekind had to put up with at school. "Filthy Berlin pig snout" is the technical term for a child, a child which does not master the Alemannic dialect, but also never set foot in Berlin. She is everything but an urchin from Berlin, namely a disguised and inconspicuous Jewish child, even if she may have inherited my lot of being beaten up by schoolchildren.

My acquaintance with it originates from Tiengen, that delightful little town at the edge of the Black Forest, next to Waldshut, and this acquaintance brought me stinging wounds and bleeding hands practically every day. For even then, that is almost forty years ago, as the only Jewish child in Tiengen, I was the most desirable target for antisemitic stone throwing and blows. It must have been a marvelous spectacle, as after school a howling mob of boys shouting "the Jews crucified our Savior, the Jews must perish" raced through the streets, hitting, biting and kicking with hob-nailed boots, without a single adult taking pity on me. That happened at the turn of the century in the Kaiser's Germany and even in the little model region of Baden!

The Special Example Land!

Next to the bullies of Tiengen of those days, the youth of Bludenz are still lambs, and Annelie is not the shy child I was at her age, and her mother has good handwriting when she sees her golden child attacked. But the adults in Bludenz are, as I said, on the whole friendly and kindly people, and so it happened that hardly a sharp word reached my ears in the district office – apart from the Briebkau affair – not between "the leaders of the workforce" and the workforce, nor among the staff. Moreover, District Inspector Briebkau has been on duty away from the office for the last two weeks, and we, the municipality accountant and I, have spread out into B's light and friendly room. That a Herr Kurt Freiherr, alias Dr. L from the Jewish community in Leipzig, not only resumes and extends his activities here, but still uses the writing implements from his earlier office, and uses them very well, that is perhaps the most unheard-of change in the last three years of my life.

Exactly three years ago, with exactly the same red and green pencils which are now useful in my auditing work, I was forced day and night to tick the names of all the Jews to whom I had to deliver the last tax notifications before they were torn away from us and shipped off to the Nazi slaughterhouses in the East; the names of our friends and the fellow occupants of our house, the names of my colleagues and the names of people of fine reputation.

"You are responsible for it!" hissed Stapo commissioner Ebeling. "If it's not done correctly...!"

Then they left us, the friends and relatives, never to be seen again. That started exactly three years ago. Even if a prophet – but not a Jewish or an Aryan one – should at that time have whispered in my ear that after three long, difficult, horrendous years, I would reach freedom with my wife and child, yes, even hold an office and regain some dignity, I would not have dared to make my way along this path of thorns. Certainly not in the midst of the Nazi people. Still, it has happened. It is only comprehensible to God.

I sit in the municipal accounts' office and work. For me, for my wife and child, and against the Nazis. I work to the satisfaction of my bosses, who cannot refrain from telling me so all the time. They cannot have had any idea how difficult I found the brainwork, deranged as I am in spirit after the time of isolation and concealment. Acting dumb is a brave description of this paralysis, understandable, but alarming. It is a little better now. Fragments form into concepts, the modern all-German governmental accounting structure rises up stone upon stone. For what purpose or aim, I do not yet know.

Any day, I could be summoned to a medical examination regarding my "suitability for military service", and this examination frightens me dreadfully. If a serious heart condition does not bring discharge papers or a medical certificate, what can one then expect? Checks with the Army? Then four-weeks of drill without a prior examination, as was the case with the first courses to which everyone was sent whether healthy or ill, unscathed or crippled?

Too many became ill from this cure, some even kicked the bucket. That is why the Party is now more careful with sending its soldiers on these constitutionals. Just the medical exam could prove my undoing. I have an enlarged heart diagnosed angiographically in July last year. But what else? In short, steering our ship of life to safety around this last cliff I will have to leave to our guardian angel, this mysterious invisible angel who blinded our enemies and let all their hearts leap towards us.

Praise for good work, which are rated all the higher as they are not among the habits of my employers, and would have given anyone else in my position a swollen head; praise despite my strict aversion to Hitlerism and Hitler's followers and the general Germanic delusion, because I seem to them a willing worker and much more.

The fact that the Chief Inspector interrupts our work practically every day for up to an hour to "have a little chat" is already sufficient. However, chatting with me, now also demands refraining from my work with a smiling face out of decency during his visit, that means a lot. That kind of behavior makes one suspect that my office being located in district leader Kühnl's vicinity is a thought springing from his wish. This may have persuaded the Chief Inspector to urge my "Sub-director", the communal auditor, quietly and in a friendly fashion, to make a more punctual start to work in the morning – usually people deliberately postpone it for half an hour. I know how to stifle all possible aggressive encounters with the Chief Inspector, and when at half past six he asked why we were not going home, I answered, "Firstly because it would be discourteous to rush out of the office, and, secondly, we would have some time to spare, tomorrow morning when we come late." Whereupon he shook with laughter, wagged a finger and disappeared.

The other side of the coin is not quite so sympathetic and amusing. I have given up hope of cleansing Kühnl of his National Socialist way of thought, which, when discerned in such an educated person, quite simply makes one perplexed and silent. This person is actually of the conviction that a teacher, who attends a religious service, especially a Catholic one, is unworthy of his office, and is even unsuitable to educate young people. Furthermore, he believes that the Germans will be obliged to wage war with poison gas, firstly because it would help bring immediate victory if used spontaneously, and secondly because it represents the fastest means of ending the war. My objection that such an undertaking could mean that the Allies will feel obliged to, indeed must, by the same means eradicate the German people, he sought to refute with the typical naive belief that the enemy would have neither the time nor the opportunity for a counterattack.

Such arguments, as I said, usually shut my mouth, and I have finally made up my mind and decided it is just as pointless to want to persuade a National Socialist of the half-hearted nature of his Nazi ideology as it is has always been to argue with a Christian about how the definition of the trinity means blasphemy to a Jew. Neither of them understands because they do not want to understand, and because their faith is enemy to understanding.

Meanwhile, the anti-Christ Bolshevik is already in Budapest, in Warsaw, in Krakov and Lodz, and prepares to trample on Hitler's sacred land and call the greatest enemy of mankind to account. The Nazi bosses do not seem to recognize this danger as being particularly acute – which shows their weakness – when they wrote, "The Soviets will come up against places" where "they won't know what hit them". They claim, even deep advances and territorial gains in southern Poland cannot alter that. When the Germans go in for the kill, the Soviets will not be able to go further. Even the all-powerful Stalin will have to come to terms with that!

How much longer may the executioners carry on striking terror into the hearts of mankind? How much longer may they cover their dictatorial belief with the cloak of virtue and justice? How much longer? Are 12 years still not enough, 12 cruel years? The guiding spirit of the world has spared three small human beings, taken them under his wing and kept them from the cruelest fate. Why does he not show mercy on the millions who have to shed their blood in this most fearful of all wars?

Why not? Now and then it seems to me that our existence in the last two and a half years has been nothing but sorrow, whereas reality would have long seen us murdered in Polish deportation camps. Our deliverance has become too much like a dream, our earthly wanderings too implausible. But only for the time being. The recognition of reality is stronger than appearances. And although I recognize that the moment when I would report to a Stapo post as so-and-so from Leipzig must mean the end of this record, our existence is real up to this day. And that is indeed a miracle performed for us.

Would that an even greater one would be performed for mankind.

January 25, 1945

A week ago, today I had to stay in bed after I had been sick as a dog for many days. I stayed at home for three days so as to get over the seemingly light attack of influenza and tried to work again, after a fashion, in the district office. Yesterday morning, however, I started to spit blood, first brown then red and in the end a deep black. At first, I thought it was a burst blood vessel in one of the air passages. The sputum remained bloody for the entire day and this morning I went to the doctor who X-rayed me and handed over a letter of referral to a tuberculosis advice center. Their consultation hours were just today, Thursday, so I reported to the tuberculosis sanatorium in Gaishübel near Nenzing by telephone. Tomorrow morning, I will go there, for I can already spit blood on command. Is it TB or not, that is the question? I am afraid it will be a positive answer, and what will follow then? Under no circumstances will I be called up to the local rifle corps of the Tyrol. That is certain. They may take miserable scum, but they will not have any use for blood spatters. Freiherr, the consumptive! Bloody hell, you've taken it a bit far! Freiherr went to Bludenz to become consumptive.

Our friends in Leipzig have likewise heard of a wasting disease that has befallen their city. The gas runs out, the lights flicker alarmingly and often enough fail, trams have gone into retirement, and there is now shooting at informers and officers. Yes, yes, the air is thick.

Piet, our Dutch friend, who is lying seriously low with a lung infection and pleurisy, is getting better despite the German doctor who voiced the opinion that one foreigner is not much of a loss. I fear that one day this error will be statistically resolved.

Only four months have elapsed since our departure from Leipzig and already the railway lines do not need to bend so often under their load. Indeed, they will even find peace enough to hear the grass grow between the sleepers, since all the fast trains have disappeared from the timetable. Whoever would like to entrust themselves to the slow train for further than 75 kilometers must first obtain approval at a branch of the relevant Reich railway office – for the people of Bludenz that means going to Feldkirch.

OK, what else? What else? The Germans are not allowed to write letters any longer, only postcards. Who has determined that? The Anglo-Americans or the Russians? Oh dear! Mr. Himmler, yes! So that his protégés can no longer snuffle around in the envelopes. Even the sending of parcels and packages has come to an everlasting German rest.

Oh, you old German twerps, have you still not noticed? By the time you notice tomorrow, there will be no Germany. Consumptive Germany and I will run a race for a bet.

January 26, 1945

At the inn near the Nenzing station I consumed appetizing dumplings after handing over coupons for 100g white bread and 10g fat and passed the time until my return to Bludenz with a reconstruction of the events since the last night.

The night was miserable, without sleep and filled with a thousand conflicting pictures of my imminent route to hell over the stages of being unfit for work and months in a sickbed. I could already hear my loved ones whimpering. I shuddered at going to the Chief Inspector, who had designated the fears of myself and my doctor as madness, to inform him of the shocking result of the specialist's examination, whereupon he would overwhelm me with a look of disappointment.

As I got up, limp and miserable, I was drenched in sweat but completed my early morning toilette without spitting too much blood. Only a small clot was to be seen. I spat the stuff into a bottle as a mild offering to the public health department. The administrator was well known to me and she ordered me to come to her to undergo a test of the blood sedimentation rate. That was more easily planned than done, for the artery in the right arm resisted the penetration of the surgical needle very unpleasantly, then gave the blackest of blood. A small pressure pain remained, like the one after the blood sample taken during my lung infection.

Thereupon I made my wife turn red with my spitting. I went with her and our little treasure to the station, spewed clots of blood on the way there, climbed into the train with looks of pain from Mutti and child and travelled onward. It was thawing under a mild January sky and the Nenzing valley already looked ready to greet the spring. On the other side of the station was the tuberculosis sanatorium Gaishübel, now the reserve hospital used to patch up bad or torn skin in the lungs. I climbed the gentle hill where the building daubed in protective colors stood in solitary splendor, past a mediocre-looking factory, which seemed to produce nothing other than – whatever can one manufacture near a hospital? – so thousands of something lie all around stapled in snow-covered crates and await transportation. It is probably from this area the military specimens come which greeted me three quarters of a year ago when I first arrived at the station in Bludenz. It's clear that if there was an air raid, the hospital too would be blown up.

The doctor in charge was not there, and his deputy was doing his rounds. I was sent to a captain in the medical corps, Dr. Maehr. A captain in the medical corps – hm! What will he ask me as a civilian? Will he be very inquisitive? I had to sit on a bench in the lowest corridor and straightaway found another patient in the shape of a lad from the Vorarlberg, with hair falling over his forehead, a snub nose, and a tangled moustache which twisted from a red cheeked childish face, and disgustingly sweaty feet. He asked me this and that. I could not answer because I did not know the movements of the doctor and nothing about the steps he would be expected to take, so I said yes to everything. Only once did he gape at me and barked: "No!" I said no – and everything was alright.

Caregivers and laboratory technicians hurried busily along the cold, echoing corridors, patients in between hobbled either in uniforms or in institutional clothing. The thought that I had to make a close and long acquaintance with Gaishübel made me feel uneasy, and the ruinous smell of chloroform, carbolic acid, iodine and other clinical substances fought with the high mountain oxygen.

Then he came, the dreaded one. He took my and my companion's letters of reference and disappeared for a while. Then he called me into the X-ray room and observed me for a moment with his red, pockmarked face, behind which I immediately felt was hidden understanding and kindness. He told me to tell him about my pain, upon which he recorded my statement in the X-ray book, and I had to unclothe the upper part of my body and step behind the screen of the huge apparatus. He turned on the power, took both my arms and moved them while watching intently from all angles. He "viewed" me also from the back and said even before he was finished the relieving words: "So, your lungs are clear. The right one is quite badly scarred and joined to the abdominal diaphragm as the result of many lung and pleurisy infections. The bleeding probably comes from one of these scars, or possibly also from the upper respiratory tract. It is not possible to be absolutely exact. Your heart is weak, yes."

I believe I fell around the man's neck. No TB! No Gaishübel. What luck! And I could see how this good military man was pleased for me. We chatted a little longer, he gave me several notes for the doctor in Bludenz and found it quite natural that I should be declared unfit for military service because of my heart condition. When I referred to my eventual call up to the local rifle corps, he advised me to sit down straightaway when they want to enlist me. Advice I promised him to obey to the letter.

That was the captain of the medical corps, Dr. Maehr. He is a reasonable chap. And the dumplings, already mixed with a delicate gravy, will become a feast, and I drink to the health of my radiologist. Cheers!

Snowflakes are whirling in the windows of the tavern. People with upturned collars are pushing in. They say it has suddenly become very cold again. In five minutes, the train for Bludenz is leaving. Young lady, I want to pay.

February 11, 1945

In spite of the negative test results with which I go home from Gaishübel, I feel really miserable. My stomach and limbs rebel, and – most alarmingly – my head. I no longer feel any appetite, the desire to eat the war feed has disappeared in spite of intensive cooking efforts by Mutti, but just as noticeable is my rapid weight loss, accompanied by the loss of thought capacity and memory. My bones stick in a wrapping of skin, my bodyweight with clothes is all of 104 pounds, and when I have finished my daily work at the municipal office I am incapable of writing, reading or conversing with my wife and child. Instead, I am overwhelmed immediately by sleep. I haven't had a regular night's sleep for many weeks, so in the morning I creep out of bed completely exhausted.

My co-worker and actual mentor, who as a devourer of Nazis is especially attached to me, has been drilled for the past week with the shameful Home Guard, which my former benefactor, the Chief Government Inspector, uses to his heart's content to pester me and confuse me with all the rules of the art. While I am happy to have found at least a solid footing in account auditing, a state of affairs which has given me a certain reassurance in view of my many years of separation from the field of public administration, the chief tries to pull this basis from under my feet with all sorts of refinements, and describes everything I have learned as the right way forward as nonsense. He tries to explain the thousands of mistakes committed daily by unskilled administrative officials as corresponding to the official regulations and representing the art of accounting he has learned through many years of dealing with subordinates.

In doing so, he smiles his most lovable smiles, and takes pleasure in continually insisting that I could do far more than I want to concede, that a qualified teacher of commerce should after five months of familiarization be capable of moving freely and confidently around the area of public administration. He says that in case my fellow worker should not return, because he is urgently needed by other authorities, I would have to carry out not only my own but also his work, and in addition certain tasks belonging to the main administration. Now, the very words "municipal audit office" trigger a vehement horror in every person in public service because of the hair-splitting, and also because of the notoriety which naturally clings to this department. It is work of a mental voracity not even a well-versed, bull-headed official wants to expose himself to, whatever the pay may be.

As for me, I have not the slightest desire to pour more oil into the administrative machine of the Nazi tyrants and thus betray my very own mission. Obviously, this idiot will not know this unless they string me up even faster than they would like to. I have to get out of this predicament as soon as possible.

The welcome opportunity may arise very soon, if on the order of the Chief Inspector I should unmask the tavern-keepers as sinners in the Nazi Reich and as swindlers, so that they can be brought in for "just punishment." Official procedures are already under way, which means I have done my task and could be let go. I have indicated to the lovable gentleman that I would under certain circumstances suggest to his chief, the Regional Councilor, to make use of his right to dismiss a person. Whether the Regional Councilor would go along with my suggestion is doubtful. At best, the labor office would decide on my further employment, a not exactly pleasant idea.

This latter "solution" would be avoidable if I finally followed the advice of my doctor to cure myself at home. If I am not much mistaken, I will be obliged to take this step in the next few days thanks to the solicitude of the Chief Inspector.

When we made our way to Bludenz in September, I dared to hope that the holy Third Reich would lie in ruins half a year later and that the war would be at an end. Then I would have bidden farewell to the emergency aid of the Regional Council Office and would have regained my inner freedom. But we are not there yet.

The Russian offensive has come to a halt near Berlin, probably due to the sudden thaw. The Anglo-Americans gain ground in the west, but so little that at this speed the heroic beasts can still smoke a good few pipes in peace. In Italy the Allies appear to have become stuck, and what is going on in the Balkans is even more obscure. No wonder that Herr Heinrich Himmler still has sufficient leisure to wait for victims to fall into his trap. There are hundreds each day, among them mayors, regional heads and other Nazi functionaries who have had their fill of Hitler's blessings.

I do not doubt that the bird catcher would carry out his threat to kill anybody who yearns for capitulation and not "until the last man", and I today doubt even less that the Allies will only find dead people when they succeed in overrunning Germany.

The few survivors, Hitler and his elects, will figure out how to avoid an encounter with the invaders as soon as the ground burns under their feet. The German people, however, are irredeemably lost. They are dying an ignominious death for fear of their debtors. They have to die because they can no longer summon the strength to free themselves from the claws of the vultures, all the more so if the wish of Herr Chief Inspector for a poison gas war should be fulfilled.

29 I WAS DOUBTLESS THE FIRST JEW

As the Vorarlberg area of Austria nears liberation by the Allies, Walter must prepare to shed his Freiherr identity and become the learned Herr Doktor Walter Leopold again.

But he understands that the revelation of his true self might not sit well with antisemitic Austrians. As a functionary of the Nazi government, he likely will be perceived as a German alien, not as a resistance fighter. And he may be dead by then if he is pressed into the Home Guard, the last-ditch squads used as cannon fodder against the Allies.

At this point Walter gives us a rare glimpse of the transformation of day-to-day life as the Nazi regime collapses. But in his mind, he is much more than an observer. He sees himself as a one-person resistance cell engaged in intelligence gathering and incitement. It's not clear if he has any comrades and he certainly has no one to report to about his findings... at least not yet.

March 2, 1945

Bludenz, I think you've got something coming to you.

Three days ago, the big birds were here and have left behind their visitation cards. They flew in very low from the Kloster valley, in large squadrons and with a great racket, swooped down left over Bludenz and disappeared towards Switzerland.

Just one of them, which seemed very much to enjoy the sky over Bludenz, circled for an hour over our heads and scattered leaflets. They turned out to be the so-called illegal newspaper *Red-White-Red*, and brought only what the dumbest German speaker and even the most benighted Nazi mind knew long ago. It is bad propaganda and even worse advertising. When the Allied lone wolf got a bit bored, he let something fall, which after the well-known whistling sound exploded with a crack which could be heard all around. Then he bolted.

A little later we learned that close to the bridge crossing the River Ill near Nenzing, several small bridges, which must have been for the railway, were blown up and a number of trees just awakening from their winter sleep went with them. For the Bludenz people this is a first-rate sensation, but also a very serious warning. They have understood, and whenever there is an alarm they rush at once into the mountain caverns, where they are safe from bombs of all calibers. We prepare ourselves for new trauma and can only hope that the Fates will not tear the last shirt from our back.

Believe it or not, there are still people who have a "good nose" as the Saxon likes to say, which one of my female co-workers has proved with amazing ostentation. This woman, who has a cool and rather overbearing central-German manner, suddenly threw me questioning looks and said she had the strangest feeling that in me she saw not Kurt Freiherr, but someone who was concealing his true existence behind this name. "A kind of mystical personality with something about him," she called it.

I never told her anything about my family, nor of my parents, siblings, nothing about the family of my wife and noticeably little about my previous life. Yes, she could even imagine that I would not be of Aryan blood, and like my wife would sometime find Jews among my ancestors. My lively spirit, my knowledge and my ability to adapt feed her suspicion. She declared all this in a no means disdainful manner, hinting that once the Nazis were sent to the devil I would one day be unmasked as a great man. I smiled at her without emotion as she made her confession and removed her prickling illusion with my regret that I unfortunately was not in the position to offer any prospect of self-elevating unmasking.

"Naturally," she said sincerely, "what I say is quite foolish. Sometimes my spleen plays up."

Spleen is good. If she knew how she had hit the bulls-eye!

Yes, how would it really be, should we come through the Nazi tumult unharmed, if Germans from the old Reich were kicked out and we were forced to acknowledge our origins? Would one not consider our odyssey a fabricated swindle, thought up only to avoid expulsion from Austria?

In fact, identification after our thorough official metamorphosis could become a delicate affair.

"You don't expect us to believe that you rescued yourself and your family in this fantastic way from the claws of the Gestapo, and furthermore as a Jew reached high office. You are surely conducting this tasteless bit of theatre only because you do not wish to share the fate of the Germans from the Reich. That's surely how it is, Herr... Herr Freiherr, isn't it?"

"No sirs, that is not it at all! Just look at our original papers: birth certificates, family registers, school and service records, our passports, insurance cards, my doctoral diploma, workbook, etc. etc.!"

"Those too in no way prove your assertions. You might have received all these papers for safekeeping from deported Jews, and you have a whole briefcase full in the name of Freiherr. Tie up your bundle and push off right now into the old Reich, Herr Freiherr!"

"May it please you, sirs! Here are our Jewish identification cards with the ominous fingerprints. Please check them!"

They will put our fingers under a magnifying glass and indeed have to come to the conclusion that we are who we already asserted we are. This is to be assumed, but cannot necessarily be taken for granted. Then only a confrontation with people who knew us under our true names would remain. Bludenz people knew us too, but these acquaintances were from 17 years ago... Our friends and acquaintances in Leipzig would be unreachable, and it will be problematic to reach our friends in Zürich.

Yes, my dear fellow, the crazy journey is still far from at an end, and until you really see yourself at the finishing post, you too are done for. Yes, you are completely and utterly done for.

But perhaps things will turn out differently from our nightmares. Maybe the solution will present itself just as automatically as our most difficult situations have resolved themselves fortuitously, even though I am of the opinion that speculation on indestructible automatism can be a very unreliable guarantee.

On the other hand, it is difficult to do anything about this now, except through my widely known hostility to the Nazis which I introduced even before I took up office. Perhaps the approaching collapse of the Nazi castle in the air will also bury us in its ruins, an eventuality which sounds probable if you take into account the recent development of the political and economic conditions in the holy Reich and make predictions regarding the future.

They look like this: millions of human beings of "German and related stock" are equivalent to their foreign deportees, moving around since the Russian incursion onto the sacred earth, in the ways of the eternal Jew so sadistically devised by their Führer.

They wander and flee in honor of their anointed one from city to city, where they can scarcely catch their breath before they are roused again and chased on further by the bombs of the omnipresent Anglo-Americans, when they are not sent to the bottom of the sea in packed ships by insidious mines.

Those who think they have safely escaped from the disaster turn up in the most remote corners of the Reich, such as here in Tyrol and Vorarlberg, where they besiege and storm the welfare offices and landlords in their thousands, reduce the already limited food supplies of this small mountain region, and look fearfully back at those following them. Their numbers will swell the more the converging eastern, western and southern fronts reduce the possibilities of escaping. Since road and rail communications may very soon be completely destroyed by incessant bombing, the only means for proceeding left to the Aryan mob are the soles of their shoes, rickety wagons, handcarts and children's push-carts.

This pooling of people corresponds to the intention of the heroic rulers of Europe, who see their devilish plan of forcing the greatest possible masses into the last stronghold ripening. Wedged here between insuperable mountains and the closing Allied troops, they will inevitably die en masse...

For four days and four nights, without pausing for a minute to catch her breath, Mrs. Crest, the snow, shook out her bedclothes. It is a very rare natural drama, also for the people of Bludenz, who are used to massive snowfalls, but today have trouble working their way through the fluffy layer more than a meter high. This is a serious problem, since the snow which fell in minus temperatures becomes wet and heavy and does not offer enough of a hold even to hobnailed mountain boots.

The roofs cannot bear it and let their unwelcome burden slide down with a fearful rumble onto the heads of unsuspecting passers-by, who scramble out of the miniature avalanches leaving imprints of their backsides like hapless sea lions. Heavy avalanches of the natural sort are reported to be already thundering down steep slopes all over the place, and one of them buried an army training camp together with its occupants on the slopes of the Arlberg. For this reason, the avalanches, guilty of a serious offence against the servants of the Third Reich, now also slide against the sacred person of the Führer. If the avalanche had overcome the

Nazi boys in uniform instead of in their nightshirts, it would be put on trial this very day. "Because what is not allowed cannot be."

March 8, 1945

The mounds of white have also halted Adolf's icy coats, and what the snow machines whirl away stacks up again behind them, heavy and wet down here in the valley, dry and almost as tall as houses before the entry into the Arlberg. For this reason, the wretched soldiers called up today to fulfil their ragged national service can be stood down. Honorable Mother Nature has lowered herself to a "venal whore", who should be scorned by every decent German by spitting out a loud Pa! "March snow hurts the plants." And splendid too those who die in a March revolution.

Meanwhile all German women, girls and even 13-year-old children are being raped by the "hordes from the Asiatic steppes," as Colonel-General Guderian[1] has controversially asserted, raising his right hand washed in innocence. To back this up, he drew out of his pocket an "order of the Russian General Zhukov dripping with hate and blood". In it he proclaimed words about the time to "finish off the Fascist animal in his own lair". "I myself have fought in the Soviet Union," Mr. Guderian declared, "but I have never noticed anything of devils' ovens, gas chambers and other creations of a sick fantasy."

So, General Guderian, if you have not seen these things, then you have let slip a shining means of compelling proof and propaganda material against the cursed international Jewry. The ill-famed devils' ovens, gas chambers and similar creations of a sick fantasy have been set up by treacherous Poles and Jews, including friends and their children, who have deported themselves to Eastern Europe to the great distress of the SS, in order to carry out their plan in the face of the advancing Bolsheviks to martyr themselves past recognition, mutilate themselves and finally dispatch themselves to the next world with the help of Jewish poison gas. And all that with the intention of wanting to make the Russians and their allies believe that valiant, honorable and god-fearing German men have committed such crimes.

It is just like when the Jews in November 1938 set fire to their synagogues and plundered their shops and whipped themselves to death in their own concentration camps. That's how it was, Mr. Guderian, wasn't it? And after all that General Zhukov dares to threaten: "The time has come for the final reckoning with the German-Fascist scoundrels. Our hatred is great and burning! We will revenge ourselves tremendously for everything."

Yes, Mr. Idiot Guderian, the time has come earlier than you and your beloved little lambs expected it! Your big-mouthed bawling has become a pitiful whimper and your lust for the death rattle of broken-down victims has slipped into your guts and knees. But you and your accomplices can expect no pardon. For atrocious are your crimes, and the time of atonement is here.

March 11, 1945

Yesterday I visited Teukert, my colleague and deputy-chief from the municipality audit office, who has returned from his wretched South Tyrol rifle force course. I decided on this on the spur of the moment in spite of the miserable travel conditions to go to Hohenems, due north of us. After I ended work at midday on Saturday, I found his letter, which he had written while still at the drill place and which made clear that this poor unwilling Party man was finally able to come home with the transport train that had passed Bludenz just a few days earlier.

Through the masses of slushy snow I stamped my way down to the station, got on one of the clapped-out coaches dreaming of final victory behind windows nailed up with boards, found myself a place. Through a crack I tried to make out the large Red Cross which the Nazi protectors who consider themselves so sly have painted on the hotel hospital opposite the station, in the hope that in case of bombing of the station building they can now have some propaganda material against the air raids.

I could also view the endless row of freight wagons, which as ordered, were lifted off the tracks and will probably fulfil their last purpose by sinking into the soft ground of the railway embankment. Why this valuable function was allotted to them by the highest authority blessed by providence I could for a long time not ascertain, however "well-informed sources" claim to know that this serves to keep a passage free in case of rapid troop movements. To manipulations of this kind belong above all intact locomotives, of which the "military idiots" of the other side, as is well known, have not left all that many. The only still-functioning repair works of the Alpine region more resembles a cemetery for electric locomotives than a rejuvenation institute.

I let myself rattle over the 38-kilometer stretch at victory speed for one and a half hours through stations slumbering in assurance of the same victory, while a grey sky provided the necessary heroic frame.

My colleague received me with loud rejoicing, for he was glad that I had felt his intention to ask me for a visit over the telephone and had brought it to realization. His face grew pale when I had to refuse his request to stay overnight, and it made no difference that his wife served me up a plate of fine-smelling ham, sausage and bread to give me a foretaste of the Sunday dishes still awaiting me. Long unaccustomed to such delicious pleasures, I had to tuck in valiantly while the friend reported on his experiences in South Tyrol:

The drill lasted from dawn to dusk. Cascades from the snouts of loyal, shoulder-striped big mouths, reckless muddling through by the fulfillers of quotas, pig's food made out of the best material, accommodation similar to concentration camps and a speech by his Glory the Gauleiter Hofer with the oh so congenial threat that cowardice, shirking and shamming of illness of any kind would be punished by extermination of the whole tribe of delinquents – all had to be borne. The conditions, which the boys of the Swastika-anointed placed their little lambs under, bear solid witness to the values of a "community bound by oath".

The winter reunion of friends came to a fitting finale in a 50-hour journey home through the Arlberg, and you can see it has taken its toll on my comrade. This man who is by nature sickly, but has won many prizes as a marksman, has become even paler and thinner. He has a bandaged left thumb, where an insignificant cut grew into an infected wound. It has the same features as the notorious concentration camp boils and is accompanied by a violent, painful cough. This does not prevent the good fellow from leading me to an acquaintance so that I can inform my wife by telephone of my late return.

The short path leads past the onetime synagogue of Hohenems. Degraded to a barn used to store hay, it stares like the end of a Menetekel[2] out of broken-in windows at its dingy, old neighborhood and in dying still bewails its many children. If it could have guessed that a functionary from afar, somebody who it thought had long perished, looks up to it in bitter sorrow and indomitable loyalty, it would have opened its half-collapsed door wide and called to me in joy: *Ma tovu ohalekha Ya'akov!*[3]

Yet it was silent, and no "barucha"[4] was sung to me as the Sabbath came to an end. Wait, dear old school, hold on for a bit and beseech the Everlasting One that He may grant me time to demonstrate love and honor to you "still in our days".

At its back it covers a little old house, in which the former Jewish tavern-keeper served his guests. My colleague leads me into this place, where he so often spent time in spite of the dark looks of dear Party comrades. The converted tavern is inhabited by friends, and a dear woman offers me two telephone calls and a little glass of schnapps, without the knowledge or consent of the important and dethroned messenger of peace.[5]

Having returned to the home of my friends, I am met by a voluminous evening meal: a portion of roast beef enough for three good eaters in the present time, and with it steamed noodles, green beans, potato salad that melts in the mouth and fruit mousse. I believe that, in the light of these treats, the saying that the mouth overflows of the person whose heart is full has now been put out into the world. That's how happy a person is whose tongue hangs out from his throat and begins to drip just at the smell of such delicacies.

And only now I really understood why the Jews are accustomed to thanking their creator with exuberant and endless praise. I too thank the good host, take leave of the wife and children, let Papa and an acquaintance take me to the station, and trundle back to where I came from.

March 15, 1945

I was very clearly reminded of my exile existence when again today Mutti served me two sausages in the middle of my municipal service – known as cudgels or cuttings – together with mustard and real butter rolls. It was a celebration of my real birthday, which for some time now we could only mark clandestinely, so that it would not betray its bearer. The sumptuous meal had to be legitimized to curious people, and it turned out that on the same day as my birthday I could celebrate my half-year jubilee in service in Bludenz. That was reason enough to convey the fine, juicy delicacies piece by piece to a greedy stomach, smacking my lips.

They did good! Two sausages and butter rolls in the Nazi war year of 1945 are finer to a narrow throat than lobster with Sekt are to a heavy peacetime stomach...

March 25, 1945

I moved into my own little room, formerly that of the Kochs' maid, who has been doing conscripted labor for several months. It is comfortably arranged with furniture from the landlord, who demands no extra rent for the additional room. I laid the light wiring myself and drilled through the wall from the neighboring bedroom, into which came also the bed which was in the child's room. In the place of the infant's bed of the NSV, Annelie thus at last has a proper bed, in which she can move and stretch to her heart's delight. The remainder of my books, which until now vegetated in the food larder, I stacked in the built-in bookshelf, and my gramophone records and the microscope have likewise found their places in the living room. With that, we are the possessors of a small home.

War in the Rhineland: the Allies have taken L'hafen, Neustadt an der Weinstrasse, Speyer with its magnificent cathedral and Landau, the former place of residence of my grandparents and other relatives and are said to have now crossed the Rhine near Mainz. The "River Main line" is again topical. The Russians will try to make their way through Czechoslovakia to shake hands with the Allies, and permanently separate North from South Germany, perhaps in the course of this spring.

The Nazi leaders are talking their snouts off and can now do nothing but hope and hope. This option is free for Hitler and his Apostles, but it costs the lives of people. I fear we will have to bite through all sorts of things until we are at the goal.

Today they made the first roll call for the Home Guard. Regional Councilor Kühnl told me a week ago that from now on I would be enrolled every Sunday. So far, however, I have received no call-up order. Could they really have forgotten me or even considered me so ill that they would fear the worst if they enrolled me? If they would think of me as my doctor does, that would be good. He is of the opinion that I should have long ago died after my horrendous loss of weight, and prescribed me three medicines instead of supplementary food, which according to official instructions is again withdrawn from the ill and is to be delivered to the communal supplies being set up. The doctor told me that all people living alone and families with three or fewer members have to contribute to these provisions. Cheers, Hitler!

The Chief Inspector will report to the front when the communal provisions are introduced, or his wife and child will throw all scruples aside and let themselves bite the dust. "If I were not a National Socialist, I would like to be a pacifist," he recently declared. They are slowly coming closer, the gentlemen, when it concerns the grub. Now it's getting amusing. Maybe life will be fun once more?

March 27, 1945

The German fortifications in the West are disintegrating. Kilometer-long snakes of tanks grind over eight Rhine crossings towards the center of Germany. The tank columns are already reported in the following places: Limburg, Gießen, Danneberg, Nürnberg, Kitzingen and Mannheim. Darmstadt and Wiesbaden are in Allied hands. Stalin reports the fall of Strehlen and Rybnik.

Speed is no hocus-pocus!

But how will the Allies be able to liberate Austria, Tyrol and Vorarlberg? Our present homeland has only a single approach from outside, the one through the Rhine valley and the narrow paths near Feldkirch. Thrusting forward with tank columns will thus not achieve much here, unless parachute troops coming via Switzerland dare to spring over the hurdle into the Bludenz valley. If this happens, the Party boars will naturally send all two-legged creatures into battle with the "crazy enemy".

I would need two hundred discreet Swiss and well-armed men to arrest the pig-dogs from regional leader down to the brown dogsbodies. But they all have their pants full – and their mouths too, but only if they don't risk anything further. That at least I have been able to achieve through diligent propaganda.

The Chief Inspector has let it be known that the deputy regional leader Piazzi has accused him of sabotage before the Regional Council. He does not give anything more away, but on April 15 he must enroll with the Home Guard. I saw hundreds of red notes on his desk stapled together and ready to be sent. A whole battalion must be the first instalment from the Bludenz area... Let's wait and see what's going on by the middle of April. Once again: Veri, vici verro.[6]

April 2, 1945

Yesterday's holiday work was informative. In the morning the Chief Inspector came to me and conveyed with a highly expressive look that great events were imminent. The upset could very easily take place next week. He wants to hear nothing more about the gas war which a short time ago he praised as a cure-all. He considers that in light of the continuous successes of the Allies its effect is no longer lasting enough to bring about the "turning point". As far as the Nazi dictatorship is concerned, the German people are not yet mature for the Führer principle, and are even unworthy of it. Still he doesn't understand that the presiding rascals are not mature or worthy of leadership, and not the other way around.

In the middle of our discourse the Captain of the Gendarmerie stumbles in in civilian clothes and, noticing my presence, betrays the real reason, which I had already guessed, for the holiday service order. It was given by telephone at the last minute. An "Action Committee" has sent threatening letters to the mayor and district deputies of Vorarlberg saying that they will be killed with their families if they send out any more call-up orders for the Home Guard.

"We know all about it already," answers Kühnl and takes the chatterbox with him into his office, where the conversation goes on for a long time.

When he comes back to me, he reminds me of official secrecy, but at the same time curses the Hitlerites, the oppressors of his boss and hitherto political comrades. Nevertheless, in the afternoon he talks further twaddle about "Victory or death!" in line with the announcement by the Führer of a "German Freedom Movement", which according to a tried and tested method is to kill all German comrades who cooperate with the enemy occupying German territory.

Kühnl believes he has to approve and defend the concept of freelance snipers, which was not long ago loudly reviled by the Hitler guard and propaganda. The Germans may have condemned such dirty dealings, but today in view of the rape of its frontiers it has been fully justified. The German people have been granted the "right to necessary self-defense".

"Well, then everything will certainly be in order, except the German people themselves," I think. For if they follow this strange freedom call, which extends to the arming of children, they will be utterly extinguished. "Better this than conquered," he concluded. If the enemy wants to win the war, they will have to suffer the largest possible bloodshed.

This morning the gendarmerie Captain honored me with a visit as usual, but could report no more about the "Action Committee" than I had already found out from yesterday's conversation with Kühnl.

This gives the appearance that these are only isolated warning shots fired from a great distance, and likely to die away without effect in view of Himmler's methods. All the more so since an edict has just been circulated, according to which every officer of the army and police should be ruthlessly executed should his attitude make apparent the slightest sign of "weakness". This will not be without lasting effect.

The naïve captain, a member of the SS and an old soldier out of conviction, today served me up the rancid rind that the coming regime would not only have to take over the Jewish question but will also accept with open arms old Nazis who are willing to cooperate. Only like that would it be possible to put a spanner in the works of the freedom movement.

There is more fatal nonsense, ideas that one can tame a captured beast of prey through plentiful feeding, or even train it to be loyal; it is a twisted way of thinking which causes comic grimaces even on the faces of the opponents of Hitler. These people are really beyond help. As a last reliquary, all that remains for them is the thought of the martyrdom of their raped women comrades. All that makes me sick, and I will in future avoid all conversation with philistines, no matter how little I wish to suspend my intelligence-gathering and incitement.

Hitler's ideology has eaten its way so deeply into the last thinking heads that its eradication would be identical with the elimination of the carriers.

Earlier I returned strengthened from a marvelous walk on the Bludenz miniature mountain range, full of cowslips, of course, accompanied by my wife and child. On the way a few former Mannheim residents claimed that two enemy reconnaissance planes had released hundreds of thousands of poisonous flies over Bludenz at midday. They themselves had seen it, even though the planes could not be seen because of the enormous height at which they travelled – they could only be heard. Good, poisonous flies! Believe it, but it won't help you. You are all lost come what may.

April 3, 1945

The SS executioners have let their masks fall completely and started on the slaughter of the German people. What I have feared for years is happening. "Werewolf" is what they call their club of murderers and give them the following recommendations as they go on their cruel way:

"*.... The blood and tears of our slain men, our raped women and our murdered children in the Eastern territories cry out for revenge. Those gathered in the "Werewolf" declare in their proclamation their firm, unshakable determination, sealed with a solemn oath, that they will never bow to the enemy, will offer unending resistance even with limited means, will proudly and stoutly oppose him with contemptuous disregard for bourgeois niceties and possible death, and avenge every misdeed he commits against members of our people with death.*"

"*For him, every means to do harm to the enemy is right. He has his own jurisdiction which decides over the life and death of the enemy, as over traitors to our people. Our mission stems from the yearning for freedom for our people and from the inalienable honor of the German nation, which we consider ourselves called upon to protect. Hatred is our command and revenge our war cry."*

To this license to murder the worthy Reich leader Martin Bormann adds the following revealing commentary:

"National Socialists! Party comrades! The battle against the opponents who have forced their way into the Reich is to be waged everywhere with unyielding ruthlessness. Gauleiter and district leaders, other political leaders and organizational leaders fight in their Gau region or district, win or perish. A mean cur is he who leaves his Gau under attack from the enemy without the express order of the Führer, who does not fight until the last breath; he will be despised as a deserter and dealt with..."

It seems to me that there are already many mean curs of this sort and that there will soon be many more – those who are not willing to share the fate of the bandits of "Werewolf".

The Allies are known to possess an excellent means to take them by the collar. It is the same instrument with which they have already forced the Atlantic Wall, and they will put it into action before they let the sons of Hitler and Himmler kill them: their 150m flame-thrower. There is no doubt anymore: they will henceforth send one summons to each German town and each German village to surrender as they approach. If this is refused, the flame-thrower will open up a path without resistance from those for whom every means of fighting is right and permitted.

There is one more thing to hope for: that an opposition movement arises with the aim of forestalling the men of the "Werewolf". If this wish also turns out to be in vain, then the downfall and the complete extermination of the German people are sealed. For whoever does not die in a treacherous attack on the enemy will be assassinated by the friends from the "Werewolf". What did I say? You drink, you die, if you don't drink, you die! So – you drink? – well, die!

April 7, 1945

From house to house wandered the gold-braided Party Fritzes as authorized arrangers of accommodation for the German and non-German comrades who have fled from the "bloodthirsty Allies", and in their hundreds have been transported, carted or "relocated". One could see them beg to be let in, hungry and shivering, but the Bludenz people made inhospitable faces and withdrew into their spacious homes with regretful gestures, leaving the intruders to their fate. Now they are being forced to be hosts, as before with the Jews, on whose homes swastika-bedecked officialdom posted "the severest scale" and crammed three, four and five families into every Jewish home, until vermin crawled over faces and hands.

Today no Gebhard or Voigt, as happened in Leipzig, banged their way into our home to carry out the much-feared inspection for Aryanization. Rather two Heil Hitler people peacefully took note of the information from our landlady about how we had been bombed out. They convinced themselves with a quick look into our rooms that all beds were made, thanked everyone and stamped out again.

Well, the new masters of the Aryanized houses could rejoice over their stolen acquisitions from the Jews for only a short time. They were ruined a long time ago by those who both contemptuously and happily looked at the expelled Jews ready to be deported.

Heaven has retaken not only what they robbed from their Jewish victims, but also everything they possessed before, and now they themselves have to beg for bread and shelter. Now they must feel in their own bodies what they did to the poor Jews and all the other peoples of Europe that they mistreated. But that is only the beginning of the expiation. The size of the sacred Nazi nation is constantly contracting. The rulers of their enemies have already pushed into the heart of the Reich and push on to Berlin, Leipzig, Bremen and Stuttgart, and are outside Vienna and Graz. They set out to forge an iron ring around Hofer's[7] defiant Alpine stronghold, but also Hitler's pilgrimage mountain, Obersalzberg.

The remnants of the once great people are starved and throttled like the butcher of Jews and Poles – Greiser – who has fallen alive into the hands of the Russians.[8] But that is not enough. The great prophet Adolph looks anxiously towards his hari-kari comrades in Japan. But Stalin has troops still available for another purpose than advancing into Germany. The land of the rising sun will see its star set in the foreseeable future.

And what will the Nazis say to all that? "*The German people are courageous people, living in their own fundamental space, nowhere overcome or lied to and deceived. The first worthy people on this side of the globe. The people who go on their way into the future. The people that will triumph also in this dreadful war!*" (*Vorarlberger Tagesblatt* of April 5, 1945)

They further affirm that "*if somebody does not want to perform a duty, he not only undergoes the deserved punishment himself, but beyond him his family and kin are liable for his dishonesty...*" (*Gauleiter Hofer* of April 3, 1945)

Finally, they proclaim how loyally the people answer the Werewolf call – in Bad Kreuznach, for example, people have poured boiling water over the entering Allied troops, and 10- and 12-year-old street urchins throw hand grenades from the roofs and hack and stab in the dark.

Well, the Allies have available a series of effective means to ease the way for such madcaps who urgently want to bite the dust, but they also know how to flavor their methods with supplements. And that they are giving the recipients a thorough going over is testified by a report in today's newspaper that the "Plunder Board" set up by the Allies in Frankfurt includes four Jews. Apparently, the Jewish police chief of Cologne does not give the population enough to eat and the Americans carry off machinery from the German industrial areas. Yes, neither the Allies nor your beloved Jews will bring you the gifts that you Nazi bandits laid claim to as victors, least of all machinery, but they will smack you over the ears so that you lose your hearing and sight. Nothing will be given to you, even if you spray boiling water a hundred times and lay Hessian mantraps. They will smoke you out so thoroughly that your "iron maidens"[9] will in a thousand years' time still smell of smoked meat.

The Jewish avenger still lives. Woe betide you!

April 22, 1945

Just now, at 2100 hours, while the Nazi bands smooth-talked through their only still intact Innsbruck radio station "about the significant successes of the German army", the last troops of Bludenz comrades marched singing songs of death and farewells to the station, from where they were to follow the Home Guard, who had been there since 1900 hours. Alarming news fly from mouth to mouth and from house to house. There are justified or premature rumors, according to which the French are said to have broken through at lightning speed to Lake Constance from their position at Rottweil.

All Bludenz is running this way and that in uproar, valuable goods and possessions are brought down into cellars, vehicles of all sorts roar through South Tyrol, some coming from Feldkirch, some from where already in the morning hours a loud thundering of cannons was audible.

Now the Vorarlberg population will have to show proof of their feelings towards Switzerland, which they showed once already in a demonstration for union, and express their long-suppressed wishes to the approaching Allies. However, the unceasing attempts at intimidation from the swastika bastion have crippled the capacity of this small people for independent thought to such an extent that news of the black French regiments triggered panic and fear in many people. Some who would much prefer to be seen as loyal to Hitler instantly collapsed and want to receive the enemy troops unconcerned by the cries and the threats of the Nazis. Already there cannot be the slightest talk of treacherous attacks.

This certainty would justify hopes that the war torch would pass Vorarlberg by without setting it alight had the "Werewolf" not formed exactly for the purpose of provoking misfortune. These dirty fellows, who feel themselves called upon to carry out such crimes, were all known to an influential Bludenz man who held all police power in his hands, but this man, a former member of the SS, and for years one of the sharpest opponents of Hitler, unfortunately all too openly, has been dismissed. The deputy regional leader Piazzi, on the denunciation of a gendarme, has been sent off to Kufstein, and from there reportedly on to a "training camp" on Lake Achen. The departure of this man is not only a hard blow for me, but leading personalities see themselves unexpectedly deprived of their best protection against the Nazi executioners.

My family and I wait for our liberators, while our Leipzig friends are already under American protection. If we survive this last trial by fire, we may again be what we are. May heaven protect us once more!

April 25, 1945

The agitation of the people of Bludenz increases hour to hour. The alarming news on Sunday that the Allies were approaching Vorarlberg like wildfire may have proved premature, the French reporting their position that evening as Ludwigshafen on Lake Constance. But today it was the wish not only of those who long foresaw the unmasking of the Nazi gangsters, but also of all others for whom the scales fell from their eyes, that the last three days would have bestowed upon Bludenz conquest and occupation. Meanwhile this little town has been transformed into a real army encampment. Thousands and thousands more cars rattle through the streets to bring the occupants to safety, mostly Nazi types, this time up behind the Arlberg, which is becoming a massive mousetrap.

In the opposite direction race motorcycles with messengers, SS pigs and all sorts of flighty and immoral trash which have been dispatched by Hofer and his middlemen to certain refuges, such as the "Adolf-Hitler-Freedom-Corps" that is said to have dug itself in at Brand, where a large number of trucks with munitions and food are also heading. Meanwhile the bosses of the regional Nazi leadership revel in the loving gift packages wrapped up for prisoners-of-war and civilian prisoners, celebrate with orgies of food, drink and sex, and in spite of the pressure of the Allies do all they can to ensure that the latter send exploding and burning greetings to the people of Bludenz. From the Chief Inspector we hear that with the help of his secretary he brought secret documents from the Regional Council Office to safety the previous night.

In Klostertal and Montafon the dogs cut down whole forests and carry off the wood to the lowland, which they plough in order to erect "impenetrable obstacles" against the advancing avengers, proclaimed by the chief rascal in Berlin to be impregnable and programmed to cause the would-be conquerors to bleed to death. But the impregnable Atlantic Wall of concrete and steel belongs just as much to war history as Berlin will breathe its last under the blows of the Red Army.

Now the Italian front has also come to life. In that place where the German soldier stood, and no other should come, the Allies chase Hitler's last followers with the support of Italian freedom fighters, until the Alps will set new challenges as a wall surmountable only with difficulty. But the Anglo-Americans have certainly prepared their solution. This is the last blow. Enjoy it, little Adolf!

April 28, 1945

In spite of pouring rain, the main feature of the Bludenz climate, the Nazi vehicles of flight and war roar through the streets and alleys. They become jammed in their dozens before the headquarters of the swastika bearers, the Nazi Regional Office, and with feverish haste take all sorts of stuff, munitions and food stocks, to bring them to safety or keep them at their disposal. Well, the Deputy Regional Leader, the fine Herr Piazzi, has reason to take these desperate measures for the protection of his person and his charges, since he knows only too well that his head will be the first of all the Bludenz sadists to roll.

For this reason, he not only permanently drums into the Home Guard that they should fight "to the last man," but furthermore intervenes in the official business of the all too obedient Regional Council with measures which are intended to make my place of work into a bulwark. The abduction of the Gendarmerie Captain, his fiercest enemy in his own ranks, and the transfer of the District Secretary who was friends with the latter, still did not satisfy him. He strives for supreme command over the whole following and has documented his "iron will" by ordering that the Regional Council should now also work on Saturdays and Sundays and do night shifts.

All my fellow workers, in particular the girls, for whom free Saturday afternoons and Sundays were a given, curse over the "wretched Nazi economy". I, however, used to worse tragedies over the last decade, bear this hardship gladly in the certainty that as the best propaganda against Nazi despotism it will cause the last faithful ones to doubt. Three years ago, as a senior worker in Leipzig's Jewish community office, I had to sacrifice my nights to the last tax assessments of the poor brothers of my race before they were dragged off to slaughter. Luckily, I could avoid further executioner tasks through all kinds of finessing, to the anger of the cunning Grunsfeld and his handyman Steinert. Then I beseeched heaven to rob me of my night's rest if it meant atoning for these most fearful crimes of history.

I thought of this when at the beginning of this week I took the place of my chief on one of those nights which are the prelude to the great court of justice over the butchers of mankind. I sunned myself in the reports from the Allied radio stations, which I listened to on the radio sets of the sacred Nazi office, telling the story of the slow suffocation of the strangler.

A pure-blooded Jew, through the mercy of heaven appointed as an official employee and saboteur of Adolf, uses his work time to listen to the enemy radio and for spreading their outrageous propaganda among the staff! What mortal was ever granted to live through a similar situation! I hope that the next night I can again gloat over the downfall of the enemies of ourselves and all good people, and this until the great day dawns when I will step before the liberators as a surviving witness from a broken community – unless a bomb or a grenade or an SS pistol has by then blown out the candle of my life.

And yet I tremble before the great moment which should bring our deliverance. To survive it will be no less difficult than going into hiding under the wings of the National Socialist authority. I will have to trust the word of the future local commander, be it a Frenchman, a Briton or an American, to keep silent about my secret until there is certainty that I with my wife and child are protected from the malicious bullet of some insidious Nazi scoundrel. Until then I must struggle on as Freiherr, even on the barricades. And I can still aim well, as the target practice with our Leipzig friends has shown.

Yes, our Leipzig friends and helpers, what has become of them? Have they survived the siege and liberation of the city or are they rotting away under the still smoking ruins? It will be a long time before I can be certain about their fate, and this certainty will perhaps be hard to bear. In one way or another they have got through it.

Here too time presses on. The people await the uprising. When it starts, it will only be a week until we are at our goal. And with us all those of good sense and courage.

April 30, 1945

My friend Captain Walch unexpectedly turned up here the day before yesterday and confirmed my fears for his head, which the boys of the Gestapo are demanding. His situation has apparently taken a turn for the better though through the intervention of the head of the gendarmerie in Innsbruck. Now he is delayed here on his way back to his exile in Eber on Lake Achen due to a fault on the Arlberg railway – low-flying aircraft have partly destroyed the overhead cables – and various revolts in which he would heartily like to participate.

Our friends in Kohlgrub near Oberammergau, who saved our lives, must by now find themselves under American protection. May they fare well. I myself feel so miserable I could spew up. The sleepless nights and overbearing treatment make me feel like a dog. We too need deliverance, in the next few days. Perhaps we are experiencing the springtime of freedom.

Encouraged by the obvious collapse of the Nazi economy, the second battalion of the Vorarlberg Home Guard, stationed in Feldkirch for the past week, have done a runner during the course of today. Not to fight against the enemy until the last man and the last bullet, but rather to walk back to their hearths with all their equipment, to Bludenz, Montafon, Walsertal and anywhere where a man considers himself more useful than on the battlefield of the swastika.

Something big will happen here tomorrow, I am advised by my Gendarmerie Captain, who despite orders from on high did not return to Eber "because of illness". He and his friends intend to liberate the hostages who languish behind bars in order to be slaughtered on the arrival of the Allies, thanks to a man among the regional leadership rogues. The rogues should take their place and be handed over unharmed to the conquerors at the regional authority. The Regional Councilor, known to be a spineless man, has collapsed again and squeals like a piglet in front of the regional head and his fellow butchers. He will fare badly.

I have told the captain who I am, and there is no need to describe the effect of my confession. At first, he considered my revelation to be fiction, then he gradually worked his way through the intricate web. Now he knows that my intention to help him is not only honest but also well-founded. He is the first person in Bludenz to become my confidant. It can go further.

May 1, 1945

When I went into the Regional Council Office this morning, all insignia and edicts from the Hitler era on the large black board in the entrance staircase had been taken away. Finally, only long outdated notices with arrival and departure times of trains to and from Bludenz and two insignificant announcements remain there, yellow on black. Even the Führer's order regarding the formation of the Home Guard battalions and the announcements of the last few days obliging all those who became resident after January 1, 1945 to report to police and the military are now being used to light fires. The same happened to the lively little motto that warned everyone in the waiting rooms against using a greeting other than that to the beloved Führer.

However, the greatest satisfaction in my life was granted to me just now. The Chief Inspector went from room to room and gave the instruction, to me too, to remove the pictures of Hitler from their frames. Most of the employees took this first step into a new era with the same ardor as I. I was doubtless the first Jew in the guise of an official employee to lay a hand on the holiest reliquary of the swastika. This clearing out would be senseless if Bludenz was not declared an open town and there was no intention of refraining from any opposition to the entry of the Allies, which is fervently awaited by the people.

Almost all noteworthy local Group Leaders in the Regional Office are said to have issued orders categorically demanding passivity and readiness to hand things over. What reply they received from the big boss astonishingly still in office is not known, and although he surrounded himself with bodyguards and sharpshooters, probably members of the locally-established "Werewolf", this time he stands there forsaken, and neither Party members, the Home Guard or the military are ready to stand up for him anymore.

Within a short time, the butchers will have disappeared over the Arlberg with their bodyguards to meet up somewhere in the Inn Valley with their companions in misfortune from all over Austria.

Perhaps they will commit a mass hari-kari in the face of the approaching Americans or will be captured together with the others. The senior official calls this a "pheasant hunt". Actually, the bosses look like anything but bright birds; they look sheepish with their milky white lips and let their heads hang, like my arch enemy in the Regional Council Office, the denouncer Brickhaus.

An hour ago, he honored me with a visit to apologize for the shameful machinations through which he tried to make me pay with my head a few months ago. He says he did not mean it like that and did not seriously intend to pull one over me. He says that as an official he felt obliged to act because of my comments. Events have now proved me right and him wrong, and he wanted to ascertain that I would not speak up against him after the fall of the Nazi regime. He now had to make out whether further witnesses, against whom he played the same shabby tricks, would take action against him, etc. That's how the denunciation scoundrels are creeping around, humbling themselves.

The Regional Councilor is preparing certificates of confirmation for police and gendarmes in the German, French and English languages, to be valid under the future occupation power. From whom he received this order, or whether he acted alone, I do not know. It confirms my assumption that he is preparing for an unconditional surrender of Bludenz.

Captain Walch, on the other hand, saw his plans to lock up the bosses of the Regional Office and liberate the hostages come to nothing, since nobody in Bludenz gave him support, as he feared. The people of Bludenz have other worries. From dawn to midnight they stand in long queues outside the clothes and food shops, which by official order hand over large quantities of wine and cloth to meet household needs. My tormented wife too trots nightly from shop to shop, takes no sleep or rest and cooks between alarms. With these bodily joys, the people of Bludenz have forgotten rationing of food and the threatening existence of their oppressors. Let's hope they do not forget the white flag!

May 3, 1945

The fact is that the white flags raised by the people of Bregenz were hauled down by the SS, whereupon the French started artillery bombardment. And if I am not deceived, Bludenz will suffer the same fate, in spite of all the pleas from the Regional Councilor and the Mayor to the District Leader, who categorically insists on the most extreme defense.

The active elements among the people of Bludenz, who want to stop the district leadership in its tracks, are alone in their resolution. The military and the Home Guard, who now wander all over the place or stand around after the partaking of bodily pleasures, are not to be torn from their lethargy by any means of persuasion, since their commander is ready to take a stand in favor of the district leadership.

Twice a day I am visited by Captain Walch, who like me is unsettled, and who was insulted over the telephone for shirking by his chief in Innsbruck. He is frantically trying to gather supporters to storm the District Leadership offices. As he has so few, he fell back on the old plan to liberate the Bludenz hostages from prison, without considering that the chief Hitler villain would immediately take revenge on other citizens with the help of his SS.

I therefore suggested to the captain to surprise the District Leader and his comrades with his trusted men and helpers, and snuff out the lights of their lives by night in their homes. In this radical cure I see the only possibility of breaking the tyranny and saving Bludenz from its downfall.

But its inhabitants, as I have long noticed, are all too comfortable as mortals, and incapacitated in their thinking by the Nazis. They will not take the smallest risk in order to keep away the greatest one. As apparently a German from the Reich, I myself am still too strange for them and can therefore certainly not expect that they would follow my call to break their servitude, in addition to which I would have to fear that they would in the end run away and leave me to the machine-gun fire.

When it was officially announced yesterday evening that the army in almost all of Austria has capitulated, the lethargic people of Bludenz broke out in noisy jubilation, shook hands, threw themselves around each other's necks and, if they had not already done so, got dead drunk.

Believing that the war and Nazi tyranny were now at an end, they sang and laughed as they had not done for many years, until shortly before midnight they were startled out of their dreams of peace and chased into safe hiding places by strong detonations accompanied by gunfire. Many people, including me, thought at first that the Nazi bosses had blown up the bridges from the Bludenz tunnel, and the Gendarmerie Captain, who had joined our joyful evening party and declared that the colorful birds would fly out around midnight, rushed off to see that it all went right.

Observing events from our window, we made out that the explosions concerned the District Leadership offices and that the crossroads at the Regional Council offices were sealed off by armed guards. The people of Bludenz now rejoiced outright about the supposed pheasant hunt and assured each other that the whole pack of Nazis had been killed. At 4 am we finally went to bed believing happily in final liberation.

This morning the Captain rushed into me excitedly and reported that the fellows who had the task of blowing up the bosses of the district leadership had been so drunk that they had shot down some of their own men, had fired off a few bazookas without aiming and shot into the windows of the Regional Council offices.

Instead of being overthrown, the fighters for Hitler's honor had assembled heavily-armed SS and "Werewolf" troops out of the building of the District Leadership and ordered that Bludenz should be declared a theatre of war and that Nazi opponents should be hunted down. The advancing French should be met with the deadliest weapons, and all preparations should be made.

I could very soon verify that these reports were correct. Let's hope the Regional Councilor and the mayor can prevail over these fellows at the last moment, otherwise disaster is unavoidable.

The birds have flown from the district leadership offices. Nobody wept. The military traffic has slackened too. The final act can begin.

PART 6
STATELESS
1945

30 HERR DOKTOR

As the French liberators come to Bludenz, Walter can come out of the closet. He rightfully expects his co-workers to react with awe, and to look to him for support and verification of their anti-Nazi inclinations so that they don't become prisoners of war. But most importantly, he needs to gain a hearing from the French commander in charge of the Vorarlberg area who has the power to give legal standing to much of Walter's agenda.

That agenda is both clear and ambitious: Walter wants to be part of the new public administration as the Regional Council transitions from the Nazis to the Austrians; he wants to live permanently in Bludenz as an Austrian citizen; he wants reparations for the years his livelihood was taken away from him; he wants to help bring the cruelest local Nazis to justice and defend those who quietly opposed Hitler; he wants to establish connections with the area's Jewish population as it returns from exile and hiding; and he wants to be part of a progressive political movement that will struggle against the surviving Austrian fascists.

But the clash of old and new identities poses a formidable set of problems. Walter is a German in Austria. He is a Jew who worked for the Nazis. He is a German Jew who wants to continue to live and serve in antisemitic

Austria. Will anyone in the French command show willingness to intervene?

Once again, the Leopold family is in danger of being placed on a list for deportation – this time to a burnt-out German city along with other Nazi refugees.

May 4, 1945 (1600 hours)

Just now the French troops entered Bludenz to joyful greetings from the inhabitants. Already in the morning hours, thunderous sound of shooting rolled through the valley, and alarming tidings spread from house to house that bitter fighting was raging between Feldkirch and Frasberg, and that troops with Pak guns would mount resistance near the neighboring village. People's fear was increased by news from Swiss radio according to which fierce fighting was raging in the Watos tunnel in our neighborhood – one could see people everywhere taking their things into safety.

In order to verify for myself the credibility of such accounts, which all too often have turned out to be mere rumors, I went to the upper village, from where the view opened up down into the Ill valley to the Feldkirch defile and the Swiss mountains. I could discover no clouds of smoke, the unmistakable sign of fighting, and so I had to assume that at most it was taking place between Feldkirch and Rankel.

I set off back home, and on the road leading up from Feldkirch I met two cyclists, one of whom was playing a harmonica. The other was singing. I stopped them and asked where they came from. From Feldkirch, they said. From Feldkirch? How come, from Feldkirch? All hell was said to be breaking out there.

They looked at me in astonishment and asked who had played this hoax on me. Everything there was in the finest order, only the German artillery were blowing up their guns. Civilian traffic on the road was continuing unhindered. As proof, they let me smell cigarettes which they had got as gifts from French soldiers, those so pungently scented fags which have been unknown among us for years.

At the mayor's office I met the Regional Councilor and Kühnl. The latter said that the French had already passed Nenzing, and it was unfortunately to be expected that there would be fighting. Indeed, there were soon heavy detonations to be heard from nearby, and salvos of cannon fire thundered onto the radio tower, the impact audible from the valley. Everybody withdrew into their houses and feared that it would finally come to a fight in the town.

Shortly before 1500 hours the leading French tank columns at last drove into Bludenz. From all houses flew flags in white or the old Austrian colors. It was almost inconceivable to see. Now we are free at last! The church bells rang out again for the first time in a long time. The noise of fighting which echoes out of the Montafon and the Kler valley is now an epilogue to the martyrdom of Nazi tyranny. Tomorrow it too will have died down and been forgotten.

May 5, 1945

Since yesterday afternoon French armed forces have been continually arriving and driving through, from the smallest two-man boxcars to the heaviest tanks. Their speed is fearful. The little town is shrouded in a thick cloud of smoke. The faces of the French are weather-beaten, however, the soldiers show an astonishing vigor, whether white men or colonial troops. There are hardly any black men, but Tunisians are strongly represented.

They occupied lodgings everywhere, and in several places shook a good few sleepy people of Bludenz out of their comfortable existence and parked their countless vehicles in every possible and impossible parking space, also on the pavements. They generally comported themselves like gentlemen though, even showing understanding for the involuntary suppliers of lodgings, while naturally giving priority to sequestering the bosses' villas.

They have brought light and heavy guns into position around Bludenz, the heaviest of them far into the Kler valley to give support to the units fighting the rest of the Nazi bandits. The rumbling salvos echoed around the Bludenz mountain bowl like mighty thunderclaps, and for a while one could follow the shells by their tell-tale smoke trails and the distant flashes of their impacts. Towards morning, however, it was calm in the east, where the trap was closing around the runaways.

During the afternoon the French had capably mopped up the "Werewolves". Whole columns were driven between tanks into the Regional Council offices, a spectacle that part of the people of Bludenz greeted with schadenfreude. Others, in particular stupid women bogged down in Hitler heroism, followed it with tears in their eyes. In between appeared the first commands of the military government, which concerned all military personnel not yet released from service, including those who had discarded their uniforms, and the handing over of all firearms.

This morning I turned up at my place of work, as directed by the Regional Councilor. However, this former chef had done his reckoning without the French innkeeper, who meanwhile had also become head of the District Administration, with the result that the Chief Inspector staggered down the steps with a long face, and accordingly also his naïve belief that everything would remain as before. I too betook myself back home and thought about whether I should not go to the French commander without further ado and give him the necessary information about my existence. But he could not be found, and when I arrived an hour later, waiting before the room in the official court building I met the Regional Councilor and other petitioners, who believed they should do what was necessary for accreditation with the new regime.

One floor higher up I had a conversation with a French captain. I identified myself using my Jewish identity card forced upon us by the Nazis in Leipzig and an American affidavit, and explained to him in the best French I could muster about my path from a deportation Jew to a Regional Council employee, but he showed no particular interest in my person – rather he wanted to have people who were prominent lackeys of Hitler, especially "Werewolves".

I brought around my Gendarmerie Captain, who could make the desired declarations to the colonel and had prepared a recommendation to the incoming commandant, but concerning my personal request I was told that its settlement could await the arrival of the permanent governor in Bludenz.

Around midday I asked two Tunisian soldiers in our courtyard about any possible Jewish commanders. They wanted to know if I was a Jew myself, and when I replied in the affirmative they threw themselves around my neck, said they were Arabs, called me "mon frère", and came up to our home to greet my wife and child. As they were hungry each of them was served an egg and bread. They asked me for a few lines in French that they could hand over to their Jewish commander so that they could call me at the next opportunity and took their leave from us after warmly kissing the child. But this attempt to get to know a French Jew would also turn out to be fruitless, just like the request which I had pressed into the hand of the French non-commissioned officer yesterday.

I also introduced myself as Dr. Leopold and gave a short explanation to a female co-worker in the Regional Accounts Office, who was at the last moment given an arbitrary Nazi order to transfer to Hohenems, and her brother, hitherto Chief Accountant, whose transfer from the Italian front to Duarte ended here. Their enthusiasm was boundless. Now I have to try to take up the case of the brother with the French authorities, so that he is not carted off into captivity like all German soldiers in civilian clothes. On my urging he quickly obtained a demobilization certificate, however, with today's instruction that also demobilized German soldiers must report, it is doubtful whether they will spare him. Already former German soldiers in uniform and civilian clothing are being brought to the command post from Bludenz and its surroundings, on foot and in trucks and are registered there and reportedly taken into captivity. It was not a long time before further measures were taken by the occupation authorities. The Regional Councilor and Mayor have already been dismissed from their posts.

The acting successor of my boss is his predecessor who was deposed by the Nazis, Count Terlego. Finally, the Gendarmerie Captain came to see me, deeply worried, and informed me that he too had been dismissed from office, and already the rumor is going around that all Germans from the Reich will lose their jobs, and even be expelled from Austria.

Confirmation of this report is not at all improbable, and I will have to speed up my rehabilitation. Otherwise, after being robbed and persecuted by the Nazis in Germany, I will have to expect the same from the French, who are our liberators; I would be treated like Germans of the Reich and be expelled from the country.

Unless the French commander gives me a hearing, I will bring the Count in on my secret tomorrow, so that at least one personality in an influential position will hear of my candidature for an undisturbed existence in Vorarlberg.

Now the moment has come which I have long been frightened of. Our recognition as much abused Jews could encounter even greater obstacles than our so masterly executed Aryanization. It is no pleasure to be ground between two millstones.

Is the day of our liberation the beginning of new torments? Impossible! No, nothing is impossible in this world!

May 6, 1945

At 1300 hours I talk with Count Terlego. At first, he was surprised by my confession, then astonished at my courage, and finally he expressed his esteem for me by immediately calling me "Herr Doktor".

However, he does not believe that the military government would be prepared to issue me with a so-called "free permit", rather he fears that I will be relieved of my job, which is said to be the plan for all officials and official employees from the old Reich.

According to him, I have just as little chance of avoiding the order to be issued generally to hand in radios, cameras, etc. However, he shares my reluctance to return to Germany and promises to take up my cause with the governor in due course. He takes leave for talks with the new masters of Bludenz and its district, and thanks me for the trust which I have showed him.

Emergency laws are said to be in preparation for Germans from the old Reich. There is a danger that we too will be placed under them.

Arrests are under way.

I made a lucky acquaintance with a French military commander on the occasion of his visit to friendly neighbors, and he has consented to introduce me to the Gouverneur tomorrow.

I then undertake to get to know the neighbors. They also display extraordinary joy at our deliverance from the new dangers.

With the entry of the French, spring has finally come after very cold days. Everything is bedecked with red-white-red or blue-white-red flags.[1]

May 8, 1945 (Morning)

The new provisional district office is coming together. The Austrian officials and employees ignore those from the old Reich. Count Terlego is silent.

We have the most beautiful spring weather with high temperatures. Everything is blooming.

I show the leader of the French Communal Department my legal documents. He and his colleague can hardly keep themselves composed out of astonishment and joy and congratulate me on my deliverance. The Frenchman drives to the command post in order to inform the Gouverneur of this remarkable news and to request that I be received.

May 8, 1945 (Afternoon)

Kühnl asks that I come to the new Regional Council offices to write a few nameplates for him. He tells me of the dismissal of two arch Nazis. One was ordered to the Labor Office in the morning to be commandeered for cleaning up work.

Then a long conversation with Count Terlego followed, to whom I reported how my affair was progressing. Amongst other things, he is interested in Jewish things. I expound on some of them and he listens with rapt attention.

Towards the evening the French acquaintance pays a visit. I willingly give further details of our path of sorrow over a glass of wine, which he savors. In the course of the following morning, he wants to take me from his office to the Gouverneur, who he says is intent on making my acquaintance. I should cease worrying, since only good can come from the meeting.

The King of England, Churchill, Stalin and Truman today officially announced the end of the war in Europe through radio announcements. Ceasefire at midnight. Gunfire from the French soldiers to celebrate victory.

My female co-worker Weite has given me her radio set for safekeeping, so that she does not lose it in case of a possible order to hand it in. The page has turned. First the Jews, now the Germans. The radio through which I have obtained my information since I moved here is good and stays in our home until the end of the war.

May 9, 1945

The head of the French Communal Affairs Department has not kept his word to present me to the Gouverneur and will not turn up again at the home of our neighbors. It is reported that the present occupation force in Bludenz will be replaced by another the day after tomorrow. The Regional Council Office, which is to be called the Local Government Head Office once more, will start using its office space again. Kühnl tries to carry out his duties conscientiously, but a large part of the Austrian employees, arch

Nazis as they were, ignore the Germans from the Reich, shrugging their shoulders.

These are hot spring days, the lilac blossoms. The snow on the mountains is melting quickly.

The house of the leader of the Home Guard serves the French now to secure their telephone lines.

Tomorrow is a holiday, Ascension Day. A great parade with raising of flags before the new Catholic Church is announced!

My colleague Weite and the dismissed Gendarmerie Captain were just here. W. again begged me to intervene for the liberation of her brother with the Jewish lieutenant who deals with prisoner-of-war affairs. From her description I recognize that the lieutenant is the Alsatian compatriot already known to me, whom I told of my Jewishness and who is the interpreter for the Gouverneur. I will try to speak to him tomorrow, although there are no office hours because of the holiday, since the day after tomorrow both he and Weite are away from Bludenz.

May 10, 1945

I spoke with Landsmann, the Jewish lieutenant. He recognized me immediately and let me speak with him despite it being a holiday. When he learned that Weite was a German, he regretted that he could not do anything. Germans of the Reich are exempt from possible liberation on principle, even if they were Communists or friends of Jews. He and others would get a bad reputation with the French military authorities. Concerning my plan, I would as a Jew without doubt fall under emergency law and therefore need not feel any anxiety whatsoever. Weite is very dismayed with my failure.

A little later Kühnl asks me to come and see him in our former office, where he pleads with me to help him search out some Nazi picture frames. On the way he told me that Brickhaus had been issued with a politically impeccable testimonial for the new times, to which I replied that the monster should immediately beat it or I would be obliged to chase him off.

The business about Brickhaus was discussed in great detail... Gunz from Bludenz, who languished for a long time in prison because Brickhaus, reported him to the authorities, and will insist on revenge.

We take the pictures to my house. Kühnl stays for almost an hour and we talk about all sorts of interesting things in great detail. I discover many things about my employment. He invites us to go for a walk with him. I decline, because I have important personal affairs to deal with.

At 11 o'clock there is a great hoisting of flags in front of the Catholic Church of the Holy Cross.

May 11, 1945

I have presented my case to the new mayor, so that as a Jew I do not have to undergo the severity of the occupation regulations. Then I revealed my identity to Kühnl.

The regional council office moves back into its former quarters. I spend two days cleaning with the others.

May 12, 1945

I called on the new military gouverneur this morning. I waited an hour and presented his interpreter and adjutant with my requests. In the meantime, the employees of the District Administration cleared their files from the room. The Gouverneur arrives at last but has no time. I leave him my written explanations, in French and English, and request the issuing of certificates that certify ourselves as Jews. I am to return on Monday.

The bastard Brickhaus is in fact in office again. He even runs the registry affairs of the District Administration in the small room next to the cash desk. Those who do not want to drop him despite his misdeeds seem to fear being dragged down with him. That is what the getting rid of the Nazi riffraff looks like. Agents provocateurs remain untroubled. I will restore things to their former state.

May 13, 1945

Rail traffic is gradually getting going. Three trains up and three down, the latter, however, circulating only as far as Bregenz. There is no need for more while the travel restrictions adopted by the Allied occupation troops are still in force. It is rumored that these are to be lifted shortly.

The residents of Bludenz, especially those who come from the old Reich, are already beginning to moan about the "unfair harshness" of the occupying forces. This unfair harshness they see in the unbridled excesses of the French soldiers, who snatch a hen here and there, grab a car, and carry off Germans, and sometimes also Austrians, as prisoners of war.

Arguments like after the last war are heard again: now there is peace others no longer have the right to make reprisals. They dig out their typical old viewpoint that Germans are entitled to do anything they please in war, to suppress people, to deprive and starve, to devastate their countries, to carry off the inhabitants or slaughter them, while the victims, heading towards triumph, are not permitted to swiftly employ the actions necessary to stifle the repetition of dreadful atrocities.

As then, the people and the general public try to shift any blame for the war and the deadly wounds inflicted on Europe, and the atrocities in the concentration camps and prisoner of war camps, on the Nazi leaders, with whom they claim they have nothing in common, hoping in that way to soften the hearts of the conquerors and to help the old military and tyrannical thinking to prevail again.

31 THE TRULY UPRIGHT... ARE BUT FEW

It is said that German Jews are more German than Jewish. For 12 years under Nazi rule, that relationship was legally severed. Jews were considered a separate species, an inferior biological and cultural "race." To enshrine these ideas, Nazi identification papers and passports add the names "Israel" to every Jewish male, and to every Jewish woman "Sarah". These are the papers Kurt Freiherr must use to re-establish his identity as Herr Doktor Walter Leopold.

Walter believes this incessant assault on Jewish identity should mean that surviving German Jews should not be treated as Germans. That right is earned, he argues, by surviving a dozen years of brutal oppression and attempted extermination. Yet, he senses the path of least resistance might be for the French authorities and the new Austrian government to exile him along with all the German Nazis.

Ironically, the French liberators and local residents are recombining these two identities into a new definition of "German Jew".

May 14, 1945

My hard-won talk with the French gendarme has taken place. The result justifies not only the fears I have held for days, but even exceeds them on one point, which will remain a black mark in the

Allies' policy. Since 1933, for more than 12 years, they have lamented the unfortunate victims of the Nazis in many words, both spoken and printed, and have sworn fearful revenge on the transgressors, placing under their special protection those Jews who would have or could have been snatched from the bloodhounds, and proclaimed a campaign against Hitler and his executioners under this slogan. But now that we are their comrades, they are breaking their word and throwing the Jews onto the rubbish heap.

"Vous êtes un Allemand," the Gouverneur informed me after looking at my Jewish identity card with a shrug. "Que voulez-vous ici?"[1]

I asked him for a certificate that as Jews we would be placed under the protection of the Allied military authorities.

"C'est n'est pas possible. Vous pouvez émigrer à la Suisse."[2]

That was all that the French Captain, as a champion of the fight against National Socialism, had to say to a Jew who for 12 years had been tortured by Hitler's representatives. "Vous pouvez émigrer à la Suisse."

Too well meant, Mr. Colonel, when he grants Jews originating from Germany, hounded, tortured and vilified by the Nazis, the strange privilege, just like the hated Reich Germans, of tying up their bundles and shaking the dust of Bludenz from their feet.

Well meant, really too good. Thank you, Mr. Captain! We are only Jews, propaganda material who must be happy to wander on the rubbish heap of what is left and worn out after the advertising campaign. I advise you to issue the joyfully parading Nazis here with letters of recommendation. You will no doubt obtain a greater profit there than from pillaged Jews. Thank you, Mr. Captain, of the proud, Grande Nation!

May 15, 1945

The attitude the French Gouverneur adopts towards us Jews seems to us indicative of the burgeoning need of certain French, English and American troublemakers to turn a blind eye to the Nazi scum. And that these dubious characters are very many is shown clearly enough by General Eisenhower's announcement made in practically every English and American radio broadcast today.

It states no less than that the Allied military has entered into friendly negotiations with Nazi leaders and Nazi generals, a way of behaving which is contrary to their responsibility. Thus, a foreign newspaper shows a picture of an American officer shaking hands with the prisoner Göring.[3] A similar photograph shows the French military government in Bludenz, which is housed in the local District Court building – the photograph is of the French, British and American national flags. That of the Soviet Union is missing.[4]

That is a telling sign and a glaring snub to the people who shed the most blood in the fight against Hitler. Daladier once before raised his hand in a Hitler greeting, and the peace of Europe was gone. The French curried favor with Hitler, became Fascists, and France lost everything including her dignity. The Allies have won the European war. Through disloyalty to their friends and ideals they will lose the peace again.

We three Jews in the Vorarlberg, however, because of Daladier, run the danger of being robbed a second time and driven out of our home, according to the model of the great prophet Hitler.

As the conclusion of my illegal presence, I today signed my work record book, which was already registered with the Regional Councilor before the entry of the French, as Kurt Freiherr.

May 16, 1945

The unambiguous behavior of the French Gouverneur compels me to take the path, despite his good advice, that leads to my goal: the way to the local district government and the town of Bludenz. The consultation with Count Terlego and the new head of the District Police Office has brought me so close to my goal that I can hope to escape the danger of being expelled from Austria with my wife and child tomorrow, to have to share the lot of most of the Germans of the old Reich. For it is already rumored that shortly they are going to be deported with very little luggage to the old Reich – according to the method applied to Jews three years ago.

So that this disaster does not befall us for a second time, I have explained that I, like all Reich Jews, was declared by the Nazi authorities to have forfeited my right to belong to the Reich. I refuse to accept it again, and prefer to be stateless. To our earlier pseudonym would merely be added the legal names with the addition of "corrected", the birth dates and places of birth corrected, the appendages Sara and Israel removed, new identity cards produced and the documents at the population registration office correspondingly supplemented.

Although such activities may seem superfluous for Jewish refugees, especially when the head of the family has even been a prisoner in the Buchenwald concentration camp, one cannot ignore what crazy ideas these circumstances inspire in the French captain. His command in Bludenz, so informed sources claim, may be of only short duration, but who will guarantee that the successor is not even more "hostile to Jews"? He and all concerned will have to more carefully enforce the orders of the Allied generals against the Nazi regime, which is externally removed but quietly still flourishes. Now they look on idly as the "Werewolves" sneak down from the mountains in the night and steal food in the villages, or bump off a family of five, or create a giant swastika glistening in the sun, visible far and wide, on the Schanzkopf high above Bludenz.

Such incidents seem of far less importance to the Gouverneur than the German origin of Jews escaped from the massacre, and it is no way an exaggeration when it is claimed that after the revolution of 1918/19, workers' and soldiers' councils, although despotic, did more thorough work than the Vorarlberg Allied municipal office.

When Kühnl shied away from taking home several picture frames, which he has saved from some of the ruined rooms of the previous NSV from the overflowing greed of the people for typewriters, lounge chairs, standard lamps, rugs, clothes, linen and shoes, because the French might ask him about the contents of the packages, I told him he could march through the little town confidently with an unfurled swastika flag without causing a stir.

Possibly Geunel,[5] who now resides in Feldkirch and then Bludenz, is entitled after the Nazi's last dance to something more than promenading, sauntering, eating and drinking well, briefly entertaining himself shooting flares or undertaking similar service obligations, which the occupying forces in Bludenz enjoy so blissfully. Until now, no sorrows afflict the Nazis in any way, as they stroll by carefree with ironic smiles. So also, our friend Brickhaus, who knew how to provide himself with a "perfect political testimonial," and tells everyone that he was out of favor with the district leadership and condemned as a "black sheep". That he was seeking to whitewash his party political blackness as an agent provocateur, and this with a success which very nearly cost my family and our friends and rescuers our heads – these services to the Third Reich only a very few people seem to know of, let alone appreciate. I will myself therefore take care that this subject disappears as quickly as possible from this office and from Austria. And because I suspect that he is already notorious in the old Reich for similar dirty tricks, one can deal with him as one sees fit. The huge swastika glows far and wide on the Schwarzkopf. When will the Palatines[6] raise their arms in Hitler greetings and hoist Hitler's flag in the place of the Soviet flag?

May 17, 1945

Reports about concentration camps – Buchenwald. Normal number of inmates 80,000, after the arrival of the Americans only 20,000, among them many children as little as six years of age tattooed with prisoner numbers on their left arms. The majority of prisoners were close to starvation and too weak to raise themselves from their stinking detention bunks. Up to 50 percent died in Theresienstadt in the last weeks, also among the medical staff as the result of transfer of infected prisoners from other camps, during which the hygienic measures taken for the Jews were illusory. The Red Cross had no access, but was able to prevent the killing of the inmates at the last moment. Dr. Ley[7] has been captured.

Gebbard, a Bludenz official, refuses to issue new identity cards on the grounds that those who have become stateless – meaning us – cannot have identity cards, but, at best, passports for the stateless, but these are no longer being issued either. He thereby ignores the instructions of the Count to issue identity cards in this exceptional special case, which also necessitates leaving us our old J-identity cards and J-passports.[8]

Gebbard also brings me papers cancelling the registration of the Freiherr family and a new registration for the Leopold family, in which the question concerning our stay before Bludenz was altered from "permanent" to "indefinite". The Freiherrs thus disappeared without trace and the Leopolds turned up all of a sudden from somewhere or other. For the purpose of confirmation, the guy then confiscated our J-identity cards and J-passports without instructions or justification, that is, the most important proof of our identity and right to recourse which we preserved from all dangers.

My report of these incidents annoys the Count considerably. I don't sleep the whole night worrying about these happenings and this bad luck, as well as about the restoration of our Jewishness. I decide to denounce Gebbard to the French commanders for seizing a document according to Nazi law, in case he does not return our papers immediately.

May 18, 1945

Immediately after my arrival at the office I set in motion my plan. It is successful; his boss runs after him to get him to hand over at least the identity cards to me immediately. In his conversation with B. today, the Count categorically orders Gebbard to comply with the orders he gives B. For the issuing of new identity cards, we are summoned to the District Police Headquarters, where we fill in the necessary application forms, give finger prints and even receive the assurance from the now tamed Gebbard that he will personally deliver the papers in the course of the afternoon.

Around midday Dr. Czinglar[9] took his leave of me, "the Herr Doktor", with all good wishes and asked me how I had actually avoided the German Territorial Army. I told him about some of our journey and our strokes of luck.

The staff gradually learns about my secret. Everyone is delighted.

In the afternoon the new identity cards are given to me without the J. German Reich, which is crossed out. It is replaced with Austria. That does not mean we have become Austrians. At the registration office, as I said, we were entered as stateless. The passports are returned to us. I thank the Count. Mutti is likewise delighted with me, but Mockel[10] still does not want to say the new name out loud. On the other hand, she wants to run to the Catholic Church at every happy and unhappy opportunity. There is a continuous, almost unbearable plague of May beetles.

I interpret for the French courier of the general in Feldkirch. I give him my address for the French army field Rabbi.

I take an evening stroll through Oberdorf and down to the River Ill. For days it has been flowing with dirty yellow melting snow through lush green meadows with flowers that my wife picks. Still that dreadful plague of May beetles.

News on the radio:

Hunt in Germany for members of the Stapo. They will be brought into concentration camps.

General Eisenhower forbids Allied military to show any kind of respect in front of Germans. Hitler had directed that all prisoners-of-war should be shot. Foiling of this order by his army commanders.

Unrest and strikes in Belgium and France, in the latter partly because of lax action against the Vichy people.

The decline and backwardness of German medical practice because of the loss of Jewish doctors.

Japan is supposed to have offered the Allies peace. The latter refuse and demand unconditional capitulation.

Heavy airstrikes against Japan.

Larger areas of German territory are to be assigned to occupation by France.

May 19, 1945

The laxity of the new French occupying troops has predictably begun to bear fruit, which is harvested by the "Werewolves". Everybody is still talking about the night-time murder in Luderel of a family of five, and already several French soldiers have fallen victim to the Nazi villains. Reprisals not only against the old Hitler plotters, but also against that part of the population which is hostile to the Nazis, who are disarmed and can no longer protect themselves, will be the consequences of the laissez-faire attitude.

It is as if the French had not painfully enough felt the bites of the Nazi spider during the German plundering of France and the long occupation with its concentration camps and deportations, to finally come to the decision to sweep away all swastika paraphernalia and the blood-stained worshippers with an iron broom.

That this does not happen seems to be due to the devastating propaganda of Hitler's apostles, the German and the French pacesetters who were able to work unhindered years before the invasion of France. They openly curried favor with representatives of the Grande Nation with the idols of the autocratic German victims disguised in pomp and plunder; they arranged things with these blackguards, who understood so brilliantly how to make relieving the people from worry about the business of government appear as the highest aim.

This devastating infection, even after the collapse of the Nazi regime, is still so latent that my admittedly unique situation should not arouse even a sign of joyful surprise in the French Gouverneur, let alone awake sympathetic emotions; even former staunch Hitler supporters remark laconically that one must have been at least a Party member to gain suitable respect with the new regime. Perhaps that is a somewhat exaggerated assumption but typical of the disappointment which is gaining ground among the population.

What use is all the vehement Allied broadcasting against the swastika bloodsuckers, what use the heart-rending reports about the conditions and events in the German concentration camps, if the troops sent to thoroughly and definitively put an end to this not only act as if nothing has happened but indulge in completely incomprehensible lethargy and court favor with Göring and other banned characters after giving them friendly looks and handshakes?

On a more positive note, just now Teukert made a short visit from Hohenems to his local pastures, told briefly of his involvement in the change-over in his hometown, and showed an official proclamation by the mayor of Hohenems which contains all important announcements by the occupying authorities and will be distributed to all families.

He further reported on the industrious work by the Hohenems section of the Austrian Freedom Fighters, who have got rid of all formerly enthusiastic Nazis without ceremony. On both counts, leadership of the population and cleaning up, they could be an example for the people of Bludenz, insofar as the latter would be inclined to accept anything that could endanger their calm.

Then Kühnl asked to speak to him for a few minutes so he could explain to him my successful unmasking. He called me over too and presented me as a real so-and-so. Teukert's delight knew no bounds. He circled me like a moth, shook my hand heartily and said repeatedly: "Wonderful, wonderful!"

"I must report that immediately to my friends in Hohenems. You did that perfectly! You must come down to us as soon as possible. The synagogue will be quickly sorted out again, the holy scrolls still partly exist, as well as the books about the Jews in Hohenems, among them a book by Dr. Tanzer[11] which I will get for you. All that is wonderful! Come soon!"

He then mounted the motorbike that "had previously had belonged to a Nazi" and went home for a week. After his return we will talk about our future plans.

I was on duty in the afternoon. That is a temporary arrangement in case the French Gouverneur should issue any orders or information.

During an evening walk with my wife, we found the station platform barrier had been removed. Apparently, this measure too is to demonstrate detachment from Germany. We could therefore go across unhindered to the train that departed for Landeck with two electric engines. There are still twin pairs of trains up and down the valley; for journeys over 10 kilometers, permits from the military administration are still required.

Incidentally Bludenz looks very dirty. Whatever the French throw away in the way of paper, cartons, and paper towels simply remains lying on the ground. Garden fences are partly destroyed by cars, the high iron fence around the tennis courts has been pushed in, an unusable motor vehicle lies at the foot of an embankment, street railings are broken, there are big black patches of oil on the pavements, the doors of halls and other premises are likewise destroyed, and the garden terraces of the restaurants among the glorious hills and flowering meadows are a miserable picture of wood shavings, paper, rags and similar rubbish.

Certainly, all that is tolerable when one considers that Bludenz has survived the war without damage – still it could be removed in a just few hours through a bit more activity on the part of the residents.

The post office, telephone and telegraph are still closed. All restaurants except one are occupied by the French. All motor vehicles, motorbikes and some bicycles too, are requisitioned and the little town is wrapped in a cloud of dust for hours on end. The blackout is abolished from today on, and I see bare windows for the first time in six years. Curfew only after 22 hours. Whit Monday and Corpus Christi are holidays again. Little work is done in local government. I myself have not made a single stroke of the pen since the arrival of the troops. Money has not yet been released. Staff has not yet been sifted out.

Duda has not yet dealt with the matter at the registration office. Tomorrow at 11 o'clock I am visiting the mayor regarding this matter and have to point out to him that I am not to be included on the list of the Reich Germans which is now being completed. The people of Bludenz are capable of anything.

My odyssey is gradually becoming well known, but only a few understand its meaning. Let it sleep on.

May 20, 1945. Whit Sunday

I met the mayor on the street opposite the district headquarters instead of in the town hall, where I was just about to go. He had received a command from the Gouverneur to obtain some venison for an officers' meal and was searching for ways of complying. That's why he was out and about. I accompanied him for a stretch, reported to him about Teukert, let him tell me about the calamities associated with the demands of the occupation and then turned to my business. On Tuesday he would make sure that I, with my wife and child, were not included on the list of members of the Reich and asked me to make whatever possible appointment since official communications would be open again as from tonight. Returning home, I told our janitor in passing of my secret, with a few bare words, which he acknowledged with a sweet-sour smile – he, his wife and his daughter are still enemies of the Jews. Then I wrote new nameplates with our proper names, and beneath them in brackets the pseudonyms.

Around midday the radio broadcast something of interest: the Jews still living in Czechoslovakia receive the same food provisions as all Czechoslovaks from now on, while Germans get Jewish food cards with reduced food and tobacco.

Sunday, May 26, 1945

A year has passed since my visit to Bludenz. Today is the anniversary of my personal and professional rebirth in Bludenz, the day that was to hold me and my loved ones in fear and tension for months. As a desperate man, whipped up and driven about by an invisible band of Nazi devils, who I already saw heating up the concentration camp ovens for people hungry for life, I stormed head over heels out of Bludenz and could hardly wait for the moment of reunion with my wife and child.

One year has passed since then and we are still alive. Heaven has protected us three hundred and 60 more days from the enemies around us, from the horrors of war, from hunger and ill health. It has led us to Bludenz, this sheltered corner on the edge of the sounds of slaughter, while still allowing us to hear the thunder of cannons, and one last time the voices of death – the hiss of bombs and grenades and the malice of informers. But God opened his arms over this town and over us too and, in return for the devotion we steadfastly showed despite misery and danger, raised us up to the creatures we were before Hitler and his butchers reached for our throats. A year, a long year, that finally led us over the threshold to freedom.

This freedom still carries the indelible traces of struggle and regeneration. The almost obsessive jumps of thought lightened my corpus down to a trembling one hundred pounds. In this physical and spiritual beggar's rags, I nevertheless dare to lead towards the goal my wife, who also had to tighten her dresses, and our child who apart from nervous requisitioning has thrown off all signs of years of lack of food and freedom and romps about with fresh cheeks, shining eyes and her little girl's mouth.

The goal is in sight, but it is undermined by the selfishly faint-hearted and the sickly victims of the Nazi instruction epidemic. Some flock around us because they hope and believe they will get personal advantages through our sudden return to grace, and others seek our friendship so they can cover their rotten Hitler inclinations with roses. In their Teutonic turned-up noses perhaps they discover Jewish characteristics, while yet others do not conceal their envy and disapproval. They preserve their antisemitic fruits in the hope that one day they can once more impose upon the Jew, who has dared to cheat their divinely blessed Führer and his evangelists.

The truly upright, who unreservedly respect our roaming and our life of suffering, our battle and victory and our loyalty to the Jewish faith, are but few. They are equally represented in Austria and the old German Reich, but not in France. Indeed, it seems to me that the Jewish soldiers of the Grande Nation are afraid to be recognized as Jews, and the attitude of their Christian officers is entirely calculated to disparage the Allies' sympathy for the poor Jews as a silly amusement for kids. No wonder that my constant efforts to befriend the French Jews have remained unsuccessful. Therefore, I would not be astonished if the Rabbi of the French division stationed in Feldkirch was strictly to ignore the letter left for him by my wife with a short description of our adventure.

I do not know whether with this *decolleté* the French want to impress the people of the Vorarlberg, in whom the hatred for the Jews still circulates, but they studiously ignore the fact that the people of the old German Reich were no greater lovers of Hitler and haters of Jews than the Austrians. They publicly sympathise with the Nazi experts, while on the other hand seizing apartments and inventory, while the Party Fritzes quietly sleep dreaming of Hitler. Thus, our landlord and landlady, known in the town as champions of National Socialist freedom, just as I expected, now enjoy the best of friendship with the French billeted with them, while they treat us with contempt as the Jewish disgracers of Hitler's honor.

I will nevertheless strive towards the goal I have set myself, undeterred, step by step. I am happy I have completely pushed through my re-legalization, and in a few days, on the basis of the photos I obtained shortly after my return from Buchenwald, and my most important personal identity papers, I will arrange the renewal of my motorbike driving license, which was invalidated by the Stapo. Here too patience is the mother of success, and the game of patience over the years has made me into a little master.

And with patience I will beat the hypocritical gentlemen, even if they so secretly hatch their plans, and with patience I hope to make companions of people of good will, who are entitled to be designated as upright and freedom-loving human beings.

Approaching peace casts its light ahead. The drone of bombers and the roar of guns have given way to an un-endangered existence, and fresh evening air once more comes through open windows, behind which the blackout blinds have disappeared. The streets at night are flooded with the invigorating light of the arched street lights and boxes and cupboards are being filled anew with household supplies and other things, goods stowed away for safety from the dangers of war, in so far as this does not awaken the greed of the occupying troops. Once more free time can be taken up by useful activities or walks in the springtime beauty of Bludenz, without the expectation of howling sirens. The people who were creeping into tunnels, weighed down with luggage, have turned into merrily chatting strollers, and the friends of Hitler have become pious churchgoers.

The other side of the coin shows the fury of war which presses against the lid of the coffin into which it has just been hammered. The lid is too weak and already shows cracks, the nails are too thin and give way, and what seems to be a corpse threatens to break out and plunge the people of Europe into further misfortune.

The Empire of the Rising Sun sees its end coming, and like the Third Reich, will fall to its knees before the Anglo-Americans. Danger does not threaten here, but rather in the northeast corner of the Apennine Peninsula where Tito stubbornly defends his rights disputed by the Allies, talks of military entanglements, and is supported in his attitude by Moscow. Syria has mobilised troops against de Gaulle, who strives for a restoration of French claims in the Levant, and Poland, is still the bone of contention between the Soviet Union and the Western Allies, who equally persistently deny recognition of the Austrian government installed in Vienna.

Austria seems to be a separate chapter. This relatively small country, which because of its high mountains offers little space for agriculture, has to put up with being split into four occupation zones, even though the Allies constantly tell us over the air that they have come not as victors but rather as liberators, and would not even in the slightest, think of forbidding the reawakening of Austria's autonomy. Their only aim is to cleanse Austria so thoroughly of the Nazi spirit that it will be rehabilitated politically once and for all.

Now, one may have a different opinion about Austria's claim to be a liberated country, in view of its almost limitless enthusiasm for the cause of the Nazis, and not forget that Hitler's Austrian mercenaries performed at least as diligently as their comrades in the old Reich.[12]

At least one cannot maintain of the French occupation that it fosters its "friendly feelings for the Austrians" in such a friendly way. Their caring supervision consists of taking away radio equipment, driving cattle out of stables and dividing farms and confiscating apartments not only from former insufferable Nazi mercenaries, but also from the old fighters against Hitler's dictatorship, who can prove that more than once they laid their heads on the line. They make their mistakes to guarantee a comfortable existence, and are not moved by earnest requests from the population that they finally bring the "Werewolves" down from the mountains and string them up. Harmless walkers are attacked by Hitler's last brood with machine-gun and rifle fire without the officers of the liberating army reacting with more than a shrug. It would have been better to have let the old Austrian liberation fighters and all those who were thoroughly fed up with the Nazi regime keep their arms, so that they themselves would be capable of clearing things up.

Now, however, Nazi revivalists armed to the teeth stand in front of helpless, moaning citizens, waiting for the appropriate time to suddenly break out and cause the threatened bloodbath. As before, the governors go no further than their promises, and one of them today reacted to the demand of a person from Bludenz, an enemy of the Nazis, to finally eliminate the danger of the "Werewolves", by saying that the animals would come down of their own accord when they have no more to eat. This little man retorted soundly that after the endless demands made on the peaceable population, the "Werewolves" with their flint guns, would remain well fed.

Remiss all along the line, my dear Allies!

32 I WILL CERTAINLY NOT CRAWL TO THE CROSS

Not only does Walter have to contend with being a German in occupied Austria and a Jew within an antisemitic population, but the title of Herr Doktor adds to the potential resentment. It is a double-edged sword. Holding a PhD in Germany is a mark of great distinction. It is a sign of professionalism that immediately qualifies one for public administration and high public office then considered to be among the most prestigious positions. Should Walter be permitted to remain in Austria and gain citizenship, as he hopes to do, he becomes an instant rival to others seeking such positions. Jealousy and rivalry are exponentially compounded by the fact that many of his Bludenz neighbors still adore Hitler and hate the Jews. However, if he is denied high employment, the competitive job threat vanishes, as do his income and dwelling.

Walter wants to be certain that the most maligned Nazis in the local administration are held accountable, starting with Brickhaus, the man who threatened to turn him in to the Gestapo. Through his actions, Walter tests the limits of his moral authority.

May 28, 1945

The affection shown by the staff since my unmasking continues. Even those who a short while ago had the reputation of being endless Nazi arm raisers, at every opportunity proudly and diligently say to me "Good day Herr Doktor!" Most people in Bludenz shake my hand with respect. Only the Count shows a noticeable restraint since Brickhaus was relieved of his duties, while Kühnl tries to address my legal status.

The landlords make an effort to show their old kindness and courtesy again, yet I still feel that envy, jealousy and a thirst for vengeance are lurking in hidden corners; the envy of those who perceive in me an emerging, surprisingly professional and political rival, the jealousy of those who rampage against all and everything at all times, and the thirst for revenge of the Nazi factotums who have learned how a cursed Jew extracted, "himself and his brood from his just punishment", and played an unheard of trick on the Führer.

And as sure as envy, jealousy and resentment accompany all radical political change, once they are let loose they will just as surely be directed towards me and the likes of me. That is why the rebirth is so difficult and the pangs worse than at the time when we slithered into using the pseudonym. Even if those fears were grounded in a realistic assessment of legions of spies, informers and Stapo executioners around us, still those fears created in every situation the necessary defenses against visible, stupid and awkward enemies. There is no effective protection against the secret and the hidden, and all predictions become worthless when evil hides behind a supposedly friendly mask. It is the defense against the disembodied villains. Those they defend remain invisible and impervious.

May 29, 1945

I have a new driving license for motorcycles. Therefore, I now have the pass that was the only document among my papers that fell into Nazi hands. Lastly there remains our material rehabilitation, that is to say compensation – the re-allocation of our worldly goods stolen by Hitler. But that will take time, knowing the French, assuming they even consider it appropriate at all.

However, it is also possible that the provisional regional government of the Vorarlberg, which is called "Regional Committee, Headquarters Feldkirch", is entrusted with these responsibilities. It has a representative from Bludenz, the former Social Democrat Nesler, who had to be brought to safety shortly before the last dance of the district leadership because the Nazis were getting too close.

Perhaps it would be good if I personally look him up, not only concerning my personal affairs but because it interests me to whom the fate of the Bludenz people is entrusted. What I would learn from that can at the same time be the test as to whether the Count and the Mayor have made the Action Committee aware of my affairs.

May 30, 1945

I have spoken to the Bludenz representative of the Regional Committee. He is an honest man with grey-brown, good-natured eyes, and listened willingly to me after it was apparent he had not been informed by anyone about me or my case. I described our tortuous life of suffering. I chatted for some time with him and expect to hear more after he has entered me into his reference book.

In the afternoon I received a written summons from the head of the local government to hand in a new curriculum vitae for completion of the records. The letter was addressed to: "Herr Dr. Phil. Walter Leopold, temporary war employee". With this it will probably be documented that I was only a very tiny office person despite everything known about me now, and am not to harbor any ambitions to compete with higher officials. On top of that Kühnl recently further tested the ground in the Brickhaus affair and informed me that the latter intended to submit an application to the military government and the Regional Committee for exceptional authorization of permanent residence in Bludenz, and to justify this by his martyrdom in the Party. Kühnl wanted to know if I would have anything against this step. As impudence has so often triumphed, at least in the case of Brickhaus, I will nip it in the bud, even if it should occur to Count Terlego to plead on behalf of this depraved subject. But even Feukert is blowing the same horn and maintains that Brickhaus never denounced me to the regional management, and so my action is not completely justified. A truly revolutionary viewpoint, one has to admit. If Brickhaus's case is not already incriminatory then I would like to know where the battle against the Nazis and their accomplices should begin.

It is true that if one is once involved with them, they become brazen, and if one shows just a trace of leniency, then they swing back into the saddle again. With the French Sirs, a Brickhaus would gain an easy hearing, and should he offer several bottles of good wine, even a friendly ear. However, I have not fought for 12 years only to throw hard-won pearls to the swine or even sell my convictions for a devious story of victory. It already sounds like the laughter of victory when a guy like Brickhaus voices his opinion that he is surprised that I deal with him so leniently and decently. That can yet change should he and his assistants wish it.

The conversation with Kühnl was interrupted by the appearance of Feukert, who asked me to come to our room where the French field Rabbi was waiting for me. My wife had brought him here from our home at Widmer Street 11, where he had unexpectedly appeared. We shook hands; he was no less moved than I and my wife. He pulled the letter which I had written from his pocket and asked me to clarify the address of my brother Max in Philadelphia once more and assured me that he would spare no effort in immediately sending the good news of our existence to my relatives there. He is still a young man, the "Qui meme Israelite,"[1] in his early thirties, medium height, with good-natured Jewish eyes. On his military shirt – the uniform is the same as all the French military – he wears the silver tablets with the typical ten Roman digits, and in a smaller size and with Hebrew decoration they can also be found on his cap. He cannot speak a word of German, so it was not easy for me to express clearly the terminus technicus necessary for my case. Still, what he comprehended without too many words was my card from

Buchenwald, the photos of our two burned-out synagogues in Leipzig and the picture of me after my return from the concentration camp.

"Terrible, terrible," he sighed, "but God has saved you and your family. That is the miracle."

Otherwise he gave a dejected, even intimidated impression; I was to understand the reason straight away. When I asked him whether he thought it right to inform the commanding general in Feldkirch about the existence of rescued Jews in Bludenz, he warned against this with alarm and interjected: "Under no circumstances! That would be very disadvantageous!"

"Why, Rabbi, I thought the French were fond of the Jews?"

"They don't hate us, but at most they tolerate us. And that is already quite something,"

So! That was shattering after the bitter experiences that I myself had already had with the French. They have already sunk so deeply into hatred of Jews that an army Rabbi cannot speak better of them than his colleagues in Germany did of Hitler's faithful in 1933. Have they come here as guardians of Hitler's inheritance, the sons of the Grande Nation?

It is truly a noble task which the "liberators of Austria" have set themselves! It can be resolved very quickly, for the Vorarlberg needs to be freed of only three full Jews. I congratulate you already today on your success, French sirs. May all be well with you!

Then the Rabbi asked me about other Jews in the Vorarlberg. I had to answer his hopeful question in the negative and could only say that the sole Jewish community was in Hohenems, where the synagogue together with several Torahs are more or less preserved, though not ready for visiting, and that I intended to go over there soon and ascertain the situation. My Christian colleague, who has warmly accepted the Jews in Hohenems, wants to facilitate the restoration of the tabernacles to the best of his ability.

In conclusion the Rabbi gave me a celebratory prayer book for Jewish soldiers and wrote a dedication inside. He took his leave with warm words and promised to pay us a longer visit on the next occasion.

If I believed I could finally close the matter of my identity, I was taught otherwise by an announcement from the military government. According to this, all men of whatever state citizenship, aged between 15 and 50 years, have to report at set times to the barracks in Bludenz, now a camp for German and Austrian prisoners of war. Now I can tell the powers that be out there the story of our adventure yet again.

It makes you sick! When will this torment begun by Adolf the Great in the year 1933 finally end? Will the French masters at least take enough notice of the clarification of my legal status, which I handed in weeks ago, to grant a general exemption for us three concerning the measures being taken against the German and Austrian population infected by Nazi propaganda and in the service of the Nazis? When?

June 6, 1945

The French Army Rabbi comes to me again in the office. He reports that he has viewed the synagogue in Hohenems. It is in a very bad state, dirty and the roof is partly destroyed. He will now have the military Gouverneur issue an order to the Mayor of Hohenems to have the house of God repaired, will then inform me and go over there together with me to consecrate the synagogue anew. The Torah rolls, about ten in number, he has put in the loft of the synagogue.

For lunch he was our guest with his Jewish chauffeur; he presented Anneli with biscuits and my wife with books and supply rarities. I ask him to make the Hamotzi,[2] which he gladly does with the snow-white soldier's bread that he cuts up for us all to eat. The inimitable ceremony was a feast not experienced for many years. The chauffeur came from Algeria. The Rabbi asks me for the book of Edmond Fleg, *Pourquoi je suis juif,* [3] which he has long been looking for and borrows until his return.

On the way to the office I speak to the French First Lieutenant Querle, consultant to the Gouverneur, and ask for a meeting. He instructs me to come outside his visiting hours at 4pm.

My conversation with the justice officer brought no significant results. He does want to arrange a certificate of protection for us, but I doubt whether he will succeed. He is glad to obtain a pass for me to visit the synagogue in Hohenems, and also for any other necessary journeys.

I have handed over the new curriculum vitae to the local government with the following accompanying note:

Further to your summons of 28.5.45, I hand over to you a new curriculum vitae as an attachment to add to my personal documents.

I note with satisfaction that I am entered by you with the fine-sounding description "war assistance employee." That, contrary to your practice towards Herr Freiherr, you choose to use this title originating from the Nazi era, precisely in the first proof of my legal status, seems to me quite a particular honor.

Sincerely, Dr. L

June 10, 1945

Yesterday the French radio played a song of praise for the Vorarlberg people over the Dornbin broadcaster. It contrasted them with the sly, reactionary Reich Germans possessed by Hitler's spirit, praised their revolutionary impulse, their direct and open attitude and their distaste for everything that smells of Fascism and militarism, and called them a friendly, obliging and always smiling breed, who distinguish themselves from everything German also through their national dress.

Well, the Frenchman, or whatever nation the radio scriptwriter may have belonged to, appears to know neither the Germans nor the Vorarlberg people. Otherwise he would have long ago had to reach the disturbing conclusion that, as far as disposition and habits are concerned, there is no essential difference at all between the Vorarlberg people and Reich Germans, indeed that the bad qualities that he attributes to the latter are true to a greater extent of the former. They may be able to be friendly and amiable when they sniff an advantage, they may well be opponents of militarism when it imposes large, uncomfortable personal duties and limitations on them, they may well hate National Socialists when they have to carry out personal business with them and at the same time appear in their national costume, in order to attract the gaze of churchgoers, or, as is particularly apparent, to distance themselves in the eyes of the French from the thrice-cursed Piefke.[4]

Piefke is the one who dares to take his pleasures in the blessed fields of Vorarlberg even after the premature death of the Thousand-Year Reich;

Piefke is everyone who comes from Germany, whether he sought to make progress as an enthusiastic Nazi, or in disregard of his heroic reputation, his personal safety and business interests, spat in front of Hitler's disciples; Piefke is the curse used for everybody who alongside the local dialect practices his own way of speaking;

And finally, everybody is degraded as Piefke who dares to express another opinion than what is current in this land, or even worse, belittles the Catholic Church by failing to pay the requisite homage of three visits a day.

However, whoever has re-discovered his Catholic heart, whoever stands on the corners in leather trousers and chamois tufts, because he does not know how else he should spend his time, whoever measures up every Reich German with a disparaging look and wishes he would go to hell once he can no longer profit from him, whoever hangs out the greatest possible number of Austrian flags, and the Tyrol one as well, he is a true Vorarlberg man, even though only a month ago he stood on a table so that his Hitler salute shamed hesitant hand raisers, including those from the old Reich.

They treat us well, the only Jewish family in the whole of Vorarlberg. We are a small sensation which they believe they should not pass over carelessly, because one can never know whether a friendly smile or a comradely nod towards the Jewish wanderers may not lead to a word being put in with the new masters. Indeed, many of my colleagues are thrilled at our courage and the unexpected unmasking, pay us all sorts of attention, and are even proud of the new doctor in the local government.

But in the background these citizens, traditionally hostile to Piefkes and Jews, look suspiciously, enviously and haughtily at the newly arrived unbeliever who even has the boldness to creep into the highest office of the local government. A person from Bludenz, yes, one would see him very gladly, also a Vorarlberg person, as long as he is a devout Catholic, but a Jew from Germany? Firstly, he is a heathen and secondly, he belongs to the clique who are known to have financed the awakening Germany with the war-cry "Jew, kick the bucket!"

In that respect the Christian Vorarlbergers were different guys! From the beginning, they now claim, they have distanced themselves from National Socialism, and sent their preachers to the devil when they tried to beguile the people. On the day that Hitler took over Austria, they turned their backs on his boys, the regional and district leaders, the officials and Gestapo bosses, the great and small Nazi rascals together with all enemies of the clergy, and they never raised their hands in greeting. And today a Jew like him, now that his friends the National Socialists have hit rock bottom, wants to suck up to the Bludenz people in the true Jewish manner? Yes, if he would let himself and his wife and child at least be baptised and thus prove that he is willing and ready to acknowledge the power of the one blessed church!

But the Jew on his odyssey knows the secret machinations of all those who imagine they must swing themselves onto the throne from which the Nazis have only just been pushed, and he will fight on in order to prevent the Hitler tyranny being replaced by another, even if it springs from the brain of the clergy.

If the Catholic Church thus tramples the wish of Jews for reconciliation by imposing its worst conditions, if it rewards trust with aggression, if its bishops and priests consider it right to continue to foster and rekindle hatred of Jews – those who are meant here know it – then the fight against race hatred becomes a fight against overbearing confessional hatred. I did not fall to my knees before Hitler. I will certainly not crawl to the cross.

June 21, 1945

A directive from the Vorarlberg Regional Committee determines that all officials and public service employees are to be dismissed if in March 1938 they belonged to the German Reich. This also goes for those who belonged to the National Socialist Party or were active as Party functionaries alongside their official duties.

Well, I too count among those belonging to the Reich before March 1938, even if I am today also officially declared "stateless". Maybe I will have to return to the Reich with my wife and child? With all those people who we have learned to love as our tormentors? Even Hitler would not have demanded that. But those who have brought him down do. I will certainly not fulfil such pious wishes, whatever they may wish to call them, even if they are German Jew-eaters or children of the Grande Nation infected by the Nazi bacillus.

Through the Dreyfus affair[5] the French have already made themselves notorious for antisemitism, and degraded their motto "Liberté, Fraternité, Egalité" to an expression for bookmarkers. Now they show it again as they declare that the French "have not come in order to clean up race laws."

The woman to whom a French officer called out these flattering words asked me to take it up with the Gouverneur here. She is the daughter of a pious Jew, lived in Berlin and nourishes the hope that through divorce[6] she can mitigate the fate of her daughter and

Reich German husband, regularized according to the Nazis as Aryan. When their home was seized and the business was destroyed by a bomb attack, the three of them sought refuge in Vorarlberg and in spite of the divorce obtained from the communal commission an authorization to continue her earlier business activities, for which she even received active support from my earlier chief, the Regional Councilor.

With a seriously ill and several times operated on husband, the involuntary divorcees lived in constant fear that the Nazi authorities would get wind of the secret of their earlier mixed marriage, which was not known in these parts, and would orchestrate an abrupt and terrible end to mother, father and daughter. The woman therefore placed all hopes on the collapse of the Hitler state and liberation by the Allies, and after the entry of the French she went to the local commandant with the request that he authorizes her Reich German husband, who was again about to have an operation, and her daughter to stay together in Vorarlberg.

"We did not come to clean up the race laws!"

That was all that the Frenchman could propose to a family destroyed by the hellhounds.

"We did not come to clean up the race laws!"

May I be allowed the question for what else you came, Mr. Commandant of Nenzing?[7] Or do you feel called upon to give a last polish to the race laws of the Third Reich? The Grande Nation will know how to praise you and your soldiers, who have learned from you and can already be heard cursing Jews.

33 OUR REGRETS, HERR DOKTOR

For more than two years of living underground and then with an assumed Aryan identity, Walter avoids any direct personal antisemitism. Now he experiences it once again, although in more muted forms. But he refuses to let the whispers and lack of support get in the way of his goals. He wants to continue to serve in the Vorarlberg regional government. He wants a permanent apartment and he wants Austrian citizenship. Reparations would be welcomed as well. (Ironically, the apartment he seeks would likely come from a dispossessed Nazi.)

Day by day the miracle of his survival threatens to crash against the massive geopolitical forces driving the establishment of a new order in Europe. His expectations for substantive aid from his French liberators begin to crumble. Frustration grows as does his sense that success is tantalizingly close. Hope competes with bitterness.

June 26, 1945

Morning: Meeting with R. in the anteroom of the District Captain's office. He announces an apartment for me soon. I have a conversation with Kühnl about the matter of the continuation of my official post. His hints, which were similar to an assurance, awaken hopes.

Afternoon: Town official Häusler telephones me and informs me that the town has allotted to me, together with its fittings, the apartment in the South Tyrol settlement of a Frau Krenfing, who was reputed and feared to be a Nazi spy and informer. I should go and see the apartment. As I hear this happy news, my wife is with me.

Later Kühnl calls me in to congratulate me. Häusler has already told him the news. The apartment is said to be one of the finest in the whole settlement, with a large corner window, and at the time was allocated to Frau Krenfing on the initiative of the local government for her loyal services to the Nazis. Kühnl's wish will thus probably be fulfilled, as long as the apartment also contains furniture for three persons.

Kühnl reports on the arrest of former Nazis. He seeks justification for the arrests. I retort that the greatest scoundrels are now appealing to the decency of the new rulers and at the same time dream of a return of the Nazis.

June 27, 1945

This afternoon at 3pm I had an interview with town official Häusler after a preceding telephone call. At my request, he showed me an inventory of the apartment I will take over, so that I can check that the fittings and utensils have not been taken away. Then he handed me an order from the Mayor of Bludenz, according to which the free-standing apartment in the South Tyrol settlement No. 13, consisting of kitchen and four rooms together with fittings, is allocated to me. "Concerning the possible taking of fittings, laundry and suchlike into your possession," it continued, "this will be decided at a later point within the framework of your compensation. For the time being all the installations will be given to you for free use."

As my wife and child also wanted to see the new apartment, he gave us a police sergeant who already lives in the settlement to accompany us to the viewing. From outside it is recognizable by the only corner window to the left above the main doorway leading to the ugly, barrack-like settlement block barking at the mountains, which represents a particular aberration of taste in this unique area. But, the apartments are light, airy, comfy and practically arranged. All the more astonished were we at the unsuitable arrangement of the home fittings allotted to us, which presently a family – husband, wife and child – are still making use of.

From a small corridor, to the left one enters the spacious child's room facing the mountains with one complete bed and one bed frame, to the right the toilet with shower, while straight on the door opens to the kitchen/living room, where the actual cooking, washing and cooking installations are built into a kitchen, while the largest part of the room is filled with a table, chairs, a chaise-longue, a smaller table and a laundry cupboard which is likely meant to be a kitchenware cupboard. This not exactly pleasant picture is further marked by the housewife fussing around and her five-year-old stark naked – the somersaulting boy is mistreating the chaise-longue. The woman bewails the misery that has been heaped on her hurting body by moving for six weeks from one apartment into another. Her husband was on the way to the Mayor to report to him that his search for new accommodation had been fruitless and he was not able to move out at short notice.

From the kitchen-living room we stepped to the left into the large but primitively furnished bedroom and go through the kitchen back into the very small dining room. It is stuffed full of furniture, a sideboard, wall clock, chest of drawers, table, chairs and a reclining sofa standing close to each other, while the walls are covered all over with marvelous oil portraits. And on the sideboard I discovered to simultaneously my greatest horror and greatest joy a splendid heavy-brass Menorah – on the chest of drawers however as a pendant was a Kiddush beaker[1] with a border of grapes, trophies of a Nazi criminal from a deported and murdered Jew.

From the corner window there is a magnificent view onto the mountains. That, however, is the only advantage of the apartment, since it does not offer me even the makeshift writing space which I have made for myself in our present apartment. The policeman therefore recommends that we view another larger apartment with four rooms – that of an arrested local cop located further up the settlement. Tomorrow morning at 10 we will see it.

June 28, 1945

We have inspected the apartment of the Nazi cop Jäger with the support of police Sergeant Hahnert. A sub-tenant opened for us, since wife had already departed. The apartment is not only more spacious than the first, but also divided up more conveniently. To the right of the corridor is the bathroom (bath fittings included here), next to it the kitchen, with electric cooker. Opposite is the child's room, next to it the bedroom for the parents, and at the end of the hallway the living room set up as a farmhouse parlor, paneled halfway up with wooden benches along the wall. To the left there is access to a further room, which we could not go into since the occupant, a second sub-tenant, had locked it and gone away.

Then the mistress turned up and stood before us almost petrified as the police sergeant told her the reason for our unexpected visit. She became bright red to behind her ears and maintained that only yesterday she was given the binding promise that she could keep the apartment with her children, to which the police sergeant let her know that a higher authority would decide about it. But the bathroom installations and the boiler in the kitchen were her own property and would be taken out in case she had to give up the apartment.

As the house is somewhat higher up behind the front building, the view over the mountains is naturally limited, but a few steps away on the neighboring meadow is a pleasant view.

On the way back, we had another meeting with the town official. I briefly reported my impression of the apartment, which was not the worst, and of the objections of the Nazi woman. The town official laughed and said she must leave Bludenz immediately and of course should leave the bathroom installations and the boiler in the apartment, while her furniture would be taken over by the town of Bludenz. Into the evacuated apartment should be brought the installations left to us in the first one offered to us, and if we wished these should be supplemented also with a kitchen cupboard, writing desk with chair, bookcase and sewing machine. Then he handed over documentation including the inventory to be handed over to us, which we looked through and on first sight found quite sufficient.

In the afternoon a letter from the Bludenz Liberation Committee arrived, in which it unanimously confirmed the compensation requested, and thereby conveyed that our sojourn in Bludenz has become definitive. One of the final goals we set ourselves is reached.

June 30, 1945

Yesterday afternoon we again took a look at our apartment in the Tyrol settlement. The Nazi woman was suddenly very friendly and open, and it seems that in the mayor's office, to which she rushed after our unexpected appearance, she was brought to reason. At any rate she made no further claim to the bathroom installations or the boiler, but she asked if she may use the bath every week against the provision of heating materials. (We have not yet granted this to her.)

Our new home is a fine thing, as long as somebody does not spit in our soup at the last moment. It really is very roomy, and this time we could also view the room selected for my work room. It is really lovely and promises to be a pleasant place to be, if as promised the town puts a writing desk and bookcase at our disposal. The view from its window looks over the roof of the front building to the Ritikon, while from the dining room one can overlook the whole area downwards from the Nordspitze. No less do I like the view from the kitchen, and even the lavatory is conceived with these accessories. At last I can have room to write again and, if I know myself, with the result that we will also feel well in this craggy Tyrol settlement.

It is a long way into the little town, and in the future I will no longer run to the office in five minutes, be able to stroll home for a bread and butter breakfast, but on the other hand this walk with the enchanting panorama is delightful and relaxing. Less so for my poor wife, who must in future do her shopping and queuing without rest. But with time this misery may be relieved too.

Concerning grub: it is looking pretty rotten since the French see their provisions from the U.S.A. diminish daily and make up for it with the meagre rations and produce of the locals. Eggs we have not seen for a long time, butter too disappears noticeably, and the weekly meat ration often does not even to suffice for one meal. Today there were no vegetables, even though they flourish in our area, and if the potato beetle which recently arrived at our altitude becomes an insatiable pest, then we can congratulate ourselves.

No wonder that we two old ones – the child has first claim on nourishment – shrivel up more and more, and my clothes which a year ago fitted tightly now hang baggily around my body. So much space is left around my ribs that today they could be used as shopping nets. We must savor the misery of hunger, which is an unpleasant memory for us, once more among our "liberator friends".

After all other Bludenz dignitaries, the French have now condescended to send us two invitations to the repetition of their "Gala welfare evening – a night to celebrate the Allied Victory". Entry free. Programme 20 Marks. Formal dress desired. Robbed and burned-out Jews in tuxedos and ball gowns and 30 Marks plus many times that for material pleasures that would certainly be the greatest achievement of the last ten years of our earthly existence. But it is not our custom to place any value on such final examinations. And as the French in any case do not reflect very much on Jewish society, they will miss us all the less this evening.

Their Gouverneur has announced today through the local government that Austrians can now travel in the whole Bludenz district without passes.

Austrians? And stateless people? And Jews? I will find out and tensely await the decision. If they say that we are subject to the same restrictions as the Reich Germans, I will know enough and will be fed up to the back teeth with the Allies' appreciation of the much-pitied Jews.

July 2, 1945

For while on the one hand they proclaim total eradication of National Socialism, they escort the Hitler Youth girl leaders to the dance floor, seduce them into everything other than a humanitarian attitude to life, and regardless of military rank enter into relationships with the wives of Hitler's scoundrels, who rejoice in securing their freedom in this diplomatic way, and in the eyes of their soldiers have the remarkable reputation of being notable antisemites.

As a further accompaniment to their "liberation actions", they tuck into the necessary victuals of the thus liberated Vorarlberg people for so long that no drop of milk and not one iota of butter passes the lips of old people and children, and the housewives queue vainly for hours in front of shops waiting for a vegetable leaf. And he, who like us, has fought for longer than a decade against the Nazi filth and during the days of endless hounding and sleepless nights has longed and begged for the hours of liberation, he may now share the same peculiar luck as the former persecutors to starve again and be deprived again of his freedom of movement, this time by the representatives of the Grande Nation, whose entry a short time ago he greeted with tears of joy.

It helps him in no way that he tries again and again to persuade them that their treatment of the Jews runs strictly counter to the decisions of the Allies. He speaks to a wall when he makes efforts to prove to the government officers that one cannot throw him as a

Jew into one pot together with the most negative clique. He constantly receives the stereotypical answer: "The Germans have stolen and eaten up everything we had. Not you, but we have the priority when it comes to living and eating again."

Yes, we the Jews have imposed war on the French and eaten them bare, we the Jews have deported your women and men, we the Jews are therefore obliged to make amends to you like the enemies in Germany and Austria. Carry on like that, friends from France! Your merits concerning the matter of Hitler would find the honor that was once accorded to the Danae,[2] of that you can be sure.

Hail to you, happy Austria!

July 7, 1945

Slowly but surely, I grasp the secrets of the tactic with which the French masters cause so much confusion in the heads of those who dared to speculate about their healthy political sense. According to them, the Nazis are to be pursued not for their Nazism, but because they have caused mayhem in France. If they had not done so, they would have been quite sympathetic messengers of Hitler. If they belong to the fair sex they even become desirable companions and more, which at least brings them the desired triumph over the Nazi enemies and delicious freedom from the heroic riff-raff. What does the lover care about the diabolical mass murders that the swastika worshippers carried out on non-French territory? What matters the groaning of the few surviving Jews, and all those who built their hopes on salvation on the "liberators?"

The Nazi girls and Nazi women with their seductive bodies are such welcome bedfellows, and during hot nights of love and abandon, the rest of humanity can be so wonderfully forgotten!

And then there is the Nazi who is unprotected because he cannot compete with sexual and alcoholic offerings. Through him one can prove that the call for the liberation of the European peoples is not only empty talk. One can lock him up and beat him half dead, and if that is not enough, also put next to one or another opponent of

Hitler, preferably a Jew. Furthermore, one can offer them a cleansing act of love by sending to the devil all Reich Germans, whether Hitler followers or untiring Nazi women, handing over their fineries as gifts. Yet for every Nazi acquaintance and relative of a French soldier's love, indiscriminately passes and other favors are provided, for which truly deserving people often have to beg fruitlessly, as is the case of the Jew Dr. Leopold.

Let him complain further about his stomach shrunk by years of hunger and his spindly body, let him keep telling people of his experiences in the "concert camp", of his enslavement, of his defiance of death in the struggle for saving his wife and child, his Freiherr identity, his courage and his convictions, his daring and his indomitable hope, which finally set him free again! Leave him in peace! He too will one day get what he requests, and if not, then one can very easily bring him to reason.

But Dr. Leopold is braver than you believe, my French lords, and he does not shy away from letting himself be locked up and beaten if you want to create a perpetual memorial for yourselves. He did not bow before Hitler, and he will certainly not submit to those who are ready to sacrifice their duty for a night of love. If you celebrate your victory over France's enemies in this way, then you did not deserve that the Anglo-Americans, when you were trampled under the Nazi boot, pulled you back up into the saddle.

Now France is withdrawing, the "Julienne" division, in order celebrate their victory orgies in Tyrol, which has been granted to the French.[3] Remaining behind, unfortunately, are the men of the Hililand government! Unfortunately! For all those whose hearts are full of disappointment and bitterness would shed no tears for you either. Will they have such a good time as in Vorarlberg, and enjoy their fat, bloated finale, and let milk, honey and bodily pleasures flow as here in Bludenz? I dare to doubt it.

Adieu gentlemen! Very happy to have made your acquaintance! Farewell! I wish you a pleasant journey!

The matter of the apartment does not get off the ground. The official Häusler constantly says: "In the next few days the apartment will be free." And that's as far as it goes. Every day I call him twice, so that he gets a move on with the matter. To every exhortation and reproach he reacts kindly as always.

July 9, 1945

Radio London reads a letter from a Jewish soldier of the American occupation army who originates from Germany and had to leave his parents behind in the clutches of the Stapo. When he heard that they were dragged off to Theresienstadt, he set off for the camp town accompanied by a comrade. In the camp office he found that the names of his parents were not registered, since the SS had destroyed the card index of deceased and killed inhabitants during the approach of the American troops.

And so, the orphaned man had to make do with the story of a long-term, emaciated inmate of the camp. The latter recounted that he knew well the parents of the searcher, and remembered that in July 1943, together with many fellow sufferers, they were shipped off to Auschwitz for execution in the gas chambers.

The informant had himself once attended one of these death transports and described how the execution happened. His report corresponds with the testimonials of earlier witnesses, including the gruesome fact that children were not poisoned but thrown alive into the cremation furnaces. That is according to the chief of the American soldiers.

After all this there is little hope that the mother of my wife is among the people rescued from Theresienstadt. It is to be assumed that we will at least hear from some of our Leipzig friends, once the post works again, provided that the Russians, under whom Leipzig falls, permit postal services.[4]

Shortly I will try to put out feelers with the Red Cross in Geneva.

July 12, 1945

Before supper I stand in the courtyard where a Moroccan soldier requests from his chief that his bicycle should be repaired. I start a conversation with him and tell him I am a Jew. I wanted to see how he would react to it.

"Juif?" he asked in consternation.

"Oui, Monsieur. Juif."

"Juif nix gut."[5]

So, the French Moroccans too are already loyal Hitler hypocrites. Just carry on like that. Vive la France!

And the day after tomorrow, July 14, is the French national day, to be celebrated also by the people of liberated Vorarlberg. Liberté! Egalité! Fraternité!

But Juif, nix gut!

July 26, 1945

In fact, we feel like summer holidaymakers in our airy lookout, especially as today the crippling heat which lasted until yesterday has given way to a refreshing breeze. From the meadows, which stretch out on the west side of our house to the woods, it carries the fragrant scent of hay through the windows. I experienced a real rebirth today as I wrote down my experiences at a writing desk filled with my utensils for the first time since 1943. For the first time in my life I have the fairy-tale view onto the high mountains and the majestic scenery in the background. Our visitors, and there are more and more of them, at first largely supplicants, are just as overcome by the view as we are. However, they admire no less the beauty of our home and the atmosphere with which they are received. No wonder that we regret every hour which is lost to us up here through unavoidable trips into the little town. For down there, noisy French traffic roars around us with its stink of petrol and pollution.

The last two days of my first week of holiday since 1940 I spend sunk dreamily into myself, for we three have not yet regained the spiritual strength which is necessary to measure the indescribable happiness of our newly-won home, let alone to bear it. For our inner beings are still too burdened with fear of jealous people, and with the setbacks and disappointments which followed one after the other for a decade. Alongside freedom, perhaps heaven will also give us the gift again of enjoying it uninhibitedly.

August 3, 1945

I spoke today with the Count about my future and asked him on his next journey to the Regional Committee in Bregenz to negotiate with Chairman Ilg about my plans to stay in the administration or take over a teacher's post, and to arrange that I should be invited for a personal interview. For this, I handed him the written explanation of my naturalization. He promised to do everything for me and to inform the Regional Committee thoroughly of my character. This step is essential if I am not only to remain in the Office but also to finally get to move on from my pitiful position as a temporary war employee.

August 14, 1945

Kühnl questioned the Count as he left the government building and received the answer that the Regional Committee has selected me for higher education teaching, specifically foreign languages. At which establishment, he did not ask. It seems that Vorarlberg has after all now recognized my right to reside and be active, and has even responded to the special desire I expressed to the Count to move into teaching. I still need to take care that I can teach in Bludenz and will make my case to both the Count and Nesler.

Tomorrow I will therefore call the office, even though I have my second week of holiday. I will ask the Count whether I can now count on back pay of my salary since that amounts to more than 500 Reich Marks, and that is a lot for a poor devil.

In all this, I absolutely do not yield to the madness of considering my employment in higher education as a fait accompli. On the contrary. I can hardly think that the Vorarlberg government employs men who have passed no teaching test, even if they have functioned as a professor in an adult education center and a teacher and educator in an orphanage in the Leipzig Jewish community. I can well imagine that applicants must complete more courses and pass a test before they are admitted. My French and English are more or less all right, the English better than the French, but it is quite enough for teaching. German I would like to include, that is my element. Well, we will see. Maybe it will come off.

I thought so. The story about the teaching post is an unlaid egg. The Count, who had told Kühnl of the apparent result of his interview in Bregenz and empowered him to report to me, when I visited him today, said not a word about it. He thought fit merely to remark that the Regional Committee must first come to a conclusion about the status of my citizenship after the delivery of my declaration.

"You actually wanted to go to Bregenz yourself, didn't you?" he asked me quietly.

"If you consider it necessary, Count, then of course."

"Well, it is not exactly necessary."

"So, the gentlemen there know enough about me to make a judgment?"

"Yes, indeed."

"And have you, Count, made a decision about my application for the adjustment of my salary?"

"No, it has not yet been presented to me."

"Yes, it has, Herr Kühnl spoke about it."

"How high is your salary?"

"About 370 Marks gross, 301 Marks net."

"Well then, 50 Marks more are always welcome. Moreover, if you had been known as Freiherr before 1942, then you would not have been deprived of your citizenship, would you?"

With this he turns away. I understand.

"But you have already convinced yourself that I only called myself Freiherr on the day of our flight. The matter is thus clear, Count."

"Yes, certainly, indeed."

"Thank you! Good day!"

And then I was outside.

Theatre, hypocritical comedy. They want to get rid of me after all. And what in particular does this have to do with the school story?

I finish the letter to Nesler in the resistance movement and send it through my wife. To continue counting on Count Terlego is pointless. Hatred of Jews is an incurable illness. And one should not burden ill people. I hope I will find a few friends among the resistance people.

Thus, the fate of a Jew seems to be tragic once again. Despised, hunted and robbed by the Nazis, preserved by the hand of heaven from terrible disaster, the outcast without a home is confronted by new enemies, who do not dare to make their hatred for the Jews openly known. They are thus more deceitful, and more dangerous than the Fascists, whom they pretended to fight against. Now that they have slipped out of the Nazi straitjacket with the help of the Allies, they turn with outlandish cunning against all freedom fighters who are not willing to submit themselves to a new tyranny, or set about trampling to death the only Jewish public employee in Vorarlberg, in order to preserve their blessed little land from Jews.

The few people who believe they have to digest these rotten deeds withdraw discouraged or believe they have to embrace the antisemitic majority or at least keep silent out of opportunism, such as Feukert, who says neither yes or no, and seems to have come to terms with the fact that Vorarlberg once was, is and will remain hostile to the Jews. Consequently, the Jew Leopold has no right to exist in these parts. Those resisting the aggressions and the fiery torches are discouraged by the attitude of the Allies, who for years puffed themselves up as liberators of the poor Jews, only to now raise their hands in appeasement and trumpet that no injustice must befall the Nazis for the sake of the Jews.

In particular the French, who after all "did not come in order to settle the race question", degrade the little Jewish doctor before the district leadership as an object of scorn by the gloating and vainglorious people of Catholic or other persuasions, while they grant the hidden Austrian Nazis freedom that nobody ever expected. They confine the Jew made stateless in a ten-kilometer radius so that he should be permanently forced to be conscious of his role as pure propaganda material. They reckon they can put the Jewish freedom fighter and Odysseus from Leipzig on the same level as outlawed Party members and officials and employees sacked because of their too brazen Nazi inclinations. One is surrounded by the stink of rotting carrion, which cannot to be banished even through sweet Catholic holy water.

August 17, 1945

I had a long talk with Nesler. As one of the few left-wing politicians, he is opposed to me leaving the district leadership to enter the school service. He would rather arrange that I be entrusted with the Commercial Office, where the Count has put one of his own rank, Baron W, and given him a high pension, all loyal and honest.

Then Nesler indicated that the occupation authority is working on decrees according to which all Nazi Germans from the Reich should be rapidly deported to Germany while the Austrian Nazis should be put in barracks.

Tomorrow, Sunday evening, I should appear at Nessler's home for a meeting of the left-wing faction of the resistance movement.

August 18, 1945

During the assembly of the left-wing faction of the resistance movement for Bludenz, when my turn came, I gave an improvised talk against reaction and antisemitism. The feedback was more than satisfactory. Regrettably Nesler made a lapse in presenting me as an old comrade of the Social Democrat Party. This embellishment with alien feathers was certainly well meant, but has to be laid aside not only for the sake of truth, but also to make clear my independence of any party, even though I am strongly orientated to left-wing socialism, since this has proved stronger through all the confusion than the party wavering of many Social Democrats, who lay in the dust before Hitler and kissed his slippers.

Nevertheless, I have the not unjustified hope that I will feel so much at home with my Bludenz comrades that they will consider me worthy to become one of their advocates and comrades-in-arms. And then the bosses in the area leadership and Bregenz will have to learn some lessons.

August 26, 1945

For the first time since I have been staying in Bludenz the dear "Jew" is recognized in a favorable light. No. 6 of the official journal cites that Jewish children can be registered for an exchange in Switzerland, without linking it to the precondition of a particular state citizenship. They are put on the same level as children of Vienna refugees and prisoners from concentration camps. Thus, the rights of the Jews seem to be gradually acknowledged, whereby I am offered two sorts of chances, one as a Jew and the other as a former inmate of Buchenwald.

Annelie, who has not been separated from us for a single day, as expected howled when Mutti spoke to her of the good fortune possibly awaiting her, but soon calmed down and even felt remorse at her refusal to go to Switzerland for a few weeks. Now she can hardly wait for the day of her departure, naturally not considering that during the first nights in the foreign country she will cry. Nevertheless, I will register her on the assumption that as the only Jewish child in the Vorarlberg area, she will go to a Jewish family in Switzerland. Good genuine food would do the child good, and this consideration is the most important.

The wretched fuss over our status makes me sick. Now it is clear once and for all that the Vorarlberg people want to have no Jews among them, and certainly not in the public service. Reich Germans and Jews must get out of this "Land of Mary" that the Lord has created for the Vorarlberg people, as long as they remain faithful children of the Catholic Church. Whoever does not belong to it or is no longer a believer (and those are above all, the Jews) has no claim on the hospitality of this blessed land.

The finest thing is that these ladies and gentlemen are still proud of their antisemitic nature, which they acknowledge quite openly among themselves. Comrade Feukert, who after the arrival of the French did not find enough space in his breast for enthusiasm about my mutation back into a genuine Jew, has recently been quite openly and confidently proclaiming that Vorarlberg is now finally free of Jews and probably will remain so, and that it would be senseless to fight against this fact. Then he said that it was written on his freedom-fighter identity card that he devoted his life to the cause of the resistance, without knowing or guessing how much he was disavowing himself through his textbook thinking concerning sacrifice for the majority. It is understood that one must swim with the strongest current if one wants to continue to be in the good books – exactly as one wore or took off one's safety pin and decorated one's hat with shooting awards.

Those who are principally concerned, that is my chief, the Count and the people of the Regional Committee, want to be seen as tactful and do not dare to openly avow their distaste for Jews and other unauthorized persons who meddle in their affairs. In order to get rid of me they will make use of a tried and tested means and will sooner or later open up with:

"Only Austrian citizens have a right to employment in the public service. And as you are stateless you do not fulfil this condition sine qua non[6] and will not be able to fulfil it for as long as there is no government which is willing and able to consider you for such a distinction.

I much regret, Herr Doktor, that I cannot give you more favorable news.

If it depended only on us, yes, certainly. But unfortunately, we have no power in this matter.

Our regrets, Herr Doktor!"

That is how they will talk, that is how they will write, and they will entertain the hope that they can indulge their antisemitic ways until eternity. If against expectations a lightning bolt should strike from heaven, then it will be picked up by a tried and tested lightning rod, that is, the Reich Germans. As long as one can curse them and demand their deportation, the antisemitic pulse can throb unheard, and one can even engage in a little bit of Nazi propaganda if one whips up hatred for the Jews and keeps it alive. As far as the French are concerned, dear God, from this side we have absolutely nothing to fear, for firstly they too cannot stand Jews, and certainly not Reich German Jews. In that way we play our trump card.

It happens differently than one thinks. It may be that they will force the Jewish travelers out of Bludenz, Vorarlberg and Austria. It may be that he will again have to tie up his bundle, take his walking stick and make off to distant lands. But he will take these notes with him and give them to the whole world to read, and they will rejoice, the Americans, the British, the Swiss and the Germans, that the brave Vorarlberg people have cleansed their little land of the Nazis and of my presence, cleansed themselves of the Reich Germans and a Jewish public employee together with his wife and child. The whole world will rejoice and hundreds of thousands will make pilgrimages to Vorarlberg, in order to get to know the only land on earth where National-Socialist leftovers have become pious keepers of reliquaries and are honored with the humility due to them. They will not come with gifts, but as curious enquirers and will look for unhallowed houses for those who find a hellish pleasure in the blessed land of Vorarlberg, free from the damned Jews and friends of Jews abroad, convinced of the saying that eating oneself makes one fat.

Fare ye well, dear Vorarlberg people, nimbly exchange your Jews for those kinds of advantages for which you exchanged your candles for the lights of war under the swastika flag. You will be well off in the land where no Jews live.

September 8, 1945

All the chaverim[7] on the survivor list – Jews 120 in number – are liberated inmates of concentration camps, one even from Auschwitz, another from Theresienstadt, who was present when the transport from Leipzig from which we ran away arrived there.

The Leipzig "old ones", that is those over 45 years of age, were dispatched to Auschwitz shortly afterwards for "extermination," very probably including the mother of my wife, for whom I have been searching without success. In order to ascertain her fate and that of my Leipzig friends, I leaf through the printed lists of Jews liberated from various concentration camps, and to my consternation I note that scarcely forty of the Leipzigers are registered. Not only my mother-in-law, also all friends and acquaintances are missing, and thus seem not to have survived their martyrdom; so too the whole leadership of the Jewish community, the last doctor of the hospital, likewise all holders of the Iron Cross, for whom the transport to Theresienstadt was designated as a special favor, and which all of them made hopeful allowances for, against my worst fears, which drove me to my reckless undertaking.

But two prominent Jews from Leipzig they spared, the SS butchers, namely the Stapo helper and informer Grunsfeld and his assistant, the decadent Jewish arch antisemite Arthur Fritz together with his wife, of whom it was earlier recounted that they performed the functions of "pool attendants". I hope that my Leipzig non-Jewish friends, to whom I told of the collaborationist deeds of Dr. Grunsfeld and his disciples, will help put them on trial. Should this not yet have happened for a lack of living witnesses, then I will ask the Allies and friends in Germany to get hold of these fellows before they slip underground... and cause new mischief.

34 DISAPPOINTMENT

Walter's dreams are imperiled. Yes, he is incredibly grateful that he and his family have survived the Nazi terror. But he wants and needs a full life commensurate with his education and skills, and he wants it in Bludenz, Austria, not Germany, not Palestine, not even the United States. The beauty of this alpine area and the openings in the public service capture him, body and soul. When visiting the Vorarlberg area with his wife Hilda after they were married, he fell in love with the mountains, meadows and fresh air. And here he is again after a victorious journey few dared to take, and even fewer survived. He wants his due.

So, he tries and tries to regain his position in this community. He fights to be recognized as a concentration camp survivor, a special status that exists at that time in Austria. He fights for Austrian citizenship. He wages battle with his pen, writing hundreds of letters, and through the force of his personality, pressing scores of officials and political activists. Surely after successfully maneuvering through the Nazi bureaucracy for 12 long years, should he not be able to master peacetime Austria?

As this quest intensifies, more and more bitterness seeps into his writing. As he writes more letters, he records his thoughts less often in this memoir. He wonders if he, like Moses, will be denied entry into his Promised Land.

September 8, 1945

The chaverim in Hohenems, who are praying the Kol-Nidre on Yom Kippur, mostly come from Eastern European lands, many from Czechoslovakia. They almost all speak fluent German and besides their native languages some also speak Hebrew and French. Some of the girls speak German perfectly, so I can converse seriously with them about the many pressing questions. Compared with the superficial conversation with the Rabbi, who has become rather invisible next to his flock, this is the first cordial and fruitful exchange of thoughts with Jews. They are largely simple, extraordinarily pleasant, straight-forward and objectively thinking human beings, who flock around their little Rabbi, whose good heart shines out of his eyes.

I take my midday meal in the dining room of the chaverim. Kosher, as they meaningfully and proudly remark. It is noodle soup, cabbage with rice in tomato sauce, and cucumber slices. For lack of free wardrobe hooks I eat sweating in my coat and hat until the Rabbi notices. He takes my coat off, gives my hat a questioning look – like all Jews I keep my hat on according to tradition – and beams all over his face when I pull a little yarmulke out of my pocket, by which he recognizes that I am really not just of Jewish ethnic origin.

At the table I make the acquaintance of many other chaverim, among whom are nice, even lovely girls. One wonders how they could maintain their pleasant looks through years of concentration camp imprisonment.

At the Regional Committee Office, after some waiting, I speak with Councilor Dr. Grabmayer, an old, gaunt gentleman with rather stiff manners. I introduced myself with the remark that on the occasion of another obligation in Bregenz I did not want to miss introducing myself personally to him, which he countered with some polite compliments about my adventurous undertaking. However, he tries to put down my allusions to further employment with a reference to my lack of Austrian citizenship.

"Now, Herr Councilor, are you of the opinion that anything stands in the way of granting Austrian citizenship to my person?"

The Councilor reacts with a not exactly affirmative movement of his hand.

"Or do other reasons than my statelessness move you to endorse my professional stagnation, perhaps my Jewishness? I don't even dare to think this thought…!"

The Councilor hesitates with embarrassment, stands up and reaches for some documents.

"Please, Herr Doktor, excuse me! I have an urgent discussion with the regional head. With the best of will I cannot give you more time. Please excuse me!"

As he stands on the threshold, I ask him: "Do you wish that I call again?"

"Oh no, not at all. Not necessary. Herr Doktor. Your matter will be discussed. Good day!"

"Goodbye, Herr Councilor!"

September 12, 1945 (*A letter sent on this day to Max, Alex and Mother in Vineland, NJ*)

My dear ones!

It's probably due to difficulties with the postal services that no more letters have followed after your first two. On our side, we now want to help shorten the period of waiting and report further to you how we have been doing.

As you can see from the place we are sending this from, after the many years of solitude and isolation from Jewish people we have received splendid company from fellow-sufferers, more than a hundred mostly young Jews, who were liberated as last remnants from the concentration camps, and founded a Comité Israélite in Bregenz for the purpose of Hachschara[1] and subsequent emigration to Erez. Their greeting and welcome was extremely cordial, and I had to tell the chaverim, who almost all came from Eastern Europe, at length of our adventures and salvation. They were both deeply shaken and amused in their reactions, and rejoiced not a little when they realized that, despite the unspeakable trials with which we were burdened during our wanderings, we had neither lost nor been stripped of any of our Jewish consciousness, nor of our Jewish attitude and purpose. And they finally took us into their community and offered to facilitate the exchange of letters with you, for as long as sending directly is not possible. Tomorrow the three of us will travel down to Bregenz to see them again and hand them these lines.

This is the gratifying side of my experiences in the last weeks. The other side of the medal however looks somewhat different. I already informed you that the final part of my daring adventure was my appointment in the Regional Council in Bludenz, in spite of my refusal to enter the Party and my pointed opposition to National Socialism, and during this time I was curiously the only one in the whole district to be spared call-up into the Home Guard. For as long as my name was "Kurt Freiherr" and I was considered by everybody as an Aryan, I could enjoy undivided affection and considerable respect among the population and the authorities, being a corollary of my constant disguise and courageous, steadfast manner. After my exposure as a Jew this was succeeded by sensation that held all people of Vorarlberg in excitement and astonishment for weeks.

This led to even greater affection and even admiration among some people, such as most of my fellow-workers, the freedom fighters and the town authorities. But among others, the anti-Jewish Catholics and the members of the Regional Government recruited out of their ranks, it caused dislike or even undisguised rejection, all the more so since they felt that I did not receive the backing from the French occupation authorities in Bludenz that I hoped for and needed, even though I am perhaps still today the only Jewish official in the whole Austrian administration. So, they began to push me gradually to the periphery of official duties, and they now believe they can dare to take the final step, without hindrance or punishment, that is, my complete exclusion or even dismissal from public service. Naturally not with an open reference to my attribute as a Jew, but rather with the stipulation that I am not an Austrian citizen, let alone a Vorarlberger, and consequently am not entitled to occupy an official post.

They are about to announce this decision and only not yet have found the person who would be prepared to communicate this to me. For they know very well that they are thereby making themselves guilty of an offence against the directives issued by the Allies for rehabilitation of Jews, and under the eyes of the Allies are doing no less than remaining loyal to Hitler's principles, according to which no Jew was allowed to be an official because he was not a German. They thus seek to apply the laws for purging the public service of National Socialist and similar politically unreliable elements, amongst whom are counted all Reich Germans who moved in after 1938, in such a way that they can realize their ideal of making Vorarlberg radiate the brilliance of being purified of Jews once again. For if they succeed in dismissing me, we are left for a second time without any means of subsistence and are forced as Jews to give up our new home and our new homeland and once more take up the wanderer's staff.

Well, a Hitler too once emphatically announced that he had calculated every possibility beforehand. He only failed to pay attention to the probability that a Jew whom his executioners had a special eye on would not only escape his claws but even creep into his sacrosanct public offices. And the masters of Vorarlberg live with the fantasy that this Freiherr, who did not bow to Hitler, they will be able to bring down without having to see with their own eyes his power of resistance and the consequences of their criminal acts. For this Jew, once his patience with the antisemitic clique is at an end, will reveal the whole repulsive humbug before the highest instance of the Allied occupation authorities, without concern for the hidden disciples of Hitler, who continue to perform their public duties in a way as to keep away or remove anybody who disturbs them in their conservation of racist idols.

This struggle against antisemitism is not my life's task. My endeavors are much more in other directions and have always tended to move on more positive paths than the "Association for Defense against Anti-Semitism," which I left long ago. Let others who know no better walk there.

However for the first time since 1933 the existence of me and my family is unquestionably at stake, and secondly I am obliged, in rigorously pursuing my principles and as a representative of the Jews who count as belonging to the "United Nations" to act in this way and no other. For this is a matter greater than little me, or a squabble with undying antisemites; it is plainly a matter of the final recognition of the Jewish human being, and in particular of the struggle against social and race crimes. Insofar as its share is allotted to me, this task must be fulfilled before I pursue my further goals.

And in this you can be helpful with your strengths, my dear ones. Firstly you can have this letter published in the newspaper mentioned, as you did with the previous reports, and thus direct the attention of the Allies preventatively towards the conditions in Vorarlberg, and secondly we cordially request you to send some money on our name to Frau Schmuklerski, in case we should really go without bread. We would then be able to draw on this reserve if needed, and otherwise return it to you. If you could furthermore send some grub through the Red Cross or the Comité Israélite in Bregenz, you would do us a great service and find a thankful recipient of your offering.

So, my dears, you see that our ever-changing Odyssey has still not found an end, and I must confess that its duration demands rather strong nerves and in no way contributes to our bodily regeneration. All the same I constantly gain plenty of material for my book and, in case I should be really broken, for the never-expected sensational ending.

Otherwise we are doing well in our cozy home, from which we can set out into the forests and up to the mountains whenever we want to. However mostly I sit in my study with its enchanting view on the Rätikon and his queen, the three-thousand-meter high Szesaplana, and write my book, for which worthy undertaking I have specially reserved the last three weeks of my holiday. Though every day I miss more my library, almost completely consumed by fire in Leipzig, my intellectual tools, and it is still an almost insoluble problem to get hold of at least the most important fine literature and scientific books again, quite apart from the immense costs. We have saved only about a hundred books, my telescope, my large microscope, the photo negatives, the cameras and almost all personal papers, along with other small things which remained by chance, while my books about Annekind and the other manuscripts were destroyed.

It scarcely needs to be mentioned that our plentiful furniture and all our household equipment fell into the hands of the Nazis. To set up our new home, it was partially replaced by Nazi belongings and it is quite acceptable.

It is one of the whims of fate, such as those which so often blessed us during our exile, that among these are a wonderful seven-branched menorah and an artistically valuable Kiddush beaker. We also received a good radio set, a Telefunken W 337, fine-tunable and with a beautiful sound, receiving America as loud as the street noise. The kitchen is completely electric and also equipped with an electric boiler, the bathroom and Annekind's room are both finely embellished, and up here in the airy heights we have sunshine the whole day long even in winter. In this respect we are quite satisfied. With grub however, poor Mutti continues to have great troubles. It is hardly sufficient for people with full tummies, let alone for our kind of emaciated wanderers of the earth. Trains have resumed running all over Austria, and we can take them with the certificate of the Comité, after having been excluded hitherto as "Non-Austrians" outside a radius of 10 kilometers from Bludenz. The dangerous Jews could otherwise enter into forbidden communication with the Nazis! But that the Austrian supporters of Hitler, and those who would wish to be, enjoy unlimited freedom of movement – about that radio and press are deliberately silent. Main thing is that they are Austrians and not Jews.

Now another request. If you should wish to hand over my letters to the newspapers, then please each time send me a copy. Don't forget! It is very important.

Enough for today. Now it is your turn. Don't be too mean with paper and ink. We think you have not sunk so low that we have to help you out with scarce Austrian supplies. So, we await a sign of life from you soon. Until then we send you heartfelt greetings and kisses, with best wishes for Rosch Haschana.

September 14, 1945

I visited the chaverim with Hilda and Anneliese. The chaverim wept when they saw the child and looked at her as a great miracle. She was passed from arm to arm and stroked like a lapdog.

October 16, 1945

It is remarkable that among all non-National Socialist, non-Austrian employees, I as a Jew am being dismissed, while three Reich Germans, among them a National-Socialist woman, are still in the service of the District Office, because they were employed before March 1938. According to the latest decree of the Allied Control Commission, they are treated equally with those non-Austrians who were persecuted on racial, religious or political grounds. This preferential treatment should be all the more given to Jews who fought against Nazism and for the liberation of Austria, putting their lives at stake.

Furthermore, the notice given to me was legally invalid, since it gave no reason for my dismissal. Even if my status as a stateless person represented sufficient cause for the action against me, everyone would have expected a generous gesture from the authorities towards the only Jewish official employee in Tyrol and

Vorarlberg, who counted moreover as one of the few resistance fighters in public service.

At half past four the engagement party begins at the Jewish synagogue in Hoenhems. The groom is a surviving brother of Rabbi Friedmann. Soup, cold fish with a horrible amount of bones, stewed plums, a bottle of beer, coffee, cake, a dozen speeches – the only good one by Dr. Rothschild – amusing recitations in Jewish singsong, Hassidic meditation which suits an engagement celebration as well as a reading from the Torah would the dance floor.

All the reciters take the greatest of trouble to stir the young couple and make them weep through sad reminiscences of the concentration camps or relatives and friends murdered elsewhere, something to which Jews do not usually pay homage. The wedding pair sit motionless, as if the one had nothing to do with the other. They gave each other no looks and appear to consider the celebration as a religious service rather than a joyous start on the path of their common life.

One of them, a Russian Jew, tearfully beseeches the gathering to foreswear any celebration and even visits to the cinema, for as long as they have not done everything for Erez Israel.[2] So, still the same unworldliness of certain Zionist, Eastern Jewish circles. They are of the naïve opinion that Palestine could offer the Jews a hundred per cent protection, and do not consider that a single people bent on war, apart from the Arabs, can destroy all Jewish achievements.

I amuse the chaverim with racy, witty Jewish jokes, while Captain Menkind tugs at his pointed red beard without pause but cannot bring himself to say a coherent sentence in honor of the bridal pair.

October 21, 2015

Nesler takes me to the Socialist Party Secretary for the Bludenz and Feldkirch districts and begs me for a consultation. I cannot, however, commit myself before the outcome of my Innsbruck matter – my citizenship – and ask him to wait for a short time, and first sound out whether my person is at all acceptable to the Party.

I handed to the military Gouverneur via the French gendarmerie:

1. Copy of my declaration submitted in May;
2. Testimonials from the most important authorities and individuals who knew me by my legal or illegal name or both, or who still know me;
3. Copy of Kühnl's conversation as to my systematic propaganda.

October 27, 1945

Nesler lets me know that he has placed me on the list of election speakers. With regard to his suggestion to elect me as the Socialist Party Secretary for the districts of Bludenz and Feldkirch, it appears from his abashed remarks that this has met no approval.

Not an Austrian, and on top of that a Jew – that appears perhaps to be too heavy a political burden for the Social Democrats.

November 13, 1945

I met Rabbi Friedmann at the entrance to the Comité. After a short greeting we go over together to the Post Hotel, the chaverim's restaurant.

On the way, I briefly tell him the story of the mix-up of the letters, but he smilingly dismisses my misgivings. Several chaverim are praying in the restaurant, others sit scattered in the corners at breakfast, and the rest hang about the kitchen or other neighboring rooms, while I am invited to a cup of coffee and a slice of bread and marmalade. The chief cook on duty greets me and whispers that parcels and shoes have arrived for the chaverim and he will quietly pass our share over to me. The "quietly" sounds suspicious for I cannot think of the reason why we cannot take our share legally like every other Comité member.

It seems that a certain fuss is being made over us "Yekken."[3] Kellermann comes over and greets me heartily, and after him Dr. Rubinstein smilingly gives me his hand...

Rabbi Friedmann says they would now finally give me an official post, as the Jews were just declared official members of the United Nations. On the radio and in the press, he says. But as usual he cannot produce a certificate black-on-white which I could use as a basis for further action. Kellermann begs him several times but to no avail for a certificate so that the shoes and parcels which have already been selected can be handed out... Then we go to lunch: soup, apple stew, vanilla pudding.

Kellermann wants to give me several tins of fish from his parcels. I decline on the grounds that I take nothing that is not officially due to me... I am told that neither I nor my wife or child are on the membership list of the Comité; in other words, our certificates issued by Rabbi Friedmann have no basis in reality. I decide then to go without the shoes and the parcels, and not to return to the Comité's office anymore – all the more because Friedmann has made himself invisible and is no longer to be spoken with.

An hour later I meet Kellermann and Frau Picher in front of the station, from where we take ourselves to Kellermann's room. He takes the heavy parcels, among them a 20-pound box of figs – for two chaverim – under his arm. At Kellermann's place we eat a few rolls with sausage. He opens the box of figs with some effort, takes half for himself and packs a paper bag full of the sweet fruit for Annelie. I beg the dear people to hand the bag over to Annelie on their visit to Bludenz the following Sunday, but without success. Then we make our way to a café opposite the station, chat convivially for a while and when the chavera has taken leave, Kellermann tells me that many chaverim have been arrested, especially for currency smuggling. The French plan to transfer all the chaverim to Hohenems and after the opening of the border to gradually deport them abroad.

Kellermann accompanies me to the train, where I take leave after repeated reminders to visit. He offers me financial aid. I see the old sloppiness in the rail traffic again. The trains either fail to arrive on time for no apparent reason, depart with delays of half or three quarters of an hour, or stop at stations in between for equally late trains to pass through in the opposite direction. Thus, I again arrive home one hour late from the short trip from Bregenz to Bludenz, tired and disheartened.

November 16, 1945

Nesler told me that my article for the new Socialist Party newspaper *The Will of the Vorarlberg People* was considered too sharp and will probably not be accepted. I have just set eyes on the first edition of this newspaper. The format and print are attractive, the content and ideology somewhat limp.

Beiner's inflammatory speech against the Jews. Cowshed muck.

December 14, 1945

Four years had to pass before we could celebrate Chanukah again. We last did this in 1941. It was a happy celebration then, to which we had invited our Leipzig friends. In the largest room of our apartment, which on the order of the Nazi Office for Promotion of Home Building we had to give up together with another room to evacuated Jews, a few dozen of our fellow sufferers gathered and waited to see the surprises which the Chanukah man had chosen for them. The small ones began to show their impatience already early in the afternoon through performances and declamations that they had made up themselves, and they warmed up so much that when dusk fell, all of them, including our Annelie, with bright red faces and quivering in their whole bodies, tried to outshout each other when the excitement reached its climax.

Meanwhile I dressed up in a multi-colored costume in the bedroom next door – a long dress, a fancy red-and-white patterned bathrobe, long woolen socks, felt slippers, galoshes, the purple silk Tallit bag[4] turned into a hood – made my face look like a pelican with cotton wool and maltreated my cheeks with lipstick. I tidily packed the many little gifts, each with the name of its recipient, into the huge rucksack together with a bag of cake for the dog, stuck a mighty bundle of rods under my arm, seized a bell with my right hand, put a whistle in my mouth and crept out into the corridor. With a great noise, ringing and whistling, I stormed up the staircase, banged and rang at the door, wailed and shouted on the landing, kicked angrily at the door to the room, stamped inside like a Jewish Wotan,[5] and looked into the eyes and gaping mouths of the little ones, and into the grinning faces of the grown-ups. I introduced myself in a faraway voice, asked if I could sit down and put down my rucksack. Mäuslein sniffed me somewhat hesitatingly and then licked me furiously, as was his custom.

I began to recount my experiences in heaven and the long journey to earth. Too much laughter from the grown-up guests, I said the same wealth exists up there as down here on earth. The Nazi angels had hung a swastika around the lights of the Jewish Menorah. Just when they were lighting the Chanukah lights, then cut off the wings of the Jewish angels and, just as the earthly Nazis do, crammed them into a few heavenly chambers. As the Gauleiter stirred up the angels in an inflammatory speech against the non-Aryan inhabitants of heaven, I could just rescue the presents prepared for me and had to make my way on foot over a long, icy-cold path, since on the heavenly ways hung a sign with the inscription "Use by Jews prohibited!" The Nazis up there also threw a few burned-out stars after me and hit me in the back, which is now hurting very much. Now I am very weary and sad and very much wanted to hear a beautiful little song again. Annelie at once intrepidly began to sing "Moaz Tzur" with her crystal-clear voice, and not even five years old, she could do it better than most grown-ups. After her the other children recited poems.

The distribution of the little presents brought the great occasion to its climax. Every gift I accompanied by a few suitable or unsuitable witty words, drew harmless confessions out of the little ones, and rattled at the weaknesses of the grown-ups, whom I made climb over tables and chairs in the over-filled room to get at their prizes. During the whole procedure, Mäuslein tripped impatiently around in circles, kept sniffing at the opening of the rucksack and sat up prettily in order to show that he was a good Chanukah dog, and then crawled with his little piece of cake into a corner, where the cake and smacking lips immediately testified to a good appetite and a contented dog. When my cotton-wool beard threatened to fall apart, I considered it the moment to take my leave with the last verse of the Chanukah song.

While I changed back into my normal clothing in the bedroom, the memories came to me of Chanukah festivities of long ago; the days of my childhood, when a wooden platter had to replace the Menorah, and the "Moaz Tzur" filled the evenings, with walnuts and ginger biscuits to follow; of the first big Chanukah service in the synagogue of Landau, where my grandparents lived, and the following young people's celebration in the great ballroom of a hotel, where the finest pastries with chocolate, coffee and small presents were served; of truly memorable event at the Jewish Cultural Association, the former theatre society in Leipzig, at which I took my leave as its dramaturgical head with my last production, and received a handsome Menorah and was celebrated in the blaze of spotlights; the much-admired Chanukah festival productions which I put on with the pupils of the Reichenheim Orphanage in Berlin; and the sublime evenings which year after year since the making of our home saw us under the lights, and which extended with partly serious and partly amusing conversation sometimes into the early hours of the morning, without leaving any hangover, mental and spiritual refreshments which were not to be repeated after this Chanukah celebration.

Back then once more our home was filled with human beings truly hungry for light, "honored" by the racist slogans of the Third Reich, once more the tables bent under the weight of the presents which our visitors had rustled up somehow and somewhere with great difficulty and sacrifice, and for a last time we sat together, ate, drank, joked and laughed. Sometimes we suddenly fell silent, when a word was spoken about those in our circle who had emigrated, were expelled, languished in concentration camps or were murdered. For the Nazi angel swept over hardly any family without seizing a victim. But the more wounds bled, the more closely hung together the ones who remained behind and survived, and tried thus to banish for a time their dismal and painful thoughts – they ate, drank, joked, laughed and fell silent forever, when they were torn from us a fortnight later and dragged off to where there were only stranglers and no human beings.

On that evening in December 1942, the Menorah died away in our home, and did not light up again for four long years, four heavy years, burdened with sorrow, fearful and dreadful. Years of flight and fear, of worry and deprivation, of horror and repugnance of death, of being weary and alone, of discouragement and hope. Once we supplanted the honorable Menorah with a Christmas tree, so that our leap towards freedom would not end in the abyss, but our hope was always to see the Chanukah lights burning again. Then the day came when the power of the evil one seemed to be broken, the Allies chased after them and planted the banner of freedom and salvation in the place of the swastika. The wounds ceased bleeding, the oppressive mask fell, and we could once again be ourselves.

Thus, in this year of our reclaimed freedom the Menorah burned again for the first time, exactly the same Menorah which greeted us when we moved into our home. It shone as hundreds of lights from snow-covered houses and mountain flickered through the night and created that fabulous atmosphere which is hard to describe, and which makes decades to have not passed, and can conjure up children's eyes and children's joys in a swelling up of nostalgia and happiness.

And Anneliese, with cheeks burning with happy excitement, listened and sang the long-forgotten Chanukah verses, which I reframed with our rescued originals from the Berlin synagogue. I thought of the choir singers and cantors whose voices were silenced forever in the gas chambers of the SS. But here in our home they can rise again, in our Jewish cell in the snow of the high mountains they can be torn away from the past, and through the frivolous-diabolical technology of our modern age can celebrate Chanukah with us.

December 19, 1945

Rumors have it that I gained the apartment by dishonest means through my good connections with the Nazis.

January 4, 1946

The Bludenz local Social Democratic organization starts operations. It declares that I am not a Party member. Certainly, in that case I cannot contest the election.

January 24, 1946

I find out from W. the sad fact that Jews have already been expelled from Austria to Germany via a petition from the Austrian authorities aimed at the expulsion of all formerly German Jews. The Austrian bands of Fascists thus want to demonstrate their political reliability through new tirades against the Jews, and the French military authorities are unlikely to be disinclined to meet their wishes. I for my part could if necessary have referred to my officially registered status as a stateless person and even at the risk of being penalized I would not have been moved from my home; otherwise all the things we saved from the Stapo and moved to Bludenz would have been lost as the confiscated property of Reich Germans. It is really true that the Jews who have already been raided by the Nazis are shaken down for a second time – by the so-called opponents. A wonderful and very telling omen for the ethics and lifespan of the "United Nations".

January 26, 1946

My old dream of measuring the shape of the surface of heavenly bodies is being fulfilled. From Washington comes the news that it has been possible with the help of "radar" instruments to establish a connection with the moon. The duration of the reflection was about two and a half seconds. Maybe through the coming radio telescopes the world will experience surprises. These may be just as great as in politics and economics, of which the most important ones are likely to be the political and economic structure of the world in view of the renewed inappropriate actions taken by the victorious states; the unceasing racial protests and strikes in America; the political and ideological confusion in France, where de Gaulle is withdrawing resignedly to a country seat; the undiminished tensions between the Soviet Union and its wartime comrades-in-arms; Persia, Syria and Palestine; and not last the not exactly healthy and sensible policy towards Germany and Austria.

The particularly clever ones thought they could recognize, in the spreading of the Nazi movement and its atrocities, the preconditions for its collapse and showed themselves accommodating to Hitler – not thinking that an area of putrefaction is not isolated by leaving it in peace, and that one cannot calm down an animal that has gone berserk by throwing it one piece of flesh after the other. In that way they were forced into the war by Hitler bringing Germany and its vassals to order after more than five years of struggle. Now Germany, and with it half a world, has gone to the devil, but Nazism lives on. Not only in the Germans who carry out Hitler's last wishes, no, also among the so-called opponents, and it does not lack a certain absurdity when one sees how the Allies continually call for the eradication of the Nazi spirit in the former Fascist states but deliberately ignore the supporters of Hitler in their own ranks.

It is shocking enough to observe that Hitler's anti-Jewish ideas now begin to be seen as respectable also among the Allies, which is why Mr. Austrian enjoys their favors, and can indulge his antisemitic desires completely unhindered. He even dared to demand the expulsion of a Jew originating from Germany and liberated from the concentration camps, and the representatives of the Jews were not disinclined to grant this inhuman desire.

No wonder then that the Austrians feel so sure of themselves that they dare not only to demand the return of South Tyrol, but stretch their hands out also towards the land of Berchtesgaden[6] and petition for the extradition of Austrian war criminals at the top of their voices. The 100 percent followers of Hitler, and their Jew-baiting apostles, now turn into pitiable martyrs, and sit in judgment over those to whom they swore never-ending loyalty a year ago, while they commit a breach of faith such as history has not yet experienced against the part of the German people that was hostile to the Nazis.

Oh, poor America! How weak the patriotic convictions of your inhabitants must be if one can become a full citizen after a stay of only five years.

January 30, 1946

I received a direct letter from mother, which was posted in Vineland, NJ, where my two younger brothers also live. She hopes to have us over there by the New Year, while at the same time emphasizing that Max and Alex are hard put to make ends meet financially. I wonder how mother imagines our existence in America.

On the radio it is announced that, at the request of the American Jewish community, the U.S.A. will bring a proposal to the Council of the United Nations that all states in which homeless Jews are staying should grant the latter their respective citizenships, insofar as they want to remain in their midst. At last I am a step closer to the goal that I indicated in my letter to the Regional Committee. If this goes through, my own problem would be solved.

January 30! Thirteen years ago, our misery began and today, on January 30, 1946, it is still not at an end. I did say, qui viva vera![7]

February 2, 1946

I begin to give up hope that I will succeed in bringing the struggle for our existence to a happy end. All of the hundred attempts that I have undertaken since the arrival of the French have failed, every new, weak glimmer of confidence is countered with doubly heavy blows, and every step that I take in order to gain just a weak hold leads all the deeper into the labyrinth.

Two years ago, the Nazis were our open, legal enemies. The dangers and the war with its terrible plundering we shared with everybody else, however, we conducted a successful struggle with the support of our friends and a merciful fate. But the French have driven away our guardian angel and summoned new opponents onto the scene, including in places where we would never have suspected them. Those with their fake faces, which on one side shouts for revenge for the victims of the Nazis while the other side smiles ironically; those who maintain they are for equality, liberty and fraternity, and seek their friendships wherever wine, women and song lures them, indifferent to whether it is in the company of Nazis or opponents of Nazis; those who lend their ear to every blackguard who understand how to impress with enticing gifts; they also have our distress on their consciences.

On that sunny May day when I was sent away from the government as a "Reich German" and put on the same footing as my tormentors, I saw the abyss open before us, and since then we totter exposed along its very edge.

Adapting to the letter of the law and whatever advantage presented itself, the Austrians soon sniffed the anti-Jewish spiritual affinity of the French and, as befits turned-around hocus-pocus Nazi democrats, immediately showed me their backs. They discovered their age-old attachment to the French spirit and are even prepared to arrange a new crusade against the Jews, if they believe that something like that would impress their new masters.

So, the side-lined concentration camp detainee cozies up with an official who was blessed under Hitler, a pimp or a Nazi with Crosses of Merit, and may jovially shake hands with would-be so-called "resistance fighters". The Thousand-year Reich office holders still firmly in the saddle are even looking forward to the submission of Austrian "revolutionaries". These "revolutionaries" find it absolutely in order that National-Socialist chameleons with their sticky tongues bite away democratic morsels from their tormented victims, and on top of everything declare them as "Nazis in disguise", all the more since the French masters do absolutely nothing to object against such masterly conjuring tricks.

But just as chameleons can adapt amazingly to their surroundings through the gift given to them by creation, so that they can be taken for a fig-leaf from paradise or a delicate little fruit, so these guys know how to divert attention from themselves and extract themselves from the clutches of the few truly sincere democrats. And that makes my struggle against these elements so futile.

This fateful predilection for chameleons has now spilled over to the so-called Jewish Committee; they deeply "regret" my attacks against the open and concealed, the private and official enemies of Jews, and find it quite in order that only Austrians may remain in public service. They do not require such trivial privileges to develop their lucrative little businesses, and are cross at the zealous Austrian officials or the French only if they are disturbed or hindered from conducting them.

Otherwise they bow and scrape before every shoulder badge, as the Jews aping Germans formerly did before officers in spurs. They arrange orgies of allegiance as at the wedding in Bregenz, where they sought to evoke admiration for their French masters through performing Hassidic rituals, while at the same time taking morsels out of each other's mouths and pulling chairs away from backsides, true to the electoral motto "Liberté, égalité, fraternité", which they have scrawled in over-large letters on the wall of their restaurant.

It remains to be hoped that they bring this slogan over unharmed to the land of Israel and there sell it to the highest bidder as a monster amulet for every Zionist, except the "Jekken" like me, who unfortunately do not value such relics. The sacred dream of seeing Jewish people again, which continued to hold us as we had to wander alone and forsaken along our thorny path, is followed by such a painful awakening. All the hope that we avidly drew from a short-wave receiver in the years of our hardship has given way to bitter disappointment.

Today all the good German human beings who saved the lives of us and other Jews are set on a par with the Nazi dregs, and we with them. The Allies continue to turn the defeat of the Fascist people into a lucrative business, as they themselves openly or discreetly admit, by now forcing undesired competitors of industry and capital, once and for all, out of the way. They force the 70 million Germans into a small space and want to debase them by turning them into peasants and manual workers – an undertaking which must be considered as absurd as it is short-sighted. If they want to tackle the Nazi problem only in its periphery, instead of going in media res[8] and separating the chaff from the wheat, then the victorious states should not continue along this dead end or one day they could be confronted with quite unpleasant surprises, the smallest of which would be the absolute failure to harness the Germans to true democratic thinking.

On the other hand, they heap mawkish praise and marks of favor on the Austrians, who are as politically stupid as they are immature and obstinate; in this they are just like a mother who allows the naughtiest of her children to do whatever he wants and thus brings him up to be a real pest and an eternal bachelor. No wonder then that the Austrians excel in heaping praise on themselves and protest to the whole world that they never were German, let alone infected by the Fascist bacillus. By their fruit you will know them! May they not become too sour to you, my Allied friends! For in the end you must digest them. So: Quo usque tandem?[9]

35 EXILED

Walter is removed from his job and his source of income. Again, he must use his survival skills to put food on the table. This requires receiving small amounts from his two brothers in America who are also struggling, and parcels from the Jewish welfare organizations. It also means he must sell off his precious belongings that he managed to save from the Nazis.

He must find ways to prevent the humiliations from crippling him. But it is hard, perhaps emotionally even harder than life under the Nazis.

Yet Walter is able to view the German people as distinct from the Nazis. He will never forget the courage shown by those who hid him. He refuses to condemn the Germans as a whole even as he continues to suffer because of Nazi sins.

February 5, 1946

If a jobless person maintains that he has no time to do this or that, one smiles at him and calls him lazybones or, as the Austrians like to say from their own experience, a lay about. However, this lack of time may be due to the jobless person, insofar as he has not chosen lazing around as his new profession, being constantly busy with the problem of how he can find a job and position again, and acquire a few pieces of money. As long as he could have his work book stamped and peacefully carry out his tasks, he was free from worry about his income, if he knew how to live on it. He drew his pay regularly and could contentedly relax when he had carried out his daily tasks, or pursue his hobbies in full enjoyment of his freedom. With the loss of his workplace this peace is gone. He broods, runs around and looks for means of existence, has to devote days, weeks, months, perhaps even years, to this often-fruitless activity and also has to give up his beloved passions. And because he has no work he is always busy, restless, worked up – the worst of work, in the truest sense of the word, without pay, without means of subsistence, without contentment.

For as long as I could earn my daily bread through peaceful work, I had leisure to walk, chat and write my memoirs. But since the brave Vorarlberg democrats have re-discovered their Austrian hearts, and in harmony with their French allies have found mine all too international and un-Christian, my letters to enemies and friends have far exceeded the length of my book and would fully occupy even a private secretary.

Thus today I wrote to Haider to get him to admit the reason for his continuing to remain distant, to at least extract from him a hint whether he has again fallen victim to whispering against me, the so-called "cleansed Nazi", or perhaps has even obtained a precise indication of the originator of that rumor. I suspect he will still bend to the influence of his political brothers rather than to the duty to find out the true facts of the matter.

I sent off another letter to the Jewish Committee in Innsbruck, which is busy trying to ape the Stapo ways and quite simply ignore letters and submissions. A third letter goes to the Bregenz government office – to Kellermann, who promised me on his last visit to issue new documents for us; a fourth to Sally Mayer in St. Gallen, to find out something about the present whereabouts or domicile of Shargo, and a fifth to Feukert, to whom I have given Haider as guarantor and verifier of my political tendencies and participation. All day long Nesler's typewriter which he has lent me clattered; it cannot know that this frantic typing is a waste of time.

Perhaps one day the world to come will amuse itself with the publication of *Kurt Freiherr's Collected Letters* and will ask itself how this afflicted and pursued man also found the time and endurance for his endless scribblings.

To preserve later educators of the German and Austrian people from the temptation to have their schoolchildren write essays about these questions, let it be here openly declared that in these lands, thanks to the special enlightenment that the Lord of the World granted to his holy Vorarlberg, the days are longer than elsewhere – as a heathen excluded from eternal salvation I can at least make secret and illegal use of this.

February 6, 1946

My so earnestly admired Lieutenant Rome, officer of the Sécurité Militaire and imitator of the Stapo, has refused ratification of the new photo identity cards for members of the Freedom Movement,[1] and declared that he must first check the latter for their political reliability.

What he means by that becomes apparent when one takes into consideration that he is very intimate with the reactionary freedom fighter and Nazi groveler Dertsch, who in his time had good connections with the men of the Nazi district leadership. He is often their hunting guest.

To make influential French officers well-disposed through epicurean and other gifts – a method which is also successfully put to use by the regional councilors of Vorarlberg – will doubtless result in the desired "cleansing" of the democratic Freedom Movement. This is made clear by today's announcement on the Vorarlberg radio, according to which the Freedom Movement will henceforth no longer be called in to weed out Nazi elements from public service. This is now exclusively the task of the regional authority.

Bellum gerunt alii, tu Austria felix, nube![2]

The secretary of the Freedom Movement wants to bring my travel fountain pen to the man. I want 350 schillings for it in order to eke out a living for a bit longer.

February 8, 1946

So, there we have the salad! How often, when they fingered my collar, did I warn the gentlemen of the resistance movement and the Socialist Party not to take my matter lightly, and I wrote clearly to the regional leadership of the resistance movement, admonishing them that if I were brought down, they would go down with me. They smiled at me and considered my affair as purely personal and with no influence on the general political constellation, with its truly democratic currents. Now it has fortunately gone so far that with me the Austrian democratic Freedom Movement will also be taken to its grave.

Requiescat in pace![3]

The secretary has not yet been able to sell my fountain pen but will keep trying. On the other hand, none of the Jewish organizations feel moved to keep our heads financially above water. We are now as good as destitute and will have to sell our much-beloved gold jewelry, which we preserved into the era of freedom. If the Blacks[4] have not also crushed or prohibited the left-wing parties within six months, then my name is Hans.

Will "the Austrian revolutionaries" mount the barricades? The Austrian revolutionaries, ha ha ha! Until now they insisted they could not utter a sound under the Nazi regime, because the Gestapo was after them. Now they say they can again do nothing, because the Allies are in the land. Yes, my good gentlemen, with pork chops, wine and card-playing one can make no revolution. One can at most use these objects of pleasure to bribe political opponents and bring them over to one's side, as the Blacks understand so brilliantly. But as the Reds are neither wealthy nor refined enough to use these methods, they do nothing at all, apart from attacking and condemning their political comrades, or sitting on the fence and blaming them.

February 23, 1946

I have to summon up the means to allow us at least to vegetate. Thus a few weeks ago I began to sell off my stamp duplicates, and the photographer here displays the little packets without fuss in his shop. He has already brought many of them to the man, by whom he means the Frenchman, and cobbled together a few hundred for me, minus a quarter in commission. I took my spare gold fountain pen to him.

Other objects such as jewelry, my electric shaver, a good photograph and my travel Mont Blanc fountain pen have attracted interest, but in view of my disinclination to give them away for free, there are no buyers.

The same goes for the people of Bludenz, concerning their needs for petitions and other written applications, for which I have advertised my services through small ads. They look around the little town until they find a foolish person who does them this favor in return for food or drink, and after they have done the work, they are left with their tongues hanging out. Yesterday I had the really unspeakable luck to be paid ten schillings and five fresh eggs for preparing an application, and I will not omit to issue the good donor with a certificate of honesty. Whatever, that is again money in the house for one month, and if the offer of a Vienna stamp dealer of all of forty schillings for 5,000 European postage stamps is not a fraud, then I will be able to play the paterfamilias for another 60 days.

That is not quite simple in my state of health. It is worse than ever, and the sleepless nights of martyring my brain are getting me down completely. If fate had not thrown us into a miracle of light and oxygen, which means no less than permanent summer and winter freshness, I would not know whether we would have withstood the after-effects of our years of hardship and hunger at all. Who could grow weary of the fairy-tale magic which every day takes us by surprise in our heavenly abode? Well, only the people of Bludenz, who like cows make a mess on the meadow on which they graze. Now they feed after they have made a mess of us. For unspoilt joy was never granted to any Jew, and no bond of friendship can be formed with the powers that be. I wonder whether all Austrians are like that, so that one cannot trust them. Probably yes, for they do not trust each other, and just like the Bavarians once cursed the "P-Prussian swine", so the Vorarlberger sounds off against his Tyrolean brother, the Bludenzer against the Bregenzer, the Bregenzer against the Innsbrucker, the Innsbrucker the Viennese, the Viennese the Bregenzer and all together against the Jews and Reich Germans. But otherwise they are blessed in Christ.

The German people, the Allies say, should not be allowed to produce themselves, they should import. In exchange for what? For agricultural products, which they will in any case always lack? Or against paper money that is worthless? Of what then should this people live? You do not know, Messrs Allies! And because you do not know, you gather everything that is called German from the whole of Europe and cram it into a Reich that is diminished by one third. You claim that you want to educate this people and make them a worthy member of the United Nations. How can you punish your earlier good intentions with such lies? I am a Jew and as a victim of Nazi Germany and surviving witness of its inhumanity I can certainly not be suspected of hyper-Germanness. I have declared that I consider my expatriation from the German Reich irrevocable and still less do I think of returning to the country of our disenfranchisement, oppression and murder of our friends and relatives.

However, that we three are still alive we owe to good German human beings, quite simple German human beings, who, apart from a few speculators on inheritance, took the life-threatening risk of providing us as outlaws and victims of persecution with shelter and sometimes (such as Granddad J.!) also food and money. And if no more of these "good-natured Saxons" offered us asylum that was only because they themselves lived in constant fear and danger, not in any way because they were bad enough not to help Jews. There were more in Leipzig who would have helped but it was indeed my aim to keep the circle of those in the know as small as possible, in order to avoid thoughtless questions, even if this also brought us into a desperate situation more than once. The inalterable fact remains that we owe our salvation in the first place to helpful and intrepid Germans, and not exclusively to our ingenuity, our daring and the benevolence of destiny.

I do not doubt that thousands and thousands of Jews would have encountered the same fortune if they had nurtured relations with the broad layers of society, as we did for years, rather than limiting themselves to frequenting the upper ten thousand who completely failed as human beings and were so pitifully stranded in terms of political importance. How often did I warn our spiritually well-situated Jews to go out more among the people, who needed us and enjoyed our company? But they remained deaf, isolated themselves and looked on as Hitler and his cronies enticed the small men and brought ruin first on us then on them.

Only in parenthesis is it to be mentioned that the representatives of the U.S.A. in Germany do not exactly get on badly with the experts of the Hitler regime. They try through pernicious interpretation and application of the immigration regulations to keep Jews from "God's own land", and this with resounding success, as my case and the death of millions prove. The greater their reputation, the more lastingly do they commit errors, and they are also bringing in our era of peace with this really disastrous disposition. How else did they come to the conclusion that the German people are more reprehensible than the Austrians, unconcernedly observing their shocking political capers and inimitable obstinacy towards the democratization?

In view of that, I would like to allow myself the innocent question whether a Jewish family would have found so many helpers ready to sacrifice themselves among the Austrians as in Germany. To ask this question means to negate it after the bitter experiences which my fellows in religion and suffering have to undergo with Messrs Austrians ten months after liberation from the Nazi yoke, having to listen to the president of the Austria Nationalist Party proudly acknowledging his hatred of Jews, and the Regional Council here brazenly daring to announce that the purging of the public services from Nazi elements has been carried out. Where is your policy taking you, my Allied friends? The coming years and events will give you the answer, and this answer will contain political crises and tribulations. This is already to be seen in the differences between the western hemisphere and the Soviet Union in the almost ridiculous quarrel about the secret of splitting the atom, the inadequate decision-making power of the United Nations, the sudden flaring up of conflicts around the whole globe, universal material distress and lack of food, and last but not least the sleepy attitude of the Big Three to reform in Franco's Spain. If it does not come to a new world war – then to a progressive breakdown of humanity.

March 8, 1946

I am ill with 'flu or something similar since a few days and feel sick as a dog. In particular the eyes and right hip ache. I got up from time to time and typed the application with witness statements on the machine, so that I would not to let my second customer down. The small exertion has after all brought us 25 schillings and half a pound of butter. Kühnl believes the Vorarlberg police – the Greens – would probably take me by the scruff of the neck, because I have no trading license. They know me, and apart from that, freelance jobs are to be valued even less than fee-paying literary work, which counts just as little as "trade".

This afternoon, when I was going through the little town, the secretary of the Freedom Movement spoke to me and said I could fetch my identity card. It was now stamped by the government. Indeed, it was no bluff and I am carrying the identity card in my briefcase. Miracles still occur. It is a sign that honest Bludenz people do dare to designate and legitimize a Jew with a document saying he is a freedom fighter and comrade, a miracle that they dare to admit a non-Austrian into their ranks. Yes, a non-Austrian. How far this attitude is to be judged as Austrian is shown by the following announcement in today's edition of the socialist *Vorarlberger Volkswillens*:

"The Association of anti-Fascist Austrian Concentration Camp Detainees Vorarlberg on Sunday March 10 is organizing a concentration camp meeting of all political detainees from the Land Vorarlberg at the Dornbirn Hotel "Mohren" at 1 pm, however only for those that possess Austrian citizenship or can show an official certificate that they can receive state citizenship."

Concentration camp detainees of Austrian citizenship! I hope and wish that they stick to this priority for life. The millions of their "alien" comrades in suffering will know how to thank them, just as the Jews of the whole world will thank and give recognition to Herr Chancellor Figl for the reservations he made when the Anglo-American Investigative Commission for Jewish Affairs asked him about receiving returning Jews in Austria. Firstly Herr Figl wished to extend a welcome only to Jews of Austrian citizenship, and secondly "nobody should have any illusions. Much of the Jewish property was dragged off by the Nazis and has disappeared. We too cannot get hold of that."

Get hold of, no, he can't do that. For it would be unreasonable to take away from the Austrian Nazis – pardon, I mean, in case there ever were any of them! – their booty and give it to the Jews. No, something like that one cannot "get hold of", all one can do is "nationalize" it, re-confiscate it in the Austrian way, so that the pillars of democracy remain firm. In Austria everything disappears, right up to reaction, antisemitism and national chauvinism.

March 14, 1946

The global political situation is worsening. Churchill is taking a stand against Russia, apparently encouraged by certain belligerent circles in America and England. Everything speaks for a war soon against Russia, but not at all with dejection, rather full of hope, as if it were a tasty snack. And over everyone looms the atomized Angel of Death. Bombs with an explosive force of two million tons of dynamite are planned. That would be the end of everyone. They seem to look upon it cheerfully. Well, yes, after death there is no regret.

March 16, 1946

Today was my first birthday celebration since 1941. Early in the morning Bregenz people came with fine gifts: valuable stamps, stationery, cigarettes, tobacco and a book. They also brought the identity cards for mother and child with them. To the astonishment of all, my little wife performed a work of art by putting unsurpassable grub on the table. In the evening the Frickes came from Nenzing and brought sweets, cigarettes and pretzels, and after them came neighbors with smoking materials, cook wares and pastries, and the illustrious birthday party ate, drank, smoked and laughed until half past one in the morning.

The Frickes and two of the people from Bregenz stay with us, a third with a neighbor. At ten o'clock everyone has gone and my little wife has indeed once again finished her work. I cannot hold it against anyone if they admire her zeal and adroitness.

March 17, 1946

Alfred Weber, now 80 years old, is said to have returned to the University of Heidelberg and is reading sociology among other things. M. is of the naïve opinion that Weber would obtain a post as lecturer at the Ruprecht Karl University for his former pupil. As if he were just waiting for me!

Weber, 80 years old. I can't imagine it at all. Weber with his monocle. Twenty-three years ago, I took leave of him and then never saw him again. And 23 years is a long time for the memory of a university teacher, whom one is recommending me to contact for my advancement. That's nonsense, I harbor no ambitions in that direction.

March 23, 1946

At last we have assembled a small sum of money. Acquaintances arrange the sale of our things. So far, we have got rid of: two gold fountain pens (collectors of the monster Montblanc masterpieces), Hilda's luxury handbag, a case of gilded teaspoons, an electric shaver, and a package of stamp duplicates. We can now live for five months without financial worries. That's done. And spring is coming. Marvelous.

March 26, 1946

Early yesterday morning I took the eight o'clock express train to Innsbruck. Hilda brought me to the station. In said place I met Mrs. M. and Mr. Fr. We three were going the same way, but Fr. disappeared soon after our departure to search for seats in other carriages and was not seen again. It was a wonderful journey up into the Arlberg, through the tunnel and then out again towards Innsbruck.

On the way my travel companion confirmed my hunch that she is Jewish. The child, however, is the daughter of her sister, who after liberation from the concentration camp stayed in Vienna. I dare to doubt this fact since the child resembles the "aunty" so much; they're two peas in a pod. She has not inherited anything noticeable from the "uncle", an interesting state of affairs. She told me of her experiences and how, covered by false papers, she had nearly been caught by a Nazi gendarme. She, her husband and the child would continue to disguise themselves so that it would be possible for them as "Aryans" to stand up for the Jews. She was a painter and looked forward to my criticism.

Concerning my district office affair, she has a surprise. Although she would like to leave it entirely to her husband to tell me about it, she reported of his intervention on my behalf in high French places, where it was declared to him that, according to the information at hand, I was no Jew at all. Who served up this story to the French she would not tell me, but she thought it was the officials in the Vorarlberg, in order to prevent my return to an official position. All the same, I could count on my rehabilitation within a very short period, and about everything else her husband would inform me at our visit on the coming Sunday. In the meantime, I must look again and again at the little one. How magnificent! I must certainly show her to Hilda and Annelie.

What Mrs. M. has told me about herself and her family is not true. I smell white lies, which are not appropriate to tell me. Then arrival at Innsbruck and meeting with P.

We see Mr. F. on the platform at Innsbruck again. He says goodbye immediately because he is in a hurry. The two of us therefore go through the "main station", a tiny emergency building replacing the completely destroyed station house, then along the wrecked row of houses across the relatively unscathed Maria-Theresien Street to 10 Adolf-Pichler Place, the residence of the Commmanté Israélite for the Tyrol. En route she showed me a hotel on the North Chain, and on the ridge the Hafelekar Lodge. The mountains appear infinitely high to me, although they only slightly exceed our Bludenz Ritikon in one spot. They are an overwhelming sight.

I was here with Hilda 20 years ago. It was summer and the North Chain shone greyish black over the Tyrolean capital. Today it is dressed in a white garment. Such a difference! Yes, that is the famous North Chain as one sees it in photos. Soaring steeply heavenward, its walls glowing dazzling white, above a deep blue sky with clinging clouds. And yet a child can climb them today, and the masts of the cable cars, like tiny Latin Ts, are stuck securely into the snowy slopes.

So, we went up to the Comité. It was closed, as it was after 12 o'clock. However, Mrs. M. called the secretary with a secret signal. She lives next to the office. A brief conversation followed, and then we went to a nearby restaurant. The grub was little and bad! We help each other out with coupons. Then we go back again to the

Comité where the American parcels are handed over to us. The weekly food ration is not yet included. I open a parcel and see a hundred top-quality American cigarettes, which I immediately grab. The same quantity is in the other parcels. I pack two into the rucksack I have brought with me. Mrs. M., who wants to return on the five o'clock slow train, takes the third.

Then Mendelsohn arrives, the chief. He is a young man, and tells me about the intervention of the Salzburg Central Committee and asks whether I would like a post in Salzburg. I decline, firstly on health grounds, for which I show a certificate from the health office in Bludenz, and secondly because of the problems arising from the management of two different households in Salzburg and Bludenz.

Mendelsohn then volunteers to intervene in my affair with Verjand and asks me for a few lines in French to write to him. My attempts to write on the defective machine are unsuccessful, and I have to write the letter at home. Mrs. M. leaves. I stay there a little longer, pack my things together after five o'clock, express my thanks and take leave. I carry the heavy stuff to a provisional luggage storage place near the station, buy a newspaper and bread roll, and trot on with my briefcase through the underpass to a nearby green space with benches. I eat my roll, smoke and read for a while.

It is a raw climate in Innsbruck compared to Bludenz, and windy despite being at the same altitude and in the same mountainous surroundings. I start on a circular walk and arrive at the valley station of the Hungerberg train, which, like 20 years ago, still crawls up the three hundred meters at a snail's pace. The backdrop is magnificent; the North Chain with the adjoining transverse ridge of the Hungerberg. There is a big mess on the embankment of the River Inn, where not only debris, but also garbage and waste, are deposited.

I comfort myself with the view of the mountains which tickle the clouds, etc. On the way back, through the theatre- and Hofburg district, I notice the same mess in the park, yet both the theatre and the castle are unscathed. There is a great bustle in the streets of the city, especially in the Maria-Theresien Street; the O-bus line, the narrow-gauge steam trains and French trucks make for almost a big city buzz. The illuminated display windows, in part patched and wooden show the usual trash which we also get in Bludenz, next to new journals, French, Russian, Communist brochures with dubious contents, many pictures which find no buyers, antiquities which have been excavated from boxes of junk and other stuff that is superfluous nowadays.

A swarm of foreigners, white and colored French, French ladies glittering with make-up and doused with perfume, next to poorly dressed countrywomen and a small number of locals. It's half past seven in the evening, it is getting dark, the streetlamps turn on, and on the way to the station, we can see the illuminated hotels on the North Chain. Kofel sends greetings. I fetch my luggage and lug it to the station, get a ticket and sit to read for half an hour in the small waiting room. The rubbish collector takes what passengers have left lying around: cardboard, hard bread remains, stubs, etc. He smoothed out the paper and tucked it neatly away in his knapsack with all the other things he had found. Mr. F is not on the platform.

The train arrives punctually. Austria is on the move. I sit with my travel companions in an unlit compartment with wooden windows. The person opposite me is a young lad on the way to Bregenz, apparently with rot on his feet; his neighbor, who tries to stop his discomfort by moving frantically in all directions soon clears out because his neck threatens to seize up, and my neighbor, a little gentleman from Bludenz, throws funny talk into the circle.

The air in Bludenz is wonderfully healing and aromatic. It is an unsurpassable climate. I breathe deeply and lug my haul home, where I spread it out for Mutti; many paper bags full of delicious consumer goods for spoiled Americans, chocolate, washing soap and cigarettes en masse. We have not seen the like for the past 13 years, and for the six months we have been members of the Comité in Bregenz we have literally lost out, the scoundrels! I knew for a long time that the leaders of the Comité in Bregenz make a roaring trade with donations meant for all the members, serving watery soup and keeping the extras for themselves.

Then I had to tell my wife everything that I had experienced on my trip to Innsbruck. Our chat lasted until half past two in the morning. I had the feeling that the lowest point of our odyssey finale was finally behind us. At last we will get enough extra donations that we no longer need to scrimp on monthly foodstuffs. And perhaps the other thing I have been fighting for over the last six months will also soon come to a happy solution.

March 28, 1946

This afternoon a man from Feldkirch appeared at my house and claimed that Frau Grenfing, the Nazi woman whose furnishings we have taken over, bequeathed him before her demise one of my favorite pictures, the park entrance to Schönbrunn.[5] He claimed that this was written on the back of the picture. However, all we could see was the remainder of a note with some illegible characters. I referred the inheriting uncle to the mayor, who had promised me I could have it, and took myself off immediately to a telephone subscriber living nearby, so as to give a city official my instructions relating to the issue, emphasizing that I was not willing to hand over the picture.

April 1, 1946

After the meal Feukert appeared after a long interval and reported that he has not been able to fulfil his mission because Haider has been arrested and sent to Innsbruck. Reason: Haider is not Haider, Haider is no Austrian, Haider is rather a concentration camp cop. That is the man who as Chairman of the Concentration Camp Association in the Vorarlberg region wanted to plead for me, and against whom I had to bring a charge before the Tribunal Militaire. I am feeling a bit giddy. Who then is actually who he pretends to be? I am, but they are trying to challenge that too.

But Haider is not Haider. What a splendid surprise!

April 6 & 11, 1946

A banker proposes 25-30,000 schillings for a favorable prospect in Switzerland. So-called bankers with considerable sums of money wish to help washed-out Jewish comrades get on their feet again. So far nobody else has offered any help. Oh, my humble Vorarlberg!

"Banker" Hoff looks me up and is amazed I do not possess the expected sum of money.

"You, as a Jew, must have been well compensated through the system of redress."

"Were I a Nazi, I would not have had to complain."

"I don't understand that. It says in the newspapers that…"

"That Aryanized property is to be nationalized, that is taken away from the Jews a second time. Incidentally, I do not have the commercial experience for the lucrative investments referred to in your letter."

"You will soon learn that. I am not worried about that."

"If I had 25-30,000 schillings, what do you think I would do with it?"

"I am curious."

"Well, I would blow it all. In four to five years literally eat it all up, i.e. lead an agreeable life for years."

"I don't understand."

"You don't understand? Just look!"

"Were I to invest this sum, as you suggest, in a Swiss enterprise, I would have no peace day or night, because I would have to worry about losing the money. I would therefore prefer more useful expenditure, which I can manage myself, for myself and my family.

To live really well without a care for longer than five years, one cannot demand more than that."

"You are not a businessman, Herr Doktor."

"Didn't I say that straight away? I am delighted that you are now convinced of it."

April 12, 1946

Furthermore, I hear of a new version of the reasons for my dismissal from public service, which an interpreter working for the government has spread. He declares that: "They dismissed poor Dr. Leopold because he was employed in a Nazi office."

I am sorry, not even a wise person can accept such arguments, but even the dullest would then demand that the other officials and employees who worked with me in the Nazi district office would also be dismissed, e.g. Count Terlego, who for years was satisfied with his demotion from head of district to departmental leader, or Dr. Längle, who was even awarded a War Merit Cross for his enthusiastic service to Hitler.

Who, apart from me, dared to oppose the demand to enter the Nazi Party, or even to turn the whole office on its head with propaganda opposing the Nazis?

Well, who?

EPILOGUE

Here the memoir abruptly ends. We do not know if Walter just stopped writing because he was too busy with his non-stop correspondence to secure Austrian citizenship and then emigration to America, or if his writings were lost along the way.

But Walter Leopold's family's journey continues. Over the next two years they attempt to emigrate to the United States, sponsored by Walter's younger brothers, Max and Alex. Then, their departure is delayed almost another year because Anneliese is quarantined after contracting a mild case of smallpox during the round of vaccinations required by the U.S.

Rather than joining his siblings and mother in rural Vineland, New Jersey, Walter, in 1950, moves his family to Cincinnati where, according to Anneliese, he was promised a teaching position at the University of Cincinnati. However, various snags in the immigration process delay the appointment. Meanwhile Walter takes a job in a textile factory to support his family.

In 1951, before the teaching job comes through, Dr. Walter Leopold dies of a heart attack, age 53.

Life again is difficult as Hilda now must support the family. She finds work as an assistant nurse and runs the housekeeping at the Jewish

ABOUT THIS TRANSLATION: "THANK YOU FOR MY LIFE"

The Leopold family was rescued in Leipzig, mainly by the family of Josephine Hüenerfeld, a 29-year-old woman whose father, Georg Jünemann was asked by a pharmacist friend in 1942 to hide Dr. Walter Leopold, his wife Hilda and five-year-old daughter Anneliese shortly before they were to be transported to Theresienstadt.

At first they stayed five weeks, then left to another hiding place, and then returned for another five weeks sharing the family's meager food in a row house that housed Josephine, a widow, a young son, and her father.

In 2000, Anneliese Leopold, now Anneliese Yosafat, went to Leipzig and arranged for Josephine, who had moved away from the city, to meet her. She gave Josephine a small photo album entitled *Thank you for my life*. When in Leipizig she also met Dr. Andrea Lorz, an academic and historian who was working on a book on the history of Jews in Leipzig. Anneliese, or Annie, as many friends call her, told Dr. Lorz about a thick folder of scraps she possessed in the U.S. that her father had written throughout the war, on the back of envelopes, on toilet paper, on anything available. Annie had no intention of opening the folder as it brought back painful memories.

Dr. Lorz wanted to see it all and Annie sent her the material. It took many years for the historian to type up the scattered remnants that totaled more than 200,000 words. Then Annie's cousin, Evelyn Leopold, engaged a translator in Britain, through a journalist colleague. The translation also took several years.

In 2005 Anneliese Yosafat honored Josephine Hüenerfeld and her father, Georg Jünemann, at Yad Vashem, the Israeli Holocaust center, under "The Righteous Among the Nations" – gentiles who took great risks to save Jews from the death camps.

NOTES

Introduction

1. Robert Allen Willingham II, *Jews in Leipzig: Nationality and Community in the 20th Century*, 2005, 16, https://repositories.lib.utexas.edu/bitstream/handle/2152/1799/willinghamr73843.pdf?sequenc.
2. Aubrey Boag, "They Expected the Worst – They Did Not Expect the Unthinkable: Jewish Emigration from Germany, 1933-1941," unpublished paper, April 2007, http://marcuse.faculty.history.ucsb.edu/classes/133b/07Projects/BoagJewishEmigration074.htm.
3. United States Holocaust Museum, "How Many Refugees Came to the United States from 1933 to 1945," https://exhibitions.ushmm.org/americans-and-the-holocaust/how-many-refugees-came-to-the-united-states-from-1933-1945.
4. Robert Allen Willingham II, *Jews in Leipzig: Nationality and Community in the 20th Century*, 2005, 16, https://repositories.lib.utexas.edu/bitstream/handle/2152/1799/willinghamr73843.pdf?sequenc.
5. Ian Kirshaw, *The Nazi Dictatorship: Problems and Perspectives of Interpretation* (London: Bloomsbury Academic, 2015), p. 214.
6. Ian Kirshaw, *Popular Opinion and Political Dissent in the Third Reich: Bavaria 1933-1945* (New York: Oxford University Press, 2002), Introduction.
7. Ibid., p. 243.
8. Bruno Blau, "The Jewish Population of Germany 1939-1945," *Jewish Social Studies*, Vol. 12, No. 2 (April 1950), pp. 161-172.
9. Bruce F. Pauley, *From Prejudice to Persecution: A History of Austrian Anti-Semitism* (Chapel Hill: University of North Carolina Press, 1991), pp. 283, 285.
10. Ibid., p. 297.
11. Ibid., p. 305.
12. https://www.adl.org/news/press-releases/adl-global-survey-of-18-countries-finds-hardcore-anti-semitic-attitudes-remain

1. They seize a Rabbi and tear out his beard

1. An inmate appointed by the SS who serves as a prison guard.
2. This bear pit is confirmed in 1988 by a Buchenwald survivor who said to the *New York Times*, "In the camp there was a cage with a bear and an eagle. Every day, they would throw a Jew in there. The bear would tear him apart and the eagle would pick at his bones." https://www.nytimes.com/1988/11/10/world/time-too-painful-to-remember.html

3. The German diplomat Ernst vom Rath who was assassinated by a Polish-Jewish student, Herschel Grynszpan, in retaliation for the mass Nazi deportation of Polish Jews in March 1938 that included his parents.
4. At this point Buchenwald was not engaged in mass exterminations. However, there appears to have been a crematorium on the site.
5. Non-Jewish camp guards, one step above the Kapos, who take care no one escapes.
6. Lennhoff died at the end of November 1938 in Buchenwald, most likely the result of non-treatment of the serious injuries to his hand.
7. The Iron Cross medal for bravery in WWI.
8. Short for Gestapo.
9. These are the middle names given to all Jews on their passports after the fall of 1938.

2. Mäuslein the martyr

1. "The Fate of Pets in the Holocaust", December 18, 2014.
2. Hilda Kean, *The Great Cat and Dog Massacre: The Real Story of World War Two's Unknown Tragedy (Animal Lives)* Chicago: University of Chicago Press, 2017.
3. "Anna child" is one of many nicknames for daughter Anneliese.

4. I ran off like a madman

1. As of September 1, 1941 all Jews in Germany had to wear a Jewish Star of David and the word "Juden" on their outer garments when in public. Walter was also a 'star-wearer.'
2. The head official of the Leipzig Jewish community administration whom Walter suspects is a Nazi collaborator.
3. German word for sparkling wine.
4. Nazi state railway director.

5. Our soul had long left

1. Heinrich Himmler, head of the SS.
2. Fritz Grunsfeld (1899-1974) was a former law student who rose to a leadership position of the Gemeinde after many of the older, more professional leaders had emigrated. Walter views Grunsfeld, one year his junior with much suspicion - even as a Nazi collaborator who was out to get rid of Walter. According to one historical account of Jews in Leipzig there is some evidence to support Walter's fears, but no definitive proof. When in 1938 the Gestapo called for the Gemeinde to fire all Polish Jews from their jobs within the Jewish community, Grunsfeld was the official who signed all the notes. Somehow he managed to avoid deportation to Theresienstadt until 1943. He claimed to have left the camp a year later. There is no record of how he

managed that or where he went. But he found his way back to Leipzig after the war and became a top leader of the reassembled Jewish community, focusing on reparations questions within East Germany (GDR). As anti-Zionist purges began in the GDR, he fled to West Berlin in January 1953. It is speculated that he avoided the worst from the Gestapo because he served as the Executive Director of the "Reich Association of Jews in German." (See next footnote.) For more information on Grunsfeld and the Jewish politics of Leipzig see *Jews in Leipzig: Nationality and Community in the 20th Century* by Robert Allen Willingham II https://repositories.lib.utexas.edu/bitstream/handle/2152/1799/willinghamr73843.pdf?sequenc.

3. Walter's WWI Iron Cross.

4. Reichsvereinigung der Juden in Deutschland was an organization of all German and Austrian Jews as well as gentiles of Jewish descent. Membership was automatic and compulsory. The Gestapo appointed its Jewish leadership. After the Wannsee conference, the Reich Association of Jews in Germany was used to round up the Jews to be sent to death camps starting on October 18, 1941. When that job was completed the leaders of this association also were supposed to be sent to the camps.

5. Suicide.

6. Walter does not know that his mother survived her arduous confinement at the French Camp de Gurs in the Pyrenees, and successfully emigrated to the U.S. in 1940-41 via Algeria and Cuba to join Walter's two younger brothers.

6. He only pretends to be so

1. From Yad Vashem *http://db.yadvashem.org/righteous/family.html?language=en&itemId=5600335.*

2. 42 kilometers north of Leipzig.

3. 70 kilometers north of Leipzig.

4. 600 kilometers south of Leipzig.

5. Grunsfeld was not deported for another year.

7. You simple-minded Jew

1. The Leipzig world trade fair dates back at least to 1165. Jewish traders and money lenders were active in the fair from at least 1250. It is estimated that between 1668 and 1764, 82,000 Jews attended the trade fair. After the anti-Jews laws were lifted in the mid-19th century, Jews were granted residency in Leipzig. The Fair survived WWII and became an important part of the East German economy. (See https://www.jewishvirtuallibrary.org/leipzig-germany.)

2. The main concert hall in Leipzig.

3. Felix Mendelssohn (1809-1847), composer, pianist, conductor born and raised in Leipzig, was the grandson of the famous Jewish philosopher Moses Medelssohn. Felix, who grew up in a prosperous family, was baptized as a Christian at age seven.

4. Karl Friedrich Goerdeler (1884-1945) was a conservative monarchist and mayor of Leipzig from 1930 to 1936 who opposed the draconian restrictions on Jews as well as the removal of the Mendelssohn statue. He served as a top finance official in the Nazi administration but opposed Hitler's rearmament and economic policies. From 1936 onward, he sought to topple Hitler and take his place as Chancellor. Using his strong relationships with the German high command he wanted a coup to replace the Nazi regime with a military dictatorship that respected human rights and that would ally with the West. He was a key leader in the July 20, 1944 failed attempt to kill Hitler and was hung on February 2, 1945.

5. The Social Democratic Party that had governed during the Weimar Republic but had succumbed to Hitler's election victories.

6. Hundred-eyed giant in Greek mythology.

7. By the very act.

8. German Tobacco Goods, Ltd.

9. Jewish officials viewed by Walter as possible Nazi collaborators.

10. WWI German Iron Cross, first-class war merit award.

8. The child cried and shivered

1. Reference to a Buchenwald torture device where the victim's weight causes extreme pain. See https://collections.ushmm.org/search/catalog/pa1168024.

2. On December 11, 1941 (four days after the Japanese attack on Pearl Harbor) Germany declares war on the U.S. At this point all legal Jewish emigration from Germany is ended.

3. Kapo usually refers to Jewish guards in a ghetto or concentration camp. He seems to be using it as a derogatory term.

4. Reference to a sanitarium in the Black Forest.

5. Likely a reference to former Communist Party associates.

6. Alpine region of southern Germany.

7. "Red Leipzig," "Red Saxony" are terms applied to this city and area because socialists and communists once vied for power there before and during the Weimar Republic. (The socialists or Social Democrats contested for local office since the days of Bismarck who, to no avail, outlawed them with Anti-Socialist Laws, 1878-1881.) However, the Nazis virtually eliminated these groups and their members beginning in 1933. Although Walter never joins a particular party, much of his survival depends on obtaining food and shelter from these political comrades.

8. This was a Nazi tourist organization that allowed working class Germans to travel on vacations. This was an attempt to show that the new regime had eliminated class distinctions.

9. Honoring the Battle of Leipzig 1813 (also called the Battle of the Nations) marking the defeat of Napoleon in Germany and Poland. The monument was completed in 1913.

10. A reference to Walter's military service for the Germans in WWI.

11. An affectionate nick-name for Anneliese.

12. The Christian holiday of Pentecost.
13. German dive bomber.
14. German conductor and composer.
15. This concerns the transportation of German victims of the bombing (not Jews) to other areas for housing. Clearly Walter does not want to travel into the unknown where it might become more difficult to hide his identity.
16. The local Nazi welfare agency.

10. Heil Hitler Herr Freiherr!

1. German hygienist, 1868-1952.
2. A reference to being unable to find employment in public administration during the years of the Weimar Republic.

12. I am not able to fight openly

1. The German initials for the Nazi Party.
2. The Tyrol regional top Nazi official.
3. The Nazi swastika pin worn by party members and others as a symbol of full support for the Third Reich.

13. Now we are in a real mess!

1. Here Walter is reflecting about how he could regain his real identity if he should live to the end of the war.
2. Chief Inspector Kulnh and Regional Councilor Dr. Czinglar, the top officials of the Bludenz Nazi civil administration who wish to hire Walter.

14. The worst of all torments

1. V1 and V2 rockets.
2. Kaiser Wilhelm II.
3. From April until June 1944 there were mass deportations of Hungarian and Greek Jews to Auschwitz. Of 400,000 Hungarian Jews, 250,000 were gassed within eight weeks.
4. The Reichstag – the German Parliament – was set ablaze on February 27, 1933 four weeks after Hitler became Chancellor. Although the fire was set by a Nazi, the incident was blamed on the Communists and used by Hitler to seize absolute power and round up the Communists. The reference to 1939 is about the attempted assassination of Hitler by Georg Elser in Munich.
5. Hermann Goering.

15. The brave were silent

1. The flag colors of the Weimar German social democratic constitutional government which ran the country from the end of WWI in 1919 to the Nazi victory in 1933.
2. Married to a gentile and therefore not subject to anti-Jewish laws.
3. Surprise attack.
4. Might be referencing the July 20, 1944 failed assassination attempt of Hitler after which Claus von Stauffenberg flew to Berlin to initiate the actual coup. He was betrayed by one of the co-plotters and was executed that very night.

16. Enlighten the fools

1. In *Every Man Dies Alone*, Hans Fallada describes the enormous dangers of such a letter-writing campaign in Nazi Germany.

17. Curing the little Hitlers

1. The Nazi regional administration in Innsbruck.
2. Prisoners appointed by the SS to guard other prisoners in concentration camps. In this context it is unclear what group he is referencing.

18. German Jew alone

1. President Roosevelt called for an international conference to encourage nations around the world to accept more emigrating Jews. Already one out of four German Jews (150,000) had fled. However, with the annexation of Austria another 185,000 were at risk. Although 32 countries sent delegates to Evian, France in July 1938, only the Dominican Republic agreed to take in more Jews. The Nazi government smugly pointed out "how 'astounding' it was that foreign countries criticized Germany for its treatment of the Jews, but none of them wanted to open the doors to them when 'the opportunity offer[ed].'" https://www.ushmm.org/educators/teaching-materials/national-history-day/research-topics/the-evian-conference
2. Social Democratic Weimar Republic, 1918-1933.
3. Flag of the German Empire until 1918.
4. Flag of the Communists.
5. German patriotic poet and composer of the German national anthem "Deutschland, Deutschland über Alles".
6. This may be a quotation from Frederick Nietzsche in *Beyond Good and Evil*, Section 251 during which he describes the stupidity of German antisemitism. It starts with, "When a people is suffering from nationalistic nervous fever and political ambition and *wants* to suffer, we have to accept the fact that

various kinds of clouds and disturbances – in short, small attacks of dullness – will pass over its spirit:" https://ebooks.adelaide.edu.au/n/nietzsche/friedrich/n67b/chapter8.html

19. That is Swastika logic!

1. The term references armed French resistance fighters.
2. The "Sicherheitsdienst des Reichsführers-SS" (SD) was the SS's intelligence agency.

21. They fear Hitler more than the enemy

1. Walter is not being ironic. In Germany postal pickup and deliveries were expected several times a day.

23. No longer the dangerous adventurer

1. A hotel and cultural center built in 1925 in the Bauhaus style.

24. My God, isn't that a great story!

1. "Nationalsozialistische Volkswohlfahrt" is the Nazi People's Welfare Organization which became the only legal welfare organization in German after Hitler banned all private charities. It provided a full range of government social support from day-care to food supplements.
2. Adored Jewish scholar from the late first century/early second century.
3. Nationalsozialistische Deutsche Arbeiterpartei (National Socialist German Workers' Party) is the official name of the Nazi Party which controlled nearly all social, cultural and political activity in the Third Reich.
4. Reichsarbeitsdienst (Reich Labour Service) was set up by the Nazi Party during the depression to provide work for the unemployed much like the U.S. Civilian Conservation Corps. During WWII it recruited workers to provide construction and supply services for the military.
5. God bless.
6. Woe to the Vanquished!
7. Reference to mountains that were 3,000 meters high, roughly 10,000 feet.
8. This is a reference to the generals who in July, 1944 plotted to kill Hitler. Many have been executed since then.

25. Revolutionary Jew

1. A reference to the Warsaw Uprising, April 1-October 2, 1944 led by the Polish underground resistance. It was timed with the advance of the Russians and the retreat of the Germans. However, the Russians stopped at the outskirts of Warsaw and allowed the Germans to crush the uprising before the Russians advanced again. It is conjectured that the Russians wanted the Polish resistance out of the way so that they could install their own partisans, hence the mention of the "shameful spectacle" of the Allies.
2. Deutsche Arbeitsfront (The German Labor Front) is the Nazi Party's labor organization, the only union of sorts that is permitted in the Third Reich.
3. Oh, that things change!

26. We have become lonely again

1. Franz Hofer, Governor of Tyrol-Vorarlberg, who in 1933 was imprisoned for 30 months, escaped to Germany, after the Anschluss of Austria returned to become in 1940 Reich governor. In 1950 he was found guilty of high treason at Innsbruck Court of Justice.
2. A condition that affects only uncircumcised males that limits blood flow to the tip of the penis and therefore requires the removal of the foreskin.

27. Agitate, until the pips squeak

1. The name is the sign.
2. The German Labor Front which is the Nazi replacement for unions all of which have been banned.
3. A reference to Kaiser Wilhelm II, the German Emperor and King of Prussia who ruled from 1888 to 1918.
4. "Rock of Ages" liturgical poem, written in the 13th century, sung after the lighting of the Chanukah candles.
5. Antiochus Epiphanes IV, who as ruler of the Syrian Kingdom in 168 BC tried to wipe out all the Jews in his domain. A group of Jews called the Maccabees resisted and finally reclaimed Jerusalem. Chanukah celebrates this story.
6. A reference to the January 7, 1919 general strike in Berlin called by left Communists inspired by the Russian Revolution. It was crushed a few days later leading to the assassination of one of its most influential leaders, Rosa Luxemburg.
7. Reference to the "Battle of the Bulge," the massive German counter-attack through the Ardennes Forest in Belgium that almost split the advancing Allied forces into two sections. This nearly led to the capture of tens of thousands of Allied troops before the "bulge" of the Nazi attack was halted and then reversed.
8. A crime proven to have occurred.

9. Again a reference to the Battle of the Bulge.

28. How much longer?

1. Reference to Karl Arno Punzeler who then was a 16-year-old Nazi enthusiast in Belgium caught spying by the Allies and then given a life sentence. He was released in 1955.

29. I was doubtless the first Jew

1. Heinz Guderian was a German general who helped create the powerful Panzer tank divisions and the concept of Blitzkrieg – the rapid attacks by German troops and tanks. After surrendering to the Allies in 1945, he claimed to be an anti-Nazi general and never was convicted of war crimes. He wrote a best-selling book after the war, *Panzer Leader,* which helped to white-wash the role of the German High Command during the war.
2. A biblical term for ominous warning.
3. "How great are your dwelling places, Jacob!" from the Ma Tovu prayer which expresses reverence for holy places of worship.
4. Hebrew word for "blessing" of which there are many in Jewish religious services.
5. A reference to Hitler.
6. By the power of truth.
7. Franz Hofer, Nazi Party chief in charge of the Tyrol and Voralberg areas of Austria.
8. Arthur Greiser, Reich governor of the Gau Wartheland in Poland, responsible for brutal Germanisation policies and mass deportations. He was captured by the Americans, tried, convicted and publicly hanged near his former Polish residence in 1946.
9. Iron maiden was a torture device built in the shape of the victim with spikes aimed at all areas of the anatomy. As the victim tired, the spikes would dig into the body.

30. Herr Doktor

1. Colors of the Austrian and French flags.

31. The truly upright... are but few

1. "You are German. What do you want here?"
2. "That's not possible. You can emigrate to Switzerland."
3. The British conservative journal, *The Spectator,* reports on May 17, 1945 that "General Eisenhower has done well to address a sharp reprimand to senior

American officers who have been treating high German officials as 'friendly enemies.' Reports of genial intercourse with Goering and Press photographs of Kesselring conversing at a hotel dinner table have shocked both American and British readers, and offer a singular example to troops who have been ordered not to fraternise with Germans." http://archive.spectator.co.uk/article/ 18th-may-1945/1/general-eisenhower-on-goering.

4. The German high command had hoped that during the surrender they could form an alliance with the U.S., Britain and France against the Soviets.

5. A little known Nazi official outside this area.

6. Reference to the German Palatine emigrants from the southern Rhine area who fled from French occupation to England and the New World in the early 18th century.

7. Robert Ley was head of the German Labor Front, the official Nazi union. He committed suicide in 1945 while awaiting trial for war crimes at Nuremberg.

8. The old documents stamped with Jewish identities by the Nazis.

9. One of top regional officials who first hired Walter.

10. Term of affection for Anneliese.

11. Aaron Tanzer was chief Rabbi of the Tyrol and Voralberg areas in the early 20th century. He was a field Rabbi during WWI and wrote a history of the Jewish community of Goppingen in the province of Württemberg, south Germany.

12. Austria remained occupied by the French, Americans, British and Russians until 1955 when it became a neutral country in the East-West Cold War.

32. I will certainly not crawl to the Cross

1. The same Israelite or maybe a term for Jew of Moroccan descent.

2. Blessing for the bread.

3. *Why I am a Jew* (1929) written as a Jewish grandfather to an unborn grandchild of what it is like living in secular France as a Jew.

4. A slur for Germans living in Austria.

5. In 1894, the French Captain Alfred Dreyfus of Jewish descent was falsely accused and convicted of treason.

6. Under the Nazis it was illegal for a Gentile man to marry a Jew, so they divorced and hoped no one would investigate.

7. Nenzing is the name of the market area of Bludenz.

33. Our regrets, Herr Doktor

1. Ceremonial beaker for the Sabbath wine blessing.

2. Reference to a Green myth of revenge.

3. Austria is divided into four areas ruled by the French, the British, the Americans and the Russians. The French occupy the two most western provinces – Voralberg and Tyrol.

4. At this point Germany is divided into two sectors: East, occupied by the Russians, and West, occupied by the Americans. Berlin is divided into four sectors similar to Austria. Leipzig is in the Russian sector.
5. Jew no good.
6. The essential condition.
7. Orthodox Jews.

34. Disappointment

1. Preparatory agricultural training for life in Israel.
2. The land of Israel.
3. Derogatory term for German Jews.
4. The bag that holds the Jewish prayer shall.
5. Mythological supreme Teutonic sky God.
6. An area in the German Alps where Hitler set up his retreat in Obersalzberg.
7. Time will tell.
8. To the core of the matter.
9. For how much longer?

35. Exiled

1. A semi-governmental body of former resistance fighters.
2. "Let others wage war; Thou, happy Austria, marry." A reference to the Habsburg's royal family's reputed ability to thrive through carefully arranged marriages.
3. Rest in peace.
4. Catholic reactionaries.
5. The Schönbrunn Palace in Vienna, the seat of the former Hapsburg dynasty.

PHOTOS

Cantor Leopold Leopold, brothers Max, Alex, Walter
and mother Bertha, circa 1920

Walter (first row left) with his class at Heidelberg
University, circa 1923

Walter, circa 1935

Anneliese's first Chanukah, Leipzig, Germany 1937

Walter, mother Berta Leopold, Anneliese, and brother
Max, Leipzig, Germany, 1938

Anneliese and Mäuslein, Leipzig, Germany circa 1940

First Chanukah after Liberation, Bludenz, Austria 1945

Anneliese, Hilda and Walter, high above Bludenz,
Austria, circa 1945

Hilda and Walter, Bludenz, Austria circa 1946

Anneliese's 10th birthday, Bludenz, Austria, February 14, 1947

Leopold family still in Bludenz, awaiting emigration to America, circa 1948

ABOUT LES LEOPOLD

After graduating from Oberlin College and Princeton School of Public and International Affairs (MPA 1975), Les co-founded the Labor Institute (1976), a non-profit organization that designs research and educational programs on occupational safety and health, the environment and economics for unions, worker centers and community organizations.

He is the author of *Runaway Inequality: An Activist's Guide to Economic Justice* (Labor Institute Press, 2015), *How to Make a Million Dollars an Hour: Why Financial Elites Get Away with Siphoning off America's Wealth* (John Wiley and Sons, 2013); *The Looting of America: How Wall Street's Game of Fantasy Finance Destroyed Our Jobs, Pensions and Prosperity, and What We Can Do About It* (Chelsea Green Publishing, June 2009); *The Man Who Hated Work and Loved*

Labor: The Life and Times of Tony Mazzocchi (Chelsea Green Publishing, June 2006). The Mazzocchi story won the Independent Publisher Award for best biography.

Dear Reader

If you've enjoyed this book I would be very grateful if you could spend a few minutes leaving a review (it can be as short as you like) on the Amazon page.

Thanks a lot in advance!
Les Leopold

ACKNOWLEDGMENTS

This book came to light because of the dogged determination of my sister, Evelyn Leopold, a freelance journalist covering the United Nations and a former 40-year employee of Reuters. Upon learning from our cousin, Anneliese, about scraps of paper written by Walter and given to a Leipzig historian, Evelyn set about to turn these notes into a manuscript. She pursued this project with Dr. Andrea Lorz, who deserves our heartfelt thanks for freely giving her time and talents to the tedious task of piecing together Walter's ruminations. Next, Evelyn contracted with Marcus Ferrar, a British journalist and author, who skilfully produced the English translation.

David Dembo, Peter Kreutzer and Kris Raab are much appreciated for their research, editing and guidance. Special thanks also to Zak Lempert, Walter's great grandson, for tracking down archival documents. We also are most grateful to Liesbeth Heenk and her team at Amsterdam Publishers for taking on this project with great care, skilfulness and patience.

And most of all, enormous thanks and love to Anneliese for her kindness and courage. It has not been easy for her to revisit this painful story. Like she has done since her perilous childhood in

Nazi Germany, Anneliese again has risen to the challenge with grace and love.

Like every writing project I've pursued, this is dedicated to our children, Lilah and Chester, and my partner in life, Dr. Sharon Szymanski. Not only do they provide loving support for my writing, but they always contribute many key insights that improve the narrative. Thank you for making my life so worth living.

HOLOCAUST SURVIVOR MEMOIRS

The Series **Holocaust Survivor Memoirs World War II** consists of the following books:

1. Outcry - Holocaust Memoirs, by Manny Steinberg

Amazon Link: getbook.at/Outcry

2. Hank Brodt Holocaust Memoirs. A Candle and a Promise, by Deborah Donnelly

Amazon Link: getbook.at/Brodt

3. The Dead Years - Holocaust Memoirs, by Joseph Schupack

Amazon Link: getbook.at/Schupack

4. Rescued from the Ashes. The Diary of Leokadia Schmidt, Survivor of the Warsaw Ghetto, by Leokadia Schmidt

Amazon Link: getbook.at/Leokadia

5. My Lvov. Holocaust Memoir of a twelve-year-old Girl, by Janina Hescheles

Amazon Link: getbook.at/Lvov

6. Remembering Ravensbrück. From Holocaust to Healing, by Natalie Hess

Amazon Link: getbook.at/Ravensbruck

7. Wolf - A Story of Hate, by Zeev Scheinwald with Ella Scheinwald

Amazon Link: getbook.at/wolf

8. Save my Children. An Astonishing Tale of Survival and its Unlikely Hero, by Leon Kleiner with Edwin Stepp

Amazon Link: getbook.at/LeonKleiner

9. Holocaust Memoirs of a Bergen-Belsen Survivor & Classmate of Anne Frank, by Nanette Blitz Konig

Amazon Link: getbook.at/BlitzKonig

10. Defiant German - Defiant Jew. A Holocaust Memoir from inside the Third Reich, by Walter Leopold with Les Leopold

Amazon Link: getbook.at/leopold

HOLOCAUST SURVIVOR TRUE STORIES

The Series **Holocaust Survivor True Stories WWII** consists of the following biographies:

1. Among the Reeds. The true story of how a family survived the Holocaust, by Tammy Bottner

Amazon Link: getbook.at/ATRBottner

2. A Holocaust Memoir of Love & Resilience. Mama's Survival from Lithuania to America, by Ettie Zilber

Amazon Link: getbook.at/Zilber

3. Living among the Dead. My Grandmother's Holocaust Survival Story of Love and Strength, by Adena Bernstein Astrowsky

Amazon Link: mybook.to/ManiaL

4. Heart Songs - A Holocaust Memoir, by Barbara Gilford

Amazon Link: getbook.at/HeartSongs

5. Shoes of the Shoah. The Tomorrow of Yesterday, by Dorothy Pierce

Amazon Link: getbook.at/shoah

9 789493 056688